THE CHURCH IN ROME

IN THE FIRST CENTURY

THE CHURCH IN ROME
IN THE FIRST CENTURY

AN EXAMINATION OF VARIOUS CONTROVERTED QUESTIONS
RELATING TO ITS HISTORY, CHRONOLOGY, LITERATURE AND
TRADITIONS

EIGHT LECTURES

PREACHED BEFORE THE UNIVERSITY OF OXFORD
IN THE YEAR 1913

ON THE FOUNDATION OF THE LATE REV. JOHN BAMPTON, M.A.
CANON OF SALISBURY

BY

GEORGE EDMUNDSON, M.A.

LATE FELLOW AND TUTOR OF BRASENOSE COLLEGE,
VICAR OF ST. SAVIOUR, UPPER CHELSEA

WIPF & STOCK · Eugene, Oregon

Wipf and Stock Publishers
199 W 8th Ave, Suite 3
Eugene, OR 97401

The Church in Rome in the First Century
An Examination of Various Controverted Questions
Relating to its History, Chronology, Literature and Traditions
By George Edmundson
ISBN 13: 978-1-55635-846-3
Publication date 2/8/2008
Previously published by Longmans, Green and Co., 1913

THE BAMPTON LECTURES

FOR 1913

CAROLO BULLER HEBERDEN
D.C.L.
AUL. REG. ET COLL. AEN. NAS. PRINCIPALI
ACAD. OXON. VICECANCELLARIO
AMICITIAE PROBATAE
TESTIMONIUM
D. D. D.
OLIM PER DECENNIUM COLLEGA

EXTRACT

FROM THE LAST WILL AND TESTAMENT

OF THE LATE

REV. JOHN BAMPTON

CANON OF SALISBURY

'. . . I give and bequeath my Lands and Estates to the Chancellor, Masters, and Scholars of the University of Oxford for ever, to have and to hold all and singular the said Lands or Estates upon trust, and to the intents and purposes hereinafter mentioned ; that is to say, I will and appoint that the Vice-Chancellor of the University of Oxford for the time being shall take and receive all the rents, issues, and profits thereof, and (after all taxes, reparations, and necessary deductions made) that he pay all the remainder to the endowment of eight Divinity Lecture Sermons, to be established for ever in the said University and to be performed in the manner following :

'I direct and appoint, that, upon the first Tuesday in Easter Term, a Lecturer be yearly chosen by the Heads of Colleges only, and by no others, in the room adjoining to the Printing-House, between the hours of ten in the morning and two in the afternoon, to preach eight Divinity Lecture Sermons, the year following, at St. Mary's in Oxford, between the commencement of the last month in Lent Term, and the end of the third week in Act Term.

'Also I direct and appoint, that the eight Divinity Lecture Sermons shall be preached upon either of the following Subjects —to confirm and establish the Christian Faith, and to confute all heretics and schismatics—upon the divine authority of the holy Scriptures—upon the authority of the writings of the primitive Fathers, as to the faith and practice of the primitive Church—upon the Divinity of our Lord and Saviour Jesus Christ —upon the Divinity of the Holy Ghost—upon the Articles of the Christian Faith, as comprehended in the Apostles' and Nicene Creeds.

'Also I direct, that thirty copies of the eight Divinity Lecture Sermons shall be always printed, within two months after they are preached ; and one copy shall be given to the Chancellor of the University, and one copy to the Head of every College, and one copy to the Mayor of the city of Oxford, and one copy to be put into the Bodleian Library ; and the expense of printing them shall be paid out of the revenue of the Land or Estates given for establishing the Divinity Lecture Sermons ; and the Preacher shall not be paid, nor be entitled to the revenue, before they are printed.

'Also I direct and appoint, that no person shall be qualified to preach the Divinity Lecture Sermons, unless he hath taken the degree of Master of Arts at least, in one of the two Universities of Oxford or Cambridge ; and that the same person shall never preach the Divinity Lecture Sermons twice.'

SYNOPSIS OF CONTENTS

LECTURE I

PAGE

Character of the theme—The Rome of Claudius and of Nero—
Intercourse—Population—Slavery—The ' Freedman ' Class—
Alien admixture—The Jewish Colony and its history—Its
privileges and characteristics—Judaism attractive—Proselytes
and ' God-fearers '—The Synagogues—Soil prepared for Chris-
tianity—The *Laureolus*—The Jews expelled by Claudius—
Aquila and Prisca at Corinth—Their antecedents and position—
Their close intercourse with St. Paul—St. Paul at Ephesus—
His Journey to Greece—He writes to the Roman Church from
Corinth—The Epistle to the Romans : an *Apologia*—St. Paul's
proposed visit to Rome—Three groups of Roman Christians
addressed—The impelling motive of the Epistle—The Judaeo-
Christians at Rome—The Salutations of Chap. xvi. 1-23—
Genuineness of the passage—Criticism dealt with—The Church
in the house of Prisca and Aquila—Was this *Ecclesia Domestica*
existent before 57 A.D. ?—The Apostles Andronicus and Junias—
The households of Aristobulus and Narcissus—The autobiographic passage Chap. xv. 14-29—' Another man's foundation '—Was the other man St. Peter ? 1-29

LECTURE II

The Lukan authorship of the Acts—Fragmentary character of the
narrative—The Acts written before 62 A.D.—The closing verses
of the Acts—The Day of Pentecost—The sojourning Romans—
The Twelve at Jerusalem—The Hellenists and St. Stephen—
Consequences of St. Stephen's martyrdom—Activity of St. Peter
—The vision at Joppa—Conversion of Cornelius—Missionaries
at Antioch—Barnabas sent to Antioch—He seeks Saul—The
name *Christiani*—Herod Agrippa persecutes the Church—St.
Peter escapes from prison—St. James and the Brethren—
Value of tradition—Oral tradition—Early Christian written
records—Their destruction—Apocryphal ' Acts '—Criteria of
authenticity—Evidence for St. Peter's martyrdom at Rome—
' Ascension of Isaiah '—Clement of Rome—Ignatius—Dionysius

of Corinth—Irenaeus—The Episcopal lists—Eusebius of
Caesarea—Jerome—The Petrine tradition universally accepted
in East and West alike—Archaeological evidence—Portraits—
Sepulchral inscriptions — Mosaics — Frescoes — The Petrine
'legends' based on fact—*The Preaching of Peter*—Local
memories—St. Peter at Rome—The envoy of the Twelve—
Precedents of Samaria and Antioch—Analogy of circumstances 30–58

LECTURE III

St. Peter encounters Simon Magus at Rome—Eusebius on the story
of Simon Magus—His visit to Rome in Claudius' reign, and
success—Weighty evidence of Justin Martyr, of Irenaeus and
Hippolytus—The theories of Baur and Lipsius untenable—
Vogue of Oriental cults and teachers at Rome—John Mark
Peter's interpreter—Origin of St. Mark's Gospel—Its date—
Jerome's version of the Petrine tradition—His sources of information—Relations with Pope Damasus—The Hieronymian
tradition and that of the Liberian Catalogue—The differences
between them—Chronological difficulties and discrepancies—
Attempted solution—The Antiochean narrative [Acts xi. and
xii.] examined—Barnabas and Paul bear alms to Jerusalem,
46 A.D.—They meet Peter on his return from Rome—Peter
makes Antioch the missionary centre of his work, 47–54 A.D.—
Peter with Barnabas at Corinth, 54 A.D.—Testimony of the
First Epistle to the Corinthians—Accession of Nero—Peter and
Barnabas journey to Italy—Evidence of Barnabas' missionary
activity in Rome and North Italy—No rivalry between St.
Peter and St. Paul at Corinth—Paul's delay in visiting Rome
due to Peter's presence there, 54–56 A.D.—First organisation
of the Roman Church—The trial of Julia Pomponia Graecina—
Inscription in the crypt of Lucina 59–86

LECTURE IV

St. Paul's visit to Jerusalem, Pentecost, 57 A.D., and captivity at
Caesarea—Character of the administration of Felix—Accuracy
and trustworthiness of the Lukan narrative—St. Paul's financial
resources—Indulgent treatment of St. Paul by Felix—Influence
of Drusilla—Recall of Felix—Elymas or Etoimos—Attitude of
Festus—St. Paul's appeal to Caesar—His motives in appealing
—St. Paul's journey from Puteoli to Rome—He is delivered in
charge to the *Stratopedarch*—The favours accorded to him—St.
Paul invites the Jewish leaders to meet him—His interviews
with the chiefs of the Synagogues—The Apostle's appeal to the
Jews is fruitless—The Epistles of the First Captivity—The
earlier group—Colossians, Ephesians, Philemon—Their tone
cheerful—Release expected—Many friends surround the Apostle

PAGE

—Mark, the cousin of Barnabas, at Alexandria—His visit to
Rome and mission to Colossae—The Epistle to the Philippians—
Changed situation—Friends absent—Issue of trial in doubt but
Paul hopeful—The letter of a friend to friends—Discords at
Philippi—The 'true yoke-fellow'—Clement—Caesar's house-
hold—St. Paul is set at liberty—Probable course of the trial 87-114

LECTURE V

A High-Priestly embassy in Rome—Growth of hostility between
Jew and Christian—The Christians accused of anarchism and
secret crimes—St. Peter's last visit to Rome in 63 A.D.—The First
Epistle of St. Peter—Its genuineness—The Epistle written at
Rome—Its literary indebtedness to other New Testament
writings—St. Peter acquainted with the Epistles to the Romans
and Ephesians—Mark and Silvanus with Peter at Rome—The
great fire of July 19, 64 A.D.—Rumour attributes the fire to
Nero—Steps taken by Nero to efface the rumour—The Pisonian
conspiracy and its suppression—The charges brought against the
Christians—The Tacitean account of their sufferings—Character
of the Neronian persecution—The personal act of Nero—
Tigellinus, the active agent of Nero's cruelty—The Christians
not implicated in the burning of Rome—Origin of the charge
of incendiarism—Apocalyptic utterances—Tigellinus and
Apollonius of Tyana : a parallel—Atheism, Thyestean feasts,
Oedipodean intercourse—Hatred of the human race, ' Institutum Neronianum'—'Crimina adhaerentia Nomini '—Christian
contemporary evidence—The spectacle in the Vatican Gardens
—The arrest of the great multitude, end of April, 65 A.D.—
Comparison of evidence from Tacitus, Suetonius and Orosius
fixes the date—Persecution in the Provinces 115-144

LECTURE VI

Deaths of St. Peter and St. Paul at Rome—Their tombs piously
preserved—They were not martyred on the same day—Manner
of their deaths—How the mistake as to a common date arose
—Statement of Prudentius—The '*Quo Vadis?*' story examined
—St. Peter's crucifixion in the early summer of 65 A.D.—The
Epistle to the Hebrews—Addressed to Judaeo-Christians at
Rome—Internal and external evidence for this—The Epistle
never received as Pauline in Rome or the West—Tertullian names
Barnabas as the author—Barnabas well qualified to write this
Epistle—Sent to Rome, as an *eirenicon*—The personal references
support the Barnabean hypothesis—The Pastoral Epistles—St.
Paul's second imprisonment at Rome—His sense of desertion—
His death, 67 A.D.—The Apocalypse written in 70 A.D.—State-
ments of Irenaeus and Origen considered—Eusebius' use of his

PAGE

authorities—Evidence of Victorinus and Jerome—The book
reflects contemporary history—Neronian Persecution—Events
of 69 A.D.—Burning of the Capitol—Domitian in power, Jan. to
June, 70 A.D.—Nerva Consul, 71 A.D.—Temple of Jerusalem
still standing—The Number of the Beast—Nero Caesar—The
Apocalypse, a Neronian document—Nero is Anti-Christ—The
Nero legend—Armageddon—Impressions of an eye-witness—
Earthquakes and convulsions of nature—The islands of Patmos
and Thera   145-179

LECTURE VII

The First Century Episcopal Succession at Rome—The Jewish
Synagoge and the Christian Ecclesia—The Official Ministry in
the early Church—Duties and position of episcopi—Pastors and
Stewards with cure of souls—They form an inner Presbyterate—
Its president The Bishop—Apostles, Prophets, Teachers and their
functions—The Didache an untrustworthy authority for the
First Century—The genuine Epistle of Clement to the
Corinthians—Not written in 96 A.D. but in beginning of 70 A.D.—
The recent examples of our own time—The Neronian persecution
fresh in memory—The sudden and successive troubles and
calamities of 69 A.D.—Internal evidence of the Epistle to its
early date—Church Organisation—Christology—New Testament Quotations—The Daily Sacrifice at Jerusalem had not
ceased—The Corinthian dissensions—Predisposing circumstances, 66-68 A.D.—Reference to the Phoenix—Episcopal
succession—Apostolical regulations—The disturbers of the
peace at Corinth rebuked—Force of the word ἀρχαίαν—
The bearers of the Epistle to Corinth—No allusion to Clement
as the writer—Authoritative position of Clement in 96 A.D.—
The Epistle belongs to an earlier time—Written by him as
secretary to the Presbyterate—Interesting inscription   .   180-205

LECTURE VIII

Attitude of the Flavian emperors to the Christians—A quarter of a
century of moderation—Titus personally hostile—' The Shepherd' of Hermas: a Flavian writing—Blunder of the Muratorian Fragmentist—The notice in the 'Liberian Catalogue'—
The Muratorian and Liberian statements derived from a common
source—Hermas confused with the presbyter Pastor—Patristic
testimony supports the early date—Irenaeus, Clement of
Alexandria, Tertullian—Unity of 'The Shepherd'—It contains a
real life story—Hermas a contemporary of Clement of Rome—
Harnack's views discussed—The book in three parts, but the
period covered by it short—Hermas' references to the Neronian
persecution—To the organisation of the Church—Its primitive
character—Signs of an evolutionary movement—Contentions

about precedence—Growth of a Monarchical Episcopate—The
persecution of Domitian—In its origin fiscal—The *didrachma*
tax—Many Christians of high position suffer—Flavius Clemens
put to death—His wife Flavia Domitilla banished—Flavius
Sabinus, father and son—Flavius Clemens the Consul and
Clemens the bishop—A third contemporary Clemens—M.
Arrecinus Clemens is Consul 94 A.D.—He is put to death by his
relative Domitian—The two Flavia Domitillas—The ' Acts of
Nereus and Achilles '—Plautilla the sister of Clemens the Consul—Relationship between the Flavian and Arrecinian families
—Is Clement the bishop brother of Árrecinus Clemens ?—The
death of M' Acilius Glabrio—The Acilian Crypt in the cemetery
of Priscilla—Conclusion   206–237

APPENDICES

NOTE A. CHRONOLOGICAL STATEMENT   .   .   .   239–241

NOTE B. AQUILA AND PRISCA OR PRISCILLA   .   .   242–3

NOTE C. THE PUDENS LEGEND   244–249

NOTE D. THE FAMILY CONNEXION OF CLEMENT THE BISHOP 250–258

NOTE E. THE TOMBS OF THE APOSTLES ST. PETER AND
         ST. PAUL   259–272

NOTE F. THE CEMETERIES OF PRISCILLA AND DOMITILLA   273–282

INDEX   283

INDEX OF SCRIPTURE REFERENCES.   295–6

THE CHURCH IN ROME

LECTURE I

Rom. i. 8 : ' First, I thank my God through Jesus Christ for you all, that your faith is spoken of throughout the whole world.'

THE subject of these lectures is in one sense a well-worn theme. The literature bearing upon the history of the Church in Rome during the first century is enormous, and unfortunately in modern times the prevailing note has been controversial. It has seemed as if it were impossible even for those who have tried to write on the beginnings of Roman Christianity in the impartial spirit of the scientific historian to free themselves from bias and prejudice. This very fact, however, only proves that this has been and is a subject of profound and indeed of absorbing interest, and it is so from whatever point of view we regard it, the political, no less than the ecclesiastical and religious. That interest indeed, so far from diminishing, has been greatly stimulated and increased by the archaeological researches and discoveries made in Rome and its immediate neighbourhood during the past half-century. Year by year additions have been made to our knowledge, and it is now generally admitted that the last word on many most important and critical questions has not yet been spoken. Already many assertions once confidently made have had to be modified or abandoned, opinions put forward with authority are constantly being revised, and a careful study of available evidence has convinced me that there are grounds

B

for questioning seriously certain conclusions now generally received, and at the same time for upholding the historical character of some ancient traditions too hastily rejected.

The first point to grasp is the character of the spell exercised over the minds of men by the very name of Rome during the period of the early Caesars. Rome in the first century of our era occupied a position of influence unique in the annals of history. It had become the magnetic centre of the civilised world, and it was itself the most cosmopolitan of cities that have ever existed. The Rome of Claudius and of Nero was the seat of an absolute and centralised Government, whose vast dominion stretched from the shores of the Atlantic to the borders of Parthia, from Britain to the Libyan deserts, over diverse lands and many races, all of them subdued after centuries of conflict and of conquest by the Roman arms, but now forming a single empire under an administrative system of unrivalled flexibility and strength, which enforced obedience to law and the maintenance of peace without any unnecessary infringement of local liberties or interference with national religious cults. One of the most remarkable features of this great Empire was the freedom of intercourse that was enjoyed, and the safety and rapidity with which travelling could be undertaken. Never until quite modern times has any such ease and security of communication between place and place been possible. And this not merely by those admirable military roads which were one of the chief instruments for the maintenance of the Roman rule and for the binding together of province with province and of the most distant frontiers with the capital; the facilities for intercourse by water also were abundant and were, except during the winter months, freely used. The Roman Empire, as a glance at the map reveals, was—even at its zenith—essentially a Mediterranean power. Its dominion consisted mainly of the fringe of territory encircling that sea. In the midst stood the capital. The greatest cities of the Empire were ports, and Rome itself, the chief among them, was dependent upon sea-borne traffic for its daily food.[1]

At the beginning of the Christian era the population of the imperial city has been estimated at not less than 1,300,000, of which more than one half were slaves. The entire number of citizens owning private property was very small—a few thousands only.[2] Each of these possessed vast numbers of slaves,[3] who were trained to perform every kind of work, so that a considerable portion of the free inhabitants found themselves without occupation or employment. ⌐In the time of Julius Caesar [4] no fewer than 320,000 were supported by the state, and though Augustus was able to reduce this multitude of paupers to 200,000,[5] the number afterwards rapidly increased.⌐ This huge population was, as has been already said, one of the most cosmopolitan that has ever been gathered together to form one community. This was due in the first instance to the practice of selling prisoners of war, and the inhabitants of captured cities, as slaves. The institution of slavery therefore implied that in every wealthy household in Rome there was a great mixture of races, and the custom of manumission on a large scale was continually admitting batches of persons of foreign extraction to many privileges of citizenship. Thus was formed the large and important class of freedmen (liberti) containing men of culture and ability, who not only filled posts of

[1] See Sir W. Ramsay's Article in Hasting's *Dict.* vol. v. ' Roads and Travel in N.T. Times '; his *Seven Churches*, p. 15, and elsewhere in his writings. Friedländer, *Sittengeschichte Roms*, ii. 3 ; Sanday and Headlam, *Ep. to Rom.* p. xxvi; Merivale, *St. Paul at Rome*, p. 5 ; Miss C. Skeet, *Travel in the First Century* ; Renan, *Hibbert Lectures*, 1880, ' The Influence of the Institutions, Thought, and Culture of Rome on Christianity and the Development of the Catholic Church,' Eng. tr., pp. 17-19.

[2] Cicero (*De Officiis*, ii. 21) speaks of the number as 2000 in 102 B.C.

[3] At the end of the Republic and under the Empire it was not a rare thing to meet rich Romans possessing many thousands. Under Augustus a simple freedman, C. Caecilius Isidorus, although he had lost a considerable part of his fortune during the civil wars, still left at his death 4116 slaves. Pliny, *Historia Naturalis*, xxxiii. 47.

[4] Suetonius, *Caesar*, 41 ; Dion Cassius, xliii. 21.

[5] Dion Cassius, lv. 10.

responsibility in their former masters' households but not seldom became rich and rose to high official positions in the state. Freedmen indeed and the descendants of freedmen played no small part in the history of the times with which we are dealing, and Christianity found among them many of its early converts and most earnest workers. But the freedmen and the slaves by no means comprised all the foreign population of Rome at this epoch. The legionaries were recruited in all parts of the empire ; the Pretorian camp contained contingents drawn from distant frontier tribes. Traders, travellers, adventurers of every kind thronged to Rome—particularly from the East. So did the preachers and teachers of many philosophies, cults, and modes of worship, Greek, Egyptian, and Phrygian. The very language of ordinary everyday life in Rome had become Greek, and the whole atmosphere of the great city was in no small measure orientalised.[1]

Amongst this large alien element in the population the Jews formed one of the most marked and important sections. Their position indeed was at once singular and exclusive, for they had privileges accorded to none others. The origin [2] of the Jewish colony at Rome may be traced back to 63 B.C., when Pompeius after the capture of Jerusalem brought back a large number of prisoners, who were sold as slaves. But the Jew, as a slave, was always difficult to deal with, through his obstinate adherence to his ancestral faith

---

[1] Among the upper classes it had become the fashion to speak and write Greek ; for trade purposes and among the lowest classes of mixed race a debased Greek was used, as the language most generally understood. Juvenal, *Sat.* iii. 60 'Non possum ferre, Quirites, Graecam urbem ' ; *ibid.* 62 'Jam pridem Syrus in Tiberim defluxit Orontes.' Also 73–80.

[2] Berliner, Abraham (*Geschichte der Juden in Rom*, one of the best monographs on the subject), thinks that there must have been Jewish settlers in Rome before 63 B.C., or else it is difficult to account for Cicero, when pleading for Flaccus in 59 B.C., affecting to be intimidated by the crowd of Jews thronging the Aurelian steps—' multitudinem Iudaeorum flagrantium nonnunquam in concionibus ' (Cic. *pro Flacco* xxviii.), and probably he was right. Cicero however was no doubt greatly exaggerating his fear for his advocate's purpose. See Sanday and Headlam, *Ep. to Rom.* p. xix.

and peculiar customs, and so many of these slaves were speedily manumitted [1] that they were able to form a community apart on the far side of the Tiber.[2] Julius Caesar from motives of expediency showed especial favour to the Jews, and his policy was continued by Augustus and, except for brief intervals, by his successors. The privileges thus conferred were very great, and included liberty of worship, freedom from military service and from certain taxes, the recognition of the Sabbath as a day of rest, the right of living according to the customs of their forefathers, and full jurisdiction over their own members.[3] Once in the reign of Tiberius [4] the worshippers of Jahveh and of Isis fell under the heavy displeasure of the emperor; some were punished, others expelled from the city, and the consuls were ordered to enlist 4000 Jews for military service in the malarious climate of Sardinia, 19 A.D. The determination of Caligula to set up a statue of himself in the Temple of Jerusalem aroused a storm of opposition, which would undoubtedly have brought a fierce persecution upon the Jews but for the assassination of the tyrant (41 A.D.), before his

[1] Philo, *Leg. ad Caium*, 568.

[2] The Transtiberine ' Ghetto,' which was first removed across the river in 1556.

[3] Schürer, *Hist. of the Jewish People in N.T. Times*, 2nd Div., vol. ii. pp. 234, 259, 264. Josephus (*Ant.* xiv.) gives a number of the edicts conferring these privileges. See also Suet. *Caesar*, 42. The action of Julius Caesar was the more remarkable as he took energetic steps to repress all *collegia* which were unable to prove ancient prescriptive rights and liberty of association generally. Consult also Harnack, *Expansion of Christianity*, vol. i. pp. 5–10, 350–371 ; Fouard, *S. Pierre*, c. xiv. ' Les Juifs de Rome ' ; Renan, *Hibbert Lectures*, Eng. tr., pp. 45–55.

[4] Josephus (*Ant.* xviii. 5) tells us that the anger of Tiberius was aroused by the complaint of Saturninus, a friend of the emperor, that his wife Fulvia, who was a proselyte, had been induced to give money for the service of the Temple at Jerusalem under false pretences. Suetonius (*Vit. Tib.* 36) writes : ' Iudaeorum iuventutes per speciem sacramenti in provincias gravioris caeli distribuit, reliquos gentis eiusdem vel similia sectantes urbe summovit, sub poena perpetuae servitutis nisi obtemperassent.' Tacitus (*Ann.* ii. 85) confirms the account of Josephus about the sending of this body of Jews to Sardinia and characteristically remarks ' si ob gravitatem caeli interiissent, vile damnum.' The action of Tiberius was confined to the Jews of Rome.

design was carried into effect.[1] Claudius, however, on his accession at once renewed all the old privileges, and took steps to allay the fanatical passions stirred up by the action of his half-insane predecessor. From this time forward the Jews were never compelled to take part in Caesar-worship.[2] To them alone of all the peoples of the empire was this concession made.

This Jewish colony in Rome seems from the descriptions of contemporary writers to have had the same characteristics as the Jewish colonies in European cities throughout the Middle Ages, and indeed much as we see them to-day. A large proportion of these Roman Jews were very poor, living in rags and squalor, making a precarious livelihood as hawkers, pedlars, and dealers in second-hand goods. Above these were then, as now, the moneylenders, larger traders, and shopkeepers, and at the head the wealthy financiers, and in the days of Tiberius and his successors many members of the Herodian family made Rome their home and lived on terms of close intimacy with the Imperial circle.[3] It is a curious fact that the Jewish race, while hated and despised by the people of Rome, should have been endowed with so many immunities by the Emperors, and above all that its exclusive religion and ceremonial rites should have possessed such an attraction as undoubtedly they did possess, and should have drawn so many adherents from all classes.[4] The truth is that the privileges, as I have said before, were granted from motives of pure expediency. The Jewish race was numerous, it had settlements in practically every important city in the empire, and it was financially indis-

---

[1] Much may be learnt about the position of the Jews in the Empire and of Caligula's disposition towards them in Philo's *Legatio ad Caium*, in which he gives an account of the reception by the emperor of a deputation from the Jews of Alexandria headed by himself.

[2] Tacitus, *Hist.* v. 5 'Non regibus haec adulatio, non Caesaribus honor.'

[3] For the Herodian family at Rome see Josephus, *Ant.* xviii. 5, 6.

[4] Harnack, *Expansion of Christianity*, i. 7-11; Schürer, 2 Div. ii. 220-242; Allard, *Hist. de Persée.* c. i. sec. 1; Hardy, *Studies in Roman Hist.* pp. 14-28; Workman, *Persecutions in Early Church*, pp. 108-115.

pensable. ⟩ The number of Jews in Rome in 5 B.C. has been estimated at 10,000 ; in Egypt, 1,000,000 ; in Palestine, 700,000 ; in the whole Roman Empire (out of a total population of fifty-four to sixty millions) four to four and a half millions.

As 4000 adult males were actually sent to Sardinia in 19 A.D. it may safely be said that a quarter of a century later, allowing for the natural growth of population, for fresh batches of slaves receiving manumission, and for immigration from outside, the total Jewish settlement in Rome would not be less than 30,000 and might reach 50,000.

Everywhere the Jew however held aloof from his Gentile neighbours, and his absolute refusal to mingle with them and to share their life could only be met either by coercion or by favoured treatment. To the wise statesmanship of the dictator Julius the latter course commended itself, and the permanence of the policy he adopted is sufficient proof of its prescience. ⌈The attractiveness of Judaism, as a religious cult, is more difficult to explain.⌋ It had neither the mysticism nor the sensuousness of the worship of Isis or of Cybele. Yet although the Jew was hated and scorned, his religion became to a surprising degree the mode in⌉ Rome, especially among ladies of the patrician houses. ⌋ The number of actual proselytes of Gentile origin was large, and still larger the number of those whom St. Luke in the Acts styles ' God-fearers ' [1] ($\sigma\epsilon\beta\acute{o}\mu\epsilon\nu\sigma\iota$ $\tau\grave{o}\nu$ $\Theta\epsilon\acute{o}\nu$), i.e. people who adopted the Jewish monotheism, attended the

[1] These people, described in the Acts and elsewhere as $\sigma\epsilon\beta\acute{o}\mu\epsilon\nu\sigma\iota$ (or $\phi\sigma\beta\sigma\acute{u}\mu\epsilon\nu\sigma\iota$) $\tau\grave{o}\nu$ $\Theta\epsilon\acute{o}\nu$ or simply as $\sigma\epsilon\beta\acute{o}\mu\epsilon\nu\sigma\iota$, were by Schürer, in the 1st ed. of his *Geschichte d. Jüdischen Volkes im Zeitalter Jesu Christi*, described as being ' the Proselytes of the Gate ' of the Talmud. He followed the commonly received opinion. He has however since then, by a careful study of inscriptions, been led to change his opinion. In his 4th ed. 1909 (iii. 173 ff.) he is able to show that the term ' proselyte of the gate ' was not used until a much later period than that with which we are dealing, and that the real meaning is that given above, heathen who had partially adopted Judaism, but without becoming proselytes. See Kirsopp Lake, *Early Epistles of St. Paul*, pp. 37–39.

synagogue [1] services, and observed the Sabbath and certain
portions of the ceremonial law.   These 'God-fearers,' in
every place where Jewish communities were to be found,
formed a fringe round the Synagogue of bodies of men and
women, who, in this age of religious electicism, without
altogether abandoning their connexion with Paganism, had
become semi-Jews.

In a city such as the Rome we have been describing it is
not difficult to see a seed-plot ready prepared for the planting
of a new religion like Christianity, oriental in its origin,
an outgrowth of Judaism, akin in so many points to the
Mystery-Religions of Egypt and Asia Minor then so much
in vogue, and bearing, as it did, in its ethical·teaching so
striking a resemblance to the moral code of the Stoics.
That the message of the Gospel of Jesus Christ in some
primitive form reached the banks of the Tiber very early
there is, as I shall show later, good reason to believe, but
of the when or how we know nothing directly.   The converts at first would be almost certainly few in number and
drawn from the humbler class of Jews.[2]   The new sect, if

---

[1] The synagogues in Rome were each separately organised and independent.   The entire body of Jews of the capital were not allowed, as at
Alexandria, to form a state within a state, self-administered with an Ala-
barch at their head.   The names of seven synagogues have been discovered
in the inscriptions of the ancient Jewish cemeteries : (1) Αὐγουστησέων,
(2) Ἀγριππησίων, (3) Bolumni, (4) Καμπησίων, (5) Σιβουρησίων, (6) Ἀιβρέων,
(7) Ἐλαίας.   The first two were probably the synagogues of the households
of Augustus and Agrippa.   The fourth and fifth belong to Jewish settlements on the outskirts of the Campus Martius and in the crowded Suburra.
The third may have been built by some one of the name of Volumnus, or
have been associated with him in some unknown way.   The seventh, the
synagogue of the Olive Tree, may have suggested the simile of Rom. xi.
17–24.   The sixth inscription does not seem to have referred to any special
synagogue but to have been a generic term, 'a synagogue of the Hebrews
(or Jews).'   In addition to settlements in the Suburra and near the Campus
Martius, the discovery of two ancient Jewish cemeteries on the Appian
Way, one of them close to the Porta Capena, bears evidence to yet another
Jewish colony at this point, not inconsiderable in numbers.   The Transtiberine, however, was always by far the largest of the Jewish quarters.
See Schürer, 2 Div., ii. 247–249; Fouard, S. Pierre, pp. 316–322; Garrucci,
Cimetero degli antichi Ebrei in Roma, and Marucchi, Eléments
d'Archéologie Chrétienne, vol. ii. pp. 208–226, 259–274.

[2] For the chronology of these Lectures see Note A of the Appendix.

it were noticed at all by the authorities, would be regarded
with contemptuous indifference as a variety of Judaism,
and therefore sheltered by the privileges which Judaism,
as a *religio licita*, enjoyed.[1]   The only possible allusion in
the first decade after the Crucifixion to the existence in Rome
of a knowledge of Christian teaching is contained in a
passage of Suetonius' ' Life of Caligula,' in which he tells of
the performance before the Emperor of a play in which a
certain *Laureolus*, who gives his name to the piece, is crucified
upon the stage.   Might there not be here a cruel parody
upon the central theme of Christian preaching ?   Probably
not, though such an exhibition is at any rate thoroughly
illustrative of the spirit of mockery with which the idea of a
crucified Saviour would be received.[2]

There is evidence, however, in the pages of the same
historian, Suetonius, that almost exactly a decade after the
aforesaid production of the *Laureolus* Christianity in
Rome had already become a force sufficiently potent to
draw down upon it the fanatical antagonism of the Jews.
Tumults and disorders seem to have arisen in the Jewish
quarter of the city in 50 A.D. of such a threatening character
as to force the Government, in spite of its favourable in-
clination to the Jews, to take strong action. This appears
to me to be nothing more than a fair interpretation of
Suetonius' words—' the Jews who were continually rioting
at the instigation of Chrestus he (Claudius) expelled from
Rome.'[3]   To write *Chrestus* for *Christus* was quite natural to
a Latin historian, for Chrestus was a name in use at Rome

---

[1] Tertullian (*Apol.* xxi.) says that the Church until the time of Nero's
persecution grew up under the shadow of the synagogue : ' quasi sub
umbraculo religionis insignissimae certe licitae.'

[2] Suet. *Calig.* 57.   See also for later notices of Laureolus, Jos. *Ant.*
xix. 18 ; Martial, *Spect.* 7 ; Tertullian, *Valent.* 14.   In Mayor's *Juvenal*,
vol. ii. p. 40, the following note appears to *Sat.* viii. 167 : ' Laureolum Schol.
In ipso mimo Laureolo figitur crux unde vera cruce dignus est Lentulus,
qui tanto detestabilior est quanto melius gestum imitatus est sceni-
cum. . . . . Hic Lentulus nobilis fuit et suscepit servi personam in
agendo mimo.'

[3] Suet. *Claudius*, 25 ' Iudaeos impulsore Chresto assidue tumultuantes
Roma expulit.'

as extant inscriptions show,[1] ⸢and both Tertullian and
Lactantius [2] tell us that in their time the common pro-
nunciation was ' Chrestus ' and ' Chrestianos ' for ' Christus '
and ' Christianos.'⸥ The French word ' chrétien ' is to this
day a living proof that this mode of spelling still survives.
Dion Cassius [3] informs us that the edict of expulsion, owing
to the disturbance that it caused, was only partially carried
out, but that the synagogues were closed and the clubs
licensed by Caligula dissolved. Among the Jews that were
expelled were no doubt the chief leaders of the contending
factions. Among these were Aquila and Priscilla or Prisca,
of whom we read in the Acts of the Apostles that in consequence of Claudius' edict of banishment they had left Rome
and taken up their abode at Corinth, and were there brought
into personal contact with St. Paul, when in the summer
of 51 A.D. he first visited that city.

The intercourse which thus began was destined to
be long-continued and intimate, and it was through this
intercourse (such at least is my firm persuasion) that that
eager desire to visit Rome, to which the Apostle gives such
strong expression in his Epistle to the Romans some five or
six years later, was first fanned into flame. Not without
purpose did St. Luke, who never wastes words, give such an
elaborate description of this husband and wife upon their
first entry on the stage of his history. ' Having departed
from Athens ' we read [4] ' Paul came to Corinth and having

---

[1] *CIL.* vi. 10233. The following inscription, which I came across,
seemed to me specially interesting from the collocation of the names
Chrestus and Paula. ' P. Ælius Chrestus et Cornelia Paula hoc scalare
adplicitum huic sepulchro quod emerunt a fisco agente Agathonico
proc [-uratore] Augustorum nostrorum quod habet scriptura infra scripta.
Gentiano et Basso cons. vii Kal. April.' Date, 211 A.D.

[2] Tert. *Apol.* 3 : ' Sed ut cum perperam Chrestianos pronuntiatur a
vobis, nam nec nominis certa est notitia penes vos ' ; Lact. *Inst. Divin.*
iv. 17: ' Sed exponenda huius nominis [Christi] ratio est propter
ignorantium errorem, qui eum immutata litera Chrestum solent dicere.'
Compare the title *Le Roy très Chréstien* of the French Kings.

[3] Dion Cassius, lx. 6 : τούς τε Ἰουδαίους, πλεονάσαντας αὖθις χαλεπῶς ἂν
ἄνευ ταραχῆς ὑπὸ τοῦ ὄχλου σφῶν τῆς πόλεως εἰρχθῆναι, οὐκ ἐξήλασε μέν, τῷ δὲ δὴ
πατρίῳ νόμῳ βίῳ χρωμένους, ἐκέλευσε μὴ συναθροίζεσθαι. τάς τε ἑταιρείας
ἐπαναχθείσας ὑπὸ τοῦ Γαίου διέλυσε.   [4] Acts, xviii. 1.

met a certain Jew, by name Aquila, a Pontian [1] by birth, who had lately come from Italy, and Priscilla his wife, in consequence of the decree of Claudius that all the Jews should depart from Rome, betook himself to them, and because they were of the same trade he abode with them and wrought at his craft, for they were tentmakers by trade.' Here undoubtedly St. Luke intended in the first place to give the reason for the strong bond of sympathy which at once sprang up between these two Asiatic Jews and fellow craftsmen. The description of Aquila as a Jew does not mean that he was not a Christian. Had he and his wife required to be converted and baptised, it is almost impossible that so important a fact should not here have been mentioned. Compare the notice about Apollos, Acts xviii. 24–27. The Jews who were actually exiled by Claudius were no doubt the leaders of the contending factions, Aquila and Prisca having been in 50 A.D. as afterwards among the foremost of the Christian congregation. In the eyes of the Roman authorities, as has already been pointed out, Christianity was as yet simply a Jewish sect. The emphatic statement that Aquila was a Jew applies, as the context shows, not to his religion but to his race, and the separate mention of Priscilla without that epithet may be taken to imply, firstly, that she was not Jewish but Roman, and secondly that she was to play an independent role in the furtherance of St. Paul's missionary work. Never indeed in the New Testament is the one name mentioned without the other, and in four out of the six places in which they occur the name of Prisca or Priscilla stands first.[2] From this fact the deduction has been made, and in my opinion rightly, that Prisca was of

---

[1] *I.e.* a native of the Roman Province of Pontus.

[2] For further details about Prisca and Aquila see Appendix, Note B. It is noteworthy that St. Paul according to the authority of the best authenticated readings always calls the wife Prisca, while St. Luke names her Priscilla. Both writers, except in one case, 1 Cor. xvi. 19, place the name of the wife first. St. Luke is wont to use the diminutive forms of names, which were usual in conversation, *i.e.* Priscilla, Silas, Sopatros ; St. Paul the forms Prisca, Silvanus, Sosipatros. See Ramsay, *St. Paul the Traveller*, pp. 267–8.

more honourable position by birth than her husband, and that she possessed private means which she freely used in furthering the cause of the Gospel.[1]

I have spoken, not without good reason, of this intercourse which began in 51 A.D. at Corinth, as being long-continued and intimate. During the whole of his eighteen months' sojourn in that city St. Paul lived under their roof, and when he sailed from Cenchraea for Ephesus in the early spring of 53 A.D. Aquila and Prisca accompanied him. At Ephesus they took up their abode,[2] and at once set about active missionary work, while awaiting the Apostle's return some six months later. During this interval it was by their instrumentality that the eloquent and learned Apollos was instructed in the full Christian faith, and probably it was by their advice that he entered upon, what we know to have been, his fruitful ministry at Corinth.[3]   Throughout the two years and a quarter [4] that St. Paul made Ephesus the centre of his labours, Aquila and Prisca resided there. Probably their house was as before the Apostle's home ; in any case we know that it was a meeting-place in which the faithful gathered for worship, for in his First Epistle to the Corinthians,[5] which was written from Ephesus some time in the autumn of 55 A.D., St. Paul sends the salutations of Aquila and Priscilla and ' of the Church that is in their house.' From these his close friends and fellow-workers, with whom he was for some five or six years in constant communication, St. Paul would therefore have ample opportunities for learning much about the condition of the Church in Rome, and this not only from Aquila and Prisca themselves but from other exiles and the many travellers and traders from the capital whom he must have met at their house, and who would bring with them the latest news as to the state of things in the Imperial City. Among other things would

[1] Plumptre, *Biblical Studies*, p. 417 ; Hort, *Romans and Philippians*, pp. 12–14 ; Ramsay, *St. Paul the Traveller*, pp. 253 f., 267 f. ; Zahn, *Intr. to N.T.* i. 265, etc. etc.

[2] Acts, xviii. 11 and 18, 19.

[3] Acts, xviii. 24–27.   [4] Acts, xix. 10.   [5] 1 Cor. xvi. 19.

come the glad tidings of the accession of the young and
popular Nero in the place of Claudius, and of the happy
prospects that his reign promised, a promise that was
justified so long as the boy emperor was content in his public
administration to place himself under the guidance of his
wise counsellors Seneca and Burrhus.[1] What is certain is
that St. Paul at the close of his two years' ministry at
Ephesus began to look ahead and to plan fresh schemes of
missionary activity. His first task was to journey through
Macedonia to Corinth, where his presence was called for and
needed ; his next to pay another visit after a long absence
to Jerusalem, but ' after I have been there,' he said, ' I must
see Rome.'[2] His departure from Ephesus was more
hurried than he expected, for in the riots raised by
Demetrius and his fellow-craftsmen against the Christians
and the Jews with whom as usual they were con-
founded,[3] Paul seems to have narrowly escaped from the
violence of the angry throng, and to have succeeded in
doing so only through the self-sacrificing courage of
Aquila and Prisca,[4] who risked their own lives in order
to save his.

It had been Paul's intention to remain at Ephesus till
Pentecost, but this serious tumult compelled [5] him to leave
much earlier in the year 56 A.D., and at the same time and
for the same reasons his friends Aquila and Prisca may have
taken the opportunity to start on their return journey to
Rome, the edict of banishment having now been allowed
to lapse by the conciliatory policy of Nero's advisers. The
friendly Asiarchs, who warned Paul not to adventure

---

[1] For the good government of the Empire during the first five years
of Nero's reign, known in history as the *quinquennium* of Nero, see
Henderson's *Life and Principate of the Emperor Nero.*

[2] Acts, xix. 21.   [3] Acts, xix. 33-4.

[4] Rom. xvi. 34 : Ἀσπάσασθε Πρίσκαν καὶ Ἀκύλαν τοὺς συνεργούς μου ἐν
Χριστῷ Ἰησοῦ, οἵτινες ὑπὲρ τῆς ψυχῆς μου τὸν ἑαυτῶν τράχηλον ὑπέθηκαν. Comp.
2 Cor. i. 8. The group of MSS. D, E, F, G, add παρ' οἷς καὶ ξενίζομαι, pointing to the tradition in the Western Church that St. Paul lived at Ephesus
in the house of Aquila and Prisca.

[5] Acts, xix. 31.

himself into the theatre, would indeed feel it their duty, as
soon as the riot was appeased, for the sake of the peace of the
city to insist that both Paul and his protectors Aquila and
Prisca should quit Ephesus for a time. Paul himself carried
out his plan of journeying by way of Troas and Philippi
to Corinth, where he passed the three winter months of
56–57 A.D. The project of a visit to Rome, so long cherished,
so often hindered, now began to assume a concrete shape in
his mind, and the result was the writing, almost certainly in
the early spring of the year 57 A.D., of the Epistle to the
Romans. Now this great epistle stands in the forefront of
the Pauline writings chiefly as a theological treatise, but
apart from its theology it has other claims, as an historical
document of the highest evidential value, deserving from
the Church historian's point of view the closest and most
attentive study.

In the first place then this Epistle bears upon its face the
clearest testimony to the existence in 57 A.D. of a distinguished and well-established Christian Church in Rome, a
Church already of some standing and in which the Gentile
element predominated.   The mere fact that the Apostle,
at a time when many cares pressed heavily upon him,[1] took
the pains to write this elaborate and carefully reasoned
statement of his doctrinal teaching to a body of Christians
that he had never visited, is evidence to the very important
place they occupied in his thoughts. His words, ' I thank
my God through Jesus Christ for you all that your faith [2]
is proclaimed in all the world,' may be somewhat hyperbolic,
but they mean at any rate that the Roman Church was well
known and highly spoken of in all the various Christian
communities with which St. Paul was acquainted.   And the
impression these words convey is emphasised by the
Apostle's later declaration affirming even in stronger terms
his personal assent to this widely received estimate of the
character of Roman Christianity, for no language could be

---

[1] 2 Cor. ii. 4, 5, 13 ; iv. 8–11 ; xi. 27–28 ; xii. 10, 20–21 ; Acts, xx.
19–25.

[2] Rom. i. 8 : ἡ πίστις ὑμῶν = your profession of Christianity.

more explicit than this—' I am persuaded, my brethren,
I myself also concerning you, that even of yourselves '—*i.e.*
without any extraneous help derived from such an epistle
as I am sending to you—' you are full of goodness, filled with
all knowledge, able also to admonish one another.' [1] Such a
declaration implies a conviction based upon trustworthy
evidence, otherwise his readers would be the first to perceive
that here was only high-flown language covering an empty
compliment. Such an utterance from a man and a writer
like St. Paul presupposes an already existing acquaintance
with a considerable number of Roman Christians, whose
goodness, knowledge, and sound judgment he has tested and
learnt to appreciate.   Indeed it is not too much to say that
Paul in writing this epistle is somewhat oppressed by a sense
that those whom he is addressing—for a reason, which will
appear presently—may possibly think that they have no
special need either of his instruction or of his admonition.
His epistle is an *apologia* for venturing to be so bold as to
propose to pay a visit to Rome, even though that visit should
be no more than a brief pause in the course of a journey
farther west.[2] He evidently had in his mind the fear that
in Rome he had, as a preparatory step, to fight down dis-
paraging rumours concerning himself, his teaching, and his
office, and that he might be regarded as an intruder. If he
had found it necessary even in Corinth, a Church which he
himself had planted, and where even now he was writing,
to defend strenuously his Apostolic claims and doctrine,[3]
how much more in Rome among Christians of old standing,
in whose conversion he had had no hand.

So in the Introductory Salutation St. Paul sets forth
his credentials.   He is no mere ordinary apostle, a man
commissioned by the Twelve or by some particular Church
to go forth to some limited field of missionary work.   His

---

[1] Rom. xv. 14 : Πέπεισμαι δέ, ἀδελφοί μου, καὶ αὐτὸς ἐγὼ περὶ ὑμῶν, ὅτι καὶ
αὐτοὶ μεστοί ἐστε ἀγαθωσύνης, πεπληρωμένοι πάσης γνώσεως, δυνάμενοι καὶ ἀλλήλους
νουθετεῖν. Notice the emphatic position of καὶ αὐτὸς ἐγώ. Compare xvi. 19 :
ἡ γὰρ ὑμῶν ὑπακοὴ εἰς πάντας ἀφίκετο.

[2] Rom. xv. 24.

[3] 2 Cor. x. 12–18 ; xii. 11–13 ; and elsewhere.

Apostleship differed from that of their own Junias and Andronicus,[1] whom later he describes as ' apostles of note,' differed—perhaps it is implied—even from that of so eminent a man as Barnabas,[2] in that he [Paul] like the Twelve had been chosen out and set apart [3] for the preaching of the Gospel by the Lord Jesus Christ Himself—chosen and set apart for preaching the Gospel among all nations and bringing them to the obedience of the faith.[4] And though the Gospel has already been preached in Rome and with such success that the faith of the Roman Christians is spoken of everywhere in terms of praise, yet Rome too lies within the bounds of his commission, and so he has many times planned, though hitherto always hindered, to come to them that he might have some fruit amongst them also. Indeed he calls God to witness that he had prayed continually that he might be prospered on his way to visit them, that he might be able to impart to them some spiritual gift for their confirmation. Immediately, however, adding lest he should offend their susceptibilities by any assumption of superiority —' that is that while I am amongst you we may be jointly strengthened by the mutual faith of you and me.' [5]

But if the note of *apologia* can be discerned here in the introductory verses, it comes out much more strongly in what may be styled the body of the epistle. The difficulties of interpretation theologically of the Apostle's reasoning and arguments, in that grand series of chapters which end with chapter xi., lie outside my province. Those difficulties, admittedly very great, are caused in no small degree by our ignorance of the circumstances, of the persons, parties, questions, and situation generally with which St. Paul was

---

[1] Rom. xvi. 7.

[2] There are grounds, as will appear in the sequel, for believing that Barnabas had already visited Rome.

[3] Rom. i. 1 : κλητὸς ἀπόστολος, ἀφωρισμένος εἰς εὐαγγέλιον θεοῦ.

[4] Rom. i. 5 : δι' οὗ ['Ιησοῦ Χριστοῦ τοῦ κυρίου ἡμῶν] ἐλάβομεν χάριν καὶ ἀποστολὴν εἰς ὑπακοὴν πίστεως ἐν πᾶσιν τοῖς ἔθνεσιν.

[5] Rom. i. 12 : τοῦτο δέ ἐστιν συνπαρακληθῆναι ἐν ὑμῖν διὰ τῆς ἐν ἀλλήλοις πίστεως ὑμῶν τε καὶ ἐμοῦ. See Zahn, *Int. to N.T.* pp. 355-8, 369. Kirsopp Lake, *Early Epist. of St. Paul*, pp. 378-9.

dealing. We lack in fact the historical background. It is my present object to try to trace out from the materials, which the epistle itself supplies in definite even though in parts but in faint outline, such features of that background as are discernible through the mist of ages. Leaving on one side for the present the extremely important auto-biographical passage in chapter xv., also the valuable testimony as to the composition of the Roman Church furnished by the list of salutations in chapter xvi., which require special and separate treatment, we can, I think, make certain well-grounded assertions concerning the three distinct groups of persons whom St. Paul had in his thoughts as he wrote this epistle. These three groups are (1) a body of Jewish Christians, (2) a larger body of converted Gentiles, (3) the mass of unbelieving Jews. St. Paul leaves in no doubt that the third group comprised the vast majority of the Roman Jews, including practically the whole of official Israel. And what is more, as yet these rabbis, elders, and rulers of the Synagogues were not so much actively hostile to the preaching of Christianity as simply deaf, contemp-tuously indifferent. Those of Group No. 1, the Jewish Christians, were relatively small in number, but though small they were divided into two very distinct sections or parties. One of these sections consisted of Jews like Aquila and others mentioned in the salutations, who were Paul's friends and fellow-workers ; the other, an extremely influential and energetic section of Judaeo-Christians, Jews rather than Christians, who, like the Judaisers who are brought before us in the Epistle to the Galatians and elsewhere, were bitterly opposed to St. Paul, disputed his Apostolic authority, traduced and misrepresented his teach-ing, and denounced him as a renegade from the faith of his fathers. The Gentiles of the second group formed the chief element in the Roman Church. Of these no doubt a certain number had been converted straight from heathen-dom, but the assumption which runs through the epistle, that they were familiar with the Jewish Scriptures in the Sep-tuagint version, and with the Jewish ceremonial law, would

seem to point to their being largely drawn from the class
of Greek-speaking ' God-fearers,' which, as I have already
stated, in all the chief towns of the Empire, and conspicuously
in Rome, formed a fringe round the synagogue. If it be
asked, what was the impelling motive which led to the
writing of this epistle, and which dictated the order and
character of the arguments, the answer surely is not far to
seek. St. Paul had made up his mind after many hesitations
to visit Rome, but from information that had come to him
he was not altogether happy about the reception he would
meet. ⌈To the Christian community of the imperial city
as a whole he was a stranger, and as I have said, he was aware
that there was a Judaising faction there busy at their usual
task of stirring up enmity against him.⌉ His own words
(Rom. iii. 8), ' as we are slanderously reported and as some
affirm that we say, let us do evil that good may come,' are a
proof that he had been informed that his great doctrine of
Justification by Faith had been seized upon by these adver-
saries to represent him as an antinomian. He therefore
felt it to be incumbent upon him to answer at once and
in advance these Judaistic attacks by a full exposition of his
teaching on the subject of *Justification by Faith*, and at the
same time he desired to make clear what was his real
attitude towards many disputed questions concerning
Judaism and the observance of the Mosaic Law, and the
relation between Jew and Gentile in the Church of Christ.

If this be granted then a flood of light is immediately
thrown on the interpretation and import of that central
portion of this epistle, which begins with the words
(Rom. ii. 17)—' but if thou bearest the name . . . of Jew
and possessest a law to rest upon '—up to the end of
chapter xi. It is unmistakably addressed to Jews.[1] Not

[1] Rom. ii. 17-29 ; iii. 1, 2 ; iv. 1.   That this body of Judaeo-Christians
were still active in Rome, and doing their utmost at a later time to counter-
act St. Paul's influence and oppose his teaching, see Phil. i. 15, 16 ; iii. 1-6.
It was to these same Jews that chap. xiv. 1-23 appears to have been
addressed. The extreme particularity about meats and rigid asceticism
were characteristic of the party of the circumcision. See Zahn, *Int. to N.T.*
pp. 366-7.

to the strict orthodox Jews of the Synagogues, who in their haughty aloofness would not be likely either to see or to read the Apostle's arguments. The Jews addressed were men who had indeed accepted Jesus as the Jewish Messiah but who perhaps only the more obstinately for that very reason clung to their Judaism, and hated the thought of losing any of those exclusive religious privileges, as Israelites, which were their pride and boast. The doors of the Christian Church, as they conceived it, might be open to Gentiles, but only if they would consent to be circumcised and to conform to the ordinances of the Mosaic Law.

But though in form he is addressing himself to Jews, Paul's thoughts are all the time directed to his Gentile readers, and it is for their sake and for their edification quite as much as for the persuasion of his Jewish fellow-countrymen that he step by step leads up to the establishment of the fundamental principles of the Gospel that he preached. This is made quite clear by his own words (chap. xi. 13–14) : 'For it is to you the Gentiles that I am speaking. Nay, more,[1] in so far as I am the Gentiles' Apostle I make-the-most-of[2] my ministry ; if by any means I may stir to jealousy my own flesh and might save some.'[3]

The lengthy list of salutations to be found in the first

[1] So Sanday and Headlam give the force of the μὲν οὖν in this verse. *Commentary on Romans*, p. 324.

[2] Lit. glorify.

[3] On St. Paul's attitude towards Jewish Christianity and Judaism see the extremely interesting section of Harnack's *Neue Untersuchungen zur Apostelgeschichte*, 1911 (Eng. tr. by Rev. J. R. Wilkinson in Crown Theol. Lib.), pp. 28–47. Of the evidence supplied by that section of the Epistle to the Romans from which these words are taken, Harnack writes : 'Der Grosse Abschnitt—c. 9–11—ist aus der Feder eines Juden geflossen der mit allen Fasern seiner Seele an seinem Volke hängt'(p..31). And again concerning the simile of the olive-tree in c. xi. : 'Man beachte wohl, das (gläubige) Israel κατὰ σάρκα ist und bleibt " der güte Ölbaum " (gegenüber dem wilden Ölbaum der Heiden) ; jeder Israelit ist ein " natürlicher Zweig " dieses guten Ölbaums, wenn er auch unter Umständen abgehauen werden muss, und er d.h. das gläubige Israel κατὰ σάρκα ist die Wurzel an deren Safte und Fettigkeit die eingepropften wilden Schösslinge teilnehmen und die sie trägt' (p. 32). See also the quotation from Herzog in note. I have already pointed out the possibility that the name of one of the Roman synagogues 'The Olive Tree' may have suggested this simile to St. Paul.

twenty-three verses of chapter xvi. is a passage of great and peculiar interest historically, for it enables us to form some estimate, not conjecturally but positively, concerning the social and racial composition of the Roman Christian community at this time. It also gives indirectly an indication of the close relations of intercourse subsisting between the Churches of the chief cities of the Mediterranean coast. The very fact of its historical importance has however caused doubts to be raised by certain critics of the hypercritical school whether the passage is really an integral part of the Epistle to the Romans. Its Pauline authorship is not assailed, but attempts have been made to show that the list where it stands has (wholly or in part) been displaced and that it should be attached to some hypothetical epistle addressed at some unknown time to another Church, most probably to that of Ephesus. It must suffice here to say that I accept without hesitation the whole of this sixteenth chapter as an original and authentic portion of the Epistle to the Romans on the following grounds. First, to quote the words of Professor Kirsopp Lake, one of the most recent advocates of the Ephesian hypothesis, ' There is no trace of any external evidence for doubting that this section has always belonged to the epistle.' [1] This then is admitted, and it counts heavily. Secondly, all the names, some of them rare and uncommon names, contained in the list of salutations have been discovered in the inscriptions found in the *columbaria* and cemeteries of Rome, of a date contemporary or nearly contemporary with the date of the epistle : an evidence in favour of authenticity, which, if not absolutely conclusive, is at least remarkably convincing. [2] The arguments in favour of the anti-Roman hypothesis are of a purely *a priori* character, and there are only two of them, it seems to me, of weight sufficient to deserve consideration. The first is the difficulty of imagining that Paul could possibly

---

[1] Kirsopp Lake, *The Early Epistles of St. Paul, their motive and origin*, p. 325 ff.
[2] Sanday and Headlam, *Ep. to Romans*, pp. xciii–xcv ; Lightfoot, *Ep. to Philippians*, see dissertation on Caesar's Household, pp. 169–176.

have been acquainted with the names of so many members of a Church he had never visited, and still more that he should have been able in quite a large proportion of cases to add personal details. With this argument I have already dealt in part. Besides the information which he must have acquired from Aquila and Prisca during those four years they spent together at Corinth and Ephesus, he would be brought into contact at those two great centres of Mediterranean traffic with a constant stream of travellers and traders from Rome. Among these would be Christians, whose first thought would be to find their way to the friendly house of their banished fellow-citizens. Criticism here, as in many other instances, has gone astray from its failure to recognise the great facilities for intercourse in Apostolic times, especially between cities on the shores of the Mediterranean, and the freedom with which those facilities were used. The travels of Apollonius of Tyana as told by Philostratus are a good instance in point, for Apollonius was a contemporary of St. Paul. The Apostle did not draw up, we may be sure, this unusually long list of salutations without an object. Diffident, as he seems to have been, of the welcome he would receive upon his visit to Rome, may we not regard these salutations as in some sense a tactful act of diplomacy? He wished to remind those who are mentioned that he bore them in his remembrance and affection, and at the same time to bespeak, as it were, their good offices with their brethren for the time when he actually came amongst them.[1] That Paul himself could not have made out such a list with its many details without assistance is possibly true, but that assistance was at his very side, as his words were being written down. Very interesting, as a mark of the genuineness of this passage, is the sudden interpolation, in the midst of the Pauline phrases, of a salutation

---

[1] Zahn (*Int. to N.T.* i. 388) says: ' Who does not see that all these personal references are due to Paul's desire to make the Church feel that it is not such a stranger to him as it seems, and at the same time are indications of an effort on his part to bring himself into closer touch with the Church where as yet he was really a stranger ? '

from another hand, ' I, Tertius, the scribe of this epistle, salute you.' [1] Tertius was then a Roman Christian, and he had doubtless been chosen by Paul on this occasion to act as his amanuensis, for this very reason.

The second argument relied upon by the critics is at first sight more plausible.   Paul in writing his First Epistle to the Corinthians from Ephesus sends salutations from Aquila and Prisca and the Church in their house, adding according to one group of authorities the words ' with whom also I am a guest.' [2]   Nothing could be more natural, and the inference seems to follow that when previously the Apostle was a guest in their house at Corinth, there likewise that house was a meeting-place for a Christian congregation. About a year and a quarter after this Paul, writing from Corinth to the Romans, again sends salutations to these same fellow-workers (Aquila and Prisca), and then after a eulogistic reference to their having risked their lives to save his, and thanking them not only in his own name but in that of all the Churches of the Gentiles, he proceeds to salute ' the Church that is in their house.'   Now to the critics with whom I am dealing it appears very improbable that if Aquila and Prisca had only returned to Rome so recently there could have been already a Church in their house with the existence of which St. Paul could have been sufficiently acquainted to deem it worthy of a special salutation.   It is pointed out, moreover, that in his Second Epistle to Timothy (an epistle, by the by, not accepted by these same critics as Paul's or contemporary) Paul sends salutations

---

[1] Rom. xvi. 22.   In the first-century Cemetery of Priscilla close to the mausoleum of the noble family of the Acilii there may be seen to-day a Greek inscription in red (a proof of its very early date) :

ΤΕΡΤΙΑΔΕΛΦΕ
ΕΤΨΤΧΙΟΤΔΙC
ΑΘΑΝΑΤΟC

The Tertius here mentioned is probably not St. Paul's amanuensis, but there is no reason why he should not be.   It is interesting that a well-authenticated tradition places the tombs of Aquila and Prisca in the vicinity of this inscription.] Horace Marucchi, *Eléments d'Archéologie Chrétienne*, ii. 419. See also i. 104.

[2] παρ' οἷς καὶ ξενίζομαι. D, F, lat, goth, Bede.

from Rome to Prisca and Aquila apparently at Ephesus, and the suggestion is put forward that during the decade which intervened between the first and last of these salutations the home of this husband and wife had always been at Ephesus.   This being so, this section of the sixteenth chapter of the Romans cannot belong to the epistle in which we find it.

It might be thought a sufficient answer to this allegation that external authority in its favour is confessedly non-existent—to say nothing of the fact that tradition with no uncertain voice connects the names of Prisca and Aquila with definite localities in Rome.[1]   But quite apart from this there is no real difficulty in accepting the usual interpretation of the salutation.

When the Apostle parted at Ephesus with the faithful companions and fellow-workers who had been so long of such service to him, one may be quite sure it would not be without full knowledge on both sides of their future intentions and plans.   On his reaching Corinth a whole twelve-month at least must have passed, ample time for news to have come, by some of those using the highway of traffic across the isthmus, that Aquila and Prisca were again settled at Rome and carrying on their work there on the same lines as at Corinth and Ephesus.   There is nothing whatever impossible in this, nothing certainly to afford the slightest pretext for the rejection of a well-authenticated text.   Personally however I do not believe that there is any necessity for entering upon the consideration of what I venture to call ' time-table calculations.'   There is nothing in St. Paul's words to warrant us in assuming that this ' Church in the house ' of Aquila and Prisca was new to Roman Christianity.   The banishment decreed by Claudius was according to Dion Cassius most leniently carried out and would not involve the confiscation of property.[2]   It is one of those minute points that are often so significant,

---

[1] The Church of St. Prisca and the Cemetery of Priscilla.   See Appendix, Special Note B.

[2] *Relegatio*, not *deportatio*.   Dion Cassius, lx. 6.

that St. Paul speaks of the house at Ephesus as that of Aquila and Prisca, of the house at Rome as that of Prisca and Aquila. If Prisca were, as is commonly supposed, when they were resident at Rome the more important person of the two spouses, and the owner of property, then the unusual inversion of the names is explicable. But at Ephesus where they were strangers the house would naturally be described as that of Aquila and Prisca, the husband's name standing first in order of precedence.[1]

Since Aquila and Prisca were expelled, it must have been, as I have already said, because they were recognised leaders of that faction of ' Chrestus ' of which Suetonius speaks. May one not be justified then in the assumption that the readiness of the exiles at Corinth and at Ephesus to offer hospitality and a room for worship in their house was but the continuation of their previous practice at their Roman home before their banishment ? But if the Church in their house was thus in existence before 50 A.D., it is scarcely likely that the owners in their enforced absence would forbid its use. It would but lessen their sense of separation, if they were thus able to be of continued service to their poorer Christian brethren in Rome. Such a supposition of course involves certain assumptions about the state of the Church in Rome in 50 A.D., but I hope to be able to show that it is a reasonable assumption, and consistent alike with the positive and traditional data that we possess.[2] The Epistle to the Romans is itself a proof that Christianity was firmly established in the metropolis some time before 57 A.D. ; there must therefore before that date have been houses where the faithful met. Tradition mentions only two such places of assembly—the house of Prisca and Aquila and the house of Pudens. The localities are still supposed to be marked by the very ancient Churches of St. Prisca and St. Pudenziana.

Granting then that this list of salutations is addressed to

[1] See Zahn, *Int. to N.T.* p. 390, for a useful comment on the movements of Aquila and Prisca.

[2] See Marucchi, *Eléments d'Archéologie Chrétienne*, iii. p. 180 ff and 364 ff.

the Roman community, let us glance very briefly at its
general features. A study of the names enables us to draw
the conclusion that the Roman Christians mainly belonged
to the class of Greek-speaking freedmen and slaves.[1] Certain of these are addressed by the Apostle as kinsmen
(συγγενεῖς), and it is safe to assume that these were Jewish
fellow-countrymen.[2] It is possible that some others not so
designated may have been Jews, but the probability is the
other way. The evidence already adduced points clearly to
a hostility to Paul among the Judaeo-Christians at Rome,
which would naturally exclude them from receiving friendly
greetings. Two names in this group deserve special
mention. ' Salute Andronicus and Junias my kinsmen and
my fellow-prisoners, who are men of mark among the
apostles, who also were in Christ before me '[3] is the remarkable language of the seventh verse. When and where these
two had been Paul's fellow-prisoners we know not. Paul
in his Second Epistle to the Corinthians—only a few months
before—had spoken of frequent imprisonments [4] of which
we know nothing./ The very fact that he describes Andronicus and Junias as ' men of mark among the apostles '
makes it probable that he had encountered them in his
journeys, for the term ' apostle ' at this early period seems to
have been applied generally to delegates sent out with a
commission by some Church for some special field of missionary work, and to have carried with it as a necessary
qualification the possession of charismatic gifts.[5] | But
a still greater distinction is conferred on these two by

[1] They would consist of people of every nationality, but among those
converted to Christianity probably a large proportion were Orientals by race.

[2] Compare Rom. ix. 3 : ηὐχόμην γὰρ ἀνάθεμα εἶναι αὐτὸς ἐγὼ ἀπὸ τοῦ χριστοῦ
ὑπὲρ τῶν ἀδελφῶν μου, τῶν συγγενῶν μου κατὰ σάρκα, οἵτινές εἰσιν Ἰσραηλῖται.

[3] ἀσπάσασθε Ἀνδρόνικον καὶ Ἰουνιᾶν τοὺς συγγενεῖς μου καὶ συναιχμαλώτους μου,
οἵτινές εἰσιν ἐπίσημοι ἐν τοῖς ἀποστόλοις, οἳ καὶ πρὸ ἐμοῦ γέγοναν ἐν Χριστῷ. It is
possible that 'Ιουνίαν might be feminine = Junia, but it is generally taken
as masculine, Junias an abbreviation for Junianus.

[4] 2 Cor. xi. 23 : ἐν φυλακαῖς περισσοτέρως.

[5] See Harnack, Expansion of· Christianity, i. 398–412 ; Lightfoot,
Epistle to Galatians, p. 93 ; Kirsopp Lake, Early Epistles of St. Paul,
pp. 108–110. Comp. 2 Cor. viii. 23 : ἀπόστολοι ἐκκλησιῶν.

Paul's admission that 'they were in Christ before me,' words which imply that their conversion dated back at least as far as the days of St. Stephen's activity. Possibly they belonged to that 'Synagogue of the Libertines'[1] in which Stephen argued, and afterwards became, a little later, the first preachers of the Gospel at Rome. Very interesting are the salutations to the households of Aristobulus and Narcissus. These would all be freedmen or slaves. Aristobulus may well have been that grandson of Herod the Great who is described by Josephus[2] as making his permanent home at Rome. This is borne out by the salutation to 'Herodion my kinsman' intervening between those of the two households. The name suggests a member of the family to which Aristobulus belonged. Narcissus can scarcely be any other than the freedman and favourite of Claudius. He had been put to death some three years before this epistle was written, but his slaves and dependents, though they would after his execution be incorporated in the Imperial household, might still retain the distinctive name of *Narcissiani*.[3] It is possible that Aristobulus may have been dead in 57 A.D., and have bequeathed his slaves to the emperor. If so, both these groups would form part of that vast body of freedmen and slaves known as Caesar's Household, to which St. Paul refers writing from Rome to the Philippians : 'all the Saints salute you, specially they of Caesar's Household.'

How vast a number composed the imperial household may be gathered from the statement of Lanciani ('Ancient Rome in the Light of Recent Discoveries,' p. 130) that in two *columbaria* of the servants and freedmen of Augustus and Livia the remains of no fewer than 6000 persons have been found. The two groups of names in verses 14–15 seem to indicate that they were members of two smaller households

---

[1] Acts, vi. 9.   Andronicus and Junias may, of course, have been among the 'strangers of Rome, Jews and Proselytes,' who were converted on the Great Day of Pentecost.

[2] Josephus, *Ant.* xx. 1. 2 ; *Bell. Iud.* ii. 11. 6.

[3] Lightfoot, *Epistle to Philippians*, Dissertation on Caesar's Household, p. 169 ; Sanday and Headlam, *Romans*, pp. 405–6.

belonging to private persons.[1] [The expression ' all the Churches of Christ salute you ' (v. 16) is unique in the New Testament, and when taken in connexion with the language of this epistle elsewhere upon the high repute of the Roman Church may be held (to quote the words of Dr. Hort) to signify that that Church was already ' an object of love and respect to Jewish and Gentile Churches alike.' [2]]

And now we come to a consideration of the all-important autobiographic passage in the fifteenth chapter,[3] which contains, if rightly interpreted, an explanation at once of St. Paul's attitude of deference to the Roman Church and the widespread esteem in which, as he declares, it was held by its sister Churches. This passage may be regarded as an expansion of the earlier autobiographic section with which the epistle opens. The object and the tone are the same, only here the Apostle enters more into detail. After recounting how ' from Jerusalem and round about even to Illyricum I have fully carried the Gospel of Christ, but in doing so making it my pride-and-care [4] to preach not where Christ was named lest I should build upon another man's foundation,' Paul proceeds ' wherefore also I was hindered many times [5] from coming to you. But now having no more place in these regions and having had these many years a keen-longing [6] to come to you, whenever I journey to Spain [I will come to you] [7] for I hope to see you, as I am journeying through, and to be sent forward on my way thitherward by you after I have first in some measure

---

[1] Lanciani (p. 132) says that in certain *columbaria* on the Esquiline at least 370 members of the household of Statilius Taurus are buried.

[2] Sanday and Headlam, *Romans*, pp. 128–9 ; Hort, *Romans and Ephesians*, i. 52.

[3] Rom. xv. 14–29.

[4] v. 20 φιλοτιμούμενον = (lit.) priding myself, or endeavouring earnestly.

[5] διὸ καὶ ἐνεκοπτόμην τὰ πολλὰ τοῦ ἐλθεῖν πρὸς ὑμᾶς. τὰ πολλὰ seems to be the equivalent of the πολλάκις of i. 13 = the many times to which I have already referred : ' οὐ θέλω δὲ ὑμᾶς ἀγνοεῖν, ἀδελφοί, ὅτι πολλάκις προεθέμην ἐλθεῖν πρὸς ὑμᾶς καὶ ἐκωλύθην ἄχρι τοῦ δεῦρο.'

[6] ἐπιποθίαν.

[7] These words are omitted in the best MSS., but are necessary to complete the sense.

enjoyed-my-fill of your company.' The meaning of this statement, though the language and sequence of thought are somewhat involved, is nevertheless, so it seems to me, as plain and direct as it is possible to be. St. Paul had been hindered hitherto from visiting Rome, because he had made it a cardinal principle of his missionary life not to trespass in fields opened out by other men's labours, in Churches whose foundations others had laid. May not this ordinance of limitation imposed by the Apostle on himself afford the explanation of Acts xvi. 6–7, ' And they went through the region of Phrygia and Galatia, having been forbidden of the Holy Ghost to preach the word in Asia; and when they came over against Mysia, they assayed to go into Bithynia; and the Spirit of Jesus suffered them not'? If the South Galatian theory be accepted (I myself accept it unreservedly), it is really remarkable how small a portion of what is now known as Asia Minor was actually evangelised by St. Paul.[1] Even now he does not propose to come to Rome with any intention of undertaking a prolonged spell of missionary work, but merely to pay a brief passing visit on his journey further west, in order to make the acquaintance of the Roman Christians, of whom he had heard so much, and to receive at their hands a friendly and encouraging send-off when he leaves them for the scene of his new labours in Spain. It has often been asked, why St. Paul, if he meant that another had preached at Rome and been the founder of the Roman Church, did not mention his name? The answer is a very simple one: he was not writing for the information of students and critics of the twentieth century, but for the Roman Christians, who knew the facts.

There had then been a founder of this great Church of world-wide fame with whom Paul was well acquainted and into whose special sphere of successful preaching he did not think it right to intrude. Who was he?[2] All tradi-

---

[1] Bigg, *Comment on* I *Peter*, pp. 73–4.

[2] Professor Kirsopp Lake in his *Early Epistles of St. Paul*, pp. 378–9, writes: ' St. Paul clearly implies that the Roman Church was another

tion answers with one voice the name of St. Peter. In the next lecture I shall attempt to set forth the grounds on which this tradition rests, and to show that its acceptance, so far from being inconsistent with those fragments of early Christian history which have been preserved to us in the Acts and in the Epistles, serves to complete and bind them together and to explain much that is otherwise inexplicable in the rapid spread of Christianity in the three decades which followed the Great Day of Pentecost.

man's foundation, and that he had hitherto refused to preach in such places where others had made a beginning : this was the reason why he had never yet been to Rome. " Wherefore " he says " I was greatly hindered from coming to you." That " you " implies that the Church was someone else's foundation and the " wherefore " explains that this was his reason for not coming. He then goes on to explain why he now proposes to depart from his principle : there is now " no place left for him in these districts," *i.e.* from Jerusalem to Illyricum. Thus with a proper exegesis the meaning of this passage is that the Church of Rome was founded by some one else, and the question will always remain, why not St. Peter ? ' A remarkable admission on the part of this writer.

LECTURE II

Romans, x. 14: 'How shall they call on Him, in whom they have not believed ? And how shall they believe in Him whom they have not heard ? And how shall they hear without a preacher ? '

THE narrative of St. Luke in that earlier part of the Acts of the Apostles which leads up and is introductory to the main theme of the work is obviously fragmentary. The object of the writer however stands out clearly. He intended to give such an account, step by step, of the beginnings of Christianity, as was necessary for a full understanding of the life-work and missionary labours of St. Paul up to the time of his captivity at Rome. Every episode appears to have been carefully selected with a definite and precise purpose, and if the story, as told by him, seems at times to be tantalisingly brief and scanty, even disjointed, we must remember that those for whom it was written had access to oral sources of information from persons who had witnessed or taken part in the events described, which would place each episode in its proper setting and give to it its rightful significance. This we cannot do now, but if we bear in mind that not only the facts recorded by Luke but even his silences are suggestive, we may, I think, by the help of evidence gathered in from various sources, from contemporary or nearly contemporary writings, from the accumulated results of archaeological research, and from well-authenticated tradition, be able to show that the spread of Christianity during the period covered by the Acts was not by any means confined to the sphere of Paul's activity, nor intended to be so confined, but that one most important field was reserved for the Apostle who fills the foreground of the Lucan narrative up to the year 42 A.D. and then, except for a single brief appearance, is seen no more.

It is, of course, evident from what I have said that I am assuming that St. Luke the physician, the travelling companion of St. Paul, was the author of the Acts of the Apostles. I do so without feeling that such an assumption at the present time requires defence. In these lectures it is my aim, as far as possible, to avoid the mere collecting or comparing of other men's opinions, or the balancing of the authority of one set of scholars against another. It is the results of personal investigation into the history of the Church in Rome in the first century that I am now specially desirous of bringing before you, not a recapitulation of what has recently been written about that history. My own experience has taught me that the only way to arrive at conclusions in historical questions satisfying to the historical conscience is to study the original authorities for oneself with an independent mind, using indeed all the light and all the suggestions that modern critical scholarship can throw upon the many problems and difficulties that have to be solved, but never accepting any of the so-called 'results of criticism' without testing for oneself with the greatest care and at first hand the grounds on which they are supposed to rest.

The case for the Lucan authorship of the Third Gospel and of the Acts I consider however to have been so thoroughly established by the remarkable series of works published by Sir William M. Ramsay[1] and Dr. Adolf Harnack[2] upon the subject, as to have been placed, if not beyond the reach of controversy—for alas! the spirit of controversy is not

[1] *The Church in the Roman Empire before* A.D. 170, 3rd ed. 1894; *St. Paul the Traveller and Roman Citizen*, 7th ed. 1903; *A Historical Commentary on St. Paul's Epistle to the Galatians*; *The Cities of St. Paul*; *Luke the Physician and other Studies in the History of Religion*, 1908; *The First Christian Century*, 1911, etc. etc.

[2] *Lukas, der Arzt, der Verfasser des dritten Evangeliums und der Apostelgeschichte*, 1906; *Sprüche und Reden Jesu. Die zweite Quelle des Matthäus und Lukas*, 1907; *Die Apostelgeschichte*, 1908; *Neue Untersuchungen zur Apostelgeschichte*, etc., 1911. All these volumes have been translated into English and published as vols. xx. xxiii. xxvii. and xxxiii. of the Crown Theological Library.

quickly laid—on a solid bedrock of reasoned and exhaustive argument against which the waves of controversy will beat in vain. And not merely have they proved the unity of authorship. They have shown that we have in St. Luke a cultured writer possessed of literary power and historical grasp and well acquainted with the details of Roman provincial administration and of the distinct characteristics, geographical and political, of different localities who in a considerable part of his work speaks as an eyewitness, and who elsewhere uses first-hand evidence, if at times with a certain freedom, yet always with honesty and intelligence. My own conviction that the book of the Acts must have been written during St. Paul's first captivity at Rome and completed before his release has long been firmly held, but this conviction has been strengthened and deepened by the extraordinarily powerfu way in which Dr. Harnack [1] has quite recently set forth in serried array the reasons which

---

[1] *Neue Untersuchungen zur Apostelgeschichte*, pp. 63-81. In this volume Dr. Harnack completes his defence of the date 62 A.D. for the Acts in favour of which he had already argued in his *Apostelgeschichte*, 5 Excurs, 217–221. How strong was the case he made out even in this earlier and more tentative argument may be judged by the following extract from *Neue Untersuchungen*, p. 64 : ' Nicht auffallend aber konnte es nur sein, dass andere sich durch die starken Argumente für die frühe Abfassung der lukanischen Schriften als vollkommen überzeugt erklärten. Nicht nur Delbrück hielt mir sofort vor, ich hätte mich in einer von mir selbst sicher entschiedenen Frage mit unnötiger Zurückhaltung ausgedrückt, sondern auch Maurenbrecher erkannte in meinen Beweisführungen die Lösung des chronologischen Problems. In seinem Werk " Von Nazareth nach Golgatha " (1909) S. 22–30, gibt er die wichtigsten der von mir geltend gemachten Beobachtungen für eine frühe Abfassungszeit der Acta zutreffend und eindrucksvoll wieder und beschliesst seine Darlegung also : " Die Annahme (eines späteren Ursprungs und geschichtlichen Wertlosigkeit der Lukasschriften) ist neuerdings immermehr gefallen und schliesslich durch eine gründliche Untersuchung von Prof. Harnack in allen Teilen gänzlich widerlegt und beseitigt worden. Viel mehr hat sich nach jeder Richtung hin, wenn auch nicht die unbedingte Glaubwürdigkeit, so doch das hohe Alter der Apostelgeschichte ergeben. Und wenn Prof. H. selbst nur zögernd und erst nur in letzten Moment seiner Arbeit die Konsequenz seiner Ergebnisse auch für die Datierung zog, so muss man doch sagen, dass nur in jener von ihm vorgeschlagenen Weise so wohl der Schlusssatz der Acta wie die ganze Tenor des Buchs verständlich wird, und dass daher schon um dieses äusseren Zeugnisses willen die Datierung auf d. J. 62 als bewiesen und nicht nur als möglich zu gelten hat." '

have slowly driven him to abandon his earlier prepossessions
on this question, and forced him (in spite of the knowledge
that he was—to use his own words—' creating a revolution
within the domain of criticism ' [1]) to fix on grounds alike
of external and of internal evidence the end of St. Paul's
imprisonment as the date when the Acts, in the form we
now possess the book, was finished.

It is needless to say that the acceptance of such a
conclusion has a very important bearing on the subject of
these lectures. For, if St. Luke wrote the Acts at Rome,
the work must have been written in the first instance for
the Roman Christians, but if so the question naturally
arises, why should there be a total omission in the book of
any reference to the founding of the Church in Rome or
to the names of those who first preached the Gospel in that
city ? This is one of those silences of St. Luke, of which
I have spoken already as being suggestive. A comparison
of the last verses of the Third Gospel and of the Acts may
help us to an answer.[2] Had the Gospel stood alone all
commentators and critics would have asserted unanimously
that the Evangelist believed the Ascension of our Lord to
have taken place on the evening of the day of the Resurrection.[3] But from the opening passage of the Acts we learn that
they would have been wrong, and that St. Luke in the
conclusion of his Gospel deliberately foreshortened the events
of six weeks in this way, because he intended to take up the
thread of the story and fill in the details later. The similar
foreshortening of the events of two years, which we find
in Acts xxviii. 30–1, suggests that St. Luke in writing this
otherwise strangely puzzling and abrupt ending to his
narrative had already planned in his mind a third book,
which should supplement the Acts as the Acts had supple-
mented the Gospel, and that this book would have begun
by taking up the account of Peter's life-work, so sharply

---

[1] *Eine Revolution innerhalb der Kritik*, p. 65.

[2] St. Luke, xxiv. 50–53 ; Acts, xxviii. 29–31.

[3] Codex Bezae D and the first hand of the Sinaitic Codex ℵ[1] omit καὶ
ἀνεφέρετο εἰς τὸν οὐρανόν.   The difficulty which these words raised was
probably the reason for their omission.

broken off at his release from prison, and that a brief
sketch would have been given of the history of the Church
in Rome previous to St. Paul's two years' ministry during
his captivity.
With this preface let us now turn to those introductory chapters of the Acts in which St. Luke sketches
for us the steps by which Christianity emerged from the
condition of a strictly Jewish sect to that of a universal
religion intended for all mankind. It will be seen that the
enlargement of view, which is so clearly traced, was very
gradual ; that it came from below rather than from above ;
from the subordinates, to some extent from the rank and
file, rather than from the acknowledged leaders. On the
Great Day of Pentecost when St. Luke so carefully enume-
rates the various nationalities from which the great crowd
of pilgrims was drawn, it should be noted that St. Peter
addresses them as ' Men of Israel,' and his whole discourse
is that of a man concerned only with proving to an assembly
of Jews that Jesus of Nazareth was the promised Messiah
of their sacred Scriptures. The passage is in fact a striking
testimony both to the wide extent of the Jewish *Diaspora*
and to the fact of the intense love and reverence for the
Holy City and for the injunctions of the Mosaic Law, which
brought together such a throng of worshippers from far-
distant regions, including people speaking many different
tongues, to this feast at Jerusalem. In the list of those
forming St. Peter's audience we find the names of six different
peoples and the inhabitants of nine different districts, and
it is implied that Jews from these various places had come
up specially for the occasion—with one exception. The
phrase ' the sojourning Romans, Jews as well as proselytes '
seems capable of only one interpretation, that St. Luke
is here referring to a body of Roman Jews and converts to
Judaism, who were temporarily residing in Jerusalem, and
whom it may be permitted with considerable probability
to identify with the ' Synagogue of the Libertines ' [1] men-

---

[1] An inscription at Pompeii contains the words ' Synagoga Liberti-
norum,' Lanciani, *Pagan and Christian Rome*, p. 310.

tioned in Acts vi. 9. Among this body may have been numbered the Roman Christians Junias and Andronicus, who were some quarter of a century later saluted by St. Paul in his Epistle to the Romans ' as men of mark among the Apostles and who were in Christ before me.'

In his record of the period that follows St. Luke makes it quite clear that the first organised Christian community was at Jerusalem, not in Galilee.[1] After the day of Pentecost when certain of the multitude exclaimed ' Are not all these that speak Galilaeans ? '—there is not a word in the Acts to indicate that the early Church had any connexion with Galilee. The Twelve, whose authority, as being derived directly from the Lord, no one called in question, made Jerusalem their headquarters from this time forward, and from this centre carried on their mission work. But that mission work was limited to Jews. The Twelve, moreover, we are expressly told, visited the Temple regularly[2] and they seem to have conformed in every way to the regulations of the Mosaic Law, and to have differed from the Jews amongst whom they lived only in that they taught that the crucified Jesus, to whose Resurrection from the Dead they bore personal testimony, had by His Resurrection proved Himself to be the Messiah.[3] Among the Twelve St. Peter on every occasion takes the lead and is the spokesman of the rest, and occupies a position of undisputed pre-eminence.[4] In all that they did during these years, which immediately followed their Lord's departure from them, it is scarcely possible that these personal disciples should not have been

[1] [A striking testimony to the authenticity of the Johannine account of our Lord's ministry.] Had our Lord's mission been confined to Galilee up to the last week of His life, as the Synoptic narratives appear to suggest, it is almost inconceivable that the home of the Christian Church should from the very first have been at Jerusalem.

[2] St. Luke, xxiv. 52, 53 ; Acts, ii. 46 ; iii. 1 ; v. 12, 25, 42.

[3] Acts, ii. 32–36 ; iii. 14, 15, 20, 21, 26 ; iv. 10, 33 ; v. 30–32, 42.

[4] St. John is singled out on several occasions by name, as being second only to St. Peter in influence and authority; see Acts, iii. 1 ; iv. 13 ; viii. 14. Compare Gal. i. 18 ; ii. 9 ; also St. John, xiii. 23–27 ; xviii. 15 ; xx. 3–10 ; xxi. 20–24. [Again the history of the Acts confirms the account given in the Fourth Gospel.]

D 2

acting in strict accordance with their Master's last commands. Eventually they were to go forth upon a wider
mission to the nations, but for awhile—an ancient tradition
of considerable weight says definitely for twelve years [1]—
they were to abide at Jerusalem, and restrict themselves to
proclaiming in its simplest form the message of the Gospel
to the Palestinian Jews, meanwhile resting in the promise
that in the future whenever fresh calls should be made
upon them they should receive illumination and guidance
from the Holy Spirit.[2]

Not until the sixth chapter of the Acts do we find any
indication of a widening of view. But here reading between
the lines of the brief narrative one cannot but feel something
more than a suspicion that the movement of which the
appointment of the Seven was the outcome, and at the
head of which St. Stephen placed himself, was not one
with which the Twelve were at the time in entire sympathy.
The work to which St. Stephen specially addressed himself
was the preaching of the Gospel to the members of those
Synagogues which were set apart for the use of the Hellenis-
tic settlers and sojourners in Jerusalem, *i.e.* for Jews of foreign
origin, speaking a foreign tongue, and trained amidst Gentile
associations. Those mentioned seem to belong in order of
importance to the chief Jewish Colonies of the Dispersion.
The first place, be it noted, is assigned to the Libertines or
Roman freedmen, men conspicuous probably alike for their
wealth and their close connexion with the Imperial City.
Then come the Alexandrians, members of a Jewish settlement of ancient date and high culture, in numbers exceeding
probably the entire population of Palestine.[3] And after

---

[1] Compare St. Luke, xxiv. 44-49; St. John, xiv. 26; xvi. 13.

[2] Harnack (*Const. and Law of the Church*, p. 31) describes this as 'a
very old and well-attested tradition.' Apollonius is stated by St. Jerome
(*De viris illust.*) ' to have learnt it from the ancients ' and it is found in
Clem. Alex. *Strom.* vi. 5.

[3] Philo, *In Flaccum* and *Leg. ad Caium*. Philo describes the Jews
at this time as occupying entirely two out of the five districts of Alexandria,
and says that in Egypt their numbers amounted to 1,000,000. See also
Josephus, *cont. Apion.* ii. 4 ; *B.J.* xii. 3. 2.

them the Cyrenians, [1] second only to the Alexandrians in number, and like them thoroughly Hellenised. Lastly, mention is made of those of Cilicia and Asia—traders no doubt connected by ties of family and business with those characteristically Graeco-Asiatic cities, Tarsus and Ephesus. Among such a body of ' Hellenists ' the message of the Gospel would naturally be interpreted in a larger and more universal sense than in those stricter ' Hebrew ' circles to which as yet the Twelve had chiefly directed their appeal.

What we do know is that St. Stephen's ardour and activity and the special character of his teaching speedily aroused the intense enmity of the Jewish rulers. He was seized, brought before the Sanhedrim, and without proper trial or condemnation in a sudden outburst of fanatic fury stoned to death. It was the signal for a persecution which scattered far and wide those who had attached themselves to him and the doctrines that he taught.[2]

But fierce though the persecution was, St. Luke expressly tells us, it did not touch the Twelve. ' They were all,' we read ' scattered abroad, except the Apostles.' [3] Apparently at this time the accusers of Stephen did not regard the Twelve, and the Judaeo-Christians who held with them, as men ' speaking against this Holy Place and trying to change the customs that Moses hath delivered unto us.' As yet they (the original Apostles) seem not to have offended the susceptibilities of the High-Priestly caste by any neglect in their outward observance of the rites and ceremonies of the Jewish law. But this scattering abroad of the friends and disciples of Stephen was to be, under God's providence, gradually productive of great results. It led directly to the conversion of Saul the persecutor. It brought Philip, one of the Seven, to Samaria, where many were converted by

---

[1] Josephus, *Ant.* xiv. 7, *Life*, 76, *B.J.* vii. last chapter. In the revolt of the Jews in the time of Trajan (116–117) the number of Jews who perished in the district of Cyrene is given as 22,000, no doubt an exaggeration but pointing to a very large Jewish population.

[2] Acts, vi. 8, vii. 54–60, viii. 1–3.

[3] πάντες δὲ διεσπάρησαν κατὰ τὰς χώρας τῆς Ἰουδαίας καὶ Σαμαρείας πλὴν τῶν ἀποστόλων.

his preaching. Such indeed was his success that for the
first time the Apostles broke through their rule of confining
themselves to Jerusalem and its neighbourhood, and Peter
and John, the two leaders, were sent to take official charge
of the new field of missionary operations. And there at
Samaria (mark the emphasis Luke lays upon the incident)
Peter was confronted with the man who, under the name
of Simon Magus, was according to tradition to exercise a
large, perhaps a decisive, influence upon his action at a
critical point in his career.[1]

Nor was this all. After an interval, probably of some
three years,[2] we find that persecution has for the time
entirely ceased, and that already the Christian Church is
p acefully and firmly established throughout the whole of
Judaea, Galilee and Samaria,[3] and Peter engaged on a tour
of visitation in all parts.[4] Finally he reaches Joppa and
there takes up his abode for some time in the house, we are
told, of one Simon a tanner. Now this very fact, that the
Apostle chose to reside with a man whose trade in the eyes of
strict orthodox Judaism was unclean, points to the advance
he had already made in casting himself loose from the
fetters of Jewish prejudice. The vision which sent him
to Cornelius was probably the reflection of the doubts and
questionings which had been previously filling his thoughts
and an answer to his prayers.[5] It was a preparation for

[1] Acts, viii. 5-24.

[2] Comp. Acts ix. 26-31 with Gal. i. 18.

[3] καθ' ὅλης τῆς 'Ιουδαίας καὶ Γαλιλείας καὶ Σαμαρείας. ix. 31.

[4] ἐγένετο δὲ Πέτρον διερχόμενον διὰ πάντων. ix. 32. Comp. xv. 41 and
xviii. 23.

[5] We are here in presence of one of those strange psychical communications of which we have been learning so much in recent years. They are far
more common than most of us dream of, and come we know not how or
whence. In the trance into which Peter, exposed on the housetop to the
full heat of the mid-day sun and faint for lack of food, fell, just in proportion to the deadening of the ordinary senses would be the sensitiveness
of those faculties which lie below the threshold of wake-a-day consciousness.
First the spirit of the Centurion in his anxious search after truth is moved
to seek out Peter, as his guide and teacher ; then the spirit of Peter, while
still unconsciously conscious of the approach of the messengers who were
on their way to seek him, receives the intimation, which is the response to

that which was to follow, for his visit to the Roman centurion was not merely to teach him that the law which forbade intercourse between Jew and Gentile was henceforth done away, but to open his eyes to the startling and all-important fact that it was the revealed will of God that uncircumcised Gentiles should be admitted to the full privileges of Christianity. The question how far such Gentiles would have to conform to the Jewish law was indeed not yet settled, nor was it to be settled without much prolonged and even embittered controversy in the years that were to come. The collocation by St. Luke in juxtaposition of the defence of St. Peter [1] to the brethren at Jerusalem for his action in regard to Cornelius, and of the news reaching those same brethren that certain men from Cyprus and Cyrene, on their own initiative, without sanction or authority from the Mother Church, were preaching to the Greeks at Antioch and had converted a large number of them to the faith,[2] was clearly intentional. St. Peter's *apologia* was apparently somewhat grudgingly accepted, for there is little of spontaneous enthusiasm about the words—' and when they had heard these things they held their peace and glorified God, saying " Then also—$\mathring{a}\rho a\ \gamma\epsilon\ \kappa a\grave{\imath}$—to the Gentiles hath God granted repentance unto life." '

On receiving information, therefore, about what was occurring at Antioch, it was only natural that those at the head of the Church in Jerusalem should determine to send to the Syrian capital one of their own body with instructions

his own prayers. Men like Peter and John and Paul were in a manner far beyond the normal, what we should now call ' sensitives ' ; their spiritual faculties attuned to constant and intimate intercourse with that Divine Spirit who, their Master had promised, should in their hours of doubt and darkness be their guide and helper towards light and truth.

[1] Acts, xi. 1–18.

[2] Acts, xi. 19–27. These men were of those Hellenist Christians who had been driven from Jerusalem by the persecution which followed the death of Stephen. The exiles, St. Luke tells, preached the word in Phoenicia, Cyprus and Antioch (and no doubt in many other places), but at first to the Jews only. Then, after an interval probably of five or six years, certain of them, who had meanwhile settled in Cyprus and Cyrene, came to Antioch, and, finding that the Greeks were willing to listen to their preaching, began with success a work of evangelisation among them.

to inquire personally into the truth of the reports that had
reached them, and to establish official control over a movement which seemed at first sight to be revolutionary, and
which was in fact a long step in advance towards a totally
new conception of the mission of Christianity in the world.

Joseph, surnamed Barnabas, whom they selected as
their emissary, was a man singularly well qualified for dealing
wisely and sympathetically with the new situation. He had
been intimately associated from the very first with the
Jerusalem Church.[1] He was at once a Levite and a Cypriote
Hellenist, and the surname which was given to him by the
Apostles themselves tells us that he was a man endowed
with prophetic gifts for the exposition and interpretation
of Scripture.[2] And he was to remain for some years, probably to the end of his life, a mediator and reconciler between
the opposing schools of thought and ideals of Christianity
associated later with the names of St. James and St. Paul.
It is noteworthy how large a part Barnabas, who had now
gone to Antioch as the representative of the Church at
Jerusalem, took in preparing the way for him who was to be
pre-eminently the Apostle of the Gentiles. The two men
may possibly have first become friends in their youth,
when Saul of Tarsus was studying at the feet of Gamaliel.
In any case when Saul, three years after his memorable
conversion, came up to Jerusalem to make the acquaintance
of Peter, he found, perhaps not unnaturally, that the
brethren looked askance at the erstwhile persecutor, until
Barnabas took him by the hand and, as it were, stood

[1] His aunt Mary resided in Jerusalem, and her house appears to have
been used as a place of assembly (Acts, xii. 12) ; indeed there is a tradition
that the upper room of the Last Supper was in this house. Barnabas
himself seems to have had property in Jerusalem or its neighbourhood.
Acts, iv. 37.

[2] Bar-nabas = son of exhortation ; Nabi = a prophet. The Greek form
υἱὸς παρακλήσεως may be illustrated by Acts xiii. 15, where Barnabas
and Paul are asked by the rulers of the Synagogue if they have any λόγος
παρακλήσεως to address to the congregation. Compare also παράκλητος
=Comforter, Advocate, Helper, St. John, xiv. 16, 26. In accordance
with his surname we find that on his arrival at Antioch Barnabas παρακάλει
πάντας. In Acts xiii. 1 Barnabas is classed as ' a prophet and teacher.'

voucher for his good faith.1 His reception, however, on this occasion appears to have been so far discouraging that Saul withdrew for a considerable time to his native place Tarsus. [Thither Barnabas after a brief sojourn at Antioch now went to seek in his retirement the man whom he knew to be specially well fitted to act as his colleague at this juncture. His judgment and prevision were more than justified. For a whole year, we read in the Acts, Barnabas and Saul taught with such success that the assemblies of the faithful, whether of Jewish or Gentile origin, met together harmoniously and in such numbers 2 that even in this vast city,3 of mixed population, professing every known variety of religion, the new sect became sufficiently large and well known to attract public attention. The scoffing nick-name, *Christiani*, was now for the first time given to the disciples of Jesus by the pagan Antiocheans—a term of shame and reproach, which soon was to become a title of glory.

While at Antioch under the leadership of Barnabas the preaching of the Gospel was thus making rapid progress, events were taking place in Judaea of critical importance for the future of the Church. The peace which the Christians in Palestine enjoyed in the period preceding the conversion of Cornelius had been due, not to any increase of good-will on the part of the Jewish rulers, but to the fact that these were too much occupied at that time with their own serious troubles. The order given by the Emperor Caligula to place his statue in the Holy of Holies had filled the whole nation with horror and made them resolve rather to be massacred than allow such a profanation of the Temple.4 The assassination of

---

1 Acts, ix. 25–27 ; Gal. i. 18–21.

2 Acts, xi. 26. This seems to be the force of the words συναχθῆναι ἐν τῇ ἐκκλησίᾳ.

3 The population of Antioch at this time was probably about half a million. Ottfried Müller (*Antiquitates Antiochenae*) has collected all that can be learnt from ancient sources about Antioch.

4 Josephus (*Ant.* xviii. 8) and Philo (*Leg. ad Caium*) tell the whole story in detail, and also the fruitless efforts made by Agrippa to induce the Emperor to abandon his intention.

Caligula alone averted a general revolt. According to
Josephus, Herod Agrippa, who was then in Rome, played a
very important part in securing the peaceful accession of
Claudius, who rewarded him for his services by bestowing
upon him, in addition to Galilee, Peraea and the territory
beyond the Jordan with which he had been invested by
Caligula, also Judaea, Samaria and Abilene, making his
kingdom thus equal in extent to that of his grandfather
Herod the Great.[1]   Claudius became emperor, January 24,
41 A.D., and towards the end of that year King Agrippa
went to Palestine with the intention of using every means to
ingratiate himself with his new subjects.   He was especially
desirous of impressing them with his careful observance of
the Mosaic law and his zeal for the national religion, being
to some extent suspect through his long residence in Rome
and alien descent.[2]   Accordingly having gone to Jerusalem
to keep the first Passover after his accession, he resolved to
give a signal mark of his fervour as a defender of the faith,
by the summary execution of James the son of Zebedee.
Possibly he was the only one of the Christian leaders on
whom for the moment he could lay hands.   But finding his
action had pleased the Jews, he proceeded to arrest Peter
also, and, as the days of unleavened bread had already begun,
he placed the Apostle in prison under the strictest guard
with the intention of bringing him forth before the people
as soon as the Passover was over.[3]   The story of his escape
as told by St. Luke, which ends so abruptly, has every
internal mark of having been derived directly from the
maid-servant Rhoda, whose name is otherwise so unneces-
sarily mentioned. We learn from this graphic narrative
that the house in Jerusalem where the disciples were

[1] Jos. *Ant.* xix. 4, 5 ;   *B.J.* ii. 11.   H. Lehmann, *Claudius und seine
Zeit* (Leipzig, 1877), pp. 118–121, 161–164.   Milman, *Hist. of the Jews*,
ii. 126–158.
[2] Jos. *Ant.* xix. 6.   Jost (*Geschichte des Judenthums*, i. 420 ff.)
quotes many anecdotes from the Talmud of Agrippa's eagerness to
give proof of his orthodoxy and piety.   See also Fouard, *S. Pierre*,
pp. 207–212.
[3] St. Luke, xii. 1–18.

accustomed to hold their gatherings for prayer was that of
Mary, the mother of John Mark, and the aunt of Barnabas.
It was to this house that the Apostle naturally turned his
steps, as soon as he found himself outside the prison gates,
but with no intention of remaining in so well known a spot.
As he entered the room with a movement of his hand he at
once checked their cries of astonishment, briefly told his
tale, probably almost in the rapid words recorded, asked his
hearers to repeat it to James and the brethren, and then
immediately, while it was still dark, he went out to betake
himself to a more secure hiding-place. And as the Apostle
disappears into the obscurity of the night, so does he, so
far as his active career is concerned, disappear henceforth
from the pages of St. Luke's history.

There are difficulties in this brief account of the Herodian
persecution of the spring of 42 A.D.   There is no hint that
the Twelve were at Jerusalem at this critical time. St.
Peter himself does not seem to have been there when St.
James was beheaded. His parting words point to two
conclusions : (1) that the other James, the Lord's Brother,
was already the recognised head of the Jerusalem community;
and (2) that the speaker had no expectation of being able to
tell his tale to ' James and the brethren ' in person. The
explanation however lies to our hand, if we accept the
ancient and well-attested tradition of which I have already
spoken, that the Lord Jesus had bidden his Apostles to make
Jerusalem the centre of their missionary activity for twelve
years, after which they were to disperse and go forth to
preach to the nations. Already before Herod Agrippa
struck his blow the Twelve had begun to set out each one to
his allotted sphere of evangelisation, the care of the Mother
Church being confided to James, the Lord's Brother, assisted
by a body of presbyters, of whom he was one, but over whom
he presided with something of monarchical authority. It
would be an anachronism to give him the Gentile title of
Bishop, but in this earliest constitution of the Jerusalem
Church we have the model which other Churches were to
follow and out of which episcopacy grew.

But even if this be granted, it throws no light on the after-life of St. Peter.

For his after-life we have again to fall back mainly upon tradition, a tradition already referred to by me at the close of my first lecture, which makes St. Peter to have been the founder of the Church in Rome. St. Paul in his Epistle to the Romans, as I have shown, speaks of that Church as already in 57 A.D. long established and of world-wide repute, into which as being built on another man's foundation he had not thought it right to intrude.[1]   The question then arises, what grounds are there for believing that the man to whom he refers was St. Peter ?

Now there are traditions and traditions. First let it be premised that we are not dealing here with a tradition handed down orally by illiterate people. Not that oral tradition is to be neglected or despised. There is abundant evidence to show with what accuracy historical traditions including long lists of names have been handed down from generation to generation even among tribes unacquainted with writing. After describing the pre-Hispanic civilisation in Peru, a recent writer remarks: ' It is not surprising, in spite of the fact that no form of writing was known, that the people capable of such political organisation had preserved in traditional form much of their early history. Feats of memory, which seem almost miraculous to civilised races, who have become dependent on written records, have been chronicled of several peoples below the Peruvians in the scale of culture. The nobility among the Polynesians received regular instruction in their past history, and the chiefs could repeat long genealogies, which had been faithfully handed down from generation to generation. Even among African races traditional records are not unknown, and in one case a list of even one hundred chiefs, together with historical details, has been recently obtained from a tribe in the heart of the Southern Belgian Congo.' [2]   In the first century, however, in Rome and in all the chief centres

[1] Supra, pp. 28–9.
[2] Joyce, South American Archaeology, 1912, p. 76.

of population, where the early Christian Churches were established, writing was familiarly employed by all classes. [At one time it was assumed, with an assurance that had absolutely no basis, that the events of early Christian history could only have been known through oral transmission, that it was most unlikely that anything was committed to writing at the time, and the idea that the separate Churches kept any records of the appointment of their officers, or any statements concerning the various vicissitudes of their fortunes, was dismissed as untenable.] ' There is a very strong body of opinion,' said Sir W. Ramsay[1] about nine years ago, ' that the earliest Christians wrote little or nothing. It is supposed that partly they were either unable to write or at least unused to the familiar employment of writing for the purposes of ordinary life. [Put aside that prejudice, and the whole body of opinion, which maintains that the Christians at first did not set down anything in writing about the life and death of Christ, strongly and widely accepted as it is, dominating as a fundamental premise much of the discussion of this whole subject in recent times, is devoid of any support. . . . One of the initial presumptions, plausible in appearance and almost universally assumed and conceded, is that there was no early registration of the great events in the beginning of Christian history. This presumption we must set aside as a mere prejudice, contrary to the whole spirit and character of that age and entirely improbable.'] Such a presumption has in fact been proved by recent discoveries to be in all probability quite erroneous, and indeed there are strong grounds for making an assumption of a precisely opposite character, *i.e.* that the chief Christian Churches did keep more or less regular archives, which, like the bulk of ancient records, perished through fire or other accidents,[2] through the ruthless sacking of the city by barbarian conquerors, and in the case of these

---

Christian archives by systematic destruction at the hands of the imperial authorities, more especially during the persecution of Diocletian. But though the documents themselves disappeared,[1] the memory of their contents would remain to be worked up afresh into new narratives tinged with the opinions, beliefs and modes of thought of the time at which they were written, and in such a setting as the pious fancy of the compilers thought to be edifying, and in harmony with their subject. What criteria then, it may be asked, have we for judging whether these later *Acts* and *Passions* of Saints and Martyrs contain in the midst of apocryphal accretion a real core of sound and trustworthy historical fact? A tradition before it can be accepted as embodying authentic history should, I think, satisfy the following conditions : (1) It must be concerned with an event or series of events that had a great number of witnesses, and of witnesses who would have a strong motive to record or bear in memory what they had seen. (2) The beginning of the tradition should appear at a time not too remote from the facts it records, at a time, that is to say, in which it should not be possible for the notices handed down by contemporaries to be obscured. (3) Shortly after that time to which the beginning of the tradition goes back there should appear in

meaning of the following facts: Rome was taken and sacked by Alaric, 410 A.D.; by Genseric, 455 A.D.; by Ricimer, 472 A.D.; by Vitiges, 537 A.D.; by Totila, 546 A.D. In 846 A.D. the Saracens plundered Rome. See Lanciani, *Ancient Rome in the Light of Recent Discoveries*, pp. 147-9; also *The Destruction of Ancient Rome*, p. 131.

[1] Horace Marucchi, *Eléments d'Archéologie Chrétienne*, vol. i. xiv. writes thus : ' Malheureusement les Actes [des Martyrs] authentiques ont presque tous disparu. . . . L'Eglise romaine non possède aucun. ⸗es actes de ces martyrs ont dû être détruits pendant la grande persécution ⸗e Dioclétien ; il est certain qu'à cette époque on a brûlé les Archives de ⸗e l'Eglise romaine ; on a d'ailleurs agi de même en Afrique, ainsi que nous l'apprend S. Augustin.' Of the principal contemporary historians of the period dealt with in these lectures—Fabius Rusticus, Cluvius Rufus, and Pliny the Elder—not a single line has survived. A. Peter (*Hist. Rom. frag.* pp. 291-324) gives a list of thirty-five historical writers upon the period from Caligula to Hadrian (37-138) all of whose writings have perished. Of the works of Tacitus only a portion have come down to us, and the *Histories* in a single MS.

the community to which it relates a firm and general
persuasion of its truth.   (4) This persuasion should spread
gradually until everywhere the facts are accepted as true
without any doubts being raised even by those who, had
they not been plainly true, would have desired to reject
them.

Let us now apply these criteria to the Petrine tradition
at Rome. That Peter visited Rome between the years
62 A.D. and 65 A.D. and that he was put to death there by
crucifixion is admitted by everyone who studies the evidence
in a fair and reasonable spirit.[1] This is not a tradition, it
may rather be described as a fact vouched for by contemporary or nearly contemporary evidence.   On this point
no statement could be stronger than that of Professor
Lanciani : [' I write about the monuments of Rome from
a strictly archaeological point of view, avoiding questions
which pertain or are supposed to pertain to religious controversy.   For the archaeologist, the presence and execution
of SS. Peter and Paul in Rome are facts established beyond
a shadow of doubt by purely monumental evidence.' [It is
now generally conceded that the first epistle bearing the
name of Peter was written from Rome.   The ' Apocalypse
of St. John ' and the ' Sibylline Oracles ' show that Babylon
was a common synonym for Rome in the second half of the
first century.[2]   The language of Clement of Rome [3] in his
Epistle to the Corinthians leaves no doubt—for it is the
witness of a contemporary—that Peter was martyred at
Rome.   ' But leaving ancient examples let us come to the
athletes who were very near to our own times, let us take
the illustrious examples of our own generation. . . .   Peter
who through unjust jealousy endured not one or two but
many sufferings and so having borne witness—μαρτυρήσας—
departed to the place of glory that was his due.'   The

[1] Lanciani, *Pagan and Christian Rome*, p. 125.
[2] In that portion of the fifth book of the *Sibylline Oracles* which was
probably written 71–74 A.D. the flight of Nero from Rome is thus described :
v. 143 φεύξεται ἐκ Βαβυλῶνος ἄναξ φοβερὸς καὶ ἀναιδής.
[3] Clement Rom. 1 *Cor.* v.

statement in the apocalyptic 'Ascension of Isaiah'[1]—also the work of a contemporary—that ' a lawless king, the slayer of his mother, will persecute the plant which the Twelve Apostles of the Beloved have planted. ⌐Of the Twelve one will be delivered into his hands' can scarcely refer to another event than the death of Peter at the time of the Neronian persecution⌐ A comparison of St. John xxi. 18, 19 with St. John xiii. 36, 37 and with 2 Peter i. 14 is evidence as to the manner of that death. The question of the authorship of the Fourth Gospel or of 2 Peter is immaterial, for the writers, whoever they were, belong to the first century, and the testimony to the received belief of the Christian Church which they give is authentic.

But a solitary brief visit to Rome after St. Paul had previously spent in that city two years of fruitful work does not account for the position assigned by tradition to St. Peter in relation to the Roman Church. Though the two names are on several occasions coupled together, as joint founders of the Roman Church, in all the earliest notices in which the two are named together the name of Peter stands first. Thus Ignatius in his Epistle to the Romans written about 109 A.D. says : ' I do not command you like Peter and Paul ; they were Apostles ; I am a condemned criminal.'[2] Dionysius of Corinth 171 A.D. writing to Soter bishop of Rome [3] speaks ' of the plantation by Peter and Paul that took place among the Romans and Corinthians.' Irenaeus a few years later is filled with respect

---

[1] See Clemen, ' Die Himmelfahrt des Isaia, ein ältestes Zeugnis für das römische Martyrium des Petrus' in *Zeitsch. für Wissensch. Theologie,* 1896. The discovery among the *papiri* of Lord Amhurst of the Greek text of the *Ascension* makes the reference clear. καὶ (τ)ῶν δώδεκα (εἶς) ταῖς χερσὶν αὐτοῦ π(αραδ)οθήσεται. Grenfell, *The Amhurst Papiri. Ascensio Isaiah, etc.,* 1900.

[2] *Ep. S. Ignatii ad Romanos,* c. iv : οὐχ ὡς Πέτρος καὶ Παῦλος διατάσσομαι ὑμῖν· ἐκεῖνοι ἀπόστολοι, ἐγὼ κατάκριτος.

[3] Quoted by Eus. *Hist. Eccl.* ii. 25 : ταῦτα καὶ ὑμεῖς διὰ τῆς τοσαύτης νουθεσίας τὴν ἀπὸ Πέτρου καὶ Παύλου φυτείαν γενηθεῖσαν 'Ρωμαίων τε καὶ Κορινθίων συνεκεράσατε. A comparison with the passage from the *Ascension of Isaiah,* from which a quotation has already been made, is most interesting. ὁ βασιλεὺς οὗτος (Nero the matricide) τὴν φυτείαν ἣν φυτεύσουσιν οἱ ἀπόστολοι τοῦ ἀγαπητοῦ διώξει καὶ τῶν δώδεκα εἶς ταῖς χερσὶν αὐτοῦ παραδοθήσεται.

for 'the most great and ancient and universally known
Church established at Rome by the two most glorious
Apostles Peter and Paul, and also the faith declared to
men, which comes down to our own time through the succession of her bishops. For unto this Church, on account
of its more powerful lead, every Church, meaning the faithful
who are from everywhere, must needs resort ; since in it
that tradition which is from the Apostles has been preserved
by those who are from everywhere. ⌐The Blessed Apostles,
having founded and established the Church, entrusted
the office of the episcopate to Linus. Paul speaks of this
Linus in his epistles to Timothy, Anencletus succeeded him,
and after Anencletus, in the third place from the Apostles,
Clement received the episcopate.'⌐ Now Irenaeus, who
was a disciple of Polycarp, and acquainted with others
who had known St. John, and who in 177 A.D. became
bishop of Lyons, had spent some years in Rome. This
passage was written, as he tells us, in the time of Eleutherus,
probably about 180 A.D.[1]

Eusebius of Caesarea has left us two lists of the Roman
bishops, one in his ' Ecclesiastical History,' the other in his
'Chronicle.' The first is the list of Irenaeus, the beginning of
which has just been quoted. The second is derived from
the lost ' Chronicle ' of Hippolytus, bishop of Portus, written
about half a century later. ⌐In the ' Chronicle ' St. Peter's
episcopate at Rome is stated to have lasted twenty-five
years.[2] ⌐In the ' Ecclesiastical History' we read—' under the

---

[1] Irenaeus, *Adv. Haereses*, iii. 3 ; Eus. *Hist. Eccl.* v. 6.

[2] Eusebius, *Hist. Eccl.* v. 6, see also iv. 22. Hippolytus' *Chronicle*
was written during the first quarter of the third century and was undoubtedly
used by Eusebius. For an account of this learned and essentially Roman
writer see Lightfoot's *Apostolic Fathers*, part i. vol. ii. pp. 317–477. The
original Greek of Eusebius' *Chronicle* or *Chronography* is lost, but it survives
in three translations, a Latin version by Jerome, a Syriac and an Armenian.
The Hieronymian and Syriac versions give twenty-five years as the length
of Peter's episcopate. On the other hand the Armenian has twenty
years, but Duchesne (*Liber Pontificalis*, p. v) says : ' Ann. XX dans
le texte arménien, évidemment fautif.' The Armenian version has
in fact many divergences from the Hieronymian, but Lightfoot, who has
discussed the matter very thoroughly (*Apost. Fathers*, part i. vol. i.

E

reign of Claudius by the benign and gracious providence of God, Peter that great and powerful apostle, who by his courage took the lead of all the rest, was conducted to Rome.' / In other passages his martyrdom with that of Paul is represented as taking place after Nero's persecution.[1] The interval between these two dates would roughly be about twenty-five years. Now it is evident that these figures, derived as they are from men like Irenaeus and Hippolytus, who had access to the archives and traditions in Rome itself, cannot be dismissed as pure fiction. They must have a basis of fact behind them. Eusebius tells us ' that after the martyrdom of Paul and Peter Linus was the first that received the episcopate at Rome.' [Now the date of this martyrdom was according to the received tradition the fourteenth year of Nero or 67 A.D. ; if then we deduct twenty-five years, we arrive at 42 A.D., which is precisely the date given for St. Peter's first visit to Rome by St. Jerome in his work ' De Viris Illustribus.'] Remembering that Jerome was a translator of the Eusebian Chronicle his words may be taken to embody a close acquaintance with Eusebius' works, including his lost ' Records of Ancient Martyrdoms,' and with the sources that he used. Jerome writes as follows : [' Simon Peter, prince of the Apostles, after an episcopate of the Church at Antioch and preaching to the dispersion of those of the circumcision, who had believed in Pontus, Galatia, Cappadocia, Asia and Bithynia, in the second year of Claudius goes to Rome to oppose Simon Magus, and there for twenty-five years he held the sacerdotal chair until the last year of Nero, that is the fourteenth.' [2]] Now here amidst a certain confusion, which will be dealt

pp. 212-246), comes to the conclusion that these divergences are due ' probably to the errors and caprice of transcribers ' (p. 245). Duchesne, Mommsen, and others hold the Latin Chronography, known as the *Liber Generationis*, to be a translation from the Greek of Hippolytus' *Chronicle* dating from about 234 A.D.

[1] Eus. *Hist. Eccl.* ii. 14—the whole of this passage will be considered later. For the death : *Hist. Eccl.* ii. 25, iii. 1, 4.

[2] Jerome, *De Viris Illust.* i. Jerome must have had access to the *Chronography* of Julius Africanus, the *Chronicle* of Hippolytus, the *Memorials* of Hegesippus, and other lost works.

with presently, a definite date is given for Peter's first arrival at Rome, and, be it noted, it is the date of his escape from Herod Agrippa's persecution and his disappearance from the narrative of the Acts.

This evidence of Jerome, it will be thus seen, rests upon that of Eusebius, and that of the earlier authorities which that historian consulted. It has been said that one of the conditions of the soundness of an historical tradition was the wideness and unanimity of its reception. Now probably never was any tradition accepted so universally, and without a single dissentient voice, as that which associates the foundation and organisation of the Church of Rome with the name of St. Peter and which speaks of his active connexion with that Church as extending over a period of some twenty-five years.

It is needless to multiply references. In Egypt and in Africa, in the East and in the West, no other place ever disputed with Rome the honour of being the see of St. Peter ; no other place ever claimed that he died there or that it possessed his tomb. Most significant of all is the *consensus* of the Oriental, non-Greek-speaking, Churches. A close examination of Armenian and Syrian MSS., [1] and in the case of the latter both of Nestorian and Jacobite authorities, through several centuries, has failed to discover a single writer who did not accept the Roman Petrine tradition.

No less striking is the local evidence (still existing) for a considerable residence of St. Peter in Rome. 'There is no doubt,' is the judgment of Lanciani, once more to quote his well-known work ' Pagan and Christian Rome ' (p. 212), ' that the likenesses of St. Peter and St. Paul have been carefully preserved in Rome ever since their lifetime, they are familiar to every one, even to school-children. These portraits have come down to us by scores. They are

---

[1] P. Martin, ' S. Pierre, sa venue et son martyre à Rome,' *Rev. des Questions historiques*, xiii. 5, xv. 5, xviii. 202. This writer gives an array of quotations from Armenian and Syrian (Jacobite and Nestorian) authors from the fifth to the thirteenth centuries.

painted in the *cubiculi* of the Catacombs, engraved in gold
leaf in the so-called *vetri cemeteriali*, cast in bronze, hammered
in silver or copper, and designed in mosaic. The type never
varies. St. Peter's face is full and strong with short curly
hair and beard, while St. Paul appears more wiry and thin,
slightly bald with a long pointed beard. The antiquity and
the genuineness of both types cannot be doubted.' Other
noticeable facts are : (1) the appearance of the name of
Peter, both in Greek and Latin, among the inscriptions of
the most ancient Christian cemeteries, especially in the
first-century catacomb of Priscilla.[1]   The appearance of
this unusual name on these early Christian tombs can most
easily be explained by the supposition that either those
who bore it or their parents had been baptised by Peter.
In any case it may be taken that his memory was held in

[1] The oldest parts of the Catacomb of Priscilla are regarded by De Rossi,
Marucchi, Lanciani and the best authorities as dating from the middle
of the first century. The most ancient inscriptions are in red and many
in the Greek language. Among them is one containing only the single

word | ΠΕΤΡΟC | . Another on the left side of the main gallery thus :—

ΠΕΤΡΟC ΕΖΗ
CEN ETH EI H
MEPAC· NA·

a third :—

| ΠΕΤΡΟC | PETRVS |
| | FILIVS · AVSANONTIS |

In this catacomb is the mausoleum of the Acilii Glabriones, the family of
the consul M. Acilius Glabrio, put to death by Domitian in 95 A.D.   His
own tomb has been destroyed. According to the *Liber Pontificalis* Pope
Leo IV, in the ninth century, removed from this catacomb the bodies of
Aquila and Priscilla, with others, into the city to protect them from profanation at the hands of the Saracen invaders. Marucchi, *Archéologie Chrétienne*, vol. ii. pp. 586 ff; *Le Memorie degli Apostoli Pietro e Paolo in Roma*,
p. 119, pp. 160-164. On p. 162 may be seen a copy of the beautiful
medallion containing the heads of SS. Peter and Paul found by Boldetti
in the first-century catacomb of Domitilla and now in the Museo Sacro
della Biblioteca Vaticana.

especial reverence by them. ⌐Again, on a large number of early Christian *sarcophagi* now in the Lateran Museum the imprisonment of Peter by Herod Agrippa and his release by the angel is represented. ⌡ The French historian of the ' Persecutions of the first two Centuries,' Paul Allard,[1] was the first to point out that the frequency with which this subject was chosen might be accounted for by the existence of a traditional belief in a close connexion between this event and the first visit of St. Peter to Rome.⌡ Orazio Marucchi, the learned and accomplished pupil and successor of De Rossi, in his latest volume upon recent researches in the catacombs, commenting upon this suggestion of Allard, adds that this scene is often united to others, in which Moses and Peter appear as the representative founders of the Jewish and Christian Churches with particular reference to the Church in Rome.[2] In some representations may be seen the Lord handing to Peter a volume on which is written Lex Domini, or beneath which is the legend Dominus Legem Dat.[3] More remarkable still are those in which Moses, with the well-known traits of St. Peter, strikes the rock out of which flow the waters of cleansing through baptism in the name of Jesus Christ.[4] ⌐Taken together all these authentic records of the impressions that had been left upon the minds of the primitive Roman Church of a close personal connexion between that Church and the Apostle Peter cannot be disregarded. They are existent to-day to tell their own tale. ⌡

[1] Allard, *Hist. des Persécutions*, vol. i. p. 15.

[2] *Roma Sotterranea Christiana* (nuova serie) Tom. I.: *Monumenti del Cemitero di Domitilla sulla Via Ardeatina descritti da Orazio Marucchi*, 1911, p. 9.

[3] Marucchi, *Le Memorie degli Apostoli Pietro e Paolo in Roma*, pp. 180–182.

[4] G. B. de Rossi, *Bullettino di Archeologia Christiana*, 1868, p. 1 ff.; 1874, p. 174; 1877, p. 77 ff.

In the Vatican museum this scene is depicted on two glasses. Behind the figure striking the Rock is written the word ' Petrus.' There is no doubt a reminiscence here of St. Paul's words, 1 Cor. x. 4: ἔπινον γὰρ ἐκ πνευματικῆς ἀκολουθούσης πέτρας· ἡ δὲ πέτρα ἦν ὁ Χριστός, and of the declaration of Christ: Σὺ εἶ Πέτρος καὶ ἐπὶ ταύτῃ τῇ πέτρᾳ οἰκοδομήσω μου τὴν ἐκκλησίαν, St. Matt. xvi. 18.

Once more the number of legends and the quantity of apocryphal literature that grew up around the Petrine tradition are witnesses not merely to the hold that it had upon popular regard but to its historical reality. Many of these legends, much of this literature may in the main be evidently fictitious, but even in those which are most clearly works of imagination, there is almost always a kernel of truth overlaid with invention.[1] It is perfectly well known that most of these documents have behind them other documents, which are now lost, but out of which those we now possess have grown by gradual accretions and interpolations.[2] But it is not impossible even now for sound and scholarly criticism to arrive with fair certainty in many cases at the ultimate basis of fact on which the edifice of fiction rests. One of these apocryphal documents we

[1] 'Les Actes des Martyrs. Supplément aux *Acta sincera* de Dom Ruinart,' par Edmond Le Blant. *Mémoires de l'Institut Nat. de France*, tom. xxx. part 2, p. 81 : 'Les gentils, aux temps de Dioclétien, avaient recherché, pour les anéantir, les livres, les écrits religieux des fidèles. Cette destruction, qui nous est attestée par des procès-verbaux contemporains, fut rigoureusement poursuivi, et l'Eglise, après la tourmente, dut pourvoir à la réfection de ses archives dévastées. Ce fut souvent à l'aide de souvenirs de traditions orales, que l'on dut réconstituer alors nombre d'*Acta* et de *Passiones* et souvent . . . ces rédactions nouvelles furent accommodées, pour le détail, à la mode du temps où elles étaient faites'; p. 81 : 'Ces interpolations, à mon avis, ne doivent donc ni déconcerter ni rébuter la critique. Sous la couche des inventions, les traits originaux existent, et un grand nombre d'entre eux apparaissent come à fleur de sol. Il les faut dégager patiemment,' p. 87.

[2] G. B. de Rossi in an Archaeological Conference held at Rome, December 11, 1881, said : 'Che nella formazione degli Atti dei martiri devono esser distinti e considerati molti periodi successivi ; il primo della relazione contemporanea dei testimoni oculari ; il secondo delle interpolazioni fatte al testo originale fino dal seculo incerca quarto e forse prima : poi vengono le amplificazioni e parafrasi composte dai retori nei secoli quinto e sesto : finalmente le abbreviazioni delle prolisse parafrasi ad uso delle *Lectiones liturgicae*, e le nuove forme di stile date alle vecchie leggende dal seculo decimo in poi per opera di scrittori diversi, i cui nome in parte conosciamo ; i quali vollero togliere ogni oscurità e rossezza al dettato e vestirlo di nuove fogge di lingua. In tutte queste trasformazioni naturalmente si venne assai alterando l'indole genuina dei documenti ; furono aggiunti prolissi discorsi, circostanze meravigliose, leggende strane, ma generalmente rimase sempre il fondo e la sostanza del primitivo discorso.' *Bullettino di Arch. Chr.* serie IV. 1882, p. 162.

have in a very early form—the Ebionite ' Preaching of
Peter'—which was produced in the first decade of the second
century ; as a proof of its early date it may be mentioned
that it was used by Heracleon in Hadrian's time.[1] The
work bears on the face of it testimony to the fact that Peter
did labour and preach at Rome, for it was written at a time
when some of those who actually saw and heard him may
have been still alive, and there must have been numbers
whose fathers were grown-up men even in the time of
Claudius. The traditions connected with the cemetery
' ad Nymphas ' where Peter baptised, with the primitive
chair now in St. Peter's Basilica, with the very ancient
churches of St. Pudenziana, St. Prisca and St. Clement, with
the *Quo Vadis ?* story, whatever their real historical value or
lack of value, undoubtedly stretch back long before the fifth
and sixth centuries, when pilgrims flocked to Rome with
their ' itineraries ' in their hands, and they spring from a
general and deep-rooted belief in a long and active ministry
of the Apostle in the See that had become identified with his
name.[2]

Returning then once more to the undisputedly historical
ground of St. Paul's Epistle to the Romans, we find that
in 57 A.D. there was in Rome a Christian community not
of yesterday, but of many years' standing : an important
community, whose faith and whose high repute were well
known in all churches of the Empire with which the writer
was acquainted. Further that St. Paul himself for some
years past had been longing to visit this Roman community,

---

[1] Clem. Alex. *Strom.* vi. 5. 6. 15; Origen, tom. xiii., comment on
St. John, c. 17. It is from Origen we learn that the κήρυγμα was known
to Heracleon. Clement regards the work as genuine, but Origen doubted.

[2] Carlo Macchi, *La Critica Storica e l'origine della Chiesa Romana*,
1903, p. 93 : ' Non tutte le memorie di S. Pietro in Roma hanno per se
stesse il medesimo valore. Altre sono d'indubitata autenticità ; altre
sono d'autenticità probabile, altre per se stesse neppur di probabile. Ma
quando anche si prescinda dai monumenti per se stessi autorevoli, l'unione
di tante memorie in Roma e nella sola Roma è un fatto che non può
spiegarsi, se non si ammetta quel che abbiamo già dimostrato con argomenti,
i quali crediamo che non possano venir dispregiati da una critica veramente
sincera.'

but had been hindered from doing so by the restriction he had imposed upon himself of not building on another man's foundation. If again the question be repeated—Who was this man ? with greater emphasis than before the same answer must be returned—It cannot be any other than St. Peter.

But having arrived so far, we are confronted with certain difficulties that arise in making this earlier ministry of St. Peter at Rome fit in with the New Testament records relating to the same period. These difficulties will be dealt with in the next lecture. To-day I shall confine myself to pointing out that the circumstances which led to St. Peter's mission to Rome very soon after his escape from prison in the second year of Claudius were strictly analogous to those described in the earlier part of the present lecture, which led first to the mission of Peter accompanied by John to Samaria, and then to that of Barnabas to Antioch.

The dispersion of the Hellenist disciples of St. Stephen, after the persecution in which their brilliant leader died a martyr's death, was the direct cause of the evangelisation first of Samaria and then some years later of Syrian Antioch. Philip, like Stephen one of the Seven, preached in Samaria meeting with great success, and there encountered a certain man, Simon by name, who gave himself out to be some great one, and who had by his sorceries astonished and drawn to him great numbers of the people. On the news of this state of affairs being brought to the Apostles at Jerusalem, Peter and John were despatched in the name of the Twelve, to deal with the situation authoritatively. The result for a time, according to the Acts, was the triumph of St. Peter, Simon himself being baptised and seeking to be endowed by the Apostle with a portion of his wonder-working spiritual gifts. And as with Samaria so it was with Syrian Antioch. Men of Cyprus and Cyrene, who had been obliged to fly from Jerusalem ' upon the tribulation that arose about Stephen,' after preaching in their own native regions found their way to Antioch, and preaching in that city of mixed nationalities, not only to Jews but also to the Greeks, converted many.

This news again, that a Church was arising in the Syrian capital with a considerable Gentile element in its midst, when it reached the Twelve at Jerusalem, led to immediate action being taken. Barnabas was sent to exercise supervision over the new movement, and to see that a precedent of far-reaching consequences should not be established without the knowledge and sanction of those in authority.

Events at Rome probably followed on precisely the same lines. Just as the men of Cyprus and Cyrene in the face of persecution made their way back to their own homes carrying with them the message of the Gospel, so would it be with some of ' the sojourners of Rome ' belonging to the Synagogue of the Libertines. They would return to the capital inspired by the spirit and example of St. Stephen to form there the first nucleus of a Christian community. As I have already suggested, St. Paul's salutation to Andronicus and Junias seems to point to these two men as the leaders of this first missionary band. Among those converted would be, as at Antioch, both Jews and Gentiles.

Some time may well have elapsed before any news of these first small beginnings of Christianity in Rome reached Jerusalem. ⌈Possibly St. Peter's intercourse with Cornelius the centurion and his relatives and friends at Caesarea first made him acquainted with the fact that the Gospel had obtained a foothold in the capital, for the body of troops to which Cornelius belonged—the *Cohors Italica*—consisted of volunteers from Italy.[1]⌋ From this source too he may in due course have learnt that Simon Magus was in Rome, and that there as in Samaria previously he was proclaiming himself ' to be the Great Power of God ' and was leading many astray by his magical arts.

This information in any case, whether derived from Cornelius or from Roman Christians, who came up for the feasts, would reach the Apostles about the time when their twelve years' residence in Jerusalem was drawing to a close, and when, according to tradition, they divided among

---

[1] Cohors Italica. Vid. Gruter, *Inscr.* p. 434: ' Cohors militum Italicorum voluntaria, quae est in Syria.'

themselves separate spheres of missionary work abroad.   To St. Peter, as the recognised leader, it may well have been that the charge of the Christian Church in the Imperial capital should have been assigned as the post of honour. If so, it will be seen that the persecution of Herod Agrippa only hastened on a journey already planned.   After his imprisonment and escape St. Peter's first object would be to place himself out of the reach of the persecutor and to set about his voyage as quickly as possible.   If so, his arrival at Rome would be in the early summer of 42 A.D., the date given by St. Jerome.

LECTURE III

Rev. xvii. 18—The great city, which reigneth over the Kings of the earth.

IN my previous lectures I have attempted to show from the internal evidence of St. Paul's Epistle to the Romans that there existed at Rome in 57 A.D. a Christian Church of high repute and many years' standing, and that this Church had been founded and built up by a man into the sphere of whose labours he [St. Paul] had been careful not to intrude. Moreover though St. Paul does not mention the name of the man, circumstantial evidence has been brought forward making a very strong *prima facie* case in favour of the ancient tradition that he was none other than St. Peter.

To-day I propose to consider how far that tradition in the form in which it has been handed down to us by Eusebius and Jerome [1] is consistent with the facts of the early Apostolic history contained in the Acts and the Pauline Epistles and fits in with the chronological framework of that history.

Eusebius, *Hist. Eccl.* book ii. cc. xiii, xiv, xv; Jerome, *De Viris Illustribus.* The evidence of Eusebius, it must be remembered, was based upon a wide acquaintance with earlier Christian literature and with a mass of official Church documents and state papers, as well as local traditions now lost to us, and that Jerome had studied Eusebius' works, and that he had access to the Eusebian sources. Eusebius for example tells us that he was acquainted with the five books of the Commentaries of Hegesippus, a Hebrew Christian who journeyed to Rome from the East expressly to learn what was the true doctrine taught there (*Hist. Eccl.* iv. 22). It appears that when at Rome Hegesippus drew up a list of the Roman bishops. See Bright, *Introd. to Eusebius' Eccl. History*, pp. xxviii-xxix; Lightfoot, *Apostolic Fathers, Clement of Rome*, i. 202-3; Lawlor, *Eusebiana.*

Eusebius [1] tells us, on the authority of Justin Martyr (a passage of whose ' Apology ' [2] he quotes at length), that a certain Simon of the village of Gitton in Samaria, whom nearly all the Samaritans worshipped, confessing him to be the Supreme God, came to Rome in the reign of Claudius Caesar and having there performed many magic rites was regarded as a god. After further describing, this time on the authority of Irenaeus, the character of this man's teaching, as being the fountain-head of all heresy, Eusebius proceeds to say that when in Judaea Simon was convicted of his wickedness by the Apostle Peter, and later journeying from the east to the west arrived at Rome and was there successful in bringing many to believe in his pretensions. ' Not for long, however,' adds the historian, ' did his success continue ; for on his steps in this same reign of Claudius, the all-good and most beneficent providence of God conducts the mighty and great one of the Apostles, Peter, on account of his virtue the leader of all the rest, to Rome against so great a corruption of life, who like some noble warrior of God armed with divine weapons, brought the precious merchandise of the light that had been made manifest from the east to those in the west, preaching the true light and the word that is the salvation of souls, the proclamation of the Kingdom of God.' [3]

It is not necessary here to enter into any detailed examination of the theories of Christian Baur [4] and his disciples of the Tübingen School or of the arguments of Richard Lipsius [5] in their attempt to prove that the Roman

[1] Eusebius, *Hist. Eccl.* ii. 13. 14.

[2] Justin, *Apologia*, i. 26.

[3] οὐ μὴν εἰς μακρὸν αὐτῷ ταῦτα προὐχώρει. Παρὰ πόδας γοῦν ἐπὶ τῆς αὐτῆς Κλαυδίου βασιλείας, ἡ πανάγαθος καὶ φιλανθρωποτάτη τῶν ὅλων πρόνοια τὸν καρτερὸν καὶ μέγαν τῶν ἀποστόλων, τὸν ἀρετῆς ἕνεκα τῶν λοιπῶν ἁπάντων προήγορον, Πέτρον, ἐπὶ τὴν Ῥώμην ὡς ἐπὶ τηλικοῦτον λυμεῶνα βίου χειραγωγεῖ, ὃς οἷά τις γενναῖος Θεοῦ στρατηγὸς τοῖς θείοις ὅπλοις φραξάμενος, τὴν πολυτίμητον ἐμπορίαν τοῦ νοητοῦ φωτὸς ἐξ ἀνατολῶν τοῖς κατὰ δύσιν ἐκόμιζεν, φῶς αὐτὸ καὶ λόγον ψυχῶν σωτήριον, τὸ κήρυγμα τῆς τῶν οὐρανῶν βασιλείας εὐαγγελιζόμενος. Eusebius, *Hist. Eccl.* ii. 14.

[4] See Baur's *Kirchengeschichte der drei ersten Christl. Jahrhunderten ; Paulus der Apostel Jesu Christi ; Die Christus Partei in Korinth &c.*

[5] Lipsius, *Die Apokryphen Apostelgeschichten und Apostellegenden, Quellen d. röm. Petrus Sage* and other works.

Petrine legend was without foundation and that Simon Magus never had any real existence, but was a lay figure concealing the personality of St. Paul; for later research has shown that their conception of the course of early Christian History is fundamentally false and it is becoming generally discredited. These distinguished scholars indeed, while brushing aside the pseudo-Clementine literature with one hand, as pure romance invented by Essene-Ebionite writers of the third and fourth centuries, at the same time laid hold with the other hand on those very fictions, on which the Clementine romance is built up, in order to erect thereon a romance of their own equally unsubstantial, and no less inconsistent with the clear evidence of the earlier authorities that we possess.   Dr. Hort as long ago as 1884 in his ' Lectures on the Clementine Recognitions ' (pp. 130–1) declared—'' all these impossible theories [of the Tübingen School] have no other real basis than the assumption that Simon is *only* St. Paul in disguise.   The true relations of the Syrian and Roman stories are much simpler, according to what seems to me the most natural interpretation.   Simon at Rome was familiar in the second century ; of Simon in conflict with Peter in Syria, we hear nothing till the third century has well begun.'

Indeed with regard to this second century evidence, how is it possible to set aside the statements of Justin Martyr and Irenaeus ?   The evidence of Justin is of great weight. He was himself born at Flavia Neapolis in Samaria in 103 A.D., a place only a few miles distant from the native place of Simon Magus.   His account of Simon's earlier activity and great success in the neighbourhood of his own home must be regarded as first-hand evidence, and it is in exact agreement with the other account of that earlier activity which we have in the eighth chapter of the Acts, an account which it is more than probable that St. Luke derived directly from that best of all witnesses, Philip the Evangelist.   I have already pointed out that the emphasis with which St. Luke dwells upon this episode of the encounter between Peter and Simon at Samaria suggests that he had in

his mind that later encounter at Rome, which would be fresh
in the memories of the first readers of the Acts.[1] Be this as
it may, Justin was himself at Rome for some years between
150 and 160 A.D., and wrote his 'Apology' to the Emperor
Antoninus Pius in that city. [In writing a defence intended
for the Imperial eyes it may surely be taken for granted that
Justin would not twice over have ventured (for in a slightly
different form in c. 56 [2] he repeats the statement from c. 26
already quoted) to declare that the Magician Simon of
Samaria visited Rome in the reign of Claudius and that a
statue was erected in his honour and that he was worshipped
as a god, unless it were well known that such had been the
case. [Yet a third time in his 'Dialogue with Trypho'[3]
Justin speaks of the Simonians as an existing sect that took
their name from the arch-heretic. Two points have been
pressed against the evidence of Justin. The first that he
states that Simon 'had been honoured with a statue as a
god in the river Tiber, (on an island) between the two
bridges, having the superscription in Latin *Simoni Deo
Sancto*, which is, To Simon the Holy God.' Now in this
same island was found in the sixteenth century an inscription to the Sabine God Semo Sancus, *i.e. Semoni Sanco Deo
Fidio*. It is of course quite possible that Justin saw this
inscription, and being a Samaritan ignorant of Latin myth-
ology mistook this for an inscription referring to Simon
Magus. It was a natural mistake. That Justin was right
in saying that a statue was erected to Simon and worshipped
is sustained, as will be seen, by other evidence. The other
point is that while Justin states that Simon was in Rome
in the reign of Claudius he makes no mention of his encounter
with St. Peter. The only argument here is that most

---

[1] See p. 38.

[2] προεβάλλοντο ἄλλους Σίμωνα μὲν καὶ Μένανδρον ἀπὸ Σαμαρείας οἳ καὶ μαγικὰς
δυνάμεις ποιήσαντες πολλοὺς ἐξηπάτησαν καὶ ἔτι ἀπατωμένους ἔχουσι. καὶ γὰρ παρ'
ὑμῖν, ὡς προέφημεν, ἐν τῇ βασιλίδι ʿΡώμῃ ἐπὶ Κλαυδίου Καίσαρος γενόμενος ὁ Σίμων
καὶ τὴν ἱερὰν σύγκλητον καὶ τὸν δῆμον ʿΡωμαίων εἰς τοσοῦτο κατεπλήξατο ὡς θεὸς
νομισθῆναι, καὶ ἀνδριάντι, ὡς τοὺς ἄλλους παρ' ὑμῖν τιμωμένους θεούς, τιμηθῆναι.
Apol. 56.

[3] *Dial. cum Trypho.* 126.

treacherous and worthless of all arguments—the *argumentum
ex silentio*. Justin was not writing for our instruction, but
was offering a defence of Christianity to a Roman Emperor.
If anyone has thought that the omission of Peter's name
here was an argument against his presence in Rome in the
reign of Claudius, let him read the summaries of Justin's
pleading in the latest edition of the ' Apologia ' by Mr.
A. W. F. Blunt (Camb. Univ. Press, 1911), and he will see
that neither in the twenty-sixth nor in the fifty-sixth
chapter was there any place for a reference to Peter.

The evidence of Irenaeus, who was in Rome some ten
or fifteen years after Justin, is equally striking. Irenaeus
writes at some length about Simon. He describes the
rudimentary gnosticism of his teaching, and, like Justin, he
mentions the tradition that an image was erected by Claudius
Caesar to his honour in the figure of Jupiter, which the
people worshipped, and he speaks of him as the father of all
heretics.[1] Even these testimonies to the still living fame of
Simon, as a religious leader whose lofty pretensions and
skilful charlatanry had made a deep impression at Rome
and elsewhere, do not stand alone. The discovery in the
middle of the last century of a MS. at Mount Athos containing
a large part of the ' Philosophumena ' or ' Refutation of all
Heresies ' by Hippolytus, the learned bishop of Portus, has
thrown much fresh light upon Simon and his teaching.[2]
Hippolytus, who is described as a disciple of Irenaeus,[3]
spent at least twenty years of his life at or near Rome and
also travelled widely. He devotes a long section of his
sixth book, which was probably written about 225 A.D., to
an account of the heresy of which Simon was the author.
Of the man himself he writes thus [4] : ' This Simon deceiving
many by his sorceries in Samaria was reproved by the
Apostles and was laid under a curse, as it has been written

[1] Irenaeus, *Adv. Haer.* (Library of Ante-Nicene Fathers, tr. by Keble),
p. 68 ; Irenaeus speaks of the Simonians as an existing sect, i. 33.

[2] Hippolytus, *Philosophumenos*, vi. 2, 3, 4, 5, 6, 7, 8, 9, 10, 11, 12, 13,
14, 15.

[3] Photius speaks of him as a disciple of Irenaeus.

[4] *Philos.* vi. 15.

in the Acts. But he afterwards abjured the faith and attempted [these practices]. And journeying as far as Rome he fell in with the Apostle, and to him, deceiving many by his sorceries, Peter offered repeated opposition.' Here then is another absolutely clear statement that Simon went to Rome and there encountered St. Peter.

Frankly then the contention that Simon is merely Paul in disguise, Paul the heretic in the eyes of all good Jews, whom the orthodox Peter is represented as triumphantly pursuing from place to place, has not a shred of early evidence behind it, and must be given up. Indeed Professor Kirsopp Lake in his recent work on the early epistles of St. Paul does not express himself a whit too strongly, when he says ' The figure of a Judaizing St. Peter is a figment of the Tübingen critics with no basis in history.' [1] So far indeed from Peter and Paul being bitterly opposed, there is every ground for believing that they worked at Rome during their latter years in the closest harmony. ⌠The First Epistle of Peter is saturated with Pauline thoughts and language, and its amanuensis was Silvanus, the companion of Paul on his second missionary journey. ⌡ St. Paul twice mentions Mark, the disciple and interpreter of Peter, as being with him during his first imprisonment, and writing to Timothy immediately before his death shows anxiety to have him at his side, because ' he is profitable to me in the ministry.' [2] Whatever misunderstandings concerning their attitude towards Judaism or divergences in practice there may have been between the two great Apostles in early days, it is evident that they have been greatly exaggerated.⌡ It was rather on questions of expediency than of principle that they differed, and the experience of years spent in earnest work had long before the end drawn them together into the friendliest co-operation. ⌡

The appearance of Simon Magus at Rome followed by Simon Peter, so far from being an extraordinary or even an

---

[1] Kirsopp Lake, *Early Epistles of St. Paul*, p. 116. See the Introduction to Dr. Bigg's *First Epistle of St. Peter* (Int. Crit. Commentary), pp. 52-67.

[2] 2 Tim. iv. 11.

unusual event, is one in complete accord with all that we know from non-Christian sources of the way in which during the reigns of Claudius and of Nero religious teachers, preachers, and wonder-workers from the East found their way to Rome. Oriental cults, especially the worship of Cybele and of Isis, were all the vogue. Judaism had great attractions for the Roman upper classes. Priests, magicians, soothsayers, astrologers crowded the capital and found a ready welcome. Claudius, we are told, was so struck by ' the progress of foreign superstitions ' that he thought it an act of sound political conservatism to re-establish the haruspices.[1] Harnack makes the statement in his ' Expansion of Christianity ' that ' the majority of the Christians with whose travels we are acquainted made [Rome] their goal,' and he admits that there are no real grounds for doubting that Simon Magus did so.[2] Of prominent Christians who were in Rome in the time of St. Peter's and St. Paul's ministry, Timothy, Apollos, Silas, Titus, Epaphras, Aristarchus, Mark and Luke are mentioned in the salutations of extant epistles, and in all probability the names of John and of Barnabas should be added to the list. The travels and experiences of Apollonius of Tyana are most instructive (even when full allowance has been made for the element of romance introduced by his biographer Philostratus), for he was an exact contemporary of the Apostles, and a kind of second Simon Magus. His vast journeys, which extended from the Ganges to the Pillars of Hercules, are a proof of the facilities with which such wonder-working teachers of philosophy and religion made their way from place to place, and the honour and respect with which they were generally received. Apollonius was in Rome in 65 and 66 A.D.[3]

---

[1] Renan, *Hibbert Lectures*, p. 54. See Lehmann, *Claudius und seine Zeit*, p. 326 : ' Widersetzte er (Claudius) sich energisch, wiewohl erfolglos der mystischen Richtung der Zeit, welche sich namentlich in der Vorliebe für *Superstitiones peregrinae* kundgab.'

[2] Harnack, *Expansion of Christianity* (Eng. tr.), i. 463.

[3] Philostratus, *Apollonius of Tyana*, iv. 35-41 ; Justin, Irenaeus and Hegesippus were all Eastern Christians who came to Rome. Also the Jews, Josephus and Philo.

F

Of St. Peter's first Roman visit and preaching early tradition has handed down few details; a series, however, of witnesses affirm that Mark accompanied the Apostle to Rome and there wrote his Gospel. Both Irenaeus and John the Presbyter, as reported by Papias, speak of Mark as Peter's 'interpreter,' [1] as do later writers. That Peter should have chosen John Mark to go with him is quite what one might expect from the narrative of the Acts, for Peter was clearly on terms of the closest intimacy with Mary, the mother of Mark and the aunt of Barnabas, whose house was a centre of reunion for the Christians of Jerusalem. There is no reason for thinking that this was the first time that Mark had acted as the Apostle's companion and interpreter; his services would 'be profitable to the ministry' in Palestine, scarcely less than in Rome, and the suggestion that he was a catechist to whom the instruction of the Apostle's Greek-speaking converts in the elements of the Gospel story was entrusted, is both plausible and probable.[2] His surname, Marcus, may be taken as indicating that his family had some Roman connexion; he may have been, like Paul and Silas, a Roman citizen. Eusebius relates that as a consequence of Peter's preaching 'the power of Simon was soon extinguished and destroyed together with the man,' but that the Apostle's hearers were not content with listening but once 'to the unwritten doctrine of the Divine Message, but they persisted in supplicating Mark, who was Peter's companion and whose Gospel is extant, that he should leave them also in writing a memorial of the doctrine that had been orally delivered. Nor did they cease their entreaties until they had prevailed with the man, and in this way that writing which is called the Gospel according to Mark is due to them. And they say that when the Apostle through the

---

[1] The testimony of Irenaeus (*Cont. Haer.* iii. i. 1) will be found in Eusebius *Hist. Eccl.* v. 8; that of Papias, iii. 39. See Chapman, *Journ. of Theol. Stud.* July 1905, p. 563 ff.; Harnack, *Neue Untersuchungen zur Apost. Geschichte*, pp. 88–93; Macchi, *Critica Storica e l'origine della Chiesa Romana*, pp. 25–29.

[2] See *The Composition of the Four Gospels* by Rev. A. Wright, ch. iii, 'St. Mark a Catechist.'

revelation of the Spirit knew what was done he was pleased with the zeal of the men and gave authority for the writing to be read publicly in the churches.' ¹ ⌈This, says Eusebius, is the account given by Clement [of Alexandria] in the sixth book of his ' Hypotyposeis ' and that it is also corroborated by Papias the bishop of Hierapolis.⌋ In other parts of his work Eusebius actually gives the quotations to which he here refers, from which it appears that he has really combined more than one passage of Clement in his statement.² The evidence of John, as recorded by Papias ³—⌈ that Mark being the interpreter of Peter wrote whatsoever he remembered with great accuracy, but not in the order in which the things were said or done by the Lord '—is interesting, for it seems to point to the Gospel in its present form having been compiled from a set of separate lections intended for public exposition and for catechetical instruction. ⌋ Harnack has come to the conclusion that ⌈internal indications place no impediment in the way of assigning Mark at the latest to the sixth decade of the first century.' ⁴ ⌋ But it is fairly certain that Mark was

---

¹ Eusebius, *Hist. Eccl.* ii. xv. : παρακλήσεσι δὲ παντοίαις Μάρκον, οὗ τὸ Εὐαγγελίον φέρεται, ἀκόλουθον ὄντα Πέτρου λιπαρῆσαι, ὡς ἂν καὶ διὰ γραφῆς ὑπόμνημα τῆς διὰ λόγου παραδοθείσης αὐτοῖς καταλείψοι διδασκαλίας, μὴ πρότερόν τε ἀνεῖναι, ἢ κατεργάσασθαι τὸν ἄνδρα, καὶ ταύτῃ αἰτίους γενέσθαι τῆς τοῦ λεγομένου κατὰ Μάρκον εὐαγγελίου γραφῆς. Γνόντα δὲ τὸ πραχθὲν φασὶ τὸν ἀπόστολον, ἀποκαλύψαντος αὐτῷ τοῦ πνεύματος, ἡσθῆναι τῇ τῶν ἀνδρῶν προθυμίᾳ, κύρωσαί τε τὴν γραφὴν εἰς ἔντευξιν ταῖς ἐκκλησίαις.

² The clause above beginning φασὶ τὸν ἀπόστολον is Eusebius' own, derived not from the *Hypotyposeis* book vii. quoted *Eccl. Hist.* vi. 14, but from some other source. The words of Clement in the *Hypotyposeis* are remarkable—ὅπερ ἐπιγνόντα τὸν Πέτρον προτρεπτικῶς μήτε κωλῦσαι μήτε προτρέψασθαι. Eusebius seems to have had in his mind another passage of Clement from *Adumb.* in 1 Peter v. 13 (quoted by Harnack, *Neue Untersuchungen*, p. 89)—' Marcus, Petri sectator, praedicante Petro evangelium palam Romae coram quibusdam Caesareanis equitibus et multa Christi testimonia proferente, petitus ab eis, ut possent quae dicebantur memoriae commendare, scripsit ex his, quae a Petro dicta sunt, evangelium quod secundum Marcum vocitatur.'

³ Eusebius, *Hist. Eccl.* iii. 39.

⁴ Harnack, *Neue Untersuchungen*, p. 88. The difficulties in accepting the Gospel of St. Mark, as we now possess it, as the common narrative source of St. Matthew and St. Luke, appear to me well-nigh insuperable. But if we suppose that this Gospel is a revised continuous narrative formed from a number of separate lections or instructions written by

not at Rome during the sixth decade, and there can therefore be no objection to accepting the voice of tradition, which makes the Gospel to have been written for the use of St. Peter's Roman converts about the year 45 A.D.

The evidence of St. Jerome, as to the form of the Petrine tradition, which was current in the Rome of Pope Damasus during the latter part of the fourth century, now demands our most careful attention, for it is of great importance. His words (to which I have already referred) are : ' Simon Peter . . . prince of the Apostles, after an episcopacy of the Antiochean Church, and after preaching to the dispersion of those of the circumcision, who had believed in Pontus, Galatia, Cappadocia, Asia and Bithynia, in the second year of Claudius journeys to Rome to combat Simon Magus, and there for twenty-five years he occupied the sacerdotal chair, until the last year of Nero, that is the fourteenth.'[1]   The biographical notice of St. Peter, which appears in the edition of the ' Liber Pontificalis ' published about 530 A.D., is, as the Abbé Duchesne states,[2] borrowed from St. Jerome, and this notice has remained as what may be justly styled the standard Roman tradition ever since.   I have said that this represents the form of that tradition as it obtained at Rome in the pontificate of Damasus (366–384).   Damasus has been well named the first Christian archaeologist. Some of his many beautifully engraved inscriptions, embodying often

Mark previously for the use of Greek-speaking converts in Judaea, the difficulty is largely removed. If St. Luke had completed the Acts in 62 A.D., it is highly probable that he composed his Gospel at Caesarea during St. Paul's captivity under Felix. Such a set of catechetical instructions correspond almost exactly to the type of διήγησις of which Luke speaks in his preface. He would find the Marcan lections, embodying as they did the teaching of St. Peter, almost certainly in the possession of such a leader among the Hellenist teachers as Philip the Evangelist, who was residing at Caesarea at the same time as Luke.

[1] Simon Petrus . . . princeps Apostolorum, post episcopatum Antiochensis ecclesiae et praedicationem dispersionis eorum qui de circumcisione crediderant, in Ponto, Galatia, Cappadocia, Asia et Bithynia, secundo Claudii anno ad expugnandum Simonem Magum Romam pergit, ibique viginti quinque annis cathedram sacerdotalem tenuit, usque ad ultimum annum Neronis, id est decimum quartum. *De Viris Illust.* i.

[2] Duchesne, *Liber Pontificalis*, i. 51, 119.

the results of personal research and investigation, above the tombs of the martyrs in the catacombs and in the churches of Rome are still extant.[1] Tradition connects the name of this Pope, coupled with that of Jerome, with the compilation of the original ' Liber Pontificalis,' as the forged letters prefixed to the work testify. Indeed so long and to such an extent did this tradition survive that in the thirteenth century and later we find the work designated as the ' Chronica Damasi ' or ' Damasus de Gestis Pontificum.' [2] In any case Damasus did make the early history of the Roman Church his special study, and Jerome was his secretary at the time of his death in 384. Nor was this all. Jerome spent some time in his earlier life at Rome, as a student, and he has himself left on record,[3] how at that time he visited the sepulchres of the Apostles and martyrs in the catacombs, and it must be borne in mind that in those days there were in existence very many tombs and inscriptions of the highest historical interest, which have long since been destroyed, and that others were then accessible, which have not yet been unearthed. Lastly in assaying the value of Jerome's evidence, as to the received Petrine tradition in the pontificate of Damasus, it is a matter of no small interest to know that he must have met at Rome in 382–84 and been the companion at the Papal Court of Furius Dionysius Filocalus.[4] This man was the artist who engraved the

---

[1] Marucchi, *Eléments d'Archéologie Chrétienne*, i. 226–240 ; Lightfoot, *Apostolic Fathers*, part i. vol. i. p. 296.

[2] Lightfoot, *Apostolic Fathers*, part i. vol. i. p. 304.

[3] ' Dum essem puer et liberalibus studiis erudirer, solebam cum caeteris eiusdem aetatis et propositi, diebus dominicis sepulchra Apostolorum et martyrum circuire, crebroque cryptas ingredi, quae in terrarum profunda defossae, ex utraque parte ingredientium per parietes habent corpora sepultorum, et ita obscura sunt omnia, ut propemodum illud propheticum compleatur : *Descendant ad infernum viventes* (Ps. liv. 16) ; et raro desuper lumen admissum horrorem temperet tenebrarum, ut non tam fenestram quam foramen demissi luminis putes et caeca nocte circumdatis illud Virgilianum proponitur : " Horror ubique animos, simul ipsa silentia terrent." ' Migne, *P.L.* t. xxv. c. 375. *In Ezeck.* xii. 40.

[4] Marucchi, *Eléments d'Archéologie Chrétienne*, i. 230, 235 ; De Rossi, *Roma Sotterranea*, i. 118 ff, ii. 196 ff. ; Lightfoot, *Apost. Fathers*, part i. vol. i. pp. 64, 249.

Damasene inscriptions, so noted for the peculiar beauty and special character of their calligraphy. He was the illuminator and probably the editor of the Liberian or Filocalian Catalogue of the Roman Bishops, which was compiled and edited in 354 A.D. and which was the basis of the later ' Liber Pontificalis.' [1] With this Liberian catalogue it is impossible that Jerome should have been unacquainted, and the differences between its form of the Petrine tradition and that given by Jerome are of interest and will demand our consideration. What is, however, important now to note is that Jerome, the later writer, in differing from the Liberian notice of St. Peter must have done so intentionally.

The quotation given above from the ' De Viris Illustribus ' losely follows the lines of the passage from the Chronicle of Eusebius about St. Peter, which in the Hieronymian version is thus rendered—' Peter the Apostle . . . when he had first founded the Antiochean Church, sets out to Rome, where as bishop (*episcopus*) of the same city he continues for twenty-five years preaching the Gospel. After Peter Linus first held the Roman Church for eleven years.'[2] The notice in the ' De Viris Illustribus ' adds the detail, which appears later in the ' Liber Pontificalis,' that it was in the second year of Claudius that Peter arrived in Rome, and as Peter's death is asserted to have taken place in the last year of Nero, the interval gives exactly the twenty-five years of the so-called episcopacy, or, as in this case it would be better rendered, overseership of the Roman Church. The Abbé Duchesne in his monumental work on the ' Liber

[1] Duchesne, *Liber Pontificalis*, i. 4 ; Lipsius, ' Die Bischofslisten des Eusebius ' in ' Neue Studien zur Papstgeschichte,' *Jahrb. f. Protest. Theol.* vi. 233 ff. 1880 ; Mommsen, ' Ueber den Chronographen vom Jahre 354 ' in *Abhandlungen der Philol. Hist. Classe d. K. Sächs. Gesellschaft der Wissenschaften*, 1854 ; Lightfoot, *Apost. Fathers*, part i. vol. i. ' Early Roman Succession,' pp. 199–345 ; vol. ii. ' Hippolytus of Portus,' pp. 317–477.

[2] ' Petrus Apostolus . . . cum primum Antiochenam Ecclesiam fundasset, Romam proficiscitur, ubi Evangelium praedicans xxv annis eiusdem urbis Episcopus perseverat. Post Petrum primus Romanam ecclesiam tenuit Linus annis xi.' See Schoene, *Die Weltchronik des Eusebius in ihrer Bearbeitung durch Hieronymus.*

Pontificalis,' while stating that it is only after the time of
Xystus I (117–126) that there is sufficient uniformity in
the catalogues to inspire confidence in the figures given for
the duration of the earlier episcopates, writes :⌉ ' As far as
regards St. Peter the figure of his twenty-five years is as
well attested as the figures of the years of his successors
after Xystus I. I have then believed myself able to note it,
but without indicating from what date one ought to count
it, for there are on this point grave incertitudes.'[1] ⎜ With
these grave incertitudes let me now deal very briefly. The
Eusebian History and Chronicle give lists of the Roman
bishops, and the Chronicle the lengths of their term-years,
while the Liberian or Filocalian Catalogue gives a list of
bishops and their term-years, but (as I have already said)
with considerable divergences. Both are based on earlier
authorities—the Eusebian on the lists of Hegesippus and
Irenaeus, i.e. on documents belonging to the second half of
the second century ; the Liberian on a chronicler, most
probably Hippolytus, about fifty years later. Now both the
Eusebian Chronicle and the Liberian Catalogue give twenty-
five years as the term of St. Peter's episcopacy, but they
differ as to the dates of its beginning and its end. We have
already seen that the Eusebian date-limits are from 42 A.D.
to 67 A.D. ; the Liberian, however, are from 30 A.D. to 55 A.D.⌋
The Liberian chronicler states that ' after the Lord's Ascension the most blessed Peter received the office of a bishop
(episcopatum).'[2] He further states that Linus succeeded him
at Rome in 56 A.D. At first sight it may appear that
these two sets of dates are hopelessly inconsistent.[3] That

---

[1] Duchesne, *Liber Pontificalis*, ccxviii : ' En ce qui regarde Saint
Pierre le chiffre de ses vingt-cinq années est aussi bien attesté que les
chiffres d'années de ses successeurs depuis Xystus Iᵉʳ. J'ai donc cru pou-
voir le noter, mais sans indiquer, à partir de quelle date il faut le compter,
car il y a, sur ce point, de graves incertitudes.'

[2] 'Post ascensum eius beatissimus Petrus episcopatum suscepit ';
'. . . Linus fuit temporibus Neronis, a consulatu Saturnini et Scipionis '
(A.D. 56).

[3] See the authorities above quoted : Duchesne, Mommsen, Harnack,
Lipsius, Lightfoot, De Rossi, &c.

this is not necessarily the case, I will now endeavour to show.

[First, let me point out that the Liberian Chronicler's account of the whole of the early history of the Roman episcopate is full of blunders ;] his errors are not confined to his statement about St. Peter. By him Clement is reckoned as the second bishop instead of the third, and Anencletus or Cletus is represented as two persons [1] instead of one. In the case of St. Peter the Chronicler apparently regards the Ascension as being the date of the assumption of a general episcopate by the Apostle, who after that date became undoubtedly the acknowledged leader of the Twelve. Moreover St. Luke emphatically mentions sojourners from Rome, Jews and proselytes as being present at the feast of Pentecost when by Peter's preaching 3000 converts were made. But what about the other date, 56 A.D. ? It will be my aim now to show that this date also may be one of real historical significance in the life-work of St. Peter.

The Hieronymian-Eusebian version of the Petrine tradition is indeed, as it stands, scarcely less in conflict with the Lukan history than is the Liberian. Jerome's statement that before Peter went to Rome in 42 A.D. he had been bishop of the Church at Antioch and had preached to the Jewish *Diaspora* in various provinces of Asia Minor is obviously irreconcilable with the narrative in the Acts. The explanation however of all these difficulties seems to me to lie in the hypothesis of a sojourn of Peter at Rome about midway between the sojourn in the early part of Claudius and the final sojourn towards the close of Nero's reign, which ended with his martyrdom. I propose therefore to

---

[1] The evidence for the order of succession (as given by Irenaeus and Hegesippus), Peter, Linus, Anencletus (or Cletus), Clemens is very strong. Lightfoot's judgment is—' We have to reckon with three conflicting statements, as far as regards the position of Clement in the Roman succession—a *tradition*, the Irenaean—a *fiction*, the Clementine—and a *blunder*, the Liberian or perhaps the Hippolytean. Under these circumstances we cannot hesitate for a moment in our verdict. Whether the value of the tradition be great or small, it alone deserves to be considered. The sequence therefore which commends itself for acceptance is Linus, Anencletus or Cletus, Clemens, Euarestus ' (*Apost. Fathers*, part i. vol. i. p. 66).

examine the possibilities of such an hypothesis, and to see whether any evidence, circumstantial or otherwise, exists to give it support.

The sequence of events as given in the Acts has been frequently misunderstood. In the eleventh chapter, verses 19-20, St. Luke tells us of the rapid spread of the Christian faith at Antioch through the efforts of evangelists from Cyprus and Cyrene, men who had once been among the Hellenist disciples of Stephen at Jerusalem, and further that in this company of the new converts were many Greeks as well as Jews. He then proceeds to state that when news of this was brought to the Apostles in Jerusalem, they resolved to send, in their name and as their representative, Barnabas, as being at once a prominent member of the Church at Jerusalem and a Cypriote by nationality, to take charge of this important new movement and to assume its leadership. Barnabas was successful in his mission and having brought Saul from Tarsus to help him in his task, by the joint efforts of these two men of special gifts and earnest zeal the growth of the Church made such conspicuous progress as to attract public notice and to gain for the new sect in the mouth of the multitude that scoffing but distinctive nickname of *Christiani* which was to be in the coming centuries a title of honour the profession of which would bring to thousands of martyrs terrible sufferings and death.

Between verse 26 and verse 27, however, a certain interval elapsed. ⌜The phrase ' now in these days '—as in the opening verse of the sixth chapter—is one of those loose chronological expressions common to the Lukan writings, implying an uncertain interval of time.⌟ In this case the statement that ' certain prophets came down from Jerusalem unto Antioch ' may be taken to have suggested the insertion at this point of the episode with which Chapter xii. opens : ' Now about that time Herod the King put forth his hands to afflict certain of the Church.' The departure of the prophets for Antioch was in fact one of the *results* of the persecution of Herod, and as the story of the persecution was essential to the writer's purpose he has interpolated it here in the

midst of his Antiochean narrative, which is resumed at
verse 25 of this same twelfth chapter.   One of these prophets,
whose name Agabus is given, is stated to have predicted the
coming of a great famine over all the world, and such was
the belief inspired by his utterance that the Christian community of Antioch determined to collect a contribution for
the relief of the brethren that dwelt in Judaea. ⌈Now the
famine, which was, in accordance with Agabus' prophecy,
of wide extent throughout the Eastern portion of the Roman
world,[1] seems to have begun in Judaea in the year 45 A.D.
and to have reached its height in the following year.⌋ According to Josephus [2] the famine took place when Tiberius
Alexander was procurator in Judaea, and his term of office
did not begin before the latter part of 45 A.D.   As this same
historian gives a circumstantial account of the relief brought
personally to Jerusalem by Queen Helena, mother of Izates,
King of Adiabene in 45 A.D., and of her remaining there
some considerable time distributing corn that she imported
from Egypt and figs from Cyprus, it is evident that the
dearth lasted for at least two years.   The probability is
that the prophecy of Agabus was delivered some time in
44 A.D. and that with the first reports of a failure of the
crops being imminent the fund in aid at Antioch was started.
The raising of a sufficient sum by weekly collections would
take some time, and it is not likely that the delegates
Barnabas and Saul left Antioch until the spring of 46 A.D.

[1] Sir W. M. Ramsay writes (St. Paul the Traveller, pp. 48–49) : ' The
famine appears to me to be singularly well attested considering the scanti-
ness of evidence for this period.   Suetonius alludes to assiduae sterilitates
causing famine prices under Claudius, while Dion Cassius and Tacitus
speak of two famines in Rome, and famine in Rome implied dearth in the
great corn-growing countries of the Mediterranean ; Eusebius mentions
famine in Greece and an inscription perhaps refers to famine in Asia Minor.'

[2] As to the famine in Judaea Josephus is full and explicit (Ant. iii. 15.
3 ; xx. 2. 5 and 5. 2).   The story of Queen Helena's munificence is told
also by Eusebius (Hist. Eccl. ii. 12).   Ramsay in a note on the date of the
famine says that Tiberius Alexander's entry into office cannot be fixed with
absolute certainty : ' July 45 A.D. is the earliest admissible date and 46 A.D.
is far more probable ' (St. Paul the Traveller, p. 68).   In the article on
' Chronology ' in Hastings's Dictionary of the Bible, Mr. C. H. Turner gives
46 A.D. as the date of the visit of the Antiochean delegates.

was sufficiently advanced for a voyage to one of the Palestinian ports to be possible. The Feast of Pentecost would have been a very fitting time for the arrival of men bringing alms to supply the needs of those suffering from the loss of the harvest.

At this point let us carry our thoughts back to St. Peter, whom we left at Rome with Mark, as his companion and interpreter. There exists no record to tell us what was the duration of this his first sojourn in that city. At this critical stage however of the development of the Christian Church the advice and guidance of so trusted a leader must have been frequently needed both at Jerusalem and at Antioch. The longest stay that St. Paul ever made in one place was at Ephesus, where he remained for three years, and three years may be safely regarded as the extreme limit of St. Peter's absence in these opening years of the reign of Claudius.[1] In any case the news of the famine would be sure to hasten his departure, and if, as I myself strongly hold, the second visit of Paul to Jerusalem in company with Barnabas, described in the second chapter of the Epistle to the Galatians,[2] be identical with their mission from Antioch as the bearers of the relief fund, then in the spring of 46 A.D. they would find both Peter and Mark on their arrival already at Jerusalem. The only other member of the

[1] Both the Latin (Hieronymian) and Syriac translation of Eusebius' *Chronicle* make Peter to have gone to Rome in the second year of Claudius and to Antioch two years later (ed. Schoene, p. 211). This two years may represent the time actually spent in Rome according to tradition.

[2] Gal. ii. 1-10. For an eminently fair and thorough examination of the arguments for identifying the Galatian visit 'after fourteen years' with (1) the visit of Paul and Barnabas described in Acts xi and (2) with the visit to the Council described in Acts xv, see Professor Kirsopp Lake, *The Early Epistles of St. Paul*, pp. 274-293. Professor Lake after stating the case for the identification with (1) says ' To my mind it is extremely strong' (p. 281). Again after weighing the objections against (1) and (2) he concludes ' my own view is that the objections [against] placing Gal. ii. at the time of the famine are much less serious, but I recognise that they are real, and prevent one from claiming the right to feel quite certain on the subject' (p. 293). It will be seen that, in the circumstances under which I suppose the interview to have taken place, the case for the identification is much strengthened.

Twelve present in the Holy City at this juncture seems to have been St. John, and no more suitable opportunity could have been afforded for a private discussion of the situation raised by the admission into the Antiochean Church, without any Jewish restrictions, of a large number of Gentile converts, and of an understanding being arrived at upon the vital issues that were in question. The five principal representatives of what may be styled the old, the moderate and the new schools of Christian thought and opinion were now brought together by the discharge of a common charitable duty, and the result was an agreement on general principles and a working arrangement as to missionary spheres, which approved itself, if not to the Judaistic extremists, to the recognised leaders Peter, John and James no less than to Paul and Barnabas, as satisfactory.

The measure of Peter's satisfaction may be gathered from the fact that John Mark accompanied the two delegates on their return to Antioch, probably in the spring of 47, and that some months later, but before the period for sailing was over, Barnabas and Saul set out on their missionary journey to Cyprus, taking Mark with them. Their work in Cyprus, for they went through the whole island, would occupy them till the spring, when they crossed to Perga in Pamphylia where Mark left them and returned to Jerusalem. Many reasons have been suggested as the cause of this abandonment at this time. It may have been due in part to dissatisfaction with Paul's methods of teaching, more probably to a feeling that now the Cyprian mission was over it was his duty to return once more to the side of his old leader in that new sphere of work with Antioch as its centre which Peter had probably been, to Mark's knowledge, for some time planning.[1]

[1] It is a curious fact that Barnabas and Paul made no attempt to preach in Pamphylia either on the outward or the return journey, nor is there any evidence to show that Paul ever revisited that country. The idea suggests itself that Pamphylia may already have become ' another man's sphere.' Possibly Peter himself may have paused on his voyage back from Rome to preach to the Jewish *Diaspora* scattered along the Southern coast of Asia Minor. If so, Mark's refusal to proceed to Pamphylia would be explained on this ground.

⌈No tradition from early Christian times is stronger or more persistent than that which asserts that before Peter entered upon his Roman 'episcopate,' he for seven years filled a similar office at Antioch.[1]⌋ Now if the so-called Roman episcopate be taken to date strictly from the second year of Claudius, it is quite clear that Peter did not spend seven years at Antioch previously.   So it has come to pass that even those who have been willing to accept the Roman visit of 42 A.D. as historical have dismissed the Antiochean tradition as baseless fable.   But in my opinion no tradition of this character can have come into existence and held its ground as this did without there being a genuine substratum of truth in it.   The real difficulty is the chronological one. Can this be overcome ?   I believe it may be. ⌈If Peter sojourned at Rome a second time in the years 54–56 A.D., and I hope to show grounds for believing that he may have done so, then there is no reason why the seven years that preceded this (47–54 A.D.) should not have been years during which Peter made Antioch the centre of his missionary work, a starting-point for journeys to Mesopotamia in the east or even to Cappadocia and Pontus in the north, an abode from which visits to the feasts at Jerusalem could be easily undertaken.⌋It is certain that he was in Antioch at the same time as Paul and Barnabas after the return of the latter from their first missionary journey in the autumn of 49 A.D.[2] The account, which Paul gives in the second chapter of his Epistle to the Galatians, of the dispute he had

<hr/>

[1] The *Liber Pontificalis*, both in its original form as restored by Duchesne and in its later recension, gives seven years as the length of the Petrine episcopate at Antioch.   Duchesne, *Liber Pontificalis*, i. 51, 118 ; also St. Gregory, *Ep.* vii. 40.

[2] Certain, that⌈is, if the second visit of Paul to Jerusalem be identical with that in Galatians ii, which I am now assuming.   It cannot fail to strike anyone how much more fittingly the dispute between Peter and Paul falls into its place with this assumption, than if it be regarded as occurring after the Council of Jerusalem.⌋ Indeed the difficulty of regarding this meeting as happening at this later time just after the Apostolic decree had been drawn up is so overwhelmingly great that some authorities, i.e. Harnack, Zahn, and Turner (Hastings's *Dict.*) have felt compelled to suggest that the order of events has been inverted by St. Paul.   See Kirsopp Lake, *Early Epistles of St. Paul*, p. 294 ff.

with Peter concerning the question of eating with the Gentiles, would indeed lead one to think that the Apostle's stay at that time had been one of some duration. As St. Luke from the thirteenth chapter of the Acts and onward confines his narrative entirely to the missionary life of St. Paul, it is with gratitude that we welcome these flashes of light from the autobiographical portions of the Pauline epistles, which from time to time suddenly illumine the darkness of these early decades of the first century, through which we are painfully striving to grope our way, and, however evanescent, prove to us at any rate that for the moment we are walking upon the right track. There is probably no epistle which is so rich in passages of this kind as St. Paul's First Epistle to the Corinthians. It is generally agreed that this epistle was written at Ephesus towards the end of St. Paul's stay of three years in that city. Now the recent discovery of an inscription at Delphi [1] practically fixes the date of Gallio's proconsulship in Achaia as 52 A.D., and with it the chronology of this part of St. Paul's life. The date of the First Epistle to the Corinthians can therefore be given with something approaching to certainty. It was written towards the end of the year 55 A.D. Now one of the chief objects of this epistle was to reprove the Corinthians for their divisions and party spirit. There was a party there which called itself by the name of Cephas. Again there is a direct reference to the fact that Cephas was accompanied in his missionary journeys by his wife.[2] What other explanation can be given of such statements than the obvious one, that Peter had been paying a visit of such duration to Corinth

---

[1] See *Revue d'Histoire et de la Littérature Religieuses*, Mars–Avril 1911 : E. Ch. Babut, p. 139 ff., describes the discovery by M. Ed. Bourget of four fragments of a letter of Claudius to the city of Delphi. In the inscription, part of which is obliterated or wanting, the twenty-sixth salutation of Claudius is mentioned and Gallio is Proconsul. M. Babut shows that the date must lie between narrow limits. Claudius had his twenty-seventh salutation on August 1, 52 A.D., and the twenty-sixth salutation probably not before April or May of that year. Also consult Adolf Deissmann's *St. Paul* (Eng. tr. 1912), where a facsimile of the inscription is given and the Proconsulate of Gallio forms the subject of a special Appendix, p. 235 ff.

[2] 1 Cor. i. 12 ; iii. 22 ; ix. 5.

as to have created a following who boasted themselves distinctively, as being the disciples of one whom they looked upon as a ' super-eminent Apostle.'[1] Further a chance reference is made to Barnabas, as working for his maintenance,[2] a reference which would be meaningless unless the Corinthians were acquainted with Barnabas personally and had seen him so working. That Peter was really regarded in the second century as a founder of the Corinthian Church conjointly with Paul is proved by the quotation, preserved by Eusebius, from a letter of Dionysius, bishop of Corinth, to Soter, bishop of Rome, who speaks of ' the plantation of Peter and Paul at Rome and at Corinth. For they both together here in Corinth planted us and taught alike ; and both together in Italy taught alike, and then were martyred about the same time.'[3]

These almost casual references preserved in the First Epistle to the Corinthians relating to an event of much significance in the history of an important Church, to which an eminent bishop of that Church bears witness as a recognised and established tradition about a century later, bring before us in a startling way how widespread were the activities of Peter and other members of the Apostolic band in those years when the narrative of the Acts is dumb as to their very existence, and therefore how little right we have to express ourselves dogmatically and without reservation upon questions of first-century Christian history, of which our knowledge is so utterly fragmentary, or to reject unceremoniously traditions which, if carefully sifted, will generally be found to contain some precious bits of authentic historical fact. The particular episode of Petrine history with which I am now dealing affords an excellent illustration of these remarks.

---

[1] 2 Cor. xii. 11 : ὑστέρησα τῶν ὑπερλίαν ἀποστόλων.   [2] 1 Cor. ix. 6.

[3] Eusebius, *Hist. Eccl.* ii. 25 : ταῦτα καὶ ὑμεῖς διὰ τῆς τοσαύτης νουθεσίας τὴν ἀπὸ Πέτρου καὶ Παύλου φυτείαν γενηθεῖσαν Ῥωμαίων τε καὶ Κορινθίων συνεκεράσατε. Καὶ γὰρ ἄμφω καὶ εἰς τὴν ἡμετέραν Κόρινθον φυτεύσαντες ἡμᾶς, ὁμοίως ἐδίδαξαν· ὁμοίως δὲ καὶ εἰς τὴν Ἰταλίαν ὁμόσε διδάξαντες, ἐμαρτύρησαν κατὰ τὸν αὐτὸν καιρόν. See also Eusebius, *Hist. Eccl.* iv. 23 and Kirsopp Lake, *Early Epistles of St. Paul*, p. 112.

Granted then that the natural interpretation of certain passages of the First Epistle to the Corinthians implies that both Peter and Barnabas were in Corinth and working there in the autumn of 54 A.D., it may well be asked is it not strange that these two Apostolic men of all others should have thus gone apparently out of their way to visit a Church so recently founded by the efforts of St. Paul, and which should have been regarded as in his special charge ? The reply is that not by a single word does St. Paul make any complaint on the subject. What then is the explanation ? It is, I believe, that Peter on hearing of the death of Claudius on October 13, 54 A.D., had thought the time opportune for revisiting his Roman converts and had asked Barnabas to accompany him. They had stopped at Corinth simply as a convenient halting-place, being the half-way house between Syria and Italy. And now let us turn to tradition. There are many traditions which associate Barnabas with Rome and Italy. The forms in which they have come down to us are, like most of the fifth and sixth century Acts, Passions and Travels, full of chronological errors and contain many impossibilities and contradictions due to the later inventions and interpolations of hagiographers careless or ignorant of history and anxious only to glorify the memory of the particular saint or martyr in whom for local or other reasons they are interested. But as the learned French writer, Edmond le Blant,[1] who is a specialist on this subject, well says ' These interpolations, in my opinion, ought not either to disconcert or to repel criticism. Under a layer of invention the original traits exist, and a great number of them appear on the very surface. One must extricate them patiently.' The earliest reference to Barnabas [2]

---

[1] ' Les Actes des Martyrs.   Supplément aux *Acta Sincera* de Dom Ruinart ' (part 2, p. 87).

[2] The traditions about Barnabas have been collected and fully treated by Braunsberger. *Der Apostel Barnabas. Sein Leben und der ihm beigelegte Brief.* Mainz, 1876.   See also Harnack in the *Theologische Literaturzeitung*, 1876, No. 19, 487 ff. and Lipsius, *Die Apokryphen Apostelgeschichten und Apostellegenden*, 2er Band, 2e Hälfte, 270 ff.   The chief document relating to Barnabas' work first at Rome then at Milan is entitled *Datiana*

is that found in the 'Clementine Recognitions.'[1] This work,
an Ebionite romance of a much later age than Clement the
supposed writer, is prefaced by an account of Clement's early
life at Rome. The author says that Clement was converted
by the preaching of Barnabas, who afterwards introduced
him to St. Peter. The object of the author of the 'Recognitions' is to magnify the authority and orthodox teaching
of Peter, so that the introduction here of Barnabas, who is
never mentioned again, is purely gratuitous, and indeed
inexplicable in such a narrative unless the fact recorded
were one based on a received and ancient tradition too
well known to be ignored. The mention of Barnabas'
preaching has nothing to do with the story. The insertion
thus of this incident without cause in an Ebionite document
of Eastern origin strongly speaks for its authenticity. The
traditions represent Barnabas as having preceded Peter [2]
as a preacher at Rome, and it is quite possible that he may
now have left Corinth some weeks or months before Peter
followed him, and that one of the first-fruits of his ministry
in the Imperial City was the conversion of the man who

historia Ecclesiae Mediolanensis ed. Biraghi, Milan 1848. Braunsberger's
conclusion is that the preaching of Barnabas in North Italy was ' zwar nicht
sicher, aber sehr wahrscheinlich ' (p. 83).

[1] Hort in his lectures on the *Clementine Recognitions* shows that this
pseud-epigraphic writing, and the *Clementine Homilies*, which closely
resemble it, are two separate Ebionite versions of a much earlier work
known as the *Circuits of Peter*—Περίοδοι Πέτρου. See also Salmon's article
in Smith and Wace's *Dict. of Christian Biography*. The date of these
versions is about the end of the third century, of the Περίοδοι about a
century earlier. Both had their origin in the East.

[2] In the *Datiana historia* the Barnabas story as told by the author,
after relating Barnabas' work with Paul at Antioch and the choice made
of him and Paul as Apostles to the Gentiles in the fourteenth year after
Christ's Passion, and his first missionary journey, and second visit to Cyprus
after his separation from Paul, proceeds to state that thereon—in the first
year of Claudius, eight years after Christ's ascension—he takes ship with
some of his disciples for Rome—' velut totius orbis dominam visere cupiens,'
where he, as the first Apostle, proclaims the Word of God and among
others converts Clement, afterwards the third successor of Peter in the
Roman episcopate (Lipsius, ii. 2, p. 311). Here it is obvious that the
chronology contradicts itself. It ought to be the first year of Claudius
Nero, i.e. 55 A.D. If the eight years be counted from Barnabas' appointment as an Apostle of the Gentiles, 47 A.D., we arrive at the same date.

G

was to occupy so important a place in the history of the Church in Rome during the latter half of the first century.[1] If certain passages of St. Paul's First Epistle to the Corinthians have suggested that St. Peter visited Corinth in 54 A.D., certain other passages of the Epistle to the Romans, sent by St. Paul from Corinth to its destination in the early spring of 57 A.D., suggest no less strongly that he [Paul] had been recently hindered from going to Rome by the presence in that Church of one who was its founder. And here I would venture to say that we may rest assured that the principle ' not to build on another man's foundation '[2] was an Apostolic and not merely a Pauline rule of action. That Peter went to Corinth with any intention of interfering with Paul's great work in that town, or of placing himself before the Corinthians as a rival and superior to the Apostle of the Gentiles, is inconceivable. But just as Paul proposed in Peter's absence to pay a passing visit to Rome on his way to Spain in order that he might be refreshed by personal intercourse with those of whose faith in Christ he had heard so much, and that he might in his turn be able to impart to them some spiritual gift,[3] so would Peter be anxious to break his voyage to Rome at the Isthmus of Corinth, so as to make acquaintance during a brief sojourn with a Christian community in whose first conversion and establishment as a Church his own Roman disciples, Aquila and Prisca, had played so considerable a part.

Now St. Paul in his Epistle to the Romans twice emphatically declares that though he had for some time longed to visit Rome, he had been many times hindered, and the cause is plainly stated, i.e. that it was his settled practice

---

[1] A *prima-facie* case is made out for the authenticity of the tradition of Barnabas' preaching in Rome and North Italy from the fact that it was so greatly in the interest of the upholders of the Petrine origin of the Roman Church to suppress it ; as Harnack points out, its existence 'musste dem römischen Bischofe höchst unbequem werden : denn sie drohte die einzigartige Bedeutung des Petrus für das Abendland und die einzigartige Stellung Roms im Abendlande zu gefährden.'—*Literatur Zeitung*, 1876. No. 19, 488.

[2] Rom. xv. 20.   [3] Rom. i. 10–12, xv. 23, 24.

not to trespass in another man's sphere of work. As I do not wish to go over old ground, I shall assume that ' the other man ' here referred to is St. Peter. But this being granted, the more often I read over these autobiographical passages from this epistle the more thoroughly am I convinced that the writer is not here simply alluding to so distant an event as the preaching of that Apostle in the Imperial City in the early days of Claudius, but to Peter being actually present at Rome in person at the times when otherwise he, Paul, might have been able to carry out his wished-for visit. For such a friendly visit of short duration need not, as I have already said, any more than the contemplated visit on the way to Spain, have been regarded as a ' building upon another man's foundation.' The ' oftentimes ' of c. i. 13 and the ' many times ' of c. xv. 22 are practically confined within somewhat narrow limits. Paul after what he must have learned from Aquila and Prisca would scarcely have thought of adventuring himself in Rome before the death of Claudius. At that date he was in Ephesus, a city that was in direct and constant communication with the capital, and during the next two years he might have found several opportunities for undertaking a voyage to Rome : one, for instance, when from Ephesus he paid that second visit to Corinth of which there is no record in the Acts, but which is mentioned in the Second Epistle to the Corinthians.[1] Another, and a most tempting one, when his tried friends and fellow helpers, Aquila and Prisca, returned home after the tumult. Yet a third when after leaving Ephesus he went to Macedonia and then apparently followed the Via Egnatia to Illyricum before making that third sojourn in Corinth, when he wrote the Epistle to the Romans. If he were hindered from doing so, it was because precisely during this period Peter was himself in Rome.

I now turn to the evidence of the Liberian or Filocalian Catalogue of 354 A.D., which has been traced back by those who speak with the highest authority upon the subject to the lost Chronicle of Hippolytus, written about

---

[1] 2 Cor. xii. 14 and xiii. 1.

234 or 235 A.D.[1] The Liberian Catalogue makes several
palpable blunders in the early part of its list of the Roman
bishops, as I have already said, but the most curious is
that which makes the twenty-five years of St. Peter's
episcopate to begin in 30 A.D. and to end in 55 A.D. Now
this last date can scarcely be intended as that of St.
Peter's martyrdom, for the Chronicler goes on to say that he suffered
with St. Paul on June 29 in the reign of Nero, showing clearly
his acquaintance with the common tradition. But the
fact that the names of the Consuls (in a corrupted form)
for the year 55 are correctly given is a piece of strong circumstantial evidence that this date was one of special importance
in the early history of the Roman Church.[2] The assertion
that Linus at this time succeeded Peter as bishop supplies,
I believe, a clue by which to arrive at a solution of the
difficulty. Later writers and the ' Liber Pontificalis ' itself
mention both Linus and Anencletus as having been ordained
by Peter as bishops and as having exercised the duties of
that office in his name during his lifetime,[3] and there is
likewise a tradition that Clement also was ordained bishop
by Peter in his lifetime. This is a quite possible representation of what really took place. The date 55 A.D. occupied
a permanent place in the records of the Roman Church
because at this date Peter personally gave to that Church
its local organisation by appointing out of the general body
of presbyters an inner presbyteral council entrusted with
special pastoral duties of administration and overseership,

---

[1] See pp. 49, n. 2, 71, *supra*.

[2] PETRUS, ann. xxv. mens. uno, d. viiii. Fuit temporibus Tiberii
Caesaris et Gai et Tiberi Claudi et Neronis, a cons. Minuci [vinicii] et
Longini [A.D. 30] usque Nerine et Vero [Nerone et Vetere A.D. 55]. Passus
autem cum Paulo die iii. Kal. Iulias, cons. s̅s̅, imperante Nerone.

LINUS, ann. xii. m. iiii, dies xii. Fuit temporibus Neronis, a consulatu
Saturnini et Scipionis [A.D. 56] usque Capitone et Rufo [A.D. 67] (Lightfoot, *Apost. Fathers*, I. i. p. 253).

[3] Hic [Petrus] ordinavit duos episcopos, Linum et Cletum, qui praesen-
taliter omne ministerium sacerdotale in urbe Roma populo vel super-
venientium exhiberent ; beatus autem Petrus ad orationem et praedicationem, populum erudiens, vacabat. . . . Hic beatum Clementem episco-
pum conservavit, eique cathedram vel ecclesiam omnem disponendam
commisit.—Duchesne, *Liber Pontificalis*, i. 118. See evidence of Epiphanius
derived from Hegesippus, Lawlor, *Eusebiana*, p. 9.

the members of which bore the name of *episcopi*, which as St. Peter himself in his first epistle tells us was virtually the equivalent of *pastores*. Not until after the death of St. Peter however did this administrative episcopal body deem it necessary to select one of their number to succeed him as presiding *episcopus* and chief pastor of the Church.

There is one event which should, I think, be connected with this visit of St. Peter in 55 A.D., of considerable interest. It has generally been assumed that the mass of the early Christians belonged to the lowest classes and that many of them were slaves. This is no doubt to a certain extent true, but not by any means altogether so. Aquila and Prisca may have belonged to the ' freedman ' class, but they were well-to-do people, and it is probable that Prisca was Roman by birth and a person of some position. Again after dismissing all that is worthless and utterly fictitious in the account given of Clement's family and their adventures in the so-called Clementine literature, that literature bears evidence that long after his death Clement was given a place apart among the men of the sub-apostolic age not merely because he was a disciple of St. Peter or the author of a well-known epistle, but because he was connected by ties of relationship with the Imperial house. It seems unlikely that Ebionite writers in Eastern lands should have gone out of their way to lay stress on this relationship, unless it had some foundation in fact. To this matter I shall return later.

The case of Julia Pomponia Graecina, the wife of Aulus Plautius, the conqueror of Britain, is exceedingly interesting. It is best told in the words of Tacitus—' Pomponia Graecina, a distinguished lady, wife of the Plautius who returned from Britain with an ovation, was accused of some foreign superstition and handed over to her husband's judicial decision. Following ancient precedent, he heard his wife's cause in the presence of kinsfolk, involving, as it did, her legal status and character, and he reported that she was innocent. This Pomponia lived a long life of unbroken melancholy. After the murder of Julia, Drusus' daughter, by Messalina's intrigues, for forty years she wore only the attire of a mourner, with a heart ever sorrowful. For this, during Claudius' reign, she escaped unpunished, and it was afterwards counted a glory to her.'[1] It had been long surmised that the ' foreign superstition ' of which this lady was accused was the profession of Christianity. At that time Christianity was still regarded by the Roman authorities as a mere sect of Judaism, and Judaism being a *religio licita* Pomponia would be entitled to acquittal. Possibly public rumour was already beginning to accuse the Christians, as distinguished from the Jews, of indulging in impure and impious orgies, but if this were the ground of the accusation, it would not be difficult to refute it. The discovery by the famous archaeologist Giovanni Battista De Rossi in 1867, in the very ancient crypts of Lucina in the catacomb of Callistus, of a Christian sepulchral inscription bearing the name, only slightly injured, of a Pomponius Graecinus is a piece of testimony of considerable weight. He may well have been a great-nephew of the Pomponia Graecina of Tacitus, for De Rossi dates the inscription as belonging to the second half of the second century. The conjecture then that Pomponia Graecina, who was not only a friend but a relative of Julia and of the Claudian family, was a Christian convert is rendered very probable. It is worthy of note that the death of Julia, when Pomponia's mourning began, was in 43 A.D. during St. Peter's first visit to Rome, and that her trial before the family tribunal occurred in 57 A.D. or about a year (according to the hypothesis I have been endeavouring to sustain) after the second visit of the Apostle. It may well have been her intercourse with him that led to this public notice being taken of her addiction to a ' foreign superstition.'

[1] Pomponia Graecina, insignis femina, Plautio qui ovans se de Britanniis rettulit nupta ac superstitionis externae rea, mariti·iudicio permissa ; isque prisco instituto, propinquis coram, de capite famaque coniugis cognovit et insontem nuntiavit. Longa huic Pomponiae aetas et continua tristis fuit ; nam post Iuliam Drusi filiam dolo Messalinae interfectam per quadraginta annos non cultu nisi lugubri, non animo nisi maesto egit ; idque illi imperitante Claudio impune, mox ad gloriam vertit.—Tacitus, *Ann.* xiii. 32.

LECTURE IV

Acts xxviii. 15—Whom when Paul saw, he thanked God and took courage.

THE hope expressed by St. Paul in his Epistle to the Romans
that he might, after accomplishing his mission of alms-
bearing to Jerusalem, be able shortly to pay a passing visit
to the Roman Christians on his way to Spain,[1] was not to
be realised in the way that he proposed. The journey to
Jerusalem was overshadowed from the first by dark fore-
bodings,[2] and it proved disastrous for a lengthened period
to all his plans of active missionary work. It lies outside
the scope of these lectures to relate in detail all that happened to St. Paul between his arrival at Jerusalem to keep
the Pentecost feast of 57 A.D. and the early spring of 60 A.D.[3]
when at length he entered Rome as a prisoner. It is,
however, necessary for a right understanding of the character
of St. Paul's captivity in the Imperial Capital to consider
with some care what St. Luke has to tell us about his treatment by the Roman authorities during his earlier captivity
in Caesarea. There are few passages in ancient historical
literatures more clearly the work not merely of a contemporary writer but of an observant eye-witness than is the
narrative contained in the last seven chapters of the Acts.
These chapters abound in first-hand material for the history
of the time, and incidentally are valuable for the side-lights

---

[1] Rom. xv. 24.

[2] Acts, xix. 22–24 ; xxi. 4, 11–14 ; Rom. xv. 30, 31.

[3] These dates can, now that the discovery of an inscription at Delphi
makes it practically certain that Gallio was proconsul in Achaia in 52 A.D.,
be regarded as ascertained results.

that they throw upon many features of the Roman provincial administration and legal procedure, and upon the state of Judaea in the years 57 to 59 A.D.

St. Paul here appears in an historical setting, the truthfulness of which we can estimate by a comparison with the narrative of the period of Felix and Festus contained in Josephus' writings, and in the less detailed but more pungent references of Tacitus. It was the period when the great revolt was preparing. (Probably there was no provincial post that was more difficult and less desirable than that of Procurator of Judaea.) The celebrated character-sketch of Felix given by Tacitus,[1] ' in the practice of all kinds of lust and cruelty he exercised the power of a king with the temper of a slave,' no less than the fierce accusations brought against this Procurator by Josephus of cruelty, rapacity, and treachery,[2] are tinted with prejudice and exaggeration. The judgment of Mr. Henderson, the historian of Nero's Principate, is very different.[3] ' Alike in Jerusalem and in the country generally Felix found a widespread turmoil and insecurity alike of person and of property. Bands of robbers were roaming up and down, sweeping in adherents from every class of malcontent debtor and malefactor. The sect of the Zealots, founded years before by one Judas of Galilee, were hardly distinguishable from the *Sicarii*, those robbers and murderers whose evil deeds load the page of Josephus, and both plagued the unhappy land, as they disturbed the unfortunate Governor's peace. Felix acted vigorously. Robber bands were dispersed yet always reappeared. Daily assassinations in Jerusalem defied the Roman garrison. The mob was always the credulous prey of any fanatic. One Jew from Egypt gathered thousands together on the Mount of Olives promising them that the walls of the city shall fall at his bidding as those of Jericho before Joshua's trumpets, and his adherents' excited belief, stimulated by their lust and

---

[1] Tac. *Hist.* v. 9 : ' Antonius Felix per omnem saevitiam et libidinem ius regium servili ingenio exercuit'; *Ann.* xii. 54 : ' Cuncta malefacta sibi impune ratus tanta potentia subnixo.'

[2] Josephus, *Ant.* xx. 8 ; *Bell. Jud.* ii. 13.

[3] Henderson, *Life and Principate of the Emperor Nero*, pp. 364-5.

hope of rapine and of plunder, was only chilled by Felix'
appearance at the head of Roman troops. The mob was
scattered, but the leader escaped. . . . Wherever Felix
appears in the history of these troubled years, we find him
struggling with disorder, and crushing, so far as he could
with the small force at his disposal, both brigandage in the
country and rioting in the city. Difficult cases he duly
refers to Nero. Pending decision he will keep the peace
firmly. ⌐There is no good evidence to warrant the accusations of cruelty and lust so lightly brought against him.'
How accurately the Lukan narrative pictures this state of
things.' [1] ⌐The strong Roman garrison in Fort Antonia
keeping watch and ward over the faction-torn city at the
time of the Feast. The swoop of the tribune Lysias to
rescue Paul from the hands of the raging and howling
crowd in the Temple Courts. His mistake in thinking that
his prisoner was ' the Egyptian.' The scene on the stairs
and within the fort.⌐ The growing respect of the officer as
he notes that the man whom he had taken to be a leader of
banditti can speak Greek, then that he is, though a Jew
by race, not merely an inhabitant but a citizen of a famous
Greek university city, and lastly, most important of all,
that he inherits from his father the privileges of Roman
citizenship. ⌐His own naive remark ' with a great sum
obtained I this citizenship ' only enhancing the superior
position of the man who can reply ' but I was Roman
born.' [2]   The scene in the Sanhedrin is quite explicable
when we read in Josephus, ' about this time King Agrippa
gave the High-Priesthood to Ishmael, the son of Fabi. And
now arose discussions between the high priests and the
leading men of the multitude of Jerusalem . . . and when
they met together, they cast reproachful words and threw

---

[1] ' The witness to Felix' or Festus' endeavours of the other contemporary writer, St. Luke, is far more trustworthy. His Christianity secured
to him a greater neutrality in his attitude alike to Jew and to Roman,
and his simple tale of proceedings in which both were concerned is of the
highest historical merit, striking with at least one shaft of clear light into
the enwrapping mist of prejudice and hatred.'—Henderson, p. 363.

[2] Acts xxi. 37–40 ; xxii. 22–30. Tarsus was an *urbs libera*.

stones at one another.'[1] If Ananias were High Priest
de facto, while Ishmael was High Priest *de jure*, the exclama-
tion of Paul, ' I wist not that he was High Priest,' was not
unjustifiable.[2] Again the request of the chief priest to
Lysias that Paul should again appear before the Council,
and the plot that was made whereby forty assassins were
bound together by an oath to waylay and murder him, is
quite in accordance with the evidence of Josephus, when he
tells us that precisely at this period ' robbers went up with
the greatest security to the festivals and having their
weapons concealed [under their garments] and mingling
themselves with the multitude, they slew both their own
enemies and those whom other men wanted them to kill
for money.'[3]

The reticences of St. Luke upon many points on which
we should like to have fuller information are quite as
remarkable as his accuracy. We would gladly know more
about the causes which secured for St. Paul such favoured
and even indulgent treatment for four or five years at the
hands of the succession of Roman officials with whom he
was brought in contact.[4] How was it, one asks, that he
was able during the whole of this time to find sufficient
means to meet the heavy expenses that must have been
thrown upon him ? Had Paul been a mere penniless Jewish
preacher of a new superstition, an ordinary commonplace
enthusiast of no position or resources, it is practically
certain that he would not have received so much attention
from Procurators like Felix and Festus, or such courtesy
as was shown by the tribune Claudius Lysias and the
Centurion Julius. At Fort Antonia he was allowed to receive visitors and to bid a centurion conduct his nephew
to the presence of his superior officer. Does this visit of
his nephew signify that some change had taken place in
Paul's relations with his family, that that family was

---

[1] Josephus, *Ant.* xx. 8. 8. See also Milman, *Hist. of the Jews*, ii. 171-2.
[2] Acts, xxiii. 5.
[3] Acts, xxiii. 12-22. Josephus, *Ant.* xx. 8. 5 ; *Bell. Jud.* ii. 13. 3.
[4] See Ramsay, *St. Paul the Traveller*, pp. 310-313 ; also pp. 30-37.

one of distinction and wealth, and that money had come to
Paul possibly on the death of his father ? We do not know.
We can only conjecture, but the fact remains that in dealing
with him (the Roman authorities treated him as if he were
a person of some consequence.]

The first mark of this was exhibited in the extraordinary
precautions taken to ensure Paul's safe convoy to Caesarea.
Four hundred and seventy troops—legionaries, horsemen,
and light-armed auxiliaries—were sent to make a swift night
march to Antipatris, and then the horsemen continued the
journey apparently without a halt to Caesarea. The next
was when Felix, after declining to condemn Paul, when
the High Priest in person with a deputation of the Sanhedrin
brought their threefold accusation against the Apostle by
the mouth of a trained advocate, not only deferred the trial
indefinitely on the pretext that he must wait until Claudius
Lysias also could appear and give evidence, but he ordered
that Paul, while kept in charge, should be treated with
indulgence, and leave was given to any of his friends to
minister unto him.[1] The reason given by St. Luke why
Felix thus deferred the trial and treated Paul well was
' that he had more accurate knowledge concerning the
Way,'[2] i.e. the Christian religion, implying more accurate
knowledge than to be deceived by the prejudiced *ex parte*
statements of the Jewish accusers. The explanation lies in
the verse which follows : ' and after certain days Felix came
with Drusilla his wife, who was a Jewess, and heard him
[Paul] concerning the faith in Christ.' And during the
long interval of two years that he kept him in captivity,
' hoping,' says St. Luke, ' that money would be given him

[1] The confinement of Paul both at Caesarea and Rome was not the
severe confinement of a prison, *custodia publica*, but the lighter one,
custodia militaris, where the prisoner was bound by a chain to an attendant
guard. There were however degrees of the *custodia militaris* and the word
here used for indulgence—ἄνεσις—is the same as is used by Josephus
(*Ant.* xviii. 6-10), where he describes how Caligula on his accession did not
liberate Agrippa (Herod Agrippa I) from custody (he had been put in
chains by Tiberius) yet gave him indulgence or relaxation—τήρησις μετὰ
ἀνέσεως.

[2] Acts, xxiv. 22 : ἀκριβέστερον εἰδὼς τὰ περὶ τῆς ὁδοῦ.

of Paul, he sent for him the oftener and had communion with him.'[1] Now these statements point to two things: first, that Felix knew about Paul and Christianity from Drusilla, and, secondly, that from what Drusilla told him he was sufficiently interested in the man and his teaching to have repeated private interviews with him, and further that he believed him to be possessed of sufficient means to offer him a bribe to secure his release. No Roman governor, more especially a man of the type of Felix, would have such consideration as all this implies for a commonplace prisoner. At this time of political unrest and ferment in Judaea the Procurator's relations with the Jewish leaders were sufficiently strained without his extending his protection to a man against whom they displayed such fierce animosity. It would not have been difficult for him to condemn Paul as a disturber of the peace, and it was his interest to do so. At the same time he clearly was afraid to release him, lest he should provoke one of those outbursts of Jewish fanaticism which actually took place in Caesarea itself after St. Paul had been confined in the barracks attached to Herod's palace for two years. The stern way in which in this year 59 A.D. the Governor dealt with the Jewish rioters led to a deputation of the principal Jewish inhabitants of Caesarea going to Rome to accuse him for his misdeeds and harshness before Nero himself, and finally to Felix' recall to Rome to answer the charges brought against him.[2] It is perhaps no wonder that in such a crisis of his life the accused man, who only narrowly escaped condemnation by the powerful influence of friends at court, should have ' desired,' as St. Luke tells us, ' to gain favour with the Jews by leaving Paul bound.'[3] There is a curious Western reading here,

---

[1] Acts, xxiv. 26 : ἐλπίζων ὅτι χρήματα δοθήσεται ὑπὸ τοῦ Παύλου· διὸ καὶ πυκνότερον αὐτὸν μεταπεμπόμενος ὡμίλει αὐτῷ.

[2] Josephus, *Ant.* xx. 8–9 : Πορκίου δὲ Φήστου διαδόχου Φήλικι πεμφθέντος ὑπὸ Νέρωνος, οἱ πρωτεύοντες τῶν κατὰ τὴν Καισάρειαν κατοικούντων Ἰουδαίων εἰς τὴν Ῥώμην ἀναβαίνουσι Φήλικος κατηγοροῦντες· καὶ πάντως ἂν ἐδεδώκει τιμωρίαν τῶν εἰς Ἰουδαίους ἀδικημάτων, εἰ μὴ πολλὰ αὐτὸν ὁ Νέρων τῷ ἀδελφῷ Πάλλαντι παρακαλέσαντι συνεχώρησε, μάλιστα δὴ τότε διὰ τιμῆς ἔχων ἐκείνοι

[3] The reading of Cod. 137 is τὸν δὲ Παῦλον εἴασεν ἐν τηρήσει διὰ Δρυσίλλαν.

which possibly records an ancient authentic tradition that Felix left Paul in confinement ' because of Drusilla.' [1] As Drusilla was the sister of Agrippa II, who had an official residence in Jerusalem and in whose hands was the appointment of the High Priest, she may well have counselled her husband, for her brother's sake even more than for his own, not to irritate Jewish fanaticism by any act that might fan it in its present state of fever heat to yet further deeds of violence.

Festus on his arrival was confronted by a difficult and critical situation. But he was a firm and just magistrate and was determined that the prisoner should despite the clamours of the Jews have a fair trial in his presence. The principal charge brought against Paul was the crime of *majestas*—the inciting of the Jewish communities through the world to treason against Caesar. The other accusations —the being a ringleader of the sect of the Nazarenes and a profaner of the Temple—on the other hand were, in the scornful words of the Procurator to King Agrippa, only

---

[1] There occurs in Josephus, *Ant.* xx. 7. 2, a passage in which he says : ' When Felix was Governor of Judaea, he saw this Drusilla and fell in love with her, for she did indeed exceed all other women in beauty, and he sent to her a person whose name was Simon, one of his friends, a Jew, born in Cyprus, who pretended to be a magician and endeavoured to persuade her to leave her present husband and marry Felix.' As Drusilla had required her first husband to become a Jewish proselyte and submit to circumcision, so it was thought that her subsequent desertion of him for the Gentile, Felix, could only have been brought about by magic arts. She was, however, at the time of her marriage with Felix still a girl in her teens, and this Magian may have been the instrument employed by the unscrupulous Felix to cajole her into an act which as an Herodian princess must have been repugnant to her. But who was this Simon, a Jew of Cyprus, who pretended to be a magician ? Professor Rendel Harris in the *Expositor*, v. pp. 190–4 (1902), identifies him with Elymas the Sorcerer of Acts xiii. 8. Now Codex Bezae for 'Ελυμας reads 'Ετοιμας, and this reading is confirmed by several other Western authorities who read either ετοιμος or its equivalent ' paratus.' Ramsay adopts Ετοιμος as the correct name in *St. Paul the Traveller* (p. 74). And there is the same uncertainty in the text of Josephus. The Ambrosian MS. A has Ατομον for Σιμονα, also the Epitome of Josephus at Vienna. Ετοιμος and Ατομος are, it may reasonably be assumed, different forms of this man's name. Was he then one source of Felix' ' more accurate knowledge ' of Paul and The Way ?

'certain questions of their own superstition.'[1] These charges, St. Luke tells us, they failed to prove, and the Apostle no doubt hoped that the Governor would pronounce judgment in his favour. But Festus, aware of the excited state of Jewish feeling, was naturally anxious not at the very outset of his official term to get himself into disfavour with these embittered representatives of the dominant faction at Jerusalem, and he asked Paul whether he would be willing to go up to that city, there to be judged by him. But the Apostle was determined not thus to place himself in the midst of enemies thirsting for his life and utterly unscrupulous about the means employed ; he was sick, too, of delay, and he no longer hesitated. ' To the Jews I have done no wrong, as thou well knowest,' he replied to the Governor (I am somewhat paraphrasing the actual words as recorded), and ' if I have committed any offence against Caesar, I, as a Roman citizen, should be tried not at Jerusalem but before Caesar's judgment seat. As you do not acquit me of treason, I claim my right of appeal— *ad Caesarem appello.*'[2] On this the Procurator, after a conference with his assessors[3] (*consiliarii*) on the legal aspects of the case, quashed all further proceedings in Judaea, ' Thou hast appealed to Caesar, to Caesar shalt thou go.'

I have dwelt at some length on the circumstances which brought about Paul's visit to Rome, in order to make it clear that the charge against him was political, not religious, the offence one of *majestas*, not of preaching new doctrines subversive of the Jewish law. And it is noteworthy that even in regard to the political charge both Festus and

---

[1] Acts, xxv. 19 : ζητήματά τινα περὶ τῆς ἰδίας δεισιδαιμονίας. The profanation of the Temple was also an offence against Roman Law—Judaism being a *religio licita.*

[2] It is more than probable that St. Paul was acquainted with the Latin language. The employment of Tertullus before Felix shows that the pleading was in Latin.

[3] Acts, xxv. 12 : συλλαλήσας μετὰ τοῦ συμβουλίου. This body was composed of *consiliarii* or *assessores*, in Greek πάρεδροι. Suet. *Tib.* 33; *Galba,* 19 ; Josephus, *Bell. Jud.* ii. 16. 1.

King Agrippa were agreed that Paul had done nothing
worthy of death or of bonds.]He had however appealed to
Caesar, and so he obtained, not indeed his liberty, but an
escape from an irksome confinement in the midst of his
deadly foes, and a prospect of at length making acquaintance
with that Church in Rome which he had so many years been
longing to visit. Whatever the risks, he would gladly face
them, for his deep faith assured him that he was going to
Rome as God's appointed instrument to do good work in
Christ's Name amidst the thronging population of that
great world-centre of Imperial rule. Those words that
came to him, as on that first night of his incarceration in
Fort Antonia he beheld in mystic vision the Lord Jesus
standing at his side—' Be of good cheer, for as thou hast
testified concerning me at Jerusalem, so must thou bear
witness even at Rome ' [1]—had, we may well believe, been
his comfort and stay during the whole of those two weary
years spent to all appearance so uselessly in the guard-rooms
of Herod's palace at Caesarea. Now, at last, the opportunity
had come of bearing witness in the presence of Caesar himself: an opportunity embraced with his whole heart and
soul, even though the witness should be that witness which
is crowned with the martyr's death.

The Apostle left Caesarea some time during the month
of August, 59 A.D., only after many hardships and life-and-
death perils to be shipwrecked in November on the coast
of Malta. Compelled with his companions in misfortune to
winter on the island, it was not until the end of February
60 A.D. that Paul landed at Puteoli, a centre of the corn
traffic with Alexandria and the chief commercial sea-port
of Italy and Rome.[2]] In this busy and prosperous place

[1] Acts, xxiii. 11. See Ramsay's article in the *Expositor*, March 1913 :
' Suggestions on the History and Letters of St. Paul,' pp. 269–76.

[2] Puteoli shared with Ostia the trade between Rome and the provinces,
more especially the corn supply. It was originally named Dicaearchia.
Three years after St. Paul, the historian Josephus (as he himself tells us)
on his way to Rome had experiences extraordinarily similar to those of
the apostle. He writes : ' I reached Rome after an extremely perilous
voyage ; for our ship, having foundered mid-way in the Adriatic, we, to

thronged with seamen and traders of many nations the Apostle found a body of Christians who gave a right brotherly welcome to him and his companions, Luke and Aristarchus, and entertained them seven days. Of the origin of this Christian community the Acts tells us nothing, but its presence here will occasion no surprise to those who have followed the arguments of the previous lectures. It is but one proof more of the early evangelisation of Rome and other towns in Italy.

From Puteoli the company of prisoners with their military guard journeyed along the Appian Way to Rome. But the news of the approach of the Apostle had already reached the Christians of the capital, and two separate deputations came to greet him, one as far as Appii Forum, one of the regular halting places on this route, the other to Tres Tabernae still nearer Rome.[1] Probably among these delegates were a number of those whose names are so affectionately mentioned in the Epistle to the Romans, Ampliatus, Urbanus, Stachys and the rest, and surely Aquila and Prisca, his old and tried friends. St. Luke mentions no names, but his one brief statement of the effect of this meeting upon the way-worn and much burdened Apostle is worth a whole volume. In the midst of a strange and foreign land, a prisoner in bonds, Paul was feeling perhaps, as was natural, somewhat lonely and depressed, but at the sight of his friends his spirit revived. How expressive are the words ' whom when Paul saw, he thanked God and took courage.' [2]

the number of about six hundred, had recourse to swimming and had already remained the entire night in the water, when, at daybreak, a vessel from Cyrene providentially hove in sight, and received on board myself and others, eighty in all—more fortunate than our companions. Thus rescued from destruction, I landed at Dicaearchia, called by the Italians Puteoli.' This passage is interesting, for here as in Acts xxvii. 27 we find the term 'Adriatic' applied to the sea between Greece and Cyrenaica. Comp. Strabo, ii. 123: Ἰόνιον πέλαγος, ὁ νῦν Ἀδρίας. Also the number on board St. Paul's ship, 276, is seen not to be excessive as compared with the 600 with whom Josephus voyaged.

[1] Appii Forum was 41, Tres Tabernae 23 miles from Rome. ' Ab Appii Foro hora quarta : dederam aliam paullo ante Tribus Tabernis.' —Cicero, *ad Atticum*, ii. 10.

[2] Acts, xxviii. 15 : οὓς ἰδὼν ὁ Παῦλος εὐχαριστήσας τῷ θεῷ ἔλαβεν θάρσος·

The Apostle after his entrance into Rome was conducted by the centurion Julius to an officer who bore the title of the *Stratopedarch*.[1] This centurion, in whose charge St. Paul with his fellow-prisoners had been for the seven months since they left Caesarea, is described in the Acts as being of the Augustan band (σπεῖρα Σεβαστή) or as it probably should be more correctly translated, of the *Imperial Service Corps*. That great authority, Dr. Mommsen, has been able to give an explanation of the meaning of these unusual terms, which affords one more example of the marked accuracy of St. Luke in his references to Roman or local officials. Professor Ramsay has thus summarised Mommsen's conclusions.[2] 'Augustus had reduced to a regular system the maintenance of communications between the centre of control in Rome and the armies stationed in the great frontier provinces. Legionary centurions, called commonly *frumentarii*, went to and fro between Rome and the armies and were employed for numerous purposes between the Emperor and his armies and provinces. They acted not only for commissariat purposes (whence the name) but as couriers and for police purposes, and for conducting prisoners. They all belonged to legions stationed in the provinces, and were considered to be on detached duty when they went to Rome ; and hence in Rome they were " soldiers from abroad "—*peregrini*. While in Rome they resided in a camp on the Coelian Hill called *Castra Peregrinorum*. In this camp there were always a number of them present, changing from day to day, as some came and others went away. This camp was under the command of the *Princeps Peregrinorum*, and it is clear that the Stratopedarch in Acts is the Greek name for that officer.'

Julius in any case had now fulfilled his duty and handed over his prisoners to his chief. But the exceptionally favoured treatment now accorded to Paul by the Roman

---

[1] It is generally admitted that the words ὁ ἑκατόνταρχος παρέδωκε τοὺς δεσμίους τῷ στρατοπεδάρχῃ, though wanting in A B, formed part of the original text.

[2] *Berlin. Akad. Sitzungsberichte*, 1895, pp. 501 ff ; Ramsay, *St. Paul the Traveller*, pp. 315 and 347-8.

H

authorities in the capital itself was even more remarkable than that which had been shown to him in Judaea, and it may be added throughout his voyage. I have already spoken of the behaviour of Felix to him as a proof that the Apostle was regarded as a man of some distinction, and that at this period of his life he was in no lack of means. This impression is deepened as the narrative of the captivity proceeds. Festus and his assessors would not have been likely to have troubled themselves to send to Caesar's judgment seat a poor and obscure man. The courtesy of Julius to him and the privileged position he occupied during the voyage must have been due in the first instance to instructions given by the Governor. It can only have been by express permission that Luke and Aristarchus were allowed to accompany the Apostle in the vessel, a most unusual thing.[1] And it was the same upon his arrival at Rome. From the very first the prisoner ' was suffered to abide by himself with the soldier that guarded him,' and to call together the chief of the Jews to meet him twice in the friend's house [2] in which for a short time he remained, and then for the whole of the next two years of his light captivity he lived in his own hired house, receiving freely and without hindrance all who came in to him. Where this friend's house or this hired dwelling was situated we have no hint, but it must have been in the immediate neighbourhood of, perhaps even within, the extensive barracks of the Praetorian Guard outside the Colline Gate, for this would be necessary for the convenience of the change of the guards to whom he was chained. The *custodia militaris* at its best was most

---

[1] Ramsay quotes Pliny, *Ep.* iii. 16, as relating that when Paetus was brought a prisoner from Illyricum to Rome his wife Arria, despite her entreaties, was not allowed to accompany him, but he was permitted to take certain slaves to wait on him, and he raises the question whether Luke and Aristarchus may not have voluntarily accompanied Paul in the capacity of slaves.

[2] St. Luke (Acts xxviii. 23) speaks of the place where St. Paul received the Jewish leaders as ἡ ξενία, and appears to distinguish it from τὸ μίσθωμα, the hired lodging in which he spent the next two years (Acts xxviii. 30). ξενία suggests a room in a friend's house. Comp. Philem. 22 and Acts xxi. 16.

irksome, and as we learn from his epistles was felt to be so by the Apostle, but he had at least the opportunity, which was so near to his heart, of being able to have unrestricted intercourse with his Roman friends, and to preach the Gospel to all who wished to hear him. This liberty, which, as we have seen, was conceded at once after his arrival, can only have been due to the contents of the official report— the *literae dimissoriae* and *relatio*—sent by Festus concerning the prisoner, which would be handed by Julius to the Stratopedarch and by him in his turn to Burrhus, who was in 60 A.D. still sole Praetorian Prefect.[1]

Three days only had passed before St. Paul saw the leading men of the Jewish synagogues gathered round him in the room where he was confined. So eager was he to be at work again in his Master's business that he must have sent out the invitations to the heads of the six or seven independent Jewish congregations in Rome immediately after his arrival. Apostle of the Gentiles as he was, he always adhered to his unbroken rule—to the Jew first. His words at the opening of his Epistle to the Romans acquire added force in the new situation in which he now found himself—' as much as in me lies I am ready to preach the Gospel to you also in Rome. For I am not ashamed of the Gospel ; for it is the power of God unto salvation to

---

[1] The *literae dimissoriae* or *apostoli* stated the simple fact of the claim made by the appellant. When the appeal was made to the Emperor, the letter was called *relatio*. The report thus sent included all the depositions necessary for the elucidation of the case. Buss, *Roman Law and the Hist. of the N.T.* p. 399. Usually there were two Praetorian Prefects, but since 52 A.D. Sextus Afranius Burrhus had held the sole command. His appointment was due to Agrippina, who wished to have a man she could trust at the head of the Praetorian Guard on the death of Claudius. He was a worthy, straightforward man, who with Seneca exercised a great influence for good upon Nero during the first five years of his reign, the *quinquennium Neronis*, which the Emperor Trajan is reported to have praised above any other period in the reigns of his predecessors. Burrus was shortly after this to fall into disfavour. He died in 62 A.D. Some said he was poisoned by the Emperor, and his death was followed by Seneca's retirement. After Burrhus' death two Praetorian Prefects were appointed, one of them the notorious Sofonius Tigellinus, a cruel, venal, and vicious man, who pandered to all Nero's lusts and extravagances.

every one that believeth, to the Jew first and also to the Greek.' [1] These words were indeed addressed to the Christians of Rome, but he knew well how small a number out of the great Jewish population in that city had been converted to the Gospel, and even at a distance the thought saddened him, and his heart yearned towards them, the more so because he felt keenly the prejudice which his preaching to the Gentiles had aroused against him in the minds of his countrymen further east. There are few more touching passages in the writings of St. Paul, none which reveal the innermost depth of his soul more fully than portions of the ninth and tenth chapters of the Epistle to the Romans. No estimate of St. Paul is complete which does not take account of these impassioned utterances : ' I say the truth in Christ, I lie not, my conscience bearing witness with me in the Holy Ghost, that I have great sorrow and unceasing pain in my heart. For I could wish that I myself were anathema from Christ for my brethren's sake, my kinsmen according to the flesh. . . . Brethren, my heart's desire and my supplication to God is for them that they may be saved.' [2]   And now, as the chiefs of the Roman synagogues stand around him, he endeavoured to persuade them that it was not for anything that he had done against the Jewish people or contrary to the customs of the fathers that he had been put upon his trial and compelled to appeal to Caesar. On the contrary, he wished to make it clear to them that all the proceedings against him were due to a misunderstanding, because—and in these words lies the whole force of his apology—' for the hope of Israel I am bound with this chain.' The reply was a purely non-committal one. The Jews declared that they had received from Judaea no letters concerning Paul, nor had any of the brethren that came to Rome spoken harm of him. They were therefore quite ready to hear what he had to say and appointed a day for a conference. But they added, with a cold hostility which must have chilled any hopes he may have had of the issue of his appeal, ' as concerning this sect

---

[1] Romans, i. 15, 16.   [2] Rom. ix. 1-3 ; x. 1.

it is known to us that it is everywhere spoken against.'[1] This declaration was no doubt strictly correct, and is of great importance. ⌐It shows that already those charges of 'atheism,' immorality, and of abominable practices at their feasts, which were shortly to be so freely brought against them, were being widely accepted, and that the Jews themselves were taking pains to dissociate Judaism from any connexion with the new sectaries, whom they disowned. ⌐ The period during which the Christians were to find shelter beneath the privileges accorded by the Imperial Government to the Jewish people and religion was well-nigh over. The essential note of the Christianity preached by Paul was universalist, that of the Judaism protected by Roman law was national and particularist : between the two there could be no reconciliation. No wonder that when a body of Jewish delegates more numerous apparently than the first gathered in the Apostle's room, they remained unconvinced by his arguments. These chiefs of the Synagogues were not of the stuff of which converts are easily made, and though St. Luke says they reasoned among themselves and had clearly some difference of opinion, yet of their generally unbending attitude the scathing words with which the Apostle closed the interview are a proof that he regarded all his efforts as thrown away and futile.[2] It was a repetition of what had happened at Antioch in Pisidia and else-where, and there his previous experiences cannot have given him much encouragement that now, as a prisoner accused by the Jews of Jerusalem, he would meet with more success. In any case his breach with official Judaism in Rome seems to have been final. At this point the actual narrative of the Acts ceases. The next two verses, which state that ' he (Paul) abode two whole years in his own hired dwelling, and received all that went in to him, preaching the Kingdom

[1] Acts, xxviii. 17-21.
[2] The passage quoted Is. vi. 9, 10 is remarkable as having been spoken at least twice by our Lord in regard to the Jewish reception of His message, St. Matt. xiii. 14, St. Mark iv. 12, St. Luke viii. 10 and St. John xii. 40. St. Paul used it of Israel's rejection of the Gospel in his Epistle to the Romans (Rom. xi. 8) as here.

of God and teaching the things concerning the Lord Jesus Christ with all boldness, none forbidding him,'[1] are a kind of appendix. The brief summary of events which it contains forms—as did the last verses of the Gospel with the opening passage of the Acts—a bridge of connexion with another narrative, in which the author intended to take up the story at the point where it is left, i.e. the departure of the Jewish delegates, and continue it in a third treatise in fuller detail.

This abrupt breaking off of the Lukan history at a most interesting point is much to be regretted. We are not however left without information about St. Paul's personal condition, his missionary activity, and his relations with the outside world during the two years he spent in his hired house. Four epistles were written by the Apostle during this period, containing a number of references to his life and to the friends who were with him or helping him. Of these a group of three, the Epistles to the Colossians and Philemon and the circular epistle (commonly called) to the Ephesians, were clearly dictated in rapid succession and were dispatched together, somewhere about the middle of the imprisonment. The fourth epistle, to the Philippians, is later; internal evidence points to a date not long before the final trial and release.

The tone of the group of three is on the whole cheerful and full of confidence. The Apostle is surrounded by a number of his most trusted disciples and fellow-workers. In each of these epistles he refers to his bonds, but in every case not to complain, nay, rather to give added weight to his advice or his pleading. To the Colossians he writes : ' Pray for us that God may open unto us a door for the Word, to speak the mystery of Christ, for which I am also

---

[1] Acts, xxviii. 30, 31. Comp. St. Luke, xxiv. 50-53, Acts, cc. i. and ii. Ramsay holds that, in the expression τὸν πρῶτον λόγον, trans. R.V. ' the former treatise ' with ' the first ' in the margin, St. Luke did not use πρῶτον as an equivalent for πρότερον. If this were the case, ' the first ' may be regarded as implying, in addition to a second treatise, also a third. Ramsay, *St. Paul the Traveller*, pp. 27-28. See also his Article in *Expositor*, March 1913, pp. 268-70, 281-4.

in bonds, that I may make it manifest as I ought to speak,'
while in a corresponding passage of the circular epistle he
asks for the prayers and supplications of his readers, ' on
my behalf that utterance may be given to me in opening
my mouth, to make known with boldness the mystery of
the Gospel for which I am an ambassador in chains ; that
in it I may speak boldly, as I ought to speak '—passages
which testify that his whole thoughts at this time were
directed to the opportunity—the door—which his position
gave him for preaching the Gospel in the very heart of the
world's capital.[1] Notice on the other hand the force of
the appeal with which the Epistle to the Colossians closes—
' the salutation of me Paul with mine own hand. Remember
my bonds,'[2] or in that most delightful passage from the
beautiful epistle to Philemon, in which he so tenderly and
affectionately pleads with the master at Colossae to receive
back the slave Onesimus, who had run away from him and
robbed him, but had now been converted by Paul at Rome
and so become Philemon's brother in the faith. ' Wherefore,
though I have all boldness in Christ to enjoin thee that
which is befitting, yet for love's sake I rather beseech,
being such an one as Paul the aged, and now also a prisoner
of Christ Jesus : I beseech thee for my child, Onesimus,
whom I have begotten in my bonds, Onesimus, who was
aforetime unprofitable to thee, but now is profitable to
thee and to me ; whom I have sent back to thee in his own
person, that is my very heart ; whom I would fain have
kept with me, that in thy behalf he might minister to me
in my bonds of the Gospel.' A few verses further on the
declaration ' if he have wronged thee at all or oweth thee
ought, put that to my account : I Paul write it with mine
own hand, I will repay it ' affords one more testimony to
those already given that the Apostle at this time did not
lack means. | One reason for St. Paul's cheerfulness was,
no doubt, that his release was approaching and not far
distant, otherwise he would not have concluded his letter

[1] Col. iv. 3 ; Eph. vi. 19, 20.
[2] Col. iv. 18 ; Philemon 8–13, 19, 22.

to Philemon with the words ' Withal prepare for me a lodging : for I hope that through your prayers I shall be granted
unto you.'] The other reason was that he had at his side
at this time a body of faithful friends,[1] who were a comfort
to him. Aristarchus and Luke, who accompanied the
Apostle on his voyage probably in the capacity of slave-
attendants, still continued their willing service. Aristarchus
is mentioned as ' my fellow-prisoner,' Luke as ' the beloved
physician.' Epaphras, a native of Colossae, one of those
who had originally carried the Gospel to that town, had
arrived in Rome bringing news of the state of the Church
of which he was so prominent a member. He also is styled
by the Apostle ' his fellow-prisoner,' and possibly all these
three lived with him in his hired house. Then, too, Tychicus
of Ephesus had joined him in company with Paul's specially
loved disciple Timothy, whom we now find acting as his
amanuensis. In addition to these were Jesus surnamed
Justus, one of the few among the circumcision who had been a
fellow-worker and a comfort to him, and Demas, of whom we
know nothing, except that he some years later deserted him.]
One name remains which deserves a longer notice.

' Mark, the cousin of Barnabas, saluteth you, touching
whom ye received injunctions, if he come unto you receive
him,' the very phraseology of this salutation sent by St.
Paul to the Colossians suggests that more lies behind the
words than they actually express. Since Barnabas and
Paul parted in anger at Antioch in 50 A.D. because of Mark,
and Paul chose Silas to be his fellow missionary, while
Barnabas took Mark and sailed to Cyprus, no mention is
made of the latter in the Acts at all nor in the pre-captivity
epistles of Paul.] What was he doing during the interval,
and how are we to account for this greeting being sent by
Paul from Rome in Mark's name in 61 A.D. to the Church
at Colossae ?

[1] Aristarchus, Col. iv. 10, Philem. 23. Luke, Col. iv. 14, Philem. 23.
Epaphras, Col. i. 7, iv. 12, Philem. 23. Timothy, Col. i. 1, Philem. 1.
Tychicus, Col. iv. 7, 8, Eph. vi. 21, 22. Onesimus, Col. iv. 9, Philem. 10.
Mark, Col. iv. 10, Philem. 23.

In studying the history of the Apostolic age it should always be remembered that the character of our extant authorities only too often has caused a one-sided and very warped view of the expansion of Christianity (during the period of which we are treating) to be taken. The happy fact that St. Paul found a sympathetic biographer in his disciple and companion St. Luke, and still more the fact that, owing to his exceptional power and weight as a writer, a very considerable collection of his letters have survived the general destruction of early Christian literature, has led to a quite false estimate being formed of the widespread and successful activity of other leading missionaries and preachers of the Gospel. The influence they exerted and the large area covered by their work have been too much overlooked and ignored. The late Professor Bigg was one of the few who have shown a really comprehensive grasp of what actually took place. In his admirable ' Introduction to the First Epistle of St. Peter ' he has pointed out how small a portion of Asia Minor was ever visited by St. Paul. He also suggests not only that many of the Churches in that part of the Empire were planted at an early date but that the reason why St. Paul deliberately refrained from entering Asia, Mysia and Bithynia on his second missionary journey was that those provinces were already being evangelised by others.[1] To say this is no disparagement to St. Paul, he would be the last to wish to take credit for other men's labours, and he himself expressly states in his Epistle to the Colossians that neither the Christians of that city nor those of Laodicea had seen his face in the flesh ! [2]

Now the emphatic mention by St. Paul in this epistle of Mark as Barnabas' cousin (with the enigmatic parenthesis that follows) appears to me to be one of those seemingly incidental notices, which, when placed in its right setting, is then seen to be the central link in a chain of circumstantial evidence drawn from a variety of sources. Once more I ask, therefore, What had been the history of Mark since in

[1] Bigg, *Internat. Commentary, Epistles of St. Peter and St. Jude,* pp. 73-4.   [2] Col. ii. 1.

50 A.D. he sailed with Barnabas for Cyprus ? ⌐According to
one of the best authenticated traditions of these early times
he went to Alexandria and spent some years in organising
the Church in that great city and in evangelising the neighbouring districts of Egypt.¹⌐ Another tradition of a less
trustworthy character, but reasonably probable, relates
that Barnabas himself went in the first instance with Mark
to Alexandria.² It is quite likely that this choice by
Barnabas of Egypt as the scene of Mark's missionary
labours may have been dictated by the fact that it lay
outside the Pauline sphere of activity. ⌐Now Eusebius tells
us—and he had exceptional opportunities of obtaining
accurate information about the Alexandrian Church—that
in the eighth year of Nero's reign Annianus succeeded
Mark the Evangelist in the administration of the Church in
Alexandria.³ ⌐The date of Mark's leaving Egypt thus
corresponds with the date at which we find him in Paul's
company at Rome, i.e. 61 A.D. When he is introduced to
us it is as one about to journey to Colossae with the Apostle's
commendation. But the question again naturally arises,
why should he from Alexandria have gone out of his way
to Rome in order to visit Colossae, what was his object ?
Those words of St. Paul—' Mark, the cousin of Barnabas,
about whom ye received injunctions '—gives, I think, the
answer. ⌐If Mark is thus described to the Colossian Christians as ' the cousin of Barnabas,' it follows that Barnabas
was well known in Colossae, and that the injunctions referred
to were Barnabas' injunctions, and, if so, that Barnabas
himself had been with Paul and had been one of those who
had furnished him with information about the state of the
Asian Churches.⌐ The course of events, that the passage

¹ Eus. *Hist. Eccl.* ii. 16. 24. Also in the Hieronymian version of
Eusebius' *Chronicle* ; Schöne, ii. 155 ; Lipsius, *Die Apokryphen Apostelgeschichten und Apostellegenden*, ii. 2nd half, p. 322 ff.
² Περίοδοι Βαρνάβα, c. 26 (Tischendorf, p. 73). Mark is supposed to
be the narrator. ἐλθόντες δὲ ἐπὶ τὸν αἰγιαλὸν [of the village Limnes in
Cyprus] εὕρομεν πλοῖον Αἰγύπτιον καὶ ἀνελθόντες εἰς αὐτὸ κατήχθημεν ἐν
Ἀλεξανδρείᾳ κἀκεῖ ἔμεινα ἐγὼ διδάσκων τοὺς ἐχομένους ἀδελφούς . . . . .
³ Eus. *Hist. Eccl.* ii. 24.

suggests to me, is this. One of the objects of the Epistles
to the Colossians and Ephesians was to give comfort to the
hearts of these Asian Christians, who were afflicted by
hearing of St. Paul's imprisonment at Rome. Barnabas,
at Colossae, on receiving the news had resolved to go to his
old friend in this crisis of his fate and at the same time
revisit the scenes of his previous labours in Rome and in
Italy. He travelled by Alexandria to see Mark, and finding
that the work of organisation there was satisfactorily
advanced, it was agreed between them that Mark should
seek a new field for his energies in Asia Minor and that
Barnabas should write to prepare the minds of the Colossians
for his cousin's coming among them. Meanwhile, as Pauline
influence was still strong in the Asian cities—he first took
Mark with him to Rome to effect a reconciliation between
him and Paul and secure a few words of commendation
from the Apostle, as a further credential to the former
deserter. It has been pointed out above that the traditional
date of Mark's departure from Egypt synchronises with the
date at which we find him at Rome with St. Paul making
ready shortly to depart for Colossae. The presence of
Barnabas at Rome at this time is vouched for by the Gnostic
Acts of Peter [*Actus Petri Vercellenses*], which state that
Barnabas accompanied Timothy, when the latter was sent
a little later by Paul to Macedonia as the bearer of the
Epistle to the Philippians.[1] The same argument holds
good here as in the case of the mention of Barnabas in the
opening of the ' Clementine Recognitions ' ; his name would
never have been introduced in documents written expressly
to exalt the position of St. Peter, unless he had actually
visited Italy and worked there. There are strong grounds
for believing that Timothy after carrying out his mission

---

[1] The *Actus Petri Vercellenses* are portions of the Περίοδοι Πέτρου
which formed the basis of the *Clementine Recognitions and Homilies*, found
in the Latin Cod. Vercellensis. See Lipsius, vol. ii. 1st half, pp. 174 ff ;
also vol. ii. 2nd half, p. 272. Speaking of the departure of Paul into
Spain the passage runs ' praeterea quod non esset Romae Paulus neque
Timotheus neque Barnabas, quoniam in Macedoniam missi erant a
Paulo.'

to Philippi went on to Ephesus and made that town the centre of his ministerial activity for some years. The Pastoral Epistles represent Timothy and Mark as together a few years later in this same district. In a future lecture I shall bring forward reasons of considerable weight for holding that the Epistle to the Hebrews was written by Barnabas and sent by him to Rome from some place not far from Ephesus, where he had been in touch with Timothy.[1] There is much that is disputable in all this, but all critics who approach the subject with an open mind must at least admit that a cumulative presumption has been established in favour of the conclusion that Barnabas and Mark were together in Italy and Rome in 61 A.D. and afterwards in Colossae.

At the time when the Epistle to the Philippians was written the circumstances and surroundings of St. Paul had undergone a complete change. He had no longer around him a group of trusted friends and companions. Only Timothy (whom in the opening salutation we find as sharing with Paul the responsibility of joint authorship of the epistle) is left of those mentioned in the earlier epistles, the rest being probably dispersed on various missions. The situation is in fact precisely similar to that described in the Second Epistle to Timothy, and curiously it was at the time of his trial in each case that the Apostle has to complain of being thus left alone.[2] As on the occasion of his second trial he sorrowfully writes ' only Luke is with me,' so now of his intimate disciples there is only Timothy. Epaphroditus, the bearer of a gift from the Church of Philippi to the Apostle, was indeed still in Rome, having been detained by a sickness that had been well-nigh unto death, but he was about to return as the bearer of the epistle, and such was the unselfishness of St. Paul, moved as he was by the tenderest feelings of gratitude and affection towards these Philippians, who had always from the very first been the most liberal and helpful of all the Churches that he founded,

---

[1] 1 Tim. i. 19, 20 ; vi. 12–14 ; 2 Tim. ii. 11 ; comp. Heb. xiii. 23.
[2] Phil. ii. 11 ; comp. 2 Tim. iv. 9–11.

that he was ready to spare even Timothy from his side to go with Epaphroditus to testify to the Apostle's deep sense that once again they had borne his needs in kindly remembrance.]He has ' no one like-minded ' with Timothy to fulfil this office, and he promises that ' as soon as I shall see how it will go with me ' he will send this beloved disciple, of whom he touchingly says ' ye know the proof of him, that as a child *serveth* a father, *so* he served with me in the furtherance of the Gospel.' [1]

Those words, ' as soon as I shall see how it will go with me,' tell their own tale. [St. Paul was no longer ' in his own hired house ' but in the Pretorian camp, where he was in closer confinement while his case was being brought at last before the Imperial Appeal Court.] This alone can be the meaning of the passage, ' now I would have you know, brethren, that the things that are happening to me have rather turned out unto the progress of the Gospel, so that my bonds became manifest in Christ in the whole Praetorium and to all the rest ; and that most of the brethren in the Lord, being confident through my bonds, are more abundantly bold to speak the Gospel without fear.' [2] The publicity of the trial, in fact, and the opportunity that it gave the Apostle in the course of his defence against the charges brought against him to set forth the true nature of the faith that he preached had caused the message of the Gospel to be known throughout the Imperial Court, the Praetorian Guards, and generally in Rome. The whole tone of the epistle shows that so far all had gone well, that the brethren were filled with confidence that the issue would be favourable, and that Paul himself, although not free from serious anxiety and quite prepared for death should it come, is full of hope that he will speedily be released and be able once more to revisit his beloved Philippians.[3]

This Epistle differs widely in character and contents

---

[1] Phil. ii. 19–30.

[2] Phil. i. 12–15. See Lightfoot, *Epist. to Philippians*, pp. 97–102 ; Ramsay, *St. Paul the Traveller*, pp. 356–360 ; *Expositor*, March 1913, pp. 277–80.

[3] Phil. i. 19–25 ; also ii. 17 and 24.

from those to the Colossians and Ephesians. In the latter
St. Paul was combating certain subtle forms of heretical
belief of a gnostic character which had been creeping in
and making headway among the mixed Greek and Oriental
populations of a group of Asian Churches, to whom he himself, though well known by name and repute was, except
at Ephesus itself, personally a stranger. ⌠To Philippi he
writes, as a Roman citizen to Roman citizens, as a friend
to dear friends, as an Apostle to a body of personal disciples
who had above all others shown him unceasing sympathy
and kindness.⌡ His Epistle is primarily a letter of thanks
called forth by the gift of money that had been sent to
him by the hands of Epaphroditus.[1] Such a letter was
bound to be rich in personal references and allusions. I
have already referred to those which relate to the hopes
and fears aroused by his pending trial. He had however
other troubles that worried him. Despite all he had endured
and was enduring for the Gospel's sake, it is clear that
there was a Judaising faction among the Roman Christians,
who even now could not abate their opposition and spite
against the Apostle of the Gentiles. ' Most of the brethren
in the Lord,' he writes, ' being confident through my bonds,
are more abundantly bold to speak the word of God without
fear. Some indeed preach Christ of envy and strife ; some
also of good will ; the one do it of love, knowing I am set
for the defence of the Gospel ; but the other proclaim
Christ of faction, not sincerely, thinking to raise up affliction
for me in my bonds. What then ? Let but in every way,
whether in pretence or in truth, Christ be proclaimed ; and
therein I rejoice, yea, and will rejoice.' Who they were of

---

[1] The supposition that Paul at this time was in no lack of financial
resources is fully borne out by the language of the passage in which he
expresses his gratitude to the Philippians for their kindly thought in
providing for his necessities. His words are quite plain on this point :
' Not that I speak in respect of want,' and again : ' Not that I seek for the
gift, but I seek for the fruit that increaseth to your account. But I have
all things and abound : I am filled, having received from Epaphroditus
the things that came from you. . . . ' The whole passage is worth careful
study. Phil. iv. 10-20.

whom he is here speaking is revealed in the later warning :
' Beware of the dogs, beware of the evil workers, beware
of the concision ; for we are the circumcision, who worship
by the spirit of God and glory in Jesus Christ and have no
confidence in the flesh.' [1]

Among the Philippian Christians there had been discords,
the opening of the fourth chapter pointing to the existence
of acute dissensions between two women, named Euodia
and Syntyche, possibly deaconesses, and probably each of
them with a following. ' I exhort Euodia and I exhort
Syntyche,' writes the Apostle, the word exhort being
repeated, as being addressed to each separately, ' to be of
one mind in the Lord.' He then proceeds, ' Yea, I beseech
thee also, true yokefellow, help them [to be reconciled] ;
seeing that they laboured with me in the Gospel together
with Clement also and my other fellow-workers, whose
names are in the book of life.' These words have caused
much difficulty to commentators, and have been interpreted
in many different ways. To myself their meaning does
not seem doubtful. The passage is a sudden parenthesis
and is addressed by St. Paul to Timothy, the man whose
name is coupled with his own at the beginning of the Epistle,
and who was sitting at his side as his amanuensis. He was
his yoke-fellow, since he was sharing with him the duty
and the burden at that very moment of a common task.
He commends him to the Philippians in the words ' I have
no man like-minded, who will truly care for your state.'
The word here descriptive of the character of that care
which Timothy alone could be trusted to give, be it noted,
is the same word which is used as the epithet qualifying
the 'yoke-fellow' of chapter iv. 3, a word which in the
original Greek signifies ' genuine.' This identity of epithet
is of some evidential significance in support of the identification of the yoke-fellow with Timothy, and it is strengthened
when we find that the Apostle again uses this same epithet
in the opening salutation of the First Epistle to Timothy,

[1] Phil. i. 14-18 ; iii. 2, 3.

where he addresses that disciple as ' my true [or genuine]
child in the faith.' [1]

The appeal of St. Paul ' to his true yoke-fellow ' to
strive to heal the dissensions between the two women
Euodia and Syntyche is accompanied by the suggestion that
he should secure the help of ' Clement and the rest of my
fellow-workers ' in the task of conciliation. Who this
Clement was, we do not know. Origen, Eusebius and others
regard this passage as a reference to the well-known Clement,
who wrote in the name of the Roman Church an Epistle to
the Corinthians, but it is extremely doubtful whether they
had any sound historical authority for their statement.
The name of Clement was not uncommon, and this Clement
may have been one of the leading Christians in Philippi.
Nevertheless it is not at all impossible that he may have
been the Roman Clement.] The title ' fellow-worker '—
σύνεργος — is frequently used by St. Paul of those like
Timothy, Titus, and others, sent out by him on some mission
as his delegates. Clement may have been thus sent to
Philippi by Paul. It will be observed that he alone is
named, and this implies that he stood apart from the rest
as a person of some authority. The final salutation is of
some interest. ' The brethren who are with me salute
you '—the brethren here being those of his companions,
not inhabitants of Rome, who were still at his side. ' All
the saints '—i.e. the body of Roman Christians—' salute
you, but especially those of Caesar's household.' Why
especially ? Surely because Paul was now during his trial
confined in the barracks close to the palace, and he had
therefore special opportunities of intercourse at this time
with those members of the Roman Church who belonged
to the vast Imperial household—numbering many thousands
of freedmen and slaves.] This phrase and the earlier one,
' my bonds have become manifest in Christ in the whole
Praetorium,' supplement and partly explain one another.
The spread of the Gospel among Caesar's household was no

---

[1] Phil. iv. 3 : γνήσιε σύνζυγε; ii. 20 : οὐδένα γὰρ ἔχω ἰσόψυχον, ὅστις
γνησίως τὰ περὶ ὑμῶν μεριμνήσει ; I Tim. I : Τιμοθέῳ γνησίῳ τέκνῳ ἐν πίστει.

new thing. Already in his Epistle to the Romans St. Paul
had sent his salutations to those who were of the households
of Aristobulus and of Narcissus. These households had
almost certainly even in 57 A.D. been incorporated in the
household of the Emperor.[1]

Over the further progress and issue of the trial a veil
falls. It was during the early months of this year 62 A.D.
that Burrhus died, and a little later Seneca retired from
public life. Burrhus had been sole Praetorian Prefect, but
Nero now reverted to the usual custom of appointing two.
One of these, Sofonius Tigellinus, has left an infamous
name as a man who encouraged the cruel propensities of
Nero and pandered to all his vicious excesses. It is probable
therefore that the trial of Paul took place while Burrhus was
still prefect, and that it may have been furthered by the
friendly offices of Seneca.[2] That he was acquitted at the
beginning of 62 A.D. there can be no reasonable doubt.
Clement of Rome, a contemporary, affirms that Paul afterwards travelled to the far West, and the fragment of the
Muratorian Canon, about 200 A.D., states that he carried
out his intention of visiting Spain. The Pastoral Epistles
also refer to extensive journeyings of the Apostle later still

[1] *Supra*, p. 26.

[2] The very remarkable coincidence in thought and phrase between the
writings of Seneca and Paul led to a tradition arising of actual intercourse
between them, and even of Seneca having secretly become a Christian.
It has been shown conclusively by Lightfoot (in his *Commentary on the
Epistle to the Philippians*) and others that there are no grounds for such
a supposition. It is however possible that he may have heard of St. Paul
from Burrhus, from his brother Gallio, or others, and have been interested
in a man whose language and moral sentiments were in certain respects
so closely akin to his own.

As Seneca was *Consul suffectus* during Paul's imprisonment he must
have had some acquaintance with the case. That a member of the
Annaean *gens* in the next century was a Christian seems to be proved
by an inscription discovered at Ostia in January 1887.

D. M.
M. ANNIO
PAVLO PETRO
M. ANNEVS PAVLVS
FILIO CARISSIMO

See Lanciani, *Pagan and Christian Rome*, p. 17.

in Asia Minor. What probably occurred was that when
Paul was brought before the Court the charges preferred
against him in the *literae dimissoriae* of Festus would be
read and considered, and then an interval of time would
be given for the appearance of witnesses. Then, as no
witnesses came, and the *relatio* of Festus was found to be
favourable, a dismissal followed.[1]

[1] Clement, 1 *Ep. to Cor.* c. v. : ἐπὶ τὸ τέρμα τῆς δύσεως.   Murat.
Canon, lines 37, 38 : ' Sed profectione Pauli ab urbe ad Spaniam proficiscentis.'   There was a law of Claudius, which permitted the discharge of
a prisoner if the prosecutors did not put in an appearance after a certain
time.   Dion Cassius, lx. 28.

LECTURE V.

1 Peter iv. 16 : ' If a man suffer as a Christian, let him not be ashamed, but let him glorify God in this name.'

THE reasons that were given at the close of the last lecture for holding that St. Paul was released from his bonds and left Rome at the beginning of the year 62 A.D. are greatly strengthened by the consideration of certain facts recorded by Josephus. He tells us that during the short procurator-ship of Festus a serious quarrel had arisen between King Agrippa and the priestly party at Jerusalem. Agrippa had built a lofty tower to his palace, from the top of which he was able to overlook the Temple courts. This the Jews bitterly resented, and in their turn erected a high wall to block out the view. Agrippa thereupon applied to Festus, who at first commanded the Jews to pull down the wall and then, fearing an outbreak of violence, afterwards permitted them to send an embassy to lay the matter before Caesar. This embassy consisted of twelve persons headed by the High Priest Ishmael, son of Fabi, and Hilkiah the treasurer. The probable date of their arrival in Rome was April or May, 62 A.D., for Festus died in the spring of this year. Nero had just married his mistress, the beautiful and profligate Poppaea Sabina, to satisfy whose ambition he had first divorced his long-suffering wife Octavia and was within a few weeks to order her murder. Now Poppaea was, if not actually a Jewish proselyte, one of that outer circle of adherents to Judaism known as ' God-fearers.' Her influence with the Emperor was now exerted on behalf of the Jewish embassy, with the result that Nero decided in their favour. Ishmael and Hilkiah were, however, retained at Rome as hostages, a very necessary precaution, for Agrippa on hearing the news had at once deposed Ishmael from the High Priesthood, and Jerusalem was in a very disturbed state.[1] [Had these two men been in Rome at the time of Paul's trial, they would have been important witnesses in support of the charges against him, and it would not have been difficult with the help of Poppaea to secure his condemnation.[2]]

The growth of a bitter feeling of hostility between the Jews and the new Christian sect which had sprung up out of their midst was in this sixth decade of the first century becoming more accentuated. The men of the synagogues hated this new faith, which had for a number of years found shelter under the protection of the privileges accorded to Judaism, as a *religio licita*, throughout the empire, but which by its principle of universalism struck a blow at the very foundations of Judaic exclusiveness. And it was against the Jewish converts, much more than against the far larger number of Gentiles who had embraced the Gospel, that their anger was especially directed. The Jewish Christians were in the eyes of their orthodox fellow-countrymen traitors to their race and to the traditions of their fathers. Hence the vindictive spite with which

---

[1] Josephus, *Ant.* xx. 8. 11 : τῇ γυναικὶ Ποππαίᾳ, θεοσεβὴς γὰρ ἦν, ὑπὲρ τῶν Ἰουδαίων δεηθείσῃ χαριζόμενος, ἢ τοῖς μὲν δέκα προσέταξεν ἀπιέναι. Poppaea was buried after the Jewish custom, Tac. *Ann.* xvi. 6 ; *Hist.* i. 22.

[2] The above was not an isolated act of interference by Poppaea on behalf of the Jews. Josephus in his autobiography tells us of the hard case of certain priests who were his friends. They had been sent in irons to Rome by Felix to be tried before Caesar, and remained there in strict confinement without trial for some four years. Josephus describes how in 63 A.D. he went to Rome to see if he could do anything on their behalf. After a perilous voyage, in which he was shipwrecked in the Adriatic, he finally, like St. Paul, landed at Puteoli, and there met a Jewish actor, named Aliturus, who was a favourite with Nero. By this man's help he obtained an introduction to Poppaea, who not only secured for him the liberation of the priests but gave to him some costly presents before his return to Judaea.—Josephus, *Vita*, c. 3. Josephus tells us that he was at this time twenty-six years of age, and as he was born in the year of the accession of Caligula, *i.e.* 37 A.D., this fixes the date of his voyage to Rome as 63 A.D.

St. Paul was pursued, and the fierce outburst of fanaticism
at Jerusalem which in this very spring of 62 A.D. had led to
the stoning of St. James the Just.[1]   The animosity of the
Roman Jews was probably much less pronounced than that
of the fierce priestly fanatics in Judaea, but they would
naturally be anxious not to add to the hatred and contempt
in which they were held by all classes of the population of
Rome, by allowing public opinion to regard Christianity
as a mere sect of Judaism.[2]   About this time it is certain
that the distinction between Jew and Christian began to be
generally recognised, and rumours to spread abroad, which
probably had their origin in Jewish malice, by which the
Christians were accused of holding impious orgies and
horrible Thyestean feasts and of being a secret society of
anarchists and criminals.   It is not difficult to see that such
slanders might be based upon distorted versions of Christian
teaching, of the baptism of infants in the Catacombs, and
of the nocturnal meetings of the brethren for the holding
of the *Agape* meal and the partaking of the Eucharist.[3]

[1] Josephus, *Ant.* xx. 9. 1 ; Eusebius, *Hist. Eccl.* ii. 23.

[2] It was not until the second century that the hatred between Jew and
Christian became irreconcilable. In the period we are considering the
Christians had no enmity against the Jews, as a race. Despite the bad
treatment he received at their hands at Antioch in Pisidia, Iconium,
Thessalonica, Corinth, Ephesus, and, above all, at Jerusalem, St. Paul
always showed the strongest affection for his fellow-countrymen, and in
his preaching held fast to the rule ' the Jew first.' But Tertullian's words
' synagogas Iudaeorum fontes persecutionum ' were true always. Tert.
Scorp. 10.

[3] The well-known Roman archaeologist, Orazio Marucchi, has dis-
covered in the 1st-century cemetery of Priscilla on the lower floor an ancient
baptistery that he has identified with the ' Coemeterium ad Nymphas
Beati Petri ubi baptizaverat,' *Acta Liberii* [according to their Acts the
Martyrs Papias and Maurus were interred ' via Nomentana ad nymphas
Beati Petri ubi baptizabat ']. In any case this baptistery dates from the
first century and the local traditions in the *Acta* are generally correct.
Marucchi, *Eléments d'Archéologie Chrétienne*, ii. 385-6, 457-61 ; also
Le Memorie degli Apostoli Pietro e Paolo in Roma, pp. 93-102.   The
language of Tacitus (*Ann.* xv. 44) and Suetonius (*Nero*, 31, 39) testifies
that the charges against the Christians in the time of Nero were of the
same kind as those mentioned in detail at a later date by Justin Martyr,
Dial. c. Tryph. 10, 17, 108 ; I *Apol.* 26 ; Athenagoras, *Apol.* 3 ; Eusebius,
Hist. Eccl. vi. 1 (as to the charges brought against the Christians at Lyons).

The exact date of the last visit of St. Peter to Rome cannot be fixed with certainty, but a number of considerations point to the year 63 A.D. as the time of his arrival. That St. Peter was martyred in Rome towards the end of the reign of Nero is a fact, as I have previously shown, established by overwhelming evidence.[1] That he resided there for some length of time before his death is witnessed to by a weight of tradition which only prejudice and prepossession can put on one side, as without evidential value. By some curious perversity of critical aberration it was precisely the Ebionite fictions, which have come down to us in the 3rd century pseudo-Clementine literature, which Baur and Lipsius and their followers adopted as historical, accepting their representation of Peter and Paul as the heads of two rival and hostile Christian factions and as passing their lives in continuous and acute conflict, while rejecting the tradition universally accepted in every part of the Christian world for fifteen centuries, which regarded these two Apostles as the joint founders of the Roman Church, working in harmony for the common cause, and sealing their testimony by death in the city where both alike spent their last days. This Tübingen theory, worked out with much literary ingenuity and all the resources of erudition, had for some decades a great vogue, but being fundamentally false it could not live long when tested by the results of scientific archaeological research, and has at length been practically abandoned. Christian archaeology indeed has during the past half century made giant strides, especially at Rome itself, and the accumulating evidence furnished by the excavations and explorations in the Catacombs and elsewhere has been most illuminating, and tends more and more by the testimony of still existing monuments, tombs, and inscriptions to verify the general correctness of early Christian tradition.[2]

St. Peter's final sojourn in Rome has a permanent

[1] See pp. 47-51.
[2] G. B. de Rossi, *Roma sotterranea cristiana*, 4 vols. 1864-1877; *Inscriptiones Christianae urbis Romae VII° saeculo antiquiores*, 1861-1888. De Rossi examined over 15,000 epitaphs in the Catacombs. *Bullettino di archeologia cristiana*, 1863-1894, etc. *Nuovo Bullettino di archeologia*

record in the first Epistle bearing his name, which is
from the historian's standpoint a document of the utmost
value. Its authenticity was never questioned in ancient
times and the external witness to its genuineness is un-
impeachable.[1] [If on subjective grounds doubts have been
thrown on its authorship, its date and the place from which
it was written, it has been simply because its contents,
being on the face of them that which they claimed to be—
Petrine, Neronian, and Roman—naturally clashed with
theories which denied to it any of these attributes.] With
the death and burial of the Tübingen fictions, let it be hoped
that the doubts about the genuineness of this Epistle may
also find decent interment.

The salutation of the Epistle is addressed to the elect
sojourners of the Dispersion, in Pontus, Galatia, Cappadocia, Asia, and Bithynia, in other words to the Jewish
Christians scattered throughout the four Roman provinces
(for Pontus and Bithynia formed one province) which lay
north and west of the Taurus mountain range.[2] This
region then, it may be assumed, had been the scene of
Peter's missionary labours for a number of years before the

cristiana (edited by Orazio Marucchi), 1895 ; Orazio Marucchi, *Eléments
d'archéologie chrétienne* : I. ' Notions générales,' II. ' Itinéraire des Cata-
combes,' III. ' Basiliques et églises 1906-9. *Roma sotterranea Christiana*
(Nuova serie) Cimitero di Domitilla,' No. 4, 1909; *Le Memorie degli
Apostoli Pietro e Paolo in Roma*, 1903, etc.; P. Wilpert, *Principien-
fragen der christlichen Archäologie*, 1892 ; R. Lanciani, *Pagan and Christian
Rome*, 1892, and *New Tales of Old Rome* ; J. S. Northcote and W. R.
Brownlow, *Roma Sotterranea*, 2 vols. 1879.

[1] On this point Renan (*L'Antéchrist*, Introd. p. vii) may be quoted :
' La *I Petri* est un des écrits du Nouveau Testament qui sont le plus
anciennement et le plus unanimement cités comme authentiques.' 1 Peter
is quoted in the Epistle to the Hebrews, of which the date is probably
66 A.D., and in Clement, 1 *Corinthians*, an epistle written by a disciple of
St. Peter.

[2] There was regular intercourse between Rome and the seaports of
provincial Pontus, especially Sinope. Possibly, as Dr. Hort suggests,
Silvanus may have had special personal reasons for beginning his journey
as the bearer of the Epistle from this point. As Bithynia adjoined Pontus
and formed part of the same province the route of Silvanus would be a
circuit ending at a point not far from that at which it began. See Dr.
Hort's special note on 'The Provinces of Asia Minor included in St. Peter's
address ' : Hort, *1st Epistle of St. Peter*, pp. 157-185 ; also the very interesting Introduction to Bigg's *1st Epistle of St. Peter*, pp. 67-80.

visit to Rome during which the epistle was written. Taken
in conjunction with the strong body of evidence from other
sources for a residence of St. Peter in Rome during the
latter part of Nero's reign,[1] and with the internal evidence
of the epistle itself—that it was written in that city during
the earlier stages of the persecution which followed the
great fire of 64 A.D., the words of ch. v. v. 13, ' the Church
(or the sister) which is in Babylon elect together with
you saluteth you,' are not difficult of interpretation.
To Jewish readers the term Babylon, as symbolically
and figuratively connoting the great city of oppression
and corruption on the Tiber, was, if one may judge by the
use made of it in the Apocalypse, so familiar as to be at once
intelligible. The 5th book of the Sibylline Oracles, in a
passage of Jewish origin referring to the misdeeds of Nero,
and possibly written not long after the fall of Jerusalem,
likewise employs the name Babylon for Rome simply and
directly, as St. Peter does.[2]

The epistle is remarkable for the extent of its indebtedness to other New Testament writings, and especially to
those of St. Paul.[3]   There is no lack of originality in either

---

[1] See Dr. Chase's article on Peter in Hastings's *Dictionary of the Bible*,
in which references will be found to the literature bearing on the subject.

[2] *The Sibylline Oracles*, Book v. p. 143 : Φεύξεται ἐκ Βαβυλῶνος ἄναξ
φοβερὸς καὶ ἀναιδής.   The subject of this passage is the flight of Nero from
Rome.   Zahn gives the date 71–74 A.D. in *Zeitschrift für Kirchliche
Wissenschaft und Leben*, 1886, p. 337 ff.

[3] St. Peter in many passages shows an acquaintance with the Epistle
of St. James. In this there is nothing remarkable, considering the close
association of the two early Christian leaders. Far more striking are the
numerous echoes and reflections of our Lord's sayings, as they are recorded
in the four Gospels. These Petrine reminiscences of the Master's words
do not, however, seem to be derived from any canonical gospel we now
possess.   Possibly St. Peter made use of some pre-canonical source, *i.e.*
that which the critics have named ' Q.' Far more probably he was in the
habit of quoting from memory in his preaching the sayings of Jesus, which
his love for the speaker had enshrined in his mind unforgettably. It is not
unlikely that 1 Peter contains many phrases and thoughts which may have
their source in sayings of the Lord unrecorded in the extant Gospels.   It
is noteworthy that the phraseology of 1 Peter contains several coincidences
with that of the Fourth Gospel, a piece of evidence strongly testifying to
the historical character of the Johannine record.

thought or diction in this essentially Petrine document, but St. Peter's mind appears to have been one of those that absorbed what he had heard or read so completely that he reproduced it almost unconsciously, and yet in reproducing transformed the borrowed phrase or idea, so as to make it his very own. ⌐It is peculiarly interesting to note that this Epistle plainly testifies that the Apostle was intimately acquainted with those two great epistles of St. Paul, the Epistles to the Romans and to the Ephesians,[1] and that he was deeply impressed by them.⌐ This being so, it follows not only that there was at this time no opposition between Peter and Paul, such as fills the foreground of Christian Baur's imaginative representation of the relations between the two men, but that any earlier divergencies of view had been replaced by the closest agreement and by practical identity in the general character of their teaching. Further the fact that the language of these two Epistles, Ephesians and Romans, should have been thus fresh in the memory of St. Peter, when dictating his own letter, is one of those undesigned coincidences which afford the strongest circumstantial proof that the historical setting is in exact accordance with that traditional interpretation of documentary evidence which I have been endeavouring to show is the correct interpretation.⌐ St. Paul, as we have seen, had sent from Rome in 61 A.D. an Epistle to the Church in Colossae and another circular epistle, commonly called the Epistle to the Ephesians, but in reality addressed to a whole group of Asian Churches. In the Epistle to Colossae the Apostle in sending the salutation of Mark, the cousin of Barnabas, who was then with him states that he (Mark) was about to visit them, and he gives to him his commendation.[2] St. Peter in writing, also from Rome, to these same Asian Churches a few years later adds to the salutation from the Church that of ' Marcus my son.'[3] ⌐ Now St. Peter, according to the opening passage of his Epistle, had been

---

[1] In the Authorised Version of 1 Peter will be found more than forty marginal references to Romans, more than twenty to Ephesians.

[2] Col. iv. 10. [3] 1 Pet. v. 13.

working himself in Asia Minor in the years preceding this
last Roman visit.   The natural inference therefrom is that
Mark had, while journeying through those Churches to
which the Epistle of the Ephesians had been sent, joined
himself to his old chief, and then accompanied him once
again to Rome, as his interpreter.   The many references
to the Epistle to the Ephesians by St. Peter in these circumstances are not more than what might reasonably be
expected.   Moreover in Christian Rome, the Apostle on his
arrival so soon after Paul's release would find himself in a
Pauline atmosphere, and being a man keenly susceptible to
influences from without, familiarity with the Epistle to the
Romans could scarcely fail to exercise that profound effect
upon his mind which is reflected in his utterances.   But not
only was Mark a living bond between the two Apostles
at this period ; ┌the concluding paragraph of this Epistle
seems to imply that Silvanus also, Paul's former missionary
associate, had been with Peter in Asia Minor, that he had
accompanied him to Rome, that he was now acting as his
amanuensis in writing his epistle to the Churches of the
Dispersion, and that he was destined to be its bearer.┘
The words ' through Silvanus, a faithful brother in my
judgement, have I written to you briefly ' stand at the
beginning of the short postscript to the epistle, which was
in all probability written by St. Peter in his own hand, and
┌it has been taken to signify that in the body of the epistle
│the more cultured scribe was allowed more or less a free
│hand in putting into literary form the rough-hewn Greek
└which fell from the lips of the Apostle.[1]

━━[1] I Pet. v. 12 : διὰ Σιλουανοῦ ὑμῖν τοῦ πιστοῦ ἀδελφοῦ, ὡς λογίζομαι, δι᾽ ὀλίγων
ἔγραψα.   Compare the words of Dionysius of Corinth quoted in Eusebius,
Hist. Eccl. iv. 2. 11, who speaks of the epistle of Clement as ἡμῖν διὰ
Κλήμεντος γραφεῖσαν.   The Epistle was sent in the name of the Church of
Rome, but the general assent of antiquity makes Clement to have been the
author.   He had no doubt general instructions agreed upon by the
Presbyterate, i.e. by Bishop Linus and the body of episcopi who were
his coadjutors and of whom Clement was one.   He appears, according
to Hermas, to have acted as the secretary of the Presbyterate in their
intercourse with foreign churches and to have been given a free hand in
. the actual composition of the letter.   To a less extent this was probably
the case with Silvanus in his transcription of Peter's dictation.

An event took place when St. Peter was in Rome, but
some months before he wrote his Epistle, which was fraught
with terrible consequences to the Christians.   On July 19,
64 A.D., a fire broke out at the end of the Great Circus
adjoining the Palatine and Caelian Hills, amidst shops
containing inflammable wares.   For nine days the conflagration raged, with most disastrous results.   Of the
fourteen districts into which Rome was divided, four only
escaped uninjured, three were totally destroyed, in the
other seven only a few scarred and half-ruined houses
remained.   Nero was at Antium at the time, but he hurried
to Rome only to see his own palace buildings on the Palatine
and Esquiline, filled with works of art, consumed by the
flames.   From 400,000 to 500,000 persons found themselves
homeless and most of them destitute.   The Emperor
threw himself with energy into the formidable work of
dealing with such an emergency.   He opened to the people
the Campus Martius, the public buildings of Agrippa and
his own gardens, where he erected temporary shelters
for the homeless.   He brought up supplies of corn and
lowered the price.   The Sibylline Oracles were consulted
and propitiations offered to the Gods.   But in spite of all
these acts, which should have won him popularity, manifold
rumours were soon afloat attributing the fire to incendiaries carrying out Nero's own orders. It was commonly
believed that he wished the ancient city to be burnt down,
with its dark, narrow, close-packed streets in order that he
might build a new one to be called after his own name.[1]
    The work of rebuilding in any case was one in which he
delighted and on which he lavished vast sums of money.
Broad, well-built streets of stone brought from the quarries
of Gabii and Alba, with long colonnades, replaced the

[1] See Tacitus, *Ann.* xv. 38–41 ; Suet. *Nero*, p. 38 ; Dion Cassius,
lxii. 16–18 ; Pliny, *Nat. Hist.* xvii. 5. Of these Suetonius, Dion and Pliny
agree in ascribing the crime of incendiarism to Nero. Tacitus does not
commit himself to any positive statement : ' sequitur clades forte an dolo
principis incertum, nam utrumque auctores prodidere.' The legend of
' Nero's fiddling while Rome burned ' is probably a fiction, but there must
always be strong doubts whether or no he was the author of the fire.

narrow and tortuous alleys which had disappeared. Above
all he now appropriated an immense area for the erection
of a magnificent palace for himself, to which the name of
the *Domus Aurea* was given, surrounded by open fields,
woods and lakes, in which nature and art vied with each
other in creating a scene of perfect sylvan beauty. All
this is told us by Tacitus, who then proceeds to describe
the effect upon the public mind of all this activity on the
part of the Emperor :—' but neither man's efforts to give
relief, nor the largess of the prince, nor the propitiations of
the Gods were able to dissipate belief in the sinister report
that the fire had been ordered. [Wherefore to efface the
rumour, Nero contrived that accusations should be brought
against a set of people hated for their abominations, whom
the populace called Christians, and subjected them to the
most exquisite torments.] The author of this name, one
Christus, had in the reign of Tiberius been executed by
the procurator Pontius Pilatus ; and the pernicious
superstition, though repressed for the moment, began to
break out afresh, not only in Judaea, the origin of that evil,
but also in Rome, where all things horrible and shameful
from every quarter collect together and are practised.'[1]

With these sentences Tacitus begins the famous passage,
so full of difficult and debateable points, in which he describes the Neronian persecution of the Christians. Before,

[1] Tac. *Ann.* xv. 44 : ' sed non ope humana, non largitionibus principis
aut deum placamentis decedebat infamia, quin iussum incendium cre-
deretur. Ergo abolendo rumori Nero subdidit reos et quaesitissimis
poenis adfecit, quos per flagitia invisos vulgus Christianos appellabat.
Auctor nominis eius Christus Tiberio imperitante per procuratorem
Pontium Pilatum supplicio adfectus erat ; repressaque in praesens exitia-
bilis superstitio rursum erumpebat, non modo per Iudaeam, originem eius
mali, sed per urbem etiam, quo cuncta undique atrocia aut pudenda con-
fluunt celebranturque.' ' Subdidit reos ' means ' brought to trial with the
malicious object of shifting the hatred of the people from himself upon
the Christians.'   Compare *Ann.* i. 6 : ' quod postquam Sallustius Crispus
, . . comperit metuens ne *reus subderetur*, iuxta periculoso ficta seu vera
promeret.'   See also Suetonius, *Nero*, 16 : ' afflicti suppliciis Christiani,
genus hominum superstitionis novae ac maleficae ' ; and Pliny in his letter
to the Emperor Trajan : ' nomen ipsum, si flagitiis careat, an flagitia
cohaerentia nomini puniantur ' . . . 'nihil aliud inveni quam superstitionem
pravam et immodicam.'

however, proceeding further, and as a necessary preliminary
to any detailed consideration of the passage as a whole, I
wish to point out what seems to me a fundamental error on
the part of almost every writer upon the subject : the error of
connecting the criminal process set on foot by Nero against
the Christians, and its culmination in the horrible fete in the
Vatican Gardens too closely with the Great Fire, either as
regards the time or the character of the charges. Most
writers assume that the Christians were accused of being
incendiaries almost as soon as the last flames were extinguished, and that the Vatican holocaust took place in the
month of August 64 A.D. Now such a supposition runs
directly counter to the Tacitean narrative and derives no
support from any other source.

The section of Book XV of the 'Annals' comprising
seven chapters (38–44) forms a continuous story and treats
of a considerable interval of time. The words 'wherefore
to efface the rumour' . . . are in strict dependence on
the sentence that precedes them—' but neither man's efforts
to give relief, nor the largesses of the prince, nor the propitiations of the Gods were able to dissipate belief in the
sinister report that the fire had been ordered.' With the
utmost distinctness and clearness of which language is capable
Tacitus here declares that Nero did not try to shift odium
from himself by inflaming odium against the Christians,
until he had exhausted all the means for gaining popularity
and diverting the suspicions of the crowd, which the historian
has just recapitulated. Now it is simply impossible that
the gigantic administrative task, first, of providing food
and temporary shelter for some hundreds of thousands of
homeless and destitute persons, and, afterwards, of clearing
away the ruins and debris of so vast a conflagration, of
laying out and planning new and spacious streets and
of setting to work to build them with stone brought from
distant quarries, can have been carried out in less than five
or six months. In all probability the Emperor did not give
instructions for the prosecution of the Christians until the
early part of 65 A.D.

It is no objection that the whole of this section (*i.e.*
cc. 38–44) is included in what appears to be the Tacitean
narrative of the events of the year 64, while the account
of the happenings of the year 65 begins at chapter 48. It is
the ordinary practice of this historian thus to group together
so as to form a single and complete episode in his narrative
a series of events having close connexion with one another
but really spread over a considerable space of time. A
conspicuous instance occurs in the account of the Pisonian
conspiracy and its suppression, which follows that of the fire
and fills the last twenty-six chapters of Book XV. The
history of the year 65 seems to begin in chapter 48 with
the words ' Silius Nerva and Atticus Vestinus then enter
on the consulship, when a conspiracy was begun and at once
gathered strength, into which senators, knights, soldiers
even women had vied with one another in giving in their
names, partly through hatred of Nero, partly through a
liking for C. Piso.' [1] But Tacitus in thus writing had
apparently forgotten that he had already spoken of the
conspiracy of Piso as being in existence in the year 63 A.D.,
and it is evident therefore that the narrative of the growth
of the plot given in chapters 48 to 53 covers the whole
intervening period. The statement that one of the leaders,
Subrius Flavus, ' had formed a sudden resolution to attack
Nero when his house was in flames and he was running
hither and thither unattended in the darkness ' shows that
as far back as the crisis of the conflagration the Emperor

[1] ' Ineunt deinde consulatum Silius Nerva et Atticus Vestinus, coepta
simul et aucta coniuratione, in quam certatim nomina dederant senatores
eques miles, feminae etiam, cum odio Neronis tum favore in C. Pisonem,'
Ann. xv. 48. Cf. xiv. 65: 'Romanus secretis criminationibus incusaverat
Senecam ut C. Pisonis socium. . . . Unde Pisoni timor, et orta insidiarum
in Neronem magna moles sed inprospera.' In xii. 56, 57 Tacitus speaks
of the piercing by Claudius of (Monte Salviano) the mountain intervening
between Lake Fucinus and the river Liris with the object of creating an
outlet for the lake into the river, and he seems to place the execution of
the work and fetes attending its inauguration all in the year 53 : ' sub idem
tempus inter lacum Fucinum amnemque Lirim perrupto monte, quo
magnificentia operis a pluribus viseretur etc.' Suetonius tells us that
the work employed 30,000 men for eleven years, *Claud.* 20. See also Pliny,
Nat. Hist. xxxvi. 15, 24.

only escaped by the lack of nerve of his would-be assailant. It will thus be seen that, while seeming to compress the rise and fall of the Pisonian conspiracy into the first few months of 65 A.D., Tacitus is really telling of the long-drawn-out drama of some two or three years. The two sections therefore of the 'Annals,' (1) that dealing with the fire, the rebuilding and the persecution, and (2) that which treats of the doings of the conspirators after the failure of Subrius Flavus, are overlapping narratives and really contemporary. What influenced Nero at this juncture to select the Christians as his victims can only be conjectured. [Possibly the suspicions of the Roman crowd had fallen upon the Jews, the objects at once of their detestation and contempt, as being incendiaries, partly because their own Ghetto across the Tiber was one of the few uninjured quarters of the city, and partly because the hated race were at that time in especial favour at the Court.] The Jews on their part, alarmed at being the objects of popular anger, would not be slow to use the influence of Poppaea with the Emperor, and to suggest that the blame should be thrown on the Christians, a sect from which they were anxious to be dissociated and on which they would be only too glad to wreak their spite.[1] A plausible reason would easily be found in distorted versions of the utterances of Christian 'prophets' and preachers concerning that approaching destruction of the world by fire, in which all Christians at that time firmly believed. However this may have been, the charge of incendiarism, if ever preferred, was only a pretext ; it was as malefactors and criminals that the Christians suffered. An examination of the extant authorities will, I think, bear out this contention.

In the first place comes the all-important passage of Tacitus (xv. 44), a part of which has been already given.

---

[1] Allard, *Hist. des Persécutions*, pp. 42-3 ; Renan, *l'Antéchrist*, pp. 154-5 ; 1 Clement, 5, διὰ ζῆλον καὶ φθόνον. Nero must have been well aware of the existence of the Christians, many of whom were to be found in his own household. Difficulties must have arisen at times with the freedmen and slaves who refused to take part in any pagan ceremonies or sacrifices or to attend public spectacles.

After his reference to the origin of Christianity he continues thus : ⌠' those therefore who confessed were first brought to trial, afterwards by the information derived from them, an immense multitude were joined with them, not so much for the crime of incendiarism, as for hatred of the human race.⌡ To their deaths mockeries were added, so that covered by the skins of wild beasts they were torn to pieces by dogs and perished or were affixed to crosses or set on fire and, when day had fallen, were burnt so as to serve as an illumination for the night. Nero had offered his gardens for the spectacle, and was exhibiting a public show in the circus. He mingled with the people in the dress of a charioteer, standing in a car. Hence compassion began to arise, although towards criminals deserving the extremest forms of punishment, on the ground that they were destroyed not for the public good but to gratify a single man's savage cruelty.' [1]

Since the publication of Mommsen's article ' Der Religionsfrevel nach römische Recht ' in 1894,[2] the views

---

[1] ' Igitur primum correpti qui fatebantur, deinde indicio eorum multitudo ingens haud proinde in crimine incendii quam odio humani generis coniuncti sunt. Et pereuntibus addita ludibria, ut ferarum tergis contecti laniatu canum interirent, aut crucibus adfixi aut flammandi, atque, ubi defecisset dies, in usum nocturni luminis urerentur. Hortos suos ei spectaculo Nero obtulerat et circense ludicrum edebat, habitu aurigae permixtus plebi vel curriculo insistens. Unde quamquam adversus sontes et novissima exampla meritos miseratio oriebatur, tamquam non utilitate publica sed in saevitiam unius absumerentur ' (*Ann.* xv. 44). *Correpti* = (1) seized by violence ; (2) dragged violently to trial. Compare ' continua hinc et vincta agmina trahi ac foribus hortorum adiacere. Atque ubi dicendam ad causam introissent ' (*Ann.* xv. 58) of the Pisonian conspirators. *Fatebantur* can only mean ' made open confession.' *Indicio eorum*: this may possibly mean that some turned renegades (see Heb. vi. 5, 6), but it includes information of all kinds. Many no doubt made no concealment about their being Christians and the views that they held as to the approaching destruction of all things by fire. It may also mean that papers and other proofs were found by search of the houses of the accused. *Coniuncti* : this is the reading of *MS. Med.* and on the ground that the more difficult reading should be preferred, I adopt it with Henderson, Ramsay, Boissier and others, and also because it seems to me to give the right interpretation of the words that precede, ' haud proinde in crimine incendii quam odio humani generis.' The other reading is *convicti*.

[2] ' Der Religionsfrevel nach römische Recht ' (*Historische Zeitung*, 1890, t. lxiv. 389 ff) (see also *Expositor*, 1893, vol. viii. 1–7).

of the writer, as the greatest authority upon the history of the early Empire, gained wide acceptance, and have now a large and growing number of adherents. ⌐According to this view stated briefly the early persecutions of the Christians were mere matters of police and were dealt with by the summary powers, *coercitio*, possessed by the executive magistrates at Rome and by the governors, proconsuls, procurators and their deputies, in the provinces.⌐ Now the subject of this article is in no sense specially the Neronian persecution or the interpretation of the passage of Tacitus which we are considering. It is a paper of a general character, dealing with what I may call the normal procedure of the Roman State in its treatment of religious offences, and no doubt it gives a perfectly correct account of the ordinary repressive measures which were continually being exercised against the Christians, as Christians, certainly after the time of Trajan's rescript, but to some extent during the whole of the Flavian period also.[1] ⌐But the Neronian persecution was not a normal repressive measure, such as those with which Mommsen is concerned. The persecution of 65 A.D. was the first act of hostility of the Roman State against those professing the Christian faith, and it was the personal act of the Emperor himself.⌐ No one can read Chapter 44 of Book XV of the ' Annals ' without

[1] Among the many modern writers on early Christian persecution the following works are specially deserving of mention: Mommsen, *Römisches Strafrecht*, 1899 ; Arnold, *Die Neronische Christenverfolgung*, 1888 ; Schiller, *Gesch. des Röm. Kaisserreichs unter der Reg. des Nero*, 1872; Allard, *Histoire des Persécutions pendant les deux premiers siècles*, 1892 ; Callewaert, 'Les premiers Chrétiens, furent-ils persécutés par édits ou par mesures de police ?' (*Rev. d'hist. ecclés.* Louvain 1901, p. 771 ff ; 1902, p. 6 ff, 326 ff, 601 ff) ; Duchesne, ' La prohibition du Christianisme dans l'Empire romain '(*Misc. di storia ecclesiastica e stud. ausil.* 1902, i. 1) ; Le Blant, *Les persécutions et les martyrs*, 1903 ; Guérin, ' Etude sur le fondement jurid. des persécutions dirigées contre les Chrétiens pendant les deux premiers siècles de notre ère ' (*Rev. Hist. de droit franç. et étrang.* 1895, pp. 600, 713) ; Renan, *L'Antéchrist*, 1873 ; Boissier, *Fin du Paganisme*, 1892 ; Parfumo, *Le fonti e i tempi dello incendio Neroniano*, 1905 ; Ramsay, *The Church and the Empire*, 4th edit. 1905 ; 'Christianity in the Roman Empire' (*Expositor*, 1893, viii. pp. 8–21, 110–119, 282–296) ; Hardy, *Christianity and the Roman Government*, 1894 ; Henderson, *Life and Principate of the Emperor Nero*, 1902 ; Klette, *Die Christenkatastrophe unter Nero*, 1907.

admitting this. From first to last Tacitus lays stress upon
the personal part taken by Nero in the whole of the proceedings. The account opens with the statement ' Ergo
abolendo rumori Nero subdidit reos et quaesitissimis poenis
adfecit, quos per flagitia invisos vulgus Christianos appellabat,' and in the closing scene ' hortos suos ei spectaculo
Nero obtulerat.' That in the popular view Nero was the
prime mover throughout could scarcely be more strongly
expressed than in the words ' in saevitiam unius.'

The evidence of Suetonius is scarcely less direct. His
biography of Nero strikes a kind of balance between the
praiseworthy and beneficent deeds of the Emperor and the
much longer list of black crimes and histrionic follies, apparently with the object of showing that the latter far outweigh
the former. Among the good and commendable deeds
comes the brief notice—' the Christians, a race of men holding
a strange and noxious superstition, were visited with punishments.' [1] The impious sect was only worthy of mention
because the severity of their punishment reflected a certain
measure of personal credit upon Nero's administration.
That of Tertullian is remarkable. In his ' Apology ' to the
Emperor Septimus Severus he writes : ' Consult your
records [commentarios] ; there you will find Nero first
savagely attacked with Caesarean sword this sect then rising
chiefly at Rome. But of such an initiator of our condemnation we are even proud. For he who knows that man
can understand that nothing except what is great and good
was condemned by Nero.' Again in the ' Scorpion '—' we
have read the lives of the Caesars ; Nero was the first to
stain with blood the rising faith at Rome.' [2] Tertullian

---

[1] ' Afflicti suppliciis Christiani, genus hominum superstitionis novae
et maleficae ' (Suet. *Nero*, 16). These words occur in the midst of a
number of sumptuary regulations enforced by Nero. The epithet *maleficae* suggests that one of the charges was that of sorcery or magic.

[2] Tertullian, *Apol.* c. 51, 21 ; *Scorp.* c. 15 ; *Ad Nat.* 1, 7 : ' sed tali
dedicatore damnationis nostrae etiam gloriamur.' The word *dedicator*
in Tertullian's writings has the signification *auctor*, *initiator*, see Oehler's
Index Verborum in his edition of Tertullian's works. In the passage from
Scorp. occur the words ' si fidem commentarii voluerit haereticus, instru-
menta Imperii loquentur.'

was himself a jurist learned in the law, and as the quotations
above testify, he bases his statements and arguments upon
documentary evidence, both the works of historians and
state records. ⌠Since, therefore, the Emperor personally
initiated the persecution of the Christians in 64-65 A.D.—
' ergo abolendo rumori Nero subdidit reos,' as Tacitus says—
the trial must have taken place in the imperial court presided
over in the Emperor's absence by the Pretorian prefects
and their assessors of the Imperial Council.¹⌡ Probably in
this matter Tigellinus took the leading part; the character
of the final tragedy in the Vatican Gardens was quite in
accord with what we are told of the fiendish ingenuity of his
cruelty. There is abundant evidence to show that Tigellinus
after 62 A.D. was not merely the instigator of many of
Nero's crimes but the active and merciless agent in the
execution of them.²

If Nero then, in the course of the winter months of
64-65 A.D., by his personal initiative brought the Christians
to trial before his court, knowing them to be held in general
odium for their crimes, in order to divert public attention
from the widely accredited rumour that it was by his secret
orders that the city had been set on fire, let us now proceed
to examine the highly condensed and somewhat enigmatic
narrative of Tacitus with the view of further investigating

¹ Tac. *Ann.* xiv. 51, 60 ; xv. 37, 50, 72 ; xvi. 19, 20 ; *Hist.* i. 72 ;
Suet. *Galba*, 15 ; Plutarch, *Otho*, c. 2 ; Tac. *Ann.* xv. 58 : ' Atque ubi
dicendam ad causam introissent . . . pro crimine accipi cum super Neronis
ac Tigellini saevas percontationes, Faenius quoque Rufus violenter urgeret.'
The trial of the Pisonian conspirators thus took place before Nero
and the two Pretorian Prefects, April 65. A little afterwards Seneca was
accused of complicity, and his answers to the charge were brought by
a tribune to the Court. Tacitus (*Ann.* c. 61) thus relates it : ' Ubi haec
a tribuno relata sunt Poppaea et Tigellino coram, quod erat saevienti
principi intimum consiliorum. . . .'
² See Juvenal, *Sat.* i. 155-157 :
        Pone Tigellinum : taeda lucebis in illa,
        Qua stantes ardent, qui fixo gutture (pectore) fumant
        Et latum media sulcum diducit arena.
On this passage an ancient *Schol.* comments : ' In munere Neronis arserunt
vivi de quibus ille iusserat cereos fieri, qui lucerent spectatoribus. . . .
Maleficos homines taeda, papyro, cera super vestiebat, sicque ad ignem
admoveri iubebat ut arderent.'

the character of the charges brought against the accused. In the first place let us clear our minds of a misapprehension. Negatively they were not accused of having had any hand in the actual conflagration of July, 64 A.D. Not a single writer, Christian or pagan, who refers to the Neronian persecution ever suggests that it had any connexion with the fire, with the single exception of the late fourth-century chronographer, Sulpicius Severus, who, however, contents himself with an almost slavish reproduction of Tacitus.[1] Neither Tertullian nor Orosius, who were well acquainted with the works of Tacitus and with other documentary sources no longer accessible to us, shows any sign of being aware of any correlation between the charges against the Christians and the burning of Rome.[2] There is not a trace in the contemporary writings—1 Peter, Hebrews, the Apocalypse or 1 Clement—that such an accusation was made.

This being so, what then is the meaning of ' those therefore who confessed were first brought to trial, afterwards by the information derived from them an immense multitude were joined with them, not so much for the crime of incendiarism as for hatred of the human race ' ?   Now in the first place it is surely plain that had any Christians confessed to the crime of setting fire to Rome in July, 64 A.D., and had they implicated the general body of their fellow-Christians in their guilt, there would have been no need of any subsidiary charges ; exemplary punishment would have been summary and immediate, and Nero's name would at once have been freed from the stigma that rested upon it.   But it was not freed.   There is something approaching unanimity in the verdict of the writers of succeeding centuries (for Tacitus scarcely conceals what was his personal opinion) in ascribing the fire to Nero, and what is more important for our present contention of contemporaries also.   The

---

[1] Sulp. Sev. *Chron.* ii. 29.

[2] This negative evidence of Tertullian comes out the more forcibly as his *Apology* was addressed to the Emperor Septimius Severus, and to the chief magistrates of the Roman Empire.   Orosius roundly charged Nero with being the incendiary : ' denique urbis Romae incendium voluptatis suae spectaculum fecit ' (*Hist. adv. Paganos*, vii. 7).

above-named Subrius Flavus, a tribune of the Pretorian guard, when on his trial before Nero, as a conspirator, in April 65 A.D., did not scruple to tell the Emperor to his face that he was an incendiary, and Tacitus is at pains to state 'I have given the man's very words.'[1] Pliny the Elder also, in his 'Natural History' published before 79 A.D., writing upon the longevity of certain trees remarks that 'they lasted until the fires of the Emperor Nero with which he burnt the city. . . ,' and he concludes in words that leave not the smallest doubt as to his conviction in this matter, 'They would have remained afterwards by cultivation green and young had not that Prince hastened the death even of trees.'[2]

The incendiarism of which the Christians were accused and of which they made open confession was an incendiarism in will not yet realised, but in their firm and absolute conviction immediately to come, and meanwhile eagerly watched for and desired. In Christian circles this one belief during the early decades of the second half of the first century overpowered all others, and transformed all men's ideas and their outlook upon life, that the second Advent of Christ was at hand, and it would be preceded by the destruction by fire of the world and with it the great city of Rome. In every part of the New Testament there are evidences that the Christians of the period with which we are dealing expected that 'the end of all things'[3] would be consummated in their own lifetime, and the Apocalyptic literature of the time dwells not only upon the fire which was to burn up the world and all its wickedness, but also upon the sign that the final judgment was at hand, by the

---

[1] 'Ipsa rettuli verba,' Tac. *Ann.* xv. 67.

[2] 'Duraveruntque, quoniam et de longissimo aevo arborum diximus, ad Neronis principis incendia quibus cremavit Urbem, annis CLXXX . . . postea cultu virides iuvenesque ni Princeps ille accelerasset etiam arborum mortem,' Pliny, *Hist. Nat.* xvii. 1.

[3] 1 Thess. iv. 16-18; 2 Thess. i. 7-10; 1 Cor. xv. 51-2 ; Rom. xiii. 11-13; Tit. ii. 12, 13 ; Heb. ix. 37 ; 1 Pet. iv. 7 ; 2 Pet. iii. 10-12 ; Rev. xviii. 1-21, xxii. 10-12, 20.—See Turner, *Studies in Early Church History*, pp. 226-7.

appearance in bodily form of Antichrist, the incarnation
of Belial or Satan, and there is evidence to show that the
enormities of Nero had before the end of his reign led
Christians to identify him as Antichrist personified.[1] The
open expression of such views at such a time would not
escape the notice of Tigellinus' secret police, and the offenders,
no doubt, when arrested (exactly as Tacitus reports) made
no attempt to deny or explain away the language they had
used. Confessing that they were Christians and that a belief
in the approaching destruction by fire of wicked Rome and
of the world of which it was the head was to them as Christians an article of faith, it is easy to see how ' by their information ' the whole body of Christians became included
in the accusation. That afterwards under torture some of
the more weak-kneed prisoners may have turned traitors
and furnished the government with the names and meeting-
places of their fellow disciples, and in the stress of agony
may even have given false evidence concerning the crimes
with which popular opinion charged them, is not impossible.
The language of the Epistle to the Hebrews rather supports
such an hypothesis, as do certain passages of ' The Shepherd '
of Hermas.[2] The proceedings against the Christians for
the use of language threatening a coming judgment upon
the world and its destruction by fire can be paralleled by
the account given by Philostratus of the visit of the sophist
and wonder-worker, Apollonius of Tyana, to Rome in 66 A.D.
We read how ' Tigellinus, who controlled the sword of Nero,
expelled from Rome ' the cynic Demetrius, a friend of
Apollonius, ' for destroying the Baths by his language,
and secretly he [Tigellinus] began to keep his eye on

[1] Rev. xiii., xvi. 10, 19, xvii. 5-9 ; *Ascension of Isaiah* [80-90 A.D.]
14 (2, 5) and 18. *Orac. Sibyllina*, iii. 63-93 [about 80 A.D.], iv. 179-182,
v. 158-162.   There are many other passages of Judaeo-Christian origin
which are difficult to date, as the books in their present form contain
many ancient fragments. See also *Apoc. of Baruch*, xxxvi.-xl., which
Dr. Charles dates before 70 A.D., and iv. Esdras a little earlier.

[2] Heb. vi. 4-6, x. 26-29, 39. The title of *Confessores* was one in which
the Christians of later centuries gloried. Compare 1 Tim. vi. 12-13.
Compare Hermas, *Pastor*, Sim. ix. 21. 3, 28. 4, Vis. iii. 2, 1, the persecution
to which Hermas refers was probably that of Nero.

Apollonius against the time when he should say something unguardedly that could be taken hold of. . . . All the eyes that Government sees with were turned to scrutinise him : his discourses or his silences ; his sitting or walking ; what he ate and with whom—all was reported. . . .' Finally, we read a little further on that Apollonius was overheard saying concerning the Emperor : ' Pardon the gods for taking pleasure in buffoons,' and on this being reported Tigellinus ' sent officers to arrest him, and he had to defend himself on a charge of sacrilege against Nero.' The representation here given of the power and methods of procedure of Tigellinus and of the action that he took in the year 66 in regard to Apollonius and his companion furnishes us with the means of filling in with detail the story of what happened to the Christians in the preceding year told by Tacitus in barest and briefest outline.[1]

The offences with which the Christians were charged under Nero appear to have been, according to Tacitus, of the same character as those of which Pliny the Younger speaks in his famous letter from Bithynia to the Emperor Trajan, as ' the crimes adhering to the name,'[2] and which we find described in the writings of the second-century Christian Apologists, perhaps more succinctly than any other by Athenagoras (about 177 A.D.), who writes ' Three things

---

[1] The translation from Philostratus' *Apollonius* is that of Prof. J. S Phillimore, recently published by the Clarendon Press, 1912, vol. ii. 43–45, bk. iv. cc. 42, 43, 44. Prof. Phillimore in his Preface sides with the majority of critics in asserting that this work of Philostratus is a Romance. At any rate, many sections of it may undoubtedly be regarded as imaginative fiction. But, as in the *Acta Sincera* of the Martyrs, the romance is built upon a basis of historical fact, and the fictitious details fill in the framework of a real biography. The portion of the book which treats of Apollonius' visit to Rome in 66 A.D. gives strong evidence of its historicity. The name of the consul Telesinus, the inauguration of the Gymnasium and Baths by Nero and his later departure for Greece, the personality of Demetrius the Cynic, and the character and activity of Tigellinus are all historical. The original Greek of two important passages stands thus : Τιγελλῖνος γάρ, ὑφ' ᾧ τὸ ξίφος ἦν τοῦ Νέρωνος, ἀπήλαυνεν αὐτὸν τῆς Ῥώμης. . . . ἀπαγγελθέντος δὲ τῷ Τιγελλίνῳ τὸν λόγον τοῦτον πέμπει τοὺς ἄξοντας αὐτὸν ἐς τὸ δικαστήριον ὡς ἀπολογήσαιτο μὴ ἀσέβειν ἐς Νέρωνα.

[2] ' Flagitia cohaerentia nomini,' Plin. *Ep.* x. 97.

are alleged against us :⌈Atheism, Thyestean feasts, Oedipodean intercourse.'⌋ The refusal to take part in the
ceremonies or to recognise the gods of the national religion
constituted the crime of Atheism. The secret assemblies,
the bringing of children to them for the rite of baptism,
the words of consecration in the Holy Eucharist, the salutation with ' a holy kiss,' were travestied by the enemies
of Christianity into charges of ⌈murder, cannibalism, and
promiscuous intercourse⌋ which were accepted as true by
public opinion already in the days of Nero, and which still
remained a fixed article of popular belief and execration
when Tertullian wrote his ' Apology ' about a century and a
half later.[1] These were the *flagitia* to which Tacitus attaches
the epithets *atrocia* and *pudenda,* abominations horrible
and shameful.

That the Christians were also condemned for the crime
of ' magic ' may be inferred from the fact that their religion
is styled by Tacitus a most pernicious superstition—*exiti-
abilis superstitio*—and by Suetonius a strange and maleficent
superstition — *superstitio nova ac malefica* — (the word
maleficus having juristically the special signification of a
magician or sorcerer), and the punishment in the Vatican
Gardens was that specially assigned to those convicted of
practising magical arts.[2]

The crime of ' hatred of the human race,' however, was
the charge which included all these other accusations, and
henceforth during the succeeding centuries was to render
the mere name of Christian a sufficient ground for summary

---

[1] Athenagoras, *Supplicatio* 3 ; also Justin Martyr, 1 *Apol.* 26, 2 *Apol.*
12, 13 ; *Dial. c. Tryph:* 10, 17, 108 ; Tertullian, *Apol.* 2, 4, 7, 8, 39 ; *Ad
Nat.* 2.   In the account of the persecution at Lyons and Vienne, 177 A.D.,
which has been preserved by Eus. *Hist. Eccl.* v. i., the same charges are
brought forward : κατεψεύσαντο ἡμῶν Θυέστεια δεῖπνα καὶ Οἰδιποδείους μίξεις.

[2] Gebhardt, *Acta Martyrum Selecta,* 119 : ' Magi estis quia novum
nescio quod genus religionis inducitis.' *Cod. Iust.* ix. tit. 18 : ' de maleficis
et mathematicis.'   Suetonius, *Nero,* 16 : ' Afflicti suppliciis christiani,
genus hominum superstitionis novae et maleficae.'   Paulus, *Sent.* v. :
' Qui sacra impia nocturnave ut quem obtruncarent, defigerent, obligarent,
fecerint faciendave curaverint, aut crucibus suffiguntur aut bestiis obii-
ciuntur. . . . Magicae artis conscios summo supplicio adfici placuit, id
est bestiis obiici aut crucibus suffigi ; ipsi autem magi vivi exuruntur.'

punishment. This charge, as we have seen, may have originated in the suggestions of Jewish malice, sustained by the reports which no doubt reached the ears of the authorities—through the agency of some of that host of spies and informers (*delatores*) employed by Tigellinus— of the incendiary discourses in which certain noxious religious fanatics, ⌐called Christians by the populace, were openly expressing their belief in the imminent destruction of the world and its inhabitants by fire without any conceal- ment of the joyful anticipation with which they awaited the Divine judgment that was impending over a city which was in their eyes the home of iniquity and of every sort of blasphemy.⌐But when those first arrested were brought before the magistrates it was soon found that the fiery words of these enthusiasts were not nearly so damning as the principles in which they gloried and which forbade them to recognise the national gods or the religion of the Roman people, or to take part in any of the public religious cere- monies or spectacles, or in that worship of the *genius* of Caesar, who was the personification of the state.   Thus that law of *maiestas*, which in the reign of Tiberius had been such a powerful instrument for the assertion of the imperial authority, and which after a period of disuse had been revived by Nero in 62 A.D., to be during this very spring of 65 A.D. employed by him with such terrible effect in securing the condemnation of those implicated rightly or wrongly in the Pisonian conspiracy, was no less a ready implement in the hands of Tigellinus for striking at the humbler Chris- tians as enemies of the Roman state. ⌐It is of this *lex de maiestate* that Tertullian writes in his appeal ' ad Nationes ' (c. 7) ' under Nero condemnation [of this Name] was firmly established.'   And a few lines further on, ' Although all his other acts were rescinded this Neronian ordinance alone remained permanent.' [1] ⌐Henceforth the mere confession

----

[1] Tertullian, *Ad Nat.* i. 7 : ' Principe Augusto nomen hoc ortum est, Tiberio disciplina eius inluxit, sub Nerone damnatio invaluit. . . . Et tamen permansit erasis omnibus hoc solum " institutum Neronianum " iustum denique ut dissimile sui auctoris.'   The *lex de maiestate* was a juridical creation of Tiberius and so would not be affected by the *rescissio*

that he was a Christian rendered a man an outlaw. It
has been argued that the name of ' Christian ' was not yet
in common use in the days of Nero, and that Tacitus and
Suetonius being writers of the second century may have
employed the term proleptically. ⸢Apart from the fact that
both these historians drew their material from contemporary sources, St. Peter in his first epistle, which, as we hold,
was written while the Neronian persecution was gathering
force, distinctly says ' If a man suffer as a Christian let him
not be ashamed, but let him glorify God in this Name,' ⸥
and, the Acts of the Apostles already completed before
62 A.D., it testifies not only that the word was popularly
used in Antioch about 40 A.D., but that it was familiar to a
man in the position of King Agrippa in 59 A.D. With the
constant intercourse between Antioch and the capital, the
nickname would be carried to Rome probably quicker than
to any other place, and the familiar Latin form of the word
would be speedily popularised even so early as the time of
Claudius. [1]   Pliny in his letter to Trajan most clearly
points out that condemnation of Christians for the name

actorum of the latter after his death : ' addito maiestatis crimine, quod
tunc omnium accusationum complementum erat,' Tac. *Ann.* iii. 38.
Nero himself was spoken of by Pliny the Elder as ' hostis generis
humani ' (*Hist. Nat.* vii. 8. 45. 46).   Attilio Profumo in his learned work
Le Fonti ed i Tempi dello Incendio Neroniano (p. 227), commenting on the
passage above quoted from Tertullian's *Ad nationes*, thus states the conclusions at which he arrived : (1) ' Non esser mai esistita nè legge nè altra
disposizione giuridica qualsiasi che colpisse nominativamente e solo, come
tali, Christiani.   (2) Le persecuzioni contro di essi furono sempre fatte in
forma giuridica e legale, applicando loro l' " *institutum* " delle tre accuse—
suntuaria, di sacrilegio, di maestà — detto " Neronianum " ; " istituto "
non già esclusivo per essi, ma ad essi solo e sempre applicato.   (3) La
natura dell' " Institutum " istesso, spiega i periodi di persecuzione e di
pace che si alternavano per i Cristiani, senza bisogno di fare o di annullare
legge alcuna ; dappoichè era affidita alla suprema autorità del Principe e
fino ad un certo limite anche a quella dei Presidi delle Province, e l'applicazione di esso e l'applicazione più o meno lata,' Tertullian, as a jurist, uses
the word ' institutum ' correctly to signify a legal procedure resting upon
custom, not necessarily written. Compare Tac. *Ann.* xiii. 32 of the domestic
court for the trial of Pomponia Graecina : ' isque (Aulus Plautius) prisco
instituto propiuquis coram de capite famaque coniugis cognovit et
insontem pronuntiavit.'   [1] Suet. *Claudius*, c. 25.

only was already of long standing in 112 A.D. His chief object in writing to the Emperor was to know whether he was to punish ' for the Name itself, if crimes were wanting, or for the crimes adhering to the Name.' [1]

Let us now see how far the evidence from contemporary Christian sources confirms that derived from Pagan authorities of a later date. That of the 1st Epistle of St. Peter has already been quoted to show that in 65 A.D. Christians were punished for the name. This epistle was written in an atmosphere of persecution. The Apostle as one who has been an eyewitness of persecution in Rome sends a letter of exhortation and warning to the Judaeo-Christians of the Roman provinces of Asia Minor, who were at the time he was writing passing through trials of the same character as those which their brethren in the capital had just been experiencing. Three times does Peter refer to the charge of being evildoers or malefactors,[2] twice to

[1] 'Ipsum nomen, si flagitiis careat, an flagitia cohaerentia nomini puniantur,' Pliny, *Ep.* x. 96. Pliny had no definite edict against Christianity to guide him : ' cognitionibus de Christianis interfui nunquam ; ideo nescio quid et quatenus aut puniri soleat aut quaeri '—so in Trajan's rescript ' Neque enim in universum aliquid quod quasi *certam formam* habeat constitui potest.' In comparing the action of Pliny with that of Tigellinus it should be noticed that there are many points of close resemblance. Pliny writes : ' interim in iis, qui ad me tanquam Christiani deferebantur, hunc sum secutus modum. Interrogavi ipsos, an essent Christiani ; confitentes iterum ac tertio interrogavi, supplicium minatus ; perseverantes duci iussi.' Thus there is the same confession before trial, and finally punishment for the name. Though he could find no specific law, there was no searching for precedents. Pliny knew that for some time past the Christians had been legally regarded as the enemies of the state and that confession of the name meant outlawry. It should be observed that he was not hasty in condemnation, but that he mentions having granted three *cognitiones* before ordering them to be executed. Finally, an anonymous paper was placed in the governor's hand implicating a large number of persons which led to his writing to the Emperor for direction and advice : ' Propositus est libellus sine auctore, multorum nomina continens. Qui negabant esse Christianos. . . . Alii ab indice nominati, esse se Christianos dixerunt.' Compare with Tacitus, *Ann.* xv. 44 : ' Igitur primo correpti qui fatebantur, deinde indicio eorum multitudo ingens. . . .' The Rescript of Trajan merely confirmed in writing the practice, which had subsisted since the time of Nero, of treating the very name of Christian as a crime against the State.

[2] 1 Pet. ii. 12, 14 ; iii. 15–17 ; iv. 15.

the ordeal of punishment by fire.[1] His exhortations are largely directed to the object of entreating his readers to prove by the goodness of their lives and their obedience to lawful authority that the accusations of being criminal evildoers was unfounded.[2] But on the other hand ' if ye be reproached by the name of Christ, blessed are ye ' ; ' if a man suffer as a Christian, let him not be ashamed but let him glorify God in this name.'[3] (The testimony of the Epistle to the Hebrews, which was most probably sent from Asia Minor to Rome in the following year 66 A.D., and of the Apocalypse, of the date 70 A.D., is similar to that of St. Peter in that both refer to the severity of the sufferings which the Roman Christians had endured, and also to the fact that the persecution which had begun in Rome had afterwards spread to Asia Minor. The evidence that Tacitus did not exaggerate either the horrors of the scene in the Vatican Gardens nor the large number of those who perished is abundantly corroborated. ' Ye endured '— says the Epistle to the Hebrews—' a great conflict of sufferings ; partly being made a public spectacle by insults and afflictions : and partly by becoming partakers with them that were so used,'[4] while the writer of the Apocalypse, to quote only one of many passages, speaks of the woman seated on the Seven Hills as ' drunken with the blood of the Saints and of the martyrs of Jesus.'[5] Still more remarkable are the added details given by Clement of Rome in what seems to be the description of an eyewitness. ' Enough of ancient examples,' he writes, ' let us pass on to the athletes of very recent times, let us take the noble examples

---

[1] 1 Pet. i. 7 : διὰ πυρὸς δοκιμαζομένου. 1 Pet. iv. 12 : τῇ ἐν ὑμῖν πυρώσει πρὸς πειρασμὸν ὑμῖν γινομένῃ.

[2] 1 Pet. ii. 11–17. Are the words (v. 14) : ἡγεμόσιν, ὡς δι' αὐτοῦ [τοῖ βασιλέως πεμπομένοις εἰς ἐκδίκησιν κακοποιῶν, a reference to instructions sent out by Nero with regard to the Christians of Asia Minor ? 1 Pet. iii. 16.

[3] 1 Pet. iv. 14–16.

[4] Heb. x. 32, 33. See also iv. 14, 15, vi. 4–6, x. 23–27, xii. 1–13, xiii. 23. For the date of Hebrews and of the Apocalypse see Lecture VI.

[5] Rev. xvii. 6. See also ii. 3, 9, 10, 13 ; iii. 8–11 ; vi. 9–11 ; vii. 13–17 ; xii. 10, 11 ; xiii. 7, 8 ; xvi. 6 ; xviii. 24 ; xx. 4.

of our own days.' Then after telling of the deaths of St. Peter and St. Paul he proceeds :—' to these men [the Apostles] of holy living was gathered together a great multitude of the elect, who having suffered through jealousy many insults and tortures, became very splendid examples amongst ourselves. Persecuted through jealousy, women after having suffered, in the guise of Danaids and Dirces, terrible and monstrous outrages, attained the goal which made sure to them the race of faith, and those who were weak in body received a noble reward.'[1]

I have already shown that the arrest of the first batch of accused Christians cannot have taken place till several months after the fire of July 64, probably in the early spring of 65 A.D. The language of Tacitus may be held to imply that there were, as in the case of Pliny's proceedings in Bithynia, several questionings and trials of the prisoners, and some time would elapse between the first confessions of which the historian speaks and the final seizing of the 'immense multitude' for the holocaust in the Gardens. One thing, moreover, may be regarded as certain : that such a nocturnal spectacle would not have been planned so long as the night air was chilly, nor would Nero with his scrupulous care for the preservation of his divine voice[2] have appeared at night in the open on a car in the garb of a charioteer in cold weather. But if this were the case then an additional motive appears for the arresting in the spring of 65 A.D. of this crowd of humble Christians in order that their execution might be a spectacle to glut the eyes of the Roman populace. In the middle of April the plot of the Pisonian conspirators to take Nero's life during the festival of Ceres was discovered. He grasped at the opportunity of getting rid of a

[1] I Clem. v. 'Αλλ' ἵνα τῶν ἀρχαίων ὑποδειγμάτων παυσώμεθα ἔλθωμεν ἐπὶ τοὺς ἔγγιστα γενομένους ἀθλητάς· λάβωμεν τῆς γενεᾶς ἡμῶν τὰ γενναῖα ὑποδείγματα . . vi. τούτοις τοῖς ἀνδράσιν ὁσίως πολιτευσαμένοις συνηθροίσθη πολὺ πλῆθος ἐκλεκτῶν, οἵτινες πολλάκις αἰκίαις καὶ βασάνοις διὰ ζῆλος παθόντες ὑπόδειγμα κάλλιστον ἐγένοντο ἐν ἡμῖν. Διὰ ζῆλος γυναῖκες Δαναΐδες καὶ Δίρκαι αἰκίσματα δεινὰ καὶ ἀνόσια παθοῦσαι ἐπὶ τὸν τῆς πίστεως δρόμον κατήντησαν.

[2] Suet. Nero, 20 ; Plin. Hist. Nat. xix. 6 108, and xxxiv. 18. 1666 Tac. Ann. xv. 22.

number of illustrious and wealthy men, the confiscation of whose goods helped to fill his treasury, depleted by the building of the *Domus Aurea* and other extravagances. Some undoubtedly were guilty, but once more public opinion condemned Nero. ' He was perpetually,' says Tacitus, ' under the lash of popular talk, which said he had destroyed men of rank, who were innocent, out of jealousy or fear.'[1] Thus confronted with a fresh crop of disquieting rumours, while those of his complicity in the conflagration were still current, it may well be that he sought at the great fetes that were given in gratitude for his escape from death to win a fleeting popularity and divert criticism from himself by devising the spectacle of the illumination with living torches and of the rest of the unspeakable barbarities of that night. But if so, the arrest of the *ingens multitudo* must have been synchronous with the trials and condemnation of the Pisonian conspirators. May it not be that in this fact may be found the explanation of that passage of Tacitus in which he relates how Nero sent out bodies of soldiers in every direction, and how ' in long succession troops of prisoners in chains were dragged along and stood at the gates of the imperial gardens ' ?[2] Mr. Henderson in his ' Life and Principate of Nero,'[3] commenting on these trials of April 65 A.D., says ' The temporary measures of repression and punishment were grossly exaggerated . . . . Forty-one persons in all were implicated ; of these twenty were certainly guilty, sixteen of them suffered death, the others were acquitted—only one certainly innocent person was slain.' Who then were these troops of prisoners in chains ? Is it not possible that the *ingens multitudo* who were arrested and convicted in chapter 44 are identical with the *continua et vincta agmina* of chapter 58 ? If the two events were really contemporaneous, Tacitus may have misread some record and converted Christian prisoners into Pisonian conspirators.

---

[1] Tac. *Ann.* xv. 73 : ' etenim crebro vulgi rumore lacerabatur, tamquam viros claros et insontes ob invidiam aut metum extinxisset.' Compare Josephus, *Ant.* xx. 8. 3 ; Suet. *Nero*, xxvi.

[2] Tac. *Ann.* xv. 58 ; ' continua hinc et vincta agmina trahi ac foribus hortorum adiacere.'   [3] Henderson, pp. 272-4.

In dealing with the question of the Neronian persecution and its date, one important authority cannot be neglected, that of Orosius, who wrote his *Historiae adversus Paganos* under the direction of his master and friend St. Augustine (410–20). In the seventh book of his history, in which is found the account of the fire and the persecution, Orosius shows himself to be thoroughly acquainted with the writings of Suetonius, Tacitus, and Josephus, all of which he quotes by name. The passage which specially concerns us runs as follows : ' The boldness of his [Nero's] impiety towards God increased the mass of his crimes, for he was the first at Rome to visit the Christians with punishments and deaths, and through all the provinces he commanded that they should be tortured with a like persecution, and having endeavoured to extirpate their very name⌈he killed the most blessed Apostles Peter by the cross, Paul by the sword.⌋ Soon calamities in heaps began on every side to oppress the wretched state, for in the following autumn so great a pestilence fell upon the city that according to the registers [in the temple] of Libitina there were thirty thousand funerals.' These last words are a direct quotation from Suetonius, who however as usual gives no date to the pestilence. This is however given by Tacitus, who thus concludes his narrative of the events of 65 A.D. : ' The Gods also marked by storms and diseases a year made shameful by so many crimes. Campania was devastated by a hurricane. . . . the fury of which extended to the vicinity of the City, in which a violent pestilence was carrying away every class of human beings . . . houses were filled with dead bodies, the streets with funerals.' [1]

[1] Orosius, vii. 7 : ' Auxit hanc molem facinorum eius temeritas impietatis in Deum, nam primus Romae Christianos suppliciis et mortibus affecit ac per omnes provincias pari persecutione excruciari imperavit ipsumque nomen exstirpare conatus beatissimos Christi apostolos Petrum cruce, Paulum gladio occidit. . . . Mox acervatim miseram civitatem obortae undique oppressere clades, nam subsequente autumno tanta Urbi pestilentia incubuit, ut triginta milia funera in rationem Libitinae venirent.' Suet. *Nero*, 39. Tac. *Ann.* xvi. 13 : ' Tot facinoribus foedum annum etiam di tempestatibus et morbis insignivere, vastata Campania turbine ventorum qui . . . pertulitque violentiam ad vicina urbi; in qua omne mortalium genus vis pestilentiae depopulabatur. . . .'

Orosius thus confirms the evidence of 1 Peter, the Hebrews, and the Apocalypse, that a general persecution in the provinces was concurrent with that in Rome ; and his express statement that the pestilence happened in the autumn following the persecution fixes the date of the trials and execution of the Christians, as having taken place in the earlier part of 65 A.D.

LECTURE VI

Rev. xii. 11 : 'They loved not their life unto death.'

THE deaths by martyrdom of the Apostles Peter and Paul at Rome towards the close of Nero's reign are among the facts of first-century Christian history which may in these days be regarded as practically outside controversy. The evidence of the letter of the Church of Rome to the Church of Corinth written by Clement,[1] a first-century document of the most authentic character, even if it stood alone, could not seriously be challenged. ' Let us take the noble examples of our own days. Through jealousy and envy the greatest and most righteous pillars [of the Church] were persecuted and contended unto death. Let us take before our eyes the good Apostles. Peter, who through unjust jealousy endured not one, or two, but many toils, and having thus borne witness went to the place of glory that was his due. Through jealousy and strife Paul showed [how to obtain] the prize of endurance. . . . To these men of holy life was gathered together a great multitude of the elect, who having through jealousy suffered many insults and tortures became very splendid examples amongst us.' The instances mentioned here, Peter, Paul, and the great multitude, cannot be separated. If language means anything, it means here that these several examples of brave and patient witness unto death took place ' amongst us,' *i.e.* recently and at Rome.

That the Church of Corinth to whom it was addressed thus interpreted the passage in the latter half of the second century appears from the letter of Dionysius bishop of

---

[1] Clement, 1 *Cor.* v. 6 ; *supra*, p. 47.

Corinth to Soter bishop of Rome written before [174 A.D.,
in which the statement appears ' Both alike [Peter and
Paul], having taught together in Italy, suffered martyrdom
about the same time.' And when we learn from this same
Dionysius that it had been the custom at Corinth to read
Clement's Epistle in the Church on the Lord's Day from the
earliest times, it may be assumed that the tradition of
events, which, at the date when Clement's epistle was first
received at Corinth, must still have been fresh in men's
memories, had been handed down continuously.[1]

Both these passages have been preserved by Eusebius
and in the same chapter of his ' Ecclesiastical History ' in
which the first Dionysian extract is found, Caius, a Roman
presbyter, who lived in the days of Pope Zephyrinus
(198–217), is quoted as saying ' I can show you the trophies
—*i.e.* the Memoriae or chapel-tombs—of the Apostles. ⌐For
if you will go to the Vatican or to the Ostian Way, you will
find there the trophies of those who founded the Church⌐
—the apostles throughout this chapter being Peter and Paul.
Irenaeus, an Oriental by birth, in his youth the disciple of
Polycarp, in later life bishop of Lyons, spent some time in
Rome about 170 A.D. ; he was thus in a special way a representative man both of Eastern and Western Christianity, and
he speaks of the ' Church at Rome, founded and established
by the two most glorious Apostles Peter and Paul, as being
the greatest, the most ancient and well known to all.' [2]
And again ' to this Church, on account of its more especial
eminence, all other Churches must gather,' and he only
spoke the truth, for as a recent writer (Rev. C. H. Turner)
quoting this passage has stated, ' in the next generation '

---

[1] Eus. *Hist. Eccl.* ii. 25 ; iv. 23 : ὁμοίως δὲ καὶ εἰς τὴν Ἰταλίαν ὁμόσε
διδάξαντες, ἐμαρτύρησαν κατὰ τὸν αὐτὸν καιρόν.

[2] Irenaeus, *adv. Haer.* iii. 3. 2 : ' Sed quoniam valde longum est in hoc
tali volumine omnium Ecclesiarum numerare successiones, *maximae
et antiquissimae et omnibus cognitae, a gloriosissimis duobus apostolis
Petro et Paulo Romae fundatae et constitutae Ecclesiae,* eam quam habet ab
apostolis traditionem et annuntiatam hominibus fidem, per successiones
episcoporum pervenientem usque ad nos indicantes, confundimus omnes
eos, qui quoquo modo, vel per sibi placentia, vel per vanam gloriam, vel
per caecitatem et malam sententiam praeter quam oportet, colligunt.'

i.e. after the Apostles—' we might say all the Churches of the Empire " made rendezvous " at Rome.' [1]   And why ? Not because it was the political capital, but because Peter and Paul there gained the crown of martyrdom, and because at Rome their hallowed remains at the Vatican and on the Ostian Way were piously preserved and held in reverence. The authority of the Church of Rome during the early centuries of Christianity obtained a general recognition accorded to no other Church, not because Rome contained the palace of the Caesars, who persecuted the faith, but because it was acknowledged everywhere and always that the Church of Rome had the distinction of having been founded by St. Peter and St. Paul and that it guarded the tombs of these ' two most glorious Apostles.' [2]

Many legends gathered round the deaths of the two Apostles, but the ' Acts ' in which they have been preserved are of late date and mainly pure fiction,[3] except in their topographical references, which the archaeological researches of De Rossi, Lanciani, Marucchi and others in recent years have shown to be generally correct. In one important point the tradition embodied in these Acts, that the martyrdom of Peter and Paul took place on the same day, *i.e.* June 29, 67 A.D.—a tradition which for centuries was universally accepted as historical—is almost certainly wrong. Considerable obscurity must always surround the actual date and manner of their death, but the only contemporary evidence we possess seems to testify clearly to an interval of time separating the two martyrdoms.

The passage of St. Clement (already quoted) mentions the examples of St. Peter and St. Paul in two distinct paragraphs, without any hint that they suffered together ;

---

[1] C. H. Turner, *Studies in Early Church History*, p. 222.

[2] Iren. *adv. Haer.* ; ' Ad hanc enim Ecclesiam propter potiorem principalitatem necesse est omnem convenire ecclesiam, hoc est, eos qui sunt undique fideles, in qua semper ab his, qui sunt undique, conservata est ea, quae est ab apostolis traditio.'   On the universal acceptance by all Churches of the martyrdom of the Apostles Peter and Paul at Rome, see P. Martin, *Revue des Questions historiques*, xiii. pp. 31 ff.

[3] Richard A. Lipsius, *Die Apokryphen Apostelgeschichten und Apostellegenden*, 2er Band, 1e Hälfte.

indeed the words about St. Paul—'when he had borne his witness before the rulers, so he departed out of this world'—by the use of the singular 'he' imply that the witness-bearer—the martyr—stood alone.[1] To this may be added the silence of the Second Epistle to Timothy as to the presence of St. Peter at Rome during the time of St. Paul's last imprisonment and trial. The evidence from silence is always a very treacherous argument to rely upon, but in this case it would indeed be strange, if St. Peter had been tried and condemned simultaneously with St. Paul, that the latter should not have referred in any way to his brother Apostle's presence. As to the manner of their death Tertullian (A.D. 200) writes : 'We read in the lives of the Caesars that Nero was the first who stained with blood the rising faith. Then is Peter girt by another, when he is made fast to the Cross. Then does Paul obtain his birthright of Roman citizenship, when in Rome he is born again ennobled by martyrdom.' The language of the African Father here shows plainly that he is referring to the undoubted first-century testimony to St. Peter's death by crucifixion from the last chapter of the Fourth Gospel.[2] Dionysius of Corinth,

---

[1] A. Harnack, *Altchristl. Lit.* 2er Theil, 1er Band, pp. 549-60. See Chase's admirable article on St. Peter in Hastings's *Dict. of the Bible*; 1 Clem. v : καὶ μαρτυρήσας ἐπὶ τῶν ἡγουμένων οὕτως ἀπηλλάγη τοῦ κόσμου.

[2] Tert. *Scorp.* 15. See also *Praescript.* 36 : 'Ista quam felix ecclesia . . . ubi Petrus passioni dominicae adaequatur'; *Adv. Marc.* iv. 5; John xxi. 18, 19 : 'Verily, verily I say unto thee, when thou wast young, thou girdedst thyself, and walkedst whither thou wouldest; but when thou shalt be old thou shalt stretch forth thy hands and another shall gird thee and carry thee whither thou wouldest not. Now this he spake signifying by what manner of death he should glorify God.' Comp. xiii. 36. Seneca (*Cons. ad Marciam*, 20) writes of those crucified 'brachia patibulo explicuerunt.' The tradition that St. Peter at his own request was crucified head-downwards was first mentioned by Origen ἀνεσκολοπίσθη κατὰ κεφαλῆς (Op. ii. 24 de la Rue), in his Commentary on Genesis to which Eusebius refers (*Hist. Eccl.* iii. 1). This shows that the tradition was known early in the third century, and the letter of Seneca quoted above is evidence that such a method of execution was not unknown in Rome, for he writes : 'Video istic cruces non unius quidem generis, sed aliter ab aliis fabricatas ; capite quidem conversos in terram suspendere.' It is impossible to say whether this tradition of the mode of St. Peter's death be true, on the whole it is improbable.

as we have seen, merely states that both Apostles suffered about the same time. ⌐The very early Judaeo-Christian Apocalypse, ' The Ascension of Isaiah ' [1] (79–80 A.D.), seems to have a clear reference to St. Peter's death at the hands of Nero, but no allusion to that of St. Paul.⌐ The Liberian Catalogue, 354 A.D., is the first document in which the death of the Apostles on the same day is mentioned, and from the Liberian Catalogue the ' Liber Pontificalis ' adopted it, and June 29 was henceforth regarded as the common anniversary of the martyrdom of the two Apostles. The origin of this mistake is however revealed by certain entries in authentic lists of the feasts of martyrs annually celebrated in the Church belonging to the second half of the fourth century, from which it appears that in the year 258 A.D., owing to the outbreak of the Valerian persecution, the relics of the two Apostles were taken from their resting-places at the Vatican and on the Ostian Way and deposited for safety in a cemetery on the Appian Way known as the Catacombs. The translation took place on June 29, and when afterwards the relics were again restored to their original tombs, a hymn of St. Ambrose tells us that henceforth on that day there were three feasts kept at Rome : one at the Vatican, a second on the Ostian Way, a third at the Catacombs.[2] From the beginning of the fourth century

---

[1] *Ascension of Isaiah*, Charles, pp. 25 and 95, iv. 2, 3 : ' A lawless king, the slayer of his mother : who himself, even this king, will persecute the plant which the Twelve Apostles of the Beloved have planted. Of the Twelve one will be delivered into his hands.' Comp. τὴν φυτείαν ἣν φυτεύσουσιν οἱ δώδεκα ἀπόστολοι and the words of the letter of Dionysius of Corinth, τὴν ἀπὸ Πέτρου καὶ Παύλου φυτείαν γενηθεῖσαν Ῥωμαίων τε καὶ Κορινθίων. Eus. *Hist. Eccl.* ii. 25. In the *Ascension of Isaiah* St. Paul is not reckoned among the Twelve.

[2] On the Liberian Catalogue, its sources and its relation to the *Liber Pontificalis*, see Duchesne's great edition of the *Liber Pontificalis* ; Lightfoot's excursus on the early Roman succession in his *Apostolic Fathers* (*St. Clement of Rome*), part I. vol. i. 201–345 ; Harnack, *Chron. der Altchristl. Literatur*, vol. i : ' Die ältesten Bischofslisten,' 79–230 ; also the chapter ' The Western Church ' in Turner's *Studies in Early Church History*, 1912. The burial and tombs of the Apostles Peter and Paul and the translation of their bodies for a time to the Catacombs are the subject of a special Note, Note E, Appendix. The fact of the date of the translation and of the triple

then the belief that the Apostles suffered together in 67 A.D. on the same day became general, though a passage in one of the poems of Prudentius written quite early in that century is a proof that with the acceptance of June 29 as the anniversary of both Apostles, a tradition remained of their martyrdoms having taken place in different years. Prudentius says [1] that St. Peter died exactly a year before St. Paul. It was the influence of St. Jerome more than any other cause that led to the universal adoption in the Western Church of the fourteenth year of Nero as the date of St. Peter's death, his account of that Apostle in the ' De Viris Illustribus ' being the basis of the notice of St. Peter which appears in the ' Liber Pontificalis.' [2]

feast being on June 29 will be found in Duchesne, pp. civ–cvii ; also in Barnes, *St. Peter in Rome*, pp. 107 ff.   In the *Hieronymian Martyrology* (in a Codex discovered by De Rossi at Berne) the following entry occurs : ' III Kal. iul. Romae, natale sanctorum Petri et Pauli : Petri in Vaticano, via Aurelia ; Pauli vero in via Ostensi ; utriusque in Catacumbas ; passi sub Nerone, Basso et Tusco Consulibus.' The words *passi sub Nerone* must be regarded as in a parenthesis, the date of the consulship of Bassus and Tuscus is 258 A.D.   A somewhat earlier and more abbreviated entry is found in the so-called *Feriale Philocalianum* (335–354 A.D., Duchesne).   The title of the document is *Depositio Martyrum*, and we find ' III. Kal. iul. Petri in Catacumbas et Pauli Ostense Basso et Tusco Consulibus.'   A hymn attributed to St. Ambrose (Daniel, *Thesaurus hymnologicus*, Halle, 1841, No. 71) has this verse :
 ' Tantae per urbis ambitum
  Stipata tendunt agmina,
  Trinis celebratur viis
  Festum sacrorum Martyrum.
This hymn was written for the Feast of St. Peter and St. Paul on June 29. The ' trinis viis ' signifies the Aurelian, the Ostian, and the Appian Ways.
 [1] Prudentius, Περιστεφανων, hymn xii.
  ' Prima Petrum rapuit sententia legibus Neronis,
   Pendere iussum praeminente ligno.

   . . . . .
  Ut teres orbis iter flexi rota percucurrit anni
   Diemque eundem sol reduxit ortus,'
  Evomit in iugulum Pauli Nero fervidum furorem,
   Iubet feriri gentium magistrum.'
St. Augustine (*Sermons*, 296–7) held a similar opinion.
 [2] Duchesne, *Lib. Pont.* vol. i. p. 119 : ' Ce début, de même que plusieurs autres parties de la notice, étant emprunté au *De Viris* de Saint-Jérôme.' C. H. Turner in his chapter on St. Cyprian's correspondence in *Studies in Early Church History*, p. 101, writes : ' The older critics, following St.

The internal evidence of St. Peter's first Epistle shows that he survived the Vatican fete and that the extension of the persecution to the provinces was the chief cause of his writing. [It follows therefore that he must have been in concealment during the climax of the Neronian attack upon the Roman Christians.] Now among the legends which have grown up around the death of St. Peter there is a very beautiful one, which may possibly have an historical foundation, I mean the well-known *Quo Vadis?* story. His friends, so runs the story, had entreated the Apostle to save his life by leaving the city. Peter at last consented, but on condition that he should go away alone. ' But when he wished to pass the gate of the city, he saw Christ meeting him. Falling down in adoration he says to Him " Lord, whither goest Thou ? " And Christ replied to him " I am coming to Rome to be again crucified." And Peter says to Him " Lord, wilt Thou again be crucified ? " And the Lord said to him " Even so, I will again be crucified." Peter said to Him " Lord, I will return and will follow Thee." And with these words the Lord ascended into Heaven . . . And Peter, afterwards coming to himself, understood that it was of his own passion that it had been spoken, because that in it the Lord would suffer.' The Apostle then returned with joy to meet the death which

Jerome's statement (*De Viris*, lxvii.) that Cyprian suffered " eodem die quo Romae Cornelius sed non eodem anno," naturally placed Cornelius with Cyprian on September 14. But we know from the *Liberian Catalogue* that Cornelius died at Centumcellae, and September 14 was perhaps the day of the translation of his remains to Rome.' Hence it appears how easily these confusions of dates may have arisen through the commemoration of a *depositio*. The passages of St. Jerome bearing upon the date are :

(1) ' Simon Petrus . . . Romam pergit, ibique viginti quinque annis cathedram sacerdotalem tenuit usque ad ultimum Neronis annum, id est, quartum decimum ' (c. i.).

(2) ' Paulus Apostolus . . . quarto decimo anno Neronis eodem die quo Petrus, Romae pro Christo capite truncatur . . . anno post passionem Domini XXXVII ' (c. v.).

(3) ' Hic [Lucius Annaeus Seneca] ante biennium quam Petrus et Paulus martyrio coronarentur, a Nerone interfectus est ' (c. xii.). Seneca was put to death end of April, 65 A.D.

the Lord had signified that he should die.⎛ Now the mere existence of this ancient tradition would indicate that the crucifixion of Peter took place while the persecution was still active, *i.e.* some time in the summer of 65 A.D.[1] ⎠

That it contains a story that is authentic in the sense of being based on events that really occurred is not improbable. The Peter described here is the Peter of the Gospels—brave, loving, but in critical moments irresolute. The persuasions of friends may have induced him to seek safety in flight, but no sooner is he on his way than his conscience reproves him. He who had just written to the persecuted disciples in Asia ' if any man suffer as a Christian let him not be ashamed ; but let him glorify God on this behalf,' [2] must have felt that he was again denying his Master, and, as in the High Priest's palace, once more did the Lord look upon Peter. The vision came to him now, as in former days the vision on the roof of the tanner's house at Joppa, as perhaps overwrought with fatigue he had flung himself on the ground to rest. ⎛There is a passage in St. John's Gospel which seems to me to support the historicity of the *Quo Vadis ?* tradition.[3] It was after the Supper on the last night of the Lord's earthly life, when (according to St. John) ' Simon Peter said unto Him, Lord,

---

[1] Lipsius, *Die Apokryphen Apostelgeschichten und Apostellegenden*, 2er Band, 1e Hälfte, p. 318. The following extract is from the *Passio Petri* by pseudo-Linus : ' Ut autem portam civitatis voluit egredi, vidit sibi Christum occurrere. Et adorans eum ait : " Domine, quo vadis ? " Respondit ei Christus : " Romam venio iterum crucifigi." Et ait ad eum Petrus : " Domine, iterum crucifigeris ? " Et dixit ad eum dominus : " Etiam, iterum crucifigar." Petrus autem dixit : " Domine, revertar et sequar te." Et his dictis dominus ascendit in coelum . . . Et [Petrus] post haec rediens in se ipsum, intellexit de sua dictum passione.' Compare St. John, xiii. 36, 37 : ' Dicit ei Simon Petrus : Domine, quo vadis ? Respondit Iesus : Quo ego vado, non potes me modo sequi : sequeris autem postea. Dicit ei Petrus : Quare non possum te sequi modo ? animam meam pro te ponam.' Wordsworth's edition of the Vulgate.

[2] 1 Pet. iv. 16 ; also see ii. 19-21, iii. 14-18.

[3] If, on the other hand, the *Quo Vadis ?* story were a pure invention of a later age, then the original romancer must have based it on the two passages St. John, xiii. 36, 37, and Hebrews, vi. 6, taken with St. John, xxi. 15-23.

whither goest Thou ? Jesus answered him, Whither I go, thou canst not follow Me now, but thou shalt follow Me afterwards. Peter saith unto Him, Lord, why cannot I follow Thee now ? I will lay down my life for Thy sake.' Two questions at once come into the mind : (1) Was the echo of those words haunting Peter's memory when he saw the vision ? (2) Did his knowledge of the cause of Peter's voluntary return to death move the Fourth Evangelist to insert those verses in his narrative ? Possibly both should be answered in the affirmative.

Before leaving the subject of the *Quo Vadis ?* tradition I should like to point out that the remarkable language of Hebrews vi. 6, if it were possible to regard it as suggested by the words of the Lord to Peter, *I am coming to Rome to be crucified again*, acquires a living force and becomes full of meaning as a reference to an event fresh in the minds of the readers. The writer of Hebrews was acquainted with 1st Peter, and if, as I venture for the moment to assume, this Epistle was addressed to the Jewish Christians in Rome about a year or a year and a half after St. Peter's death then the solemn words in which those who in times of persecution shall fall away were warned that it was impossible to renew them again to repentance—' seeing that (by such an act of apostasy) they crucify the Son of God afresh and put him to an open shame '—recalling, as they did, the very words which had caused Peter to turn back and welcome martyrdom, would strike home to the hearts and consciences of any waverers that heard them. For the *Quo Vadis ?* story, if in any sense historical, must have been widely known from the first.

Having made this reference to the Epistle to the Hebrews let us now turn to the consideration of the problems that it presents.

The internal evidence tells us that this epistle was sent to a Church containing a considerable body of Jewish Christians, who though they spoke Greek and used the LXX. version, were accustomed to style themselves ' Hebrews.' They had been exposed to a severe persecution, ' having endured a great conflict of sufferings, being made a gazing-stock both by reproaches and afflictions '—a conflict in which certain persons had apostatised.[1] Further it would appear that persecution had not ceased, but that some were still in bonds.[2] Among those who had suffered were leaders, who had set an example to be followed.[3] The place of martyrdom is plainly indicated as lying outside the city walls.[4] [Those who would be the readers of the Epistle had not yet themselves resisted unto blood, but they needed encouragement to persevere, and as a deterrent to the weak-kneed and faint-hearted the terrible judgments of God against apostasy are painted in the sternest colours.[5] Now all this applies to the Judaeo-Christian community of Rome in the year 66 A.D.]

That there was such a body of Judaeo-Christians at Rome and that the writer of this Epistle should address them as Hebrews, there is a sufficiency of evidence, apart from that furnished by the document itself. In the Epistle to the Philippians, which was written at Rome some four years before the Epistle to the Hebrews, St. Paul makes mention of a party among the Christians there, who 'preach Christ of envy and strife, of contention and not sincerely, supposing to add affliction to my bonds.' And in this same epistle he warns the Philippians 'Beware of dogs, beware of the concision, for we are the circumcision which worship God in the spirit,' and then proceeds 'if any other man thinketh that he hath whereof he might trust in the flesh, I more. Circumcised the eighth day, of the stock of Israel, an Hebrew of the Hebrews.' We may gather from this that the party who tried to add affliction to the Apostle's bonds 'of envy, strife, and contention,' were the party that held that circumcision was binding on Christians, and who styled themselves Hebrews.[6] Of this extreme Jewish party, who

[1] Heb. x. 32, 33, comp. vi. 6, x. 39, xii. 15–25.   [2] Heb. xiii. 3.
[3] Heb. xiii. 7.   [4] Heb. xiii. 12, 13.   [5] Heb. xii., the whole chapter.
[6] Phil. i. 13, 14, iii. 2–5. [The very words St. Paul uses of these opponents at Rome, διὰ φθόνον καὶ ἔριν, are the words used by Clement of the causes which led to St. Peter's death, διὰ ζῆλος καὶ φθόνον, and to St. Paul's διὰ ζῆλος καὶ ἔριν.]

were Jews first and Christians afterwards, some under the
stress of persecution seem to have apostatised, probably
by reverting to Judaism and seeking protection under its
privilege. Moreover in an extant inscription one of the
Jewish congregations at Rome is described as the synagogue
of the Hebrews.[1] And Professor Lanciani writes ' the whole
district outside the Porta Portese has retained its connexion
with the Ghetto of Ancient Rome up to our own days, being
called *Ortaccio degli Ebrei*, just as in bygone times it bore
the name of *Campus Iudaeorum* or *Contrata Hebreorum*.[2]
The external evidence that the Epistle to the Hebrews
was addressed to Roman Christians is circumstantially
strong and convincing. It was so familiar to Clement of
Rome that in his own epistle to the Church of Corinth he
incorporates its phrases and its ideas freely, but without
mentioning the writer's name. This proves that Hebrews
was well known in Rome during the last half of the first
century and that it had for Clement an attraction which
may reasonably be attributed to an acquaintance with and
respect for the author. The extent of Clement's indebtedness may be gathered from the fact that at a later time the
actual authorship of Hebrews, despite the great dissimilarity
of style, was ascribed at him.[3] Again the frequency with
which the anchor appears as the emblem of Christian hope,
in the most ancient inscriptions found in the Catacombs,

---

[1] *Corp. Inscr. Graec.* 9909, see Garrucci's *Cimitero degli antichi Ebrei*,
p. 39.   This synagogue doubtless belonged to a small isolated settlement
of Jews, which had only one place of worship ; it therefore had no distinctive name, but was known simply as the synagogue of the Hebrews.

[2] Lanciani, *New Tales of Old Rome*, p. 248.   The love of the Hellenist
Jews of the Dispersion, living as strangers and sojourners in a foreign land,
for the name of Hebrews was probably due to the desire to emphasise the
fact that they were the heirs of the promises made to Abraham who ' by
faith sojourned in the land of promise as a stranger ' (Heb. xi. 9).   *Corp.
Inscr. Graec.* 9922 is a striking proof that the Roman Jews called themselves ' Hebrews ' : Ἀλύπις Τιβεριεὺς καὶ οἱ αὐτοῦ, Ἰοῦστος καὶ Ἀλύπις, Ἑβρέοι,
μετὰ τοῦ πατρὸς αὐτῶν ὧδε κίντε.

[3] Origen, *Hom. in Hebr.* quoted by Eus. *Hist. Eccl.* vi. 25 ; Philastrius,
de Haeres. 89 ; Jerome, *de Viris Illustribus*, 15.   Others suggest that
Clement was the translator into Greek of an Epistle of Paul written in
Hebrew.   Eus. *Hist. Eccl.* iii. 37.   Euthalius, Migne, *P.G.* lxxv, 776.

may be regarded as a testimony to a very early and wide-spread knowledge of the Epistle to the Hebrews among Roman Christians.[1] Into the whole question of patristic evidence of a later date I cannot enter here, space forbids it, but it may be stated broadly that in the middle of the second century Hebrews was accepted at Alexandria by Pantaenus and his school as an epistle of St. Paul's ; that the great Alexandrian Fathers, Clement and Origen, both quote Hebrews frequently as St. Paul's, though Clement expressed doubts whether it was actually written by St. Paul, and Origen goes further and declares that the name of the writer was absolutely unknown. The same indecision and indefiniteness of opinion appear in Eusebius' ' Ecclesiastical History ' in a number of passages, and he may be taken as reflecting the general attitude of the Alexandrian and Eastern Churches at the beginning of the fourth century.[2] Very different was the attitude of the Roman or Western Church during the same period. There never seems to have been the smallest doubt in Rome and the West at any time that the epistle was not Paul's. Not until the middle of the fourth century does any Western writer cite any passage from Hebrews as Pauline. Indeed, in the course of the second century a distinct line of division between canonical and uncanonical writings began to be drawn, and there seems to have been no hesitation in the Western Church in placing the Epistle to the Hebrews among the uncanonical. Irenaeus in all his works never appears to have cited the epistle, though in his ' Treatise against Heresies ' many passages would have been effective. He may be regarded as a representative man of the last quarter of the second century. Tertullian and Hippolytus, the one at the beginning, the other in the second quarter of the third century, both deny the Pauline authorship.

---

[1] Marucchi, *Arch. Chrét.* ii. 173.

[2] Eus. *Hist. Eccl.* vi. 14, 25, 41. Origen believed the thoughts to be those of St. Paul, the actual language and argument those of a disciple. As to the authorship however he declares—τίς δὲ ὁ γράψας τὴν ἐπιστολὴν τὸ μὲν ἀληθὲς θεὸς οἶδεν. Later the opinion at Alexandria that Paul himself was the author became dominant and at last accepted by all.

Later still in that century neither Novatian at Rome nor
Cyprian at Carthage, in their controversy about ' the
Lapsed,' ever brings forward the passage from Hebrews vi.
2–6 which bears directly upon it, nor do they make any
quotations from this epistle in their writings. This affords
conclusive evidence that Rome and the West, unlike Alexandria and the East, were not in two minds about this
epistle : it was not Paul's and therefore not authoritative.
But there is evidence to show that their knowledge was not
merely negative.   They were sure it was not Paul's because
they were acquainted with the name of the actual writer.

Tertullian in his treatise ' De Pudicitia ' makes the
following statement : [1] ' for there is extant [a testimony] of
Barnabas with the title " To the Hebrews "—a man moreover
sufficiently accredited, as one whom Paul had placed next
to himself in the observance of abstinence. . . . And at any
rate the Epistle of Barnabas is more received among the
Churches than that apocryphal " Shepherd " of adulterers.'
Then, after quoting the passage at the opening of the sixth
Chapter of Hebrews, Tertullian adds ' He who learnt this
from Apostles, and taught it with Apostles, never knew
of any second repentance promised to the adulterer and

---

[1] Tertullian, *De Pudicitia*, 20 : ' Volo tamen ex redundantia alicuius
etiam comitis apostolorum testimonium superinducere, idoneum confirm-
andi de proximo iure disciplinam magistrorum.   Extat enim et Barnabae
titulus ad Hebraeos, adeo satis auctoritatis viri, utquem Paulus iuxta se
constituerit in abstinentiae tenore (1 Cor. ix. 6).   Et utique receptior
apud ecclesias epistola Barnabae illo apocrypho pastore moechorum.'
Another and a much later witness, that in the Western Church the authorship of the Epistle to the Hebrews was assigned to Barnabas, is to be found
in the *Index Claromontanus*, D. 2, a MS. of the sixth century.   In the
stichometrical catalogue of the books of the Old and New Testaments
at the end of this codex there is no mention of the Epistle to the Hebrews.
After Jude, however, and before the Apocalypse comes ' the epistle of
Barnabas,' the length of which is set down as 850 *stichoi* or lines, the
Apocalypse as 1200.   This corresponds to the length of the Epistle to the
Hebrews and not to that of the epistle of the pseudo-Barnabas, which the
stichometry of Nicephorus, 850 A.D., shows to be practically the same as the
Apocalypse, *i.e.* pseudo-Barnabas, 1360 *stichoi* ; Apocalypse, 1400.   The
position of the epistle in the *Codex Claromontanus* and the length assigned
are well-nigh positive proof that the Epistle of Barnabas here signifies the
Epistle to the Hebrews.

fornicator.' [Now here it will be noticed that the great
African Father is not attempting to reckon the Epistle to
the Hebrews as authoritative, or to place it among the
Apostolical Scriptures ; he quotes the epistle as the work
of a man whose credentials are simply that he was a companion and fellow-worker with Apostles.\ But on the question of authorship there is not a sign that he was making
an assertion about which there was any doubt.   He assumes
that his readers were aware of it and would admit it.   In
fact as he is inveighing, as a Montanist, against what he
regarded as ' the lax discipline of the Church of Rome,' he
would not be likely to have quoted this passage in support
of his argument as written by Barnabas, unless he knew
that his opponents would not impugn his assertion. ʃ It is
clear then from this that the tradition of the Barnabas
authorship was held without dispute not only in Provincial
Africa but in the Church of Rome itself in the time of
Tertullian. ɹ But if so, does   not   the   existence   of   such
an   accepted   tradition   in   a   Church   where   no   counter-
tradition existed, except that the author of Hebrews was
not St. Paul, virtually postulate its truth ?

Now it is needless for me to dilate on the fact here
that Barnabas was peculiarly qualified to be the writer
of such a hortatory homily or dissertation as the Epistle
to the Hebrews.ʃ He was at once a Cypriote Jew, brought
up in close contact with Alexandrian influences and modes
of thought, and a Levite by descent, who had relatives living
at Jerusalem.ɹ The writer himself styles his epistle a
' Word of Exhortation '—λόγος παρακλήσεως—a technical
expression for those expositions or interpretations of Scripture which it was customary to deliver in the synagogues,
and Barnabas' very name in its Greek form, υἱὸς παρακλήσεως,
signifies a man gifted with powers of such exhortation.   The
addresses of St. Stephen to the Sanhedrin or of St. Paul
at Antioch are specimens of such hortatory expositions of
Scripture, and it has been noted how closely the Epistle to
the Hebrews follows in many places the lines of St. Stephen's
speech.   The influence of St. Stephen is particularly observ-

able in the eleventh chapter. ⌜The whole character of this
Epistle is moreover exactly in accordance with what we
should expect from the man who in the Acts of the Apostles
is brought before us as the mediator between the two schools
of Judaistic and Pauline conceptions of Christianity.⌟ His
epistle, possibly written at Paul's wish and with his full
approval, was sent to Rome as an *eirenicon*, with the aim
of drawing nearer together the Hebrews and the Gentiles—
the party of the circumcision and those converts who were
followers of St. Paul's doctrines. His object is to show
that Christianity is the historical outcome of Judaism, and
that, so far from being in any way opposed, the Law,
the Temple, and all the characteristic Jewish rites and
ceremonies were but types and shadows of the more perfect
dispensation that was to come; and that they all found their
spiritual fulfilment in Christ.

It only remains to point out that the personal references
in the epistle support the hypothesis of a Barnabas authorship. The tone of authority is marked,[1] and has led some
commentators on this ground to hold that, even if St. Paul
was not the actual writer, the epistle was sent to its destination in his name. But there was one man who could write
with an authority second only to that of the chief Apostles,
Barnabas, and, if the destination of the epistle were Rome,
from what has already been said of the connexion of Barnabas
with the Roman Church [2] it is certain that after St. Peter's
death the words of no other leader would carry so much
weight with the Judaeo-Christians there as his. From one
passage we gather that the writer had not been a personal
hearer of the Lord, and from the Acts it would appear
that Barnabas did not become a Christian until some short
time after the Great Day of Pentecost.[3] Lastly, the writer,

---

[1] Renan, *L'Antéchrist*, xvi–xvii : ' Il (l'auteur) n'en tenait pas moins
un rang élevé dans l'Eglise ; il parle avec autorité ; il est très-respecté des
frères auxquels il écrit ; Timothée paraît lui être subordonné. Le seul
fait d'adresser une épitre à une grande Eglise indique un homme important,
un des personnages qui figurent dans l'histoire apostolique et dont le
nom est célèbre . . . L'attribution à Barnabé est la plus vraisemblable.'

[2] *Supra*, pp. 80–2. [3] Acts, iv. 36–7.

who had himself been in bonds, sends the news that Timothy
had been released,[1] and that he was hoping that he would
shortly be able to pay a visit to his readers with Timothy
as his companion. But according to the First Epistle to
Timothy, that disciple had at Ephesus ' confessed a good
confession before many witnesses '[2]; this city, then, it may
be safely inferred, had been the scene of Timothy's imprisonment and release. But it will be remembered that in the
last lecture some reasons were given for believing that
Barnabas and Timothy were the joint bearers from Rome
of the Epistle to the Philippians, and that from Philippi
they went on to Asia Minor.[3] If then Barnabas were the
author of Hebrews, nothing would be more natural than
that they should be in 66 A.D. the one in Ephesus, the other
in some neighbouring town, and that Barnabas should be
planning in company with Timothy to journey once again
to Rome. The words ' they of Italy salute you ' are a fitting
greeting, if sent to Rome by a man well known to the
Christian congregations in Italy, and to whom Italian
Christians sojourning in the province of Asia would resort
as a proved friend and teacher : conditions which, unless
tradition be altogether untrustworthy, apply pre-eminently
to Barnabas and to no one else,

At the close of the year 66 A.D. or the beginning of
67 A.D. we find St. Paul again at Rome. In the interval
that had elapsed since his release in the year 62 A.D., he
seems first to have carried out his intention of making a
missionary journey to Spain and then to have revisited the
scenes of his former labours in Asia Minor and Greece.
Clement in his Epistle to the Corinthians speaks of his having
reached ' the farthest bounds of the West,'[4] and the Mura-

---

[1] Heb. x. 32, xiii. 23. [2] 1 Tim. vi. 12 and i. 3. [3] *Supra, p.* 121.

[4] Clement, 1 *Cor.* v. : ἐπὶ τὸ τέρμα τῆς δύσεως ἐλθών. In the
year 66 A.D., according to Philostratus, Apollonius of Tyana being banished
from Rome ' turned westwards to the land which they say is bounded by the
Pillars. He intended to see Gades and the tides of the ocean, for he heard
some report of the philosophy of the men in those parts and their proficiency
in religion.' In 68 or 69 A.D. he was once more in Greece. See Phillimore's
Philostratus, ii. 48, 63 ff.

torian fragment on the Canon speaks of ' the departure of Paul from the city on his journey to Spain.' [1] The authorities for his later travels are the Pastoral Epistles. With those travels, or with the authenticity of the Pastoral Epistles as a whole, these lectures have no necessary concern. It is enough that the autobiographical sections of the Second Epistle to Timothy should be recognised as derived from a genuine Pauline source, and this recognition is generally conceded even by some who most strenuously deny that the entire epistle as we possess it was written by Paul,[2] for it is these sections only which deal with the second imprisonment of the Apostle in Rome. At the same time I should like at this point to record my complete agreement with the conclusion of Sir William Ramsay that ' it is far more difficult to frame any rational theory how these letters came into existence, if they are not the work of Paul, than it is to understand them as composed by him, and as completing our conception of his character ' ; and again, ' regarded in the proper perspective, they [the Pastorals] are historically perhaps the most illuminative of all the Pauline epistles ; and this is the best and the one sufficient proof that they are authentic compositions.' [3]

[1] ' Profectione Pauli ab urbe ad Spaniā proficiscentis.' The Muratorian fragment is generally supposed to be of the age of Hippolytus, if not his work. Lightfoot (*Apostolic Fathers*, part i. vol. ii. 405 ff) places its date towards the close of the second century. Also Zahn and Harnack.

[2] Salmon (*Int. to N.T.* p. 511) writes : ' As for the general Pauline character of these letters there cannot be a better witness than Renan, who, while continuing to assert them not to be genuine, every now and then seems staggered by the proofs of authenticity that strike him. (He says in one place " Some passages of these letters are so beautiful that we cannot help asking if the forger had not in his hands some authentic notes of Paul which he has incorporated in his apocryphal composition " (*L'Eglise Chrétienne*, p. 95).' Of those who reject the Epistle (2 Tim.) Hausrath, Pfleiderer and Ewald recognise the sections i. 15-18, iv. 9-22 as fragments of a genuine Pauline letter. Salmon, p. 503.

[3] Ramsay, ' Hist. Commentary on 1st Epist. to Timothy,' *Expositor*, Ser. vii. 7, June 1909, p. 488, and Ser. vii. 8, p. 1. Prof. Vernon Bartlett (*Expositor*, Ser. viii. 25, Jan. 1913, p. 29) writes : ' When one approaches these Epistles fresh from the few pages on them in Hort's *Lectures on Judaistic Christianity*, and in *The Christian Ecclesia*, and from Sir W. M.

In the Second Epistle to Timothy we find Paul at Rome in prison awaiting inevitable death in the calm consciousness of having fought the good fight and finished his course.[1] Of what befell him on his arrival at Rome we know nothing. But his previous captivity of two years and trial would make him well known as a Christian leader, and the swarms of informers [2] would lose no time in denouncing him to the authorities as suspect. Possibly he may have been arrested under the edict of 66 A.D. forbidding philosophers to reside in Rome, which had sent Apollonius into banishment. Clement tells us he was brought 'before the governors,' [3] which, in the absence of Nero in Greece accompanied by Tigellinus, may be taken to mean the freedman Helius, to whom the government had been entrusted, and Nymphidius Sabinus, the Pretorian Prefect.[4] In any case, whatever the original cause of his arrest, it was as a malefactor (κακοῦργος) that he was—at the time he was writing—suffering hardship even unto bonds; in other words, he was being charged with the crimes imputed to those who bore the name of Christian.[5] Already he had been once before the tribunal, and bitterly does he complain that he could find no one to stand by his side and aid him in his defence, but by God's help he had been able fully to proclaim his message so that all the Gentiles might hear, and he had for the time been delivered ' from the mouth of the lion '[6] and escaped immediate condemnation. But he was still in prison, his enemies were busy, and he does not anticipate any issue but death. In his captivity, however, he is feeling lonely and deserted. Of his personal friends and disciples some

Ramsay's recent" Historical Commentary on the Epistles to Timothy " in the *Expositor*, one feels the subject has been lifted to a new level of reality and that much criticism between Baur and Jülicher is simply out of date and irrelevant.'   [1] 2 Tim. iv. 6-8.

[2] Henderson's *Principate of Nero*, p. 392.

[3] Clement, 1 *Cor.* v. : μαρτυρήσας ἐπὶ τῶν ἡγουμένων.

[4] Dion Cassius, lxiii. 12: οὕτω μὲν δὴ τότε ἡ τῶν Ῥωμαίων ἀρχὴ δύο αὐτοκράτορσιν ἅμα ἐδούλευσε, Νέρωνι καὶ Ἡλίῳ· οὐδὲ ἔχω εἰπεῖν ὁπότερος αὐτῶν χείρων ἦν.

[5] Comp. 1 Pet. ii. 12, iii. 16, iv. 13, 16, 19.

[6] 2 Tim. iv. 17 : Helius—probably.

like Demas had openly forsaken him, others were engaged
on various missions, Prisca and Aquila probably in consequence of the persecution had left Rome and were once
more at Ephesus. Only the faithful Luke was with him.[1]
For some reason or other the Apostle appears in these last
months of his life to have been under a cloud. Sadly he recalls
to Timothy—'this thou knowest, that all that are in Asia
turned away from me,'[2] and the whole tone of the Epistle
shows that the Roman Christians as a body were, if not
unfriendly, at least unsympathetic. There were of course
exceptions, such as Eubulus, Pudens, Linus, and Claudia,
who send their salutations by him to Timothy, and well-
authenticated tradition points to two of these, Pudens and
Linus, as being among the foremost leaders of the Roman
Church at the close of the seventh decade of our era.[3] The
whole soul of Paul however is filled with a longing desire
to see once more his own beloved son Timothy before the
end, and twice does he earnestly in the course of the concluding verses of this most touching and noble letter beseech
him—' do thy diligence to come shortly unto me '—' do thy
diligence to come to me before winter.'[4] And then the veil
falls. Whether Timothy arrived in time to comfort the
Apostle in the final hours of his life we shall never know.
We trust it was so. All tradition says that St. Paul, as
became his status as a Roman citizen, suffered martyrdom
by decapitation, being led out of the city to the third
milestone upon the Ostian Road, at the spot known as
Aquae Salviae. The site of his tomb is now covered by
the basilica which bears his name.[5]

A document now claims our attention which has a closer
relation to Rome and throws more light upon the feelings
with which first-century Christianity regarded the World-

---

[1] 2 Tim. iv. 10-13, 19, 20.   [2] 2 Tim. i. 15.

[3] 2 Tim. iv. 21. Linus is no doubt the man who appears in the episcopal lists as the first bishop of Rome after Peter. Pudens was a man of
senatorial rank, who according to tradition played a considerable part
in the early history of the Church in Rome. See Appendix, Note C.

[4] 2 Tim. iv. 9, 21.

[5] See Appendix, Note E, The Tombs of St. Peter and St. Paul.

Empire of the Caesars than any other book of the New
Testament. I mean the Apocalypse of St. John. The
Apocalypse is full of references to historical events of which
the author had quite recently been himself an eyewitness at
Rome, or which were fresh in the memories of the Roman
Christians with whom he had been associating, and it can
be dated with great exactitude from internal evidence as
having been written at the beginning of the year 70 A.D.
The witness of the contents of the book itself, as will be
shown, amply justifies such an assertion. There is however a certain amount of external evidence, which has had
much more weight than it deserves, apparently supporting
a later date. I think it best to deal with this first, with the
object of tracing to its source the error on which I believe
it rests. The witness of Irenaeus, 180 A.D., is no doubt
important, especially on the question of the authorship of
the Apocalypse, for he had himself in Asia been instructed
by Polycarp, who was a personal disciple of St. John. Now
Irenaeus several times states that John the disciple of the
Lord, whom he identifies with the author of the fourth
Gospel, was the writer.[1] The vexed question of this identity
only concerns us now in as far as it throws light on the
passage of Irenaeus bearing upon the date, which I proceed
to quote. It is commonly rendered as follows : ' We are
not bold enough to speak confidently of the name of Antichrist. For if it were necessary that his name should be
declared clearly at the present time, it would have been
announced by him who saw the revelation. For *it* was
seen no such long time ago, but almost in our generation
toward the end of the reign of Domitian.' But surely this
rendering is wrong. It should be ' for *he* [St. John the
writer] was seen . . . almost in our generation toward the

---

[1] For the question of the identity of John the Apostle the son of
Zebedee, John the disciple of the Lord, who reclined cn His Breast at
Supper, John the author of the Epistles and the Fourth Gospel, and
John the Presbyter—see the convincing arguments of Dom John Chapman,
O.S.B., in his *John the Presbyter and the Fourth Gospel* : Clarendon Press,
1911.

end of the reign of Domitian.'[1] It is of the Seer and his ability to declare the name of Antichrist that Irenaeus is speaking. The misunderstanding about the meaning of the passage is largely due to Eusebius, who after a reference to Domitian's persecution proceeds 'in this [persecution] report affirms that the Apostle and Evangelist John, who was still living, in consequence of his testimony to the divine word was condemned to dwell on the island of Patmos,' and then he quotes Irenaeus in support of his statement. Now Eusebius was very familiar with the works of Origen, and more particularly his commentaries, and it seems to me that in making this statement he had in his mind the following comment by Origen upon St. Matthew xx. 22 : ' And the sons of Zebedee were baptised with the baptism, since Herod killed James the [brother] of John with the sword, while the king of the Romans, as tradition teaches, condemned John bearing testimony through the word of truth unto the island Patmos. And John speaks of the things concerning his testimony, not saying who condemned him . . '. and he seems to have beheld the Apocalypse in the island.'[2] Origen does not give the name of the Roman king, since, as he says, John does not tell us who condemned him. He certainly does not say that the Roman king was Domitian, indeed he is but repeating what Irenaeus had said before, who after discussing the meaning of ' the number of the Beast ' declares himself in doubt, 'for if it were necessary that his name should be declared clearly at the present time, it would have been announced by him who saw the vision.' But the enigma, which Irenaeus and Origen both left unsolved, is no longer sealed to us. In his

---

[1] Irenaeus, *Adv. Haer.* v. 30. 1-3; Eus. *Hist. Eccl.* iii. 18 and v. 8 : τοὔνομα αὐτοῦ δι' ἐκείνου ἂν ἐρρέθη, τοῦ καὶ τὴν ἀποκάλυψιν ἑωρακότος· οὐδὲ γὰρ πρὸ πολλοῦ χρόνου ἑωράθη, ἀλλὰ σχεδὸν ἐπὶ τῆς ἡμετέρας γενεᾶς, πρὸς τῷ τέλει τῆς Δομετιανοῦ ἀρχῆς. That John is the subject before ἑωράθη seems to follow necessarily from the words which precede in the same passage—μαρτυρούντων αὐτῶν ἐκείνων τῶν κατ' ὄψιν Ἰωάννην ἑωρακότων. . . .

[2] ὁ δὲ 'Ρωμαίων βασιλεύς, ὡς ἡ παράδοσις διδάσκει, κατεδίκασε τὸν Ἰωάννην μαρτυροῦντα διὰ τὸν τῆς ἀληθείας λόγον εἰς Πάτμον τὴν νῆσον· διδάσκει δὲ τὰ περὶ τοῦ μαρτυρίου αὐτοῦ Ἰωάννης, μὴ λέγων τίς αὐτὸν κατεδίκασε.

'Life and Principate of the Emperor Nero' Mr. Henderson writes 'The number of the Beast is now fairly generally admitted to be' Nero Caesar.[1] Eusebius, again, after speaking of Trajan succeeding Nerva in the Empire writes : 'About this time also, John, the beloved disciple of Jesus, at once Apostle and Evangelist, still surviving in Asia, supervised the Churches there, having returned from his banishment to the island after the death of Domitian.' He then refers to Clement of Alexandria and Irenaeus as his authorities. With Irenaeus we have already dealt. The words of Clement are : 'For when the tyrant was dead he (John) departed from the island of Patmos to Ephesus ; he also, when called upon, went to the neighbouring districts of the Gentiles, in some appointing bishops, in some organising entire Churches.'[2] But Clement does not say 'the tyrant' was Domitian, the name might with even greater propriety be applied to Nero.

The evidence of Victorinus and of Jerome next calls for notice. Victorinus, who suffered martyrdom in 303 A.D., is a pre-Eusebian witness to the tradition. In his commentary on the Apocalypse, which is the earliest extant, he writes 'When John saw these things, he was in the island Patmos, condemned to the mines by Domitian Caesar. There it was therefore that he saw the Apocalypse ; and when already the Elder had thought that he through his passion would receive acceptance, Domitian having been slain all his sentences were quashed and John, freed from the mines, then afterwards published this same Apocalypse, which he had received from God.'[3]   Jerome is still more explicit : 'In his fourteenth year when Domitian was stirring up the second persecution after Nero, John having been banished into the island Patmos wrote the Apocalypse . . . but when Domitian had been slain and his acts on account of their excessive cruelty repealed by the Senate in the reign of Nerva he returned to Ephesus.'[4]

[1] Henderson, *Life of Nero*, p. 440. See *infra*, p. 173.
[2] Eus. *Hist. Eccl.* iii. 23.   [3] Migne, *P.L.* v. 1665.
[4] *De Viris Illust.* 9.

Now the first comment I make on all these passages is, that one and all of these early Christian writers that I have quoted had no doubt that the author of the Apocalypse was John the Apostle, the son of Zebedee ; rightly or wrongly that was their belief, yet he is at the close of Domitian's reign condemned to exile in a lonely island as a criminal (to work in the mines according to Victorinus), and after his release by Nerva he returns to Ephesus, and as Clement of Alexandria (quoted by Eusebius) tells us—' he also when called upon went to the neighbouring districts of the Gentiles, in some appointing bishops, in others organising Churches &c. . . .' But John, son of Zebedee, must in the year 96 A.D. have been well-nigh a centenarian ; is it seriously contended that he at such an age could have survived the hardships of such an exile, even without the mines, or that he would have been able physically, had he survived, to have taken in hand in the reign of Nerva the organisation over a large area of the Churches in Asia and the neighbouring districts ? It is on the face of it absurd. The evidence for this late date is moreover, when critically examined, decidedly weak. It is extremely doubtful whether any of the three earliest authorities which refer to the exile at Patmos support it. Eusebius, as we have seen, read his own interpretation of the words of Irenaeus into the passages from Origen and Clement, neither of whom here names Domitian. Of the other two witnesses, however, Victorinus certainly did not write under the influence of Eusebius, and the similarity of his version of the tradition to that of Jerome seems to point to their common derivation from some documentary source, which connected the condemnation to Patmos and the subsequent release with the names of Domitian and Nerva. But, as I shall now proceed to show, a condemnation by Domitian and a release by Nerva is not merely not inconsistent with but is strongly confirmatory of the fact, attested so strongly by the internal evidence of the book, that the Apocalypse was written in the early part of the year 70 A.D.

Let us examine that portion of the internal evidence which chiefly concerns us in this lecture, the portion which reflects the events of contemporary history in the city of Rome.

In the seventeenth chapter of the Revelation ' the great city which reigneth over the kings of the earth ' is brought before us under the likeness of a woman seated on a scarlet-coloured beast with seven heads, which are explained to be seven hills, and on her forehead is written her name of Mystery—Babylon the Great, the Mother of Harlots and the Abominations of the Earth. On this woman drunken with the blood of the saints and with the blood of the martyrs of Jesus [1] judgment is pronounced. Again in the following chapter the Seer repeats this last indictment : ' And in her was found the blood of prophets and of saints and of all that were slain upon the earth.' [2] There are other passages of similar import, but these two are sufficient to make it clear that the writer is referring to the Neronian persecution with its multitude of victims, and not to that of Domitian, which was not a general persecution at all, but a series of isolated acts directed chiefly against a few influential persons, including members of his own family.

Again both in chapter xiv. 8, and chapter xviii. 2, an angel is represented as crying with a mighty voice ' Fallen, fallen is Babylon the Great,' and the lurid picture which is given of that fall is no mere effort of ecstatic imagination, it is the picture of a real event, fresh in the memory. As we read of the kings of the earth and the merchants of the earth standing afar off and weeping and lamenting for her, as they see the smoke of her burning, and crying out ' Alas, alas that great city Babylon, that mighty city ; for in one hour is thy judgment come,' and as we read again—' of the winepress of the wrath of God being trodden without the city and blood came out of the winepress even to the horses' bridles '—there is but one occasion in the whole

---

[1] Rev. xvii. 3-7, 9.
[2] Rev. xviii. 24. Compare vi. 9-11, 14, xiii. 15, xvi. 5-7.

of the first century to which such a description could be
applied : the writer had seen it with his own eyes—the
storming and burning of the Capitol by the foreign
mercenaries of Vitellius, and the subsequent capture and
sacking of the city by the infuriated Flavian army under
Mucianus and Antonius Primus on December 19 to 21,
69 A.D. At no other time, certainly not in the end of
Domitian's reign, was it possible to speak of Rome as
fallen, or for the Seer to have raised his triumphant cry
'Rejoice over her, thou heaven, and ye holy apostles
and prophets ; for God hath avenged you on her'
(Rev. xviii. 20).

The following passages from the 'Histories' of Tacitus,
if read side by side with the passages telling of the fall of
Babylon the Great in the Apocalypse, will carry conviction
that both writers are describing one and the same unique
event. Of the burning of the Capitol Tacitus writes :
'The fire extended itself to the porticoes adjoining the
temples ; soon the eagles that supported the cupola caught
fire, and as the timber was old they fed the flame. Thus
the Capitol . . . was burned to the ground. . . . From
the foundation of the city to that hour the Roman republic
had felt no calamity so deplorable, so shocking as that.'
And again of the capture of the city by the Flavian troops :
'The city exhibited one entire scene of ferocity and abomina-
tion. . . . Rivers of blood and heaps of bodies at the same
time ; and by the side of them harlots, and women that
differed not from harlots—all that unbridled passion can
suggest in the wantonness of peace—all the enormities that
are committed when a city is sacked by its relentless foes—
so that you could positively suppose that Rome was at
one and the same time frantic with rage and dissolved
in sensuality. . . . lamentation was heard from every
quarter, and Rome was filled with cries of despair and the
horrors of a city taken by storm.' [1] Well might they who
stood afar off as they saw the smoke of her burning and the

---

[1] Tac. *Hist.* iii. 72, 83, iv. 1.   Rev. xiv. 8, 17-20, xvii. 16, xviii.
passim.

terror of her torment exclaim ' Alas, alas that great city
Babylon, that mighty city; for in one hour is thy judgment
come.' [1] Even the description—' mother of harlots and
of the abominations of the earth '—what a realistic intensity
and force it gains, as the utterance of one who had seen
with his own eyes the scenes in the streets of Rome on those
terrible December days.

In the course of eighteen months four emperors had
perished and Italy had been the scene of continuous and
savage civil war. In consequence of the events just
described Vespasian became emperor, but at the opening
of the year 70 A.D. both he and his elder son Titus were
abroad, Vespasian in Egypt, Titus in Judaea. Domitian
was the sole representative of his family in Rome, and he
was at once presented to the people by the victorious
Flavian general, Mucianus, was saluted as Caesar, and
made praetor. His father and brother were appointed
consuls, but as they were absent, Domitian was invested
with full consular authority—*imperio consulari.* For six
months he in conjunction with Mucianus acted as regent,
administered public affairs, restored order and distributed
offices. His name, says Tacitus,[2] was placed at the head
of all despatches and edicts. Though but a boy of eighteen
his head became filled with ambitious ideas, and he began,
says Suetonius,[3] to use his power in so arbitrary a manner
as to give proof of what he was to become later. To such
an extent was this the case that Dion Cassius [4] tells us
that Vespasian wrote to him from Alexandria ' I am
much obliged to you, my son, for letting me still be emperor,
and for not having as yet deposed me.'

Such incendiary language as we find in the Apocalypse,
if used publicly, would at such a time soon bring down
upon the offenders the repressive arm of those charged
with the maintenance of order in the capital after the

---

[1] Rev. xviii. 10.
[2] Tac. *Hist.* iv. 3, 44–47, 51, 68; Josephus, *Bell. Iud.* iv. 11. 4.
[3] Suetonius, *Domitian*, 1.
[4] Dion Cassius, lxv. 22, lxvi. 1–3.

terrible experiences of the year 69 A.D. Tradition says
that John narrowly escaped martyrdom [1]; however this
may be, there is a high probability that his deportation
to Patmos took place very early in the year 70 A.D. (in
January or February) through a sentence passed in Domitian's name. In the month of June of that year Domitian
and Mucianus left Rome to take part in a campaign in
Gaul, and a little later Vespasian arrived in Rome and at
once assumed the direction of affairs.[2] Suetonius informs
us that from the beginning he was anxious to conduct
himself with great moderation and clemency.[3] One of
his first cares was to take in hand the administration of
justice, which had been sadly interrupted by the civil wars,
and to examine into the accumulation of law-suits which
had arisen, and to provide for the restitution of what had
been seized by violence in the disorders of the time. Now
Vespasian associated Titus with himself in the government
in the course of the year 71 A.D. and was very jealous during
the whole of his reign of allowing authority to be vested
in any but members of his own family. But Vespasian
took as his colleague in the consulship in 71 A.D. M. Cocceius
Nerva. Now Nerva—the future emperor—was the representative of a family distinguished for three generations
as jurists, and no doubt his appointment at this particular
time was due to Vespasian's desire to have a skilled lawyer
at his side for dealing with the mass of sentences of exile
and of confiscation which were the legacy of the successive
revolutions. Nerva held office during the first *nundinum*
of 71 A.D., and it is permissible to believe that in accordance
with tradition one of the sentences quashed by him was
that which sent John to Patmos. If by an order of Nerva

[1] Tertullian (*Praescrip.* 36), after speaking of the martyrdoms of
Peter and Paul, relates that John was cast into burning oil but escaped
unhurt. Jerome in his commentary on Matt. xx. 23 refers to the same
tradition. Whatever the grounds of the tradition, there can be no
question that the writer of the Apocalypse speaks of himself 'as a
partaker in the tribulation.'
[2] Gsell, *Règne de l'Empéreur Domitien*, pp. 13-14.
[3] Suetonius, *Vespasian*, 8, 10.

he were now released, his exile would have lasted almost exactly one year.[1]

The external evidence, which was supposed to be adverse to the acceptance of the early date for the writing of the Apocalypse, having thus been transformed into an argument in its favour, we will now proceed by a further examination of certain crucial passages of the book to make assurance on this matter doubly sure.

[The opening verses of chapter xi. imply that the Temple of Jerusalem was still standing, and that there was no expectation of the destruction of the Shrine itself.] But the outer court was to be given to the nations, who for a period represented by 42 months would trample it under foot.[2] [This statement must have been made at the time when the legions of Titus were already closing round Jerusalem and its doom was sealed, but before it was known that the desperate character of the defence would carry with it the entire destruction of the city and its world-famous sanctuary. [That Jerusalem was not destroyed when the words (xi. 8) were written—' their dead bodies lie in the street of the Great City, which spiritually is called Sodom and Egypt, where also their Lord was crucified '— is evident. In 95 A.D. the city was in ruins.

The central theme of the Apocalypse is the struggle between Christ and Antichrist, between Christianity and the Imperial World-Power of Rome. To St. John the Roman World-Power is Antichrist and both of them are personified by Nero. The baleful figure of Nero dominates the entire picture of the struggle between the forces of good and evil.

---

[1] Gsell, 17–18. C.I.L. vi. 1984. In the ten years from 70 to 79, Vespasian filled the office of [ordinary] consul nine times, Titus seven times, Domitian once. Domitian was *consul suffectus* five times during the same period. In 80 Titus and Domitian were consuls. For complete list see Bouché-Leclerc, *Institutions Romaines*, p. 603. For Nerva and his father and grandfather, see Profumo, *Le fonti ed i tempi dello Incendio Neroniano*, p. 511 ff. Pauly, *Real-Encyclopädie*, under Cocceius.

[2] Rev. xi. 1, 2. See Daniel, vii. 25, three and a half years or 42 months. [It is the time of the duration of the Fourth Kingdom or Roman Empire.]

The wild beast,[1] coming up out of the sea with its seven heads and ten horns, and the imagery connected with it, was suggested to the Seer by the apocalyptic visions of Daniel vii., the fourth kingdom of Daniel being identified by him with the Roman Empire. The name of the beast [2] is expressed by a number—' the number of a man '—and the number is Six Hundred and Sixty-Six. Irenaeus discusses the meaning of this number which concealed the name of Antichrist, and already when he wrote his treatise ' Against Heresies ' in 180 A.D. the key had been lost. And he is puzzled by the fact that he found in some MSS. the number 616 instead of 666—one such MS. exists still—and he supposes it due to the error of copyists. But there is a solution now generally accepted, and whose correctness this very variant reading actually confirms. For if the Greek spelling of Nero Caesar be transliterated into Hebrew and the numerical values of the Hebrew letters added together they make 666. If however the Latin spelling be treated in the same way, the total comes to 616. Nero then was Antichrist, and the interpretation of the seven heads, the ten horns and the other symbolic imagery of this portion of the Apocalypse must be approached from the point of view that they all belong to the Neronian period. St. John was not an historian, his mind was stored with the language and ideas of Daniel and Ezekiel and other Apocalyptic writers,

[1] Rev. xiii. 1. At a short distance from Patmos the island of *Thera* or ' the Wild Beast ' rises out of the sea.

[2] Rev. xiii. 18. Irenaeus, *cont. Haer.* v. 30. C. 11 gives the reading 616. In Philostratus, *Apollonius of Tyana*, Apollonius is represented as saying on his arrival at Rome—' In my travels, which have been wider than ever man yet accomplished, I have seen many, many wild beasts of Arabia and India ; but this beast, which is commonly called a Tyrant, I know not how many heads it has, nor if it be crooked of claw, and armed with horrible fangs. However they say it is a civil beast and inhabits the midst of cities ; but to this extent it is more savage than the beasts of mountain and of forest, that whereas lions and panthers can sometimes by flattery be tamed and change their disposition, stroking and petting this beast does but instigate it to surpass itself in ferocity and devour at large. And of wild beasts you cannot say that they were ever known to eat their own mothers, but Nero has gorged himself on this diet.'— Phillimore's tr. vol. ii. p. 38.

who had preceded him ; and his own Apocalypse was but one out of a number of Jewish or Judaeo-Christian Apocalypses of the first century, with some of which he shows himself to be acquainted. Nevertheless in all that he writes there is a distinctive historical background, and it is limited to what he himself knew of the actual contact of Christianity with the Imperial power at Rome : a contact which began in the days of Claudius and which had issued in the reign of Nero in a conflict for life and death, which was still undecided. Indeed I may go further and say that it is only when the Apocalypse is treated historically as a Neronian document that any satisfactory interpretation can be found for the imagery of certain difficult passages. For example, nothing is more remarkable in the years which followed Nero's death than the belief that gained firm possession of the popular imagination, that the Emperor was not really dead, but that he had fled to the East and would speedily reappear and once more possess himself of power. In 69 A.D. a false Nero was put to death in the island of Cythnus, and twenty years later another Nero pretender raised a revolt in Asia.[1] The Christian Sibylline Oracles are evidence as to the character and prevalence of this Nero legend in the reign of Vespasian,[2] and the re-

---

[1] Henderson's *Life and Principate of Nero*, p. 440. Tac. *Hist.* ii. 8 : ' vario super exitu eius rumore eoque pluribus vivere eum fingentibus credentibusque.' Sueton. *Nero*, 57 : ' edicta quasi viventis et brevi magno inimicorum malo reversuri.' The pretender of 69 A.D., driven by stress of weather to the island of Cythnus, was taken by Calpurnius Asprenas, Governor of Galatia, and put to death. Tac. *Hist.* ii. 8, 9. Dion Cassius, lxiv. 9 ; also Tac. *Hist.* i. 2 : ' mota prope etiam Parthorum arma falsi Neronis ludibrio.'

[2] *Sibylline Oracles*, v. 143-147, 361-373. This portion of the *Sibylline Oracles* was written 71-74 A.D.: so Bousset, Zahn and Charles.

> Φεύξεται ἐκ Βαβυλῶνος [Rome] ἄναξ φοβερὸς καὶ ἀναιδής
> ὃν πάντες στυγέουσι βροτοὶ καὶ φῶτες ἄριστοι·
> ὤλεσε γὰρ πολλοὺς καὶ γαστέρι χεῖρας ἐφῆκεν.   143-5.

> ἥξει δ' ἐκ περάτων γαίης μητροκτόνος ἀνὴρ
> ὃς πᾶσαν γαῖαν καθελεῖ καὶ πάντα κρατήσει.   363-4.

See also iv. 119-122, 137-139 ; this part of the *Sibylline Oracles* is dated about 80 A.D. See also *Ascension of Isaiah*, iv. 2-4. It is of importance to notice, says Dr. Charles in his note on this passage, that the persecution under Nero is the only one known to the writer (p. 25).

ferences to it in the Apocalypse are a proof of the strong
impression which it had made upon the writer. In the
thirteenth chapter, after describing the beast with its seven
heads and ten horns, St. John proceeds : ' and I saw one
of his heads as though it had been smitten unto death ;
and his death-stroke was healed ' ; and in chapter xvii.
verses 7, 8, he writes ' I will tell thee the mystery of
the woman, and of the beast that carrieth her, which hath
the seven heads and the ten horns. The beast that thou
sawest was, and is not ; and is about to come up out of
the abyss, and goeth into perdition.' Then a few verses
further on comes the passage which has caused so much
trouble to commentators, in no small measure because they
allow themselves to wander out of a strictly limited field
of investigation—i.e. the Neronian cycle. St. John says
(verses 9–12) 'The seven heads are seven mountains, on which
the woman sitteth : and they are seven kings ; the five
are fallen, the one is, the other is not yet come ; and when
he cometh, he must continue a little while. And the beast
that was, and is not, is himself also an eighth, and is of the
seven ; and he goeth into perdition.' Now the key to this
passage is found as soon as it is recognised that it deals
with no other period of Roman history than that which
I have called ' the Neronian cycle '—the period during
which the Church and the Empire, Christ and Antichrist,
were first brought face to face as forces irreconcilably
opposed. For note that throughout Nero is not merely
one of the seven heads, he is identified with the Beast
itself.[1] In one passage (xiii. 3) he is the head that ' was
smitten unto death and his wound was healed,' in another
(xiii. 14) ' the beast that had the wound of a sword and did
live,' and again (xvii. 8) the beast ' that was, and is not, and
yet is.' Now the words ' five are fallen ' ($\check{\epsilon}\pi\epsilon\sigma\alpha\nu$) imply
that in each of these five cases there was a violent death

---

[1] Rev. xi. 7 : ' And when they shall have finished their testimony the
beast that cometh up out of the abyss shall make war with them, and
overcome them, and kill them.' Dr. Charles in the Introduction to the
Ascension of Isaiah (p. lxiv) makes the following comment on this passage :
' The Antichrist in this instance makes his advent *in Jerusalem* (see v. 8),
therefore before 70 A.D.'

Augustus and Tiberius could not be described as 'fallen,' even had their reigns come within the Seer's purview. The five are Claudius, who adopted Nero as his son and heir, Nero himself, Galba, Otho, and Vitellius. 'The one who is' signifies the man for the moment invested with imperial power, Domitian, the acting Emperor, who banished the writer. 'The one not yet come' is the real Emperor Vespasian, who had not yet arrived at Rome to take into his hands the reins of government, and 'he will continue only a short while,' for Nero—'the beast that was, and is not, who is also an eighth, and is of the seven'—will quickly return from the East whither he had fled, and once more seat himself on the throne. And 'his end is perdition,' for after his return will immediately follow the great struggle between Christ and Antichrist, when the latter will be overthrown and cast alive into the lake of fire.[1]   Again 'the ten horns with ten diadems,' of chapter xiii. verse 1, are generally considered to be the governors of the chief provinces of the Empire, and this is borne out by the reference to them in chapter xvii. verses 12–13: 'And the ten horns that thou sawest are ten kings, which have received no kingdom as yet, but they receive authority as kings, with the beast, for one hour'; and then a few verses lower 'and the ten horns that thou sawest, and the beast, these shall hate the harlot, and shall make her desolate and naked, and shall eat her flesh, and burn her utterly with fire.'   Is there not a direct reference here to the events of the two preceding years?   The revolt of Vindex was the signal for the overthrow of Nero. The armies of Galba, Otho, Vitellius, and Vespasian in succession occupied Rome, and the imperial city was held in subjection by foreign troops, sacked, and its most sacred edifices burnt. All these five men were governors of provinces.

Lastly it seems to me impossible to dissociate the gathering together of the nations to battle at Armageddon, 'the nations which are in the four corners of the earth, Gog and Magog, to gather them together to the war, the number

[1] Rev. xix. 20.

of whom is as the sand of the sea,[1] from the actual gathering of the nations in those battles near Bedriacum which had taken place in the year 69.] Gog and Magog had come to signify in the Apocalyptic literature the uncivilised tribes of the earth, and surely if ever Armageddon was realised in the history of the world it was in that second battle of Bedriacum ending in the sack of Cremona in which the armies of Vitellius and Vespasian contended for the mastery. On the one side were troops from Italy, Spain and Portugal, Gaul, the German Rhine frontier, even from far distant Batavia and Britain ; on the other, legions from the Danube frontier, and behind these the armies of Syria, Judaea and Egypt, with auxiliaries from the furthermost East, from the borderlands of the Euphrates and Tigris.[2] The Seer is not describing these battles, but he saw the medley of troops from every nation under heaven actually fighting in the streets of Rome, and the scenes he witnessed still so freshly imprinted in his mind are vividly reflected in the imagery of his vision.

Renan[3] has pointed out in his well-known work ' L'Anté-christ ' that the portents, scourges, and convulsions of nature which in the Apocalypse follow upon the opening of the seals, the blowing of the trumpets, and the emptying of the vials were far from being merely imaginative. The years that preceded 70 A.D. were years marked by every kind of disaster and catastrophe. Earthquakes were frequent and violent, especially in that part of Asia to which John addressed his seven letters.[4] The great pestilence at Rome in 65 A.D. was followed by a wild hurricane, which laid waste the Campagna.[5] All sorts of portents were said to have foreshadowed the death of Nero in 68 A.D. and the succession of political convulsions that followed.[6] This same year 68

---

[1] Rev. xvi. 14–16, xx. 8.

[2] Henderson, *Civil War in the Roman Empire*, pp. 21–35, 128–144.

[3] Renan, *L'Antéchrist*, pp. 327–329.

[4] Tac. *Ann.* xiv. 13, 27 ; Suet. *Nero*, 20 ; Philostratus, *Apollonius*, vi. 38, 41 ; Seneca, *Quaest. Nat.* vi. 1 : ' Mundus ipse concutitur . . . consternatio omnium ' ; *Sibyll. Orac.* iii. 471 ff.

[5] Tac. *Ann.* xvi. 13 ; Suet. *Nero*, 39.

[6] Tac. *Ann.* xv. 47 ; *Hist.* i. 18, 86 ; Dion Cassius, lxiii. 26.

was marked by a famine at Rome,[1] the year 69 by a very disastrous inundation of the Tiber.[2] It was no wonder that a visionary mystic like St. John should have perceived the signs of the consummation of all things in such a series of catastrophes, political and physical. ⌠Surely there could not be a more convincing piece of circumstantial evidence for fixing the date of the book. ⌡

Moveover as the Seer in the island of Patmos sat brooding over and recording his visions, before his very eyes there was a spectacle which has left its traces upon his language. ⌠The volcano in the neighbouring island of Thera was in violent activity during the greater part of the first century, after which it had a long period of quiescence until 726 A.D.⌡ No one can read a number of passages in the Apocalypse [3] without feeling that the writer must have been the witness of a volcanic eruption on a grand scale, and there are other passages which point to familiarity with such scenes. Now the very remarkable fact stands recorded, that on two separate occasions, in 196 B.C. and in 46 A.D., so extraordinary was the violence of the eruptive forces in the very neighbourhood of this island that new islands came into existence, whose modern names still recall the character of their origin. A vivid description is given by Strabo of the eruption of 196 B.C. : ' Midway between Thera and Therasia flames rushed forth from the sea, causing the whole of it to boil and be on fire, and afterwards an island, twelve stadia in circumference, composed of the burning mass was thrown up as if raised by machinery.' [4] ⌠Compare with this the language of Rev. viii. 8, 9 : ' and the second angel sounded, and as it were a great mountain burning with fire was cast into the sea : and the third part of the

---

[1] Suet. Nero, 45 ; Sibyll. Orac. iii. 475 ff.
[2] Tac. Hist. i. 86 ; Plutarch, Otho, 4.
[3] Rev. vi. 12-17, viii. 5-9, xvi. 3, 18, 20, 21.
[4] See Pauly, Real-Encyclopädie under ' Thera.'   The name of the island described by Strabo as thrown up was Hiera, now Nea Kaumeni ; that thrown up in 46 A.D. Theia, now Mikra Kaumeni. Seneca, Nat. Quaest. vi. 21 ; Dion Cassius, lx. 29 ; Orosius, vii. 6.   The modern name of Thera is Santorin (a corruption of St. Irene), see Encyclopaedia Britannica (ed. 1911) under ' Santorin.'

sea became blood ; and the third part of the creatures that
were in the sea and had life died, and the third part of the
ships were destroyed.'   All these graphic touches are such
as we should expect from a writer who had actually resided
in a group of islands where such catastrophic convulsions
had recently taken place. There was an eruption in Thera
in 60 A.D., and the following decade was marked by continued
seismic and volcanic disturbances.

LECTURE VII

I Cor. i. 10 : 'Now I beseech you, brethren, by the name of our Lord Jesus Christ that ye all speak the same thing, that there be no divisions among you.'

BEFORE proceeding to the consideration of that earliest official document of the Roman Church commonly known as the 'First Epistle of Clement to the Corinthians,' some reference should be made to the order of the episcopal succession in that Church. It is only necessary to touch upon it briefly here, for it has been treated so fully and thoroughly by many writers that it appears sufficient to state the conclusion arrived at and generally accepted, viz. that the order of names is that given by Irenaeus, Linus, Anencletus or Cletus, Clemens, and that the traditional terms assigned to their episcopates, Linus twelve years, Anencletus twelve years, and Clemens nine years, are approximately correct. If Linus became bishop in 68 A.D. this would make the close of the episcopate of Clemens to coincide with the first year of the second century.[1]

As to the exact character of the office that they held, and of the organisation of the Church during these decades, there has been much difference of opinion, and from lack of the necessary material to clear up doubtful points such difference of opinion will probably always continue to exist. The constitution of the Mother Church of Jerusalem after 42 A.D. seems to have followed strictly the Jewish model, James and the elders or presbyters corresponding to the

---

[1] Lightfoot, *Apost. Fathers*, part i. vol. i. pp. 63-7, 79-81. The whole subject is exhaustively discussed and examined in his Excursus No. 5, pp. 201-345, on the 'Early Roman Succession,' see *supra*, pp. 70, 71 ; and p. 84, note 3.

High Priest and the Sanhedrin.[1] The position of James was undoubtedly monarchical, but there is no strict analogy between his position and that of the Christian bishop of the time of Ignatius. James's position was exceptional. His authority, derived at once from near relationship to the Lord and from his own lofty personal character, placed him on a level with the acknowledged leaders of the Twelve. He ranked with Peter and John, as one of the pillars of the Church.[2] But just as the earliest local organisation of the Church at Jerusalem followed the Jewish model that was at its side, so did that of the Christian communities which sprang into being among the *Diaspora*. There is no hint given that the presbyters that were ordained in every city were officials of a type unknown to the Synagogue.[3] Each Christian *ecclesia* like each Jewish synagogue had its presbyters, and in large cities, like Rome, as there were a number of distinct synagogues, so there were several distinct Christian congregations or Churches, such as the Church in the house of Aquila and Prisca. In so far as there was a new departure, it lay in the fact that the Christian presbyter was a spiritual as well as an administrative official. Little as we are told in the New Testament on the subject, the picture drawn in the Apocalypse of the four and twenty presbyters seated round the throne of God and taking the leading part in the worship of Heaven seems to place this beyond reasonable question.

But though the original model of Christian organisation was the Synagogue, more and more as the Gentile element increased and became predominant would the separate congregations or *ecclesiae* gradually acquire Gentile characteristics, derived from the constitution of the various associations for religious cults and other purposes, known as *collegia*, *sodalitates*, θίασοι or ἔρανοι, which, with the licence or at least the connivance of the state, were to be

---

[1] Harnack, *Constitution and Law of the Church*, p. 34.

[2] Gal. ii. 9; also i. 19, and ii. 12.

[3] Hort, *Christian Ecclesia*, pp. 62-3; Lightfoot, *Philippians*, pp. 191-2.

found in every part of the empire.[1] The choice, for instance, by the early Christians of the word *ecclesia* in preference to *synagoge* was probably deliberate. ⌐Both words are used in the LXX, *ecclesia* as the translation of the Hebrew *Qātal* signifying a religious assembly, *synagoge* as that of the Hebrew word *ēdhāh*, a general assembly of the whole people.⌐The adoption of the term *ecclesia*, says Harnack, ' was the happiest stroke which the primitive (Christian) community accomplished in the way of descriptive titles.'[2] Its choice was at once distinctive and would have familiar associations to Gentile ears.

So, too, with the term *episcopus*. This word in the sense of ' overseer ' occurs many times in the LXX, and its ecclesiastical use was probably suggested by familiarity with certain passages in this Greek version of the Old Testament, which was the only Scriptures with which the vast majority of the early Christians were acquainted.[3] But again it must not be forgotten that the name would be the more readily adopted by Greek-speaking Christians of Gentile origin, since it was already well known as the title of officials engaged in secular duties, as Overseers or Superintendents. When it first passed into Christian use is unknown⌐but its earliest appearance is in the remarkable words addressed by St. Paul to the presbyters of the Ephesian Church, whom he had summoned to meet him at Miletus as he was journeying to Jerusalem in 57 A.D. ' Take heed to yourselves and to all the flock in which the Holy Spirit set you as overseers (ἐπισκόπους) to shepherd (ποιμαίνειν) the Church of God, which He purchased with His Blood.'[4] Here we find certain presbyters described

[1] Hardy, *Studies in Roman History*, ' Christianity and the Collegia,' pp. 129-43.
[2] Schürer, *Hist. of the Jewish People*, 2 Div., vol. ii. pp. 59 ff.; Harnack, *Const. and Law*, pp. 15-6 ; Hort, *Christ. Eccl.* pp. 3-18.
[3] Such passages as Ps. cviii. (cix.) 8, quoted by St. Peter, Acts, i. 20, and Ezekiel, xxxiv. 11, or again Is. lx. 17, as quoted by Clement of Rome, xlii. 5 : καταστήσω τοὺς ἐπισκόπους αὐτῶν ἐν δικαιοσύνῃ καὶ τοὺς διακόνους αὐτῶν ἐν πίστει.
[4] Acts, xx. 28. See Hort, *Christ. Eccl.* pp. 97-104 ; Harnack, *Const. and Law*, p. 53. Among the numerous works on the subject of the early

as 'overseers' and their special function as that of shepherding or tending the flock, implying that in the local organisation of the Church their duty was not only that of government, guidance, and discipline, but of the provision of spiritual food. Again in the Epistle to the Philippians St. Paul salutes 'the saints in Christ Jesus with the overseers and deacons.' Turning to the Pastoral Epistles we have the qualifications set forth carefully, which should guide Timothy and Titus in their choice of persons fit for the Church's official ministry.[1] From these instructions two facts seem to come out clearly: that while all *episcopi* were presbyters, only a limited number of the presbyters were *episcopi*. In other words these titles cannot be used convertibly. An *episcopus*, or presbyter-bishop if one may so style him, differed from the ordinary presbyter in that he had certain superadded duties of oversight and superintendence such as were connoted by his name. There is a spiritual side to his office: he must be 'apt to teach,' 'able to exhort in the sound doctrine and to convict the gainsayers'; and a business or administrative side: 'he must be blameless, as God's steward.'[2] The language of St. Peter, 'Ye were as sheep going astray but are now returned to the Shepherd and Bishop of your souls,'[3] while

organisation of the Christian Church are the following: Hatch's well-known and most important *Bampton Lectures* of 1881; also his *Hibbert Lectures* of 1888, 'The Influence of Greek Ideas and Usages upon the Christian Church' [edited by Dr. Fairbairn and published 1907]; Sohm, *Kirchenrecht*, 1892; Michiel, *Les Origines de l'épiscopat*, 1900; Knopf, *Das Nachapostolische Zeitalter*, 1906; Batiffol, *L'Eglise naissante et le Catholicisme*, 1909; Gwatkin (articles in Hastings's *Dictionary*) 'Bishops,' 'Church Government,' &c.

[1] Comp. 1 Tim. iii. 2 with v. 17 and Titus, i. 7.

[2] 1 Tim. iii. 2; Titus, i. 7, 9: δεῖ γὰρ τὸν ἐπίσκοπον ἀνέγκλητον εἶναι, ὡς Θεοῦ οἰκονόμον.

[3] The words of St. Peter deserve careful consideration. In 1 Peter ii. 25 the Apostle writes: Ἦτε γὰρ ὡς πρόβατα πλανώμενοι· ἀλλ' ἐπεστράφητε νῦν ἐπὶ τὸν ποιμένα καὶ ἐπίσκοπον τῶν ψυχῶν ὑμῶν. The Shepherd here, whose office is described by the additional term ἐπίσκοπος (note there is only one article), being the Good Shepherd Himself, the Lord Jesus Christ, of Whom all earthly ποίμενες καὶ ἐπίσκοποι were the delegates and representatives. Can it be doubted that the Apostle had here in his mind his Master's

it seems to point to an equivalence of the two terms
Shepherd and Bishop—*pastor* and *episcopus*—no less
significantly marks out the sphere of duty—as the pastorate
of souls. That it was possible to be a presbyter without
having a specific local charge, just in the same way as in
modern days there are priests without cure of souls, seems
to be conveyed in another passage of this epistle, where
St. Peter addresses the presbyters, as their fellow presbyter,
exactly as St. John at a later date styled himself simply ' the
presbyter ' in the opening salutation of his second and third
Epistles, and indeed it was as John *the Presbyter* that he
was best known in his old age.[1] Certainly neither Peter
nor John was a local official. The whole passage runs as
follows : ' the presbyters therefore among you I exhort
who am your fellow-presbyter . . . tend (shepherd) the
flock of God which is among you, exercising the oversight
(acting as *episcopi*) not of constraint but willingly like
God ; nor yet for filthy lucre, but of a ready mind ; neither
as lording it over your allotted charges,[2] but making yourselves ensamples to the flock.' The presbyters therefore
who were addressed were presbyter-bishops, and it may be
gathered they had each of them a separate cure, over which
they had independent spiritual rule, and moreover that they

commission so emphatically and lovingly repeated Ποίμαινε τὰ πρόβατά
μοῦ—βόσκε τὰ προβάτιά μου ? A very interesting passage is that at the
opening of the fifth chapter of this same First Epistle of St. Peter, *vv.* 1, 2 :
Πρεσβυτέρους οὖν ἐν ὑμῖν παρακαλῶ ὁ συμπρεσβύτερος . . . ποιμάνατε τὸ ἐν
ὑμῖν ποίμνιον τοῦ Θεοῦ [Comp. Acts, xx. 28] ἐπισκοποῦντες. This last word
is not found in Aleph and B, possibly omitted for ecclesiastical reasons.
Consult the excellent notes of Bigg's commentary on ii. 25 and v. 1, 2
(Int. Crit. Commentary Series), pp. 149–50, 182–8.

[1] 2 John, *v.* 1 ; 3 John, *v.* 1. For the identity of John the son of
Zebedee, the Apostle, with John the Presbyter—see Chapman's *John
the Presbyter*. This writer's arguments go to the very root of the
question.

[2] μηδ' ὡς κατακυριεύοντες τῶν κλήρων. The word κλήρων is ambiguous,
but its most natural interpretation is that of separate allotted charges or
cures, otherwise the expression κατακυριεύοντες would be unmeaning.
Dr. Bigg (*Commentary on* 1 *Peter*, p. 189) remarks that St. Paul warns the
presbyter-bishop that he is to be ' no striker ' (1 Tim. iii. 3 ; Tit. i. 7) and
that this implies that discipline in a congregation, many of whom were
converted slaves, might be roughly administered.

received stipends, otherwise it would not have been necessary to warn them against the danger of seeking after
filthy lucre. It will be at once seen how appropriate is
the name of ' rulers ' which is applied to these officers of
the Church in the Epistle to the Hebrews. The exhortation ' obey your rulers and submit to them ; for they watch
in behalf of your souls, as they that shall give account ' [1]
at once emphasises the authority which, as we have seen,
these presbyter-bishops exercised, and likewise defines the
double sphere of their jurisdiction and the two aspects
of their office, as at once ' shepherds of souls ' and ' God's
stewards.'

Thus after the martyrdom of the Apostles Peter and
Paul such evidence as we possess points to the government
of the Church in Rome passing into the hands of that inner
committee of the presbyterate consisting of those who had
spiritual charge of the several congregations or domestic
Churches in the capital. At their head we find a president,
either elected or chosen by seniority of office, bearing the
title of The Bishop, but at first differing in no way from the
other presbyter-bishops except in precedence, as *primus
inter pares.*

The analogy between the earliest Christian organisation
and that of the Synagogue has already been pointed out.
The presbyters ordained by the Apostles from city to city
were to a certain extent the Christian counterparts of the
Jewish presbyters, but, as the Christian Church had no
Temple and no priestly caste entrusted with the conduct
of sacrificial worship, the Christian presbyter differed from
the Jewish in that his functions were not merely administrative but spiritual and liturgical. In the same way the
government of the Church by a committee of presbyter-
bishops representing the several congregations with a
Bishop-president at their head was analogous to that of
cities like Alexandria, in which the Jewish population was

[1] Heb. xiii. 17 ; also xiii. 7 and 24. Twice in Clement (1 *Cor.* i. 3 and
xxi. 6) are the ἡγούμενοι and the πρεσβύτεροι distinguished from one another,
i.e. there was an inner committee of presbyter-bishops.

large, where the government was entrusted to a *gerousia* or
committee of *archons* representing the several synagogues,
whose president bore the name of *Gerousiarch*.[1] The
contention of Dr. Hatch in his Bampton Lectures that the
Christian presbyters were purely administrative and judicial
officers is not, as we have shown, borne out by a careful
examination of the scriptural references to their functions,
nor is the supposed evidence of the ' Didache ' to the existence in the latter part of the first century of a hierarchy of
Apostles, Prophets and Teachers, whose authority was
supreme in spiritual matters and to whom the presbyters
and deacons were subordinate, really tenable. Notably to
the Prophet a lofty position is assigned in the ' Didache,'
especially in the conduct of worship and in the celebration
of the Eucharist.[2] The discovery of this work and its first
publication in 1883 has had an immense influence in mould-
ing the opinions of recent writers on the early organisation
of the Church, particularly those of Harnack,[3] but it may
be asked what proof is there that its picture of first-century
Church life and order is trustworthy? We have indeed the
witness of many passages in the Acts and Epistles to the
fact that the prophet with his peculiar charismatic gift of
ecstatic (chiefly eschatological) utterance occupied a prominent place in the early Christian communities, but these
passages also testify not merely that the prophet, as such,
had no definite place in Church organisation, but that his
influence was intermittent and even spasmodic, and that,
at Corinth for instance, he might be a disturbing factor in
the assemblies, an element, to use St. Paul's words, ' of

---

[1] The analogy is made the more complete by the fact that the Greek title
ἄρχων was the equivalent of a Hebrew word signifying ' shepherd.' See
Schürer, *Hist. of the Jewish People*, 2 Div., vol. ii. pp. 59ff, 247ff. In the
inscriptions in the Jewish cemeteries at Rome the titles ' archon ' and
' gerousiarch ' are frequent. ' Presbyter ' has according to Schürer never
been found.

[2] *Didache*, x. 7, xiii. 3, xv. 1, 2.

[3] Harnack, *Expansion of Christianity*, vol. i. pp. 407 ff. ; *Constitution
and Law of the Church*, p. 78 ff. ; *Die Lehre der Zwölf Apostel* [*Texte und
Untersuchungen*, ii. 1, 2, pp. 193–241] ; *Chronologie*, pp. 428–38.

confusion rather than of peace.' [1] The truth is that there are very cogent reasons for holding the 'Didache' to be a fourth-century document, whose author in his presentation of first-century Christianity drew largely upon his imagination.[2] It is not wise therefore to base any arguments or theories about the true character of the earliest organisation of the Church upon a writing whose date is very disputable and whose origin and sources are unknown.

Leaving therefore the 'Didache' on one side let us now try to supplement the evidence as to the state of the Church in Rome and elsewhere about 68 A.D. that has been gathered from the canonical books of the New Testament, evidence that on the face of it is very incomplete and obscure,

---

[1] See especially 1 Cor. xiv. *passim*, also xii. 28, 29 ; and Eph. ii. 20, iii. 5, iv. 11. The passages which the author of the *Didache* had chiefly in his mind were no doubt 1 Cor. xii. 28, where St. Paul writes ' God hath set some in the Church, first apostles, secondly prophets, thirdly teachers,' and Eph. iv. 11 : ' He gave some apostles, and some prophets, and some evangelists, and some pastors and teachers.' Hort remarks (*Christian Ecclesia*, pp. 157–61) ' much profitless labour has been spent on trying to force the various terms used into meaning so many different ecclesiastical offices. Not only is the feat impossible, but the attempt carries us away from St. Paul's purpose, which is to show how many different functions are those which God has assigned to the different members of a single body . . . ; these passages give us practically no evidence respecting the formal arrangements of the *ecclesiae* of that age ; though they tell us much of the forms of activity that were at work within them.' Dr. Bigg's account of New Testament prophets and prophecy in his Introduction to 1 *Peter*, pp. 43–48, is clear and illuminating. He comments on the fact that in 1 Peter there is no allusion to Christian prophecy. For the ' prophet ' in sub-Apostolic times and in the *Didache* see his introduction to the *Doctrine of the Twelve Apostles*, pp. 28–38.

[2] In Dr. Bigg's *Doctrine of the Twelve Apostles* (Early Church Classics, S.P.C.K., 1898) just referred to, he gives a series of reasons for holding this document to have been written early in the fourth century. More recently in the *Journal of Theological Studies*, April 1912, Dean Armitage Robinson announces his adhesion to Dr. Bigg's view as to a probable late date for the *Didache*. The author, he argues, was trying to represent the state of the Church in accordance with what he thought to be the Apostles' teaching, not as it was in his own days. His description is not derived from contemporary knowledge. See also an article in the same journal, October 1911, by Rev. A. S. Duncan Jones, on ' The Nature of the Church,' in which the writer criticises the views of Harnack and of Sohm on the constitution of the early Church.

by an examination of two works both of them Roman and at one time regarded as almost canonical, I mean the (so-called) 'First Epistle of Clement to the Corinthians' and ' The Shepherd of Hermas.' These writings with the Epistles of Ignatius are first-class authorities, but clearly much depends upon a knowledge of the date of their first appearance. [That of Ignatius' epistles has been determined within very narrow limits, 107 to 109 A.D.] The notice about Hermas in the Muratorian fragment and the Liberian catalogue is, as I shall attempt to show later, most probably a blunder. [The date of Clement's Epistle was at one time regarded as uncertain, but since the publication of Lightfoot's great work on the Apostolic Fathers, the opinion of scholars has become practically unanimous that it was written at the close of the reign of Domitian, about 96 A.D] ; indeed this date may be regarded as one of the ' accepted results' of present-day criticism. I feel therefore how very bold it is on my part to venture even to hint at a difference of view. I have never however been able to convince myself that this ' accepted result ' is correct, and I welcome the opportunity afforded me by these lectures for stating my reasons for doubting the soundness of the arguments on which it is based.

Of the authenticity of the anonymous epistle which opens with the words [1] ' the Church of God sojourning in Rome to the Church of God sojourning in Corinth ' or of the accuracy of the early, continuous, and widespread tradition, which assigned the actual authorship to that Clement who in the earliest lists of the bishops of Rome stands the third in order from the Apostles, there is absolutely no question.[2]   The patristic evidence is conclusive, and is admitted as such. But the corollary to this postulate, that because Clement was the author therefore the epistle was written during the time of his episcopate, 92 to 101 A.D.,

---

[1] ἡ ἐκκλησία τοῦ Θεοῦ ἡ παροικοῦσα Ῥώμην τῇ ἐκκλησίᾳ τοῦ Θεοῦ τῇ παροικούσῃ Κόρινθον.

[2] Eus. *Hist. Eccl.* iii. 16, 37.   The epistle is called by Eusebius μεγάλη, θαυμασία, ἀνωμολογημένη παρὰ πᾶσιν.

does not follow. Nevertheless the assumption has been made with surprising unanimity, and it has led to the date at which this letter was sent to Corinth being assigned to the time when the Church found deliverance from the persecution of Domitian by that tyrant's assassination. Nay, to such an extent has this pre-supposition gained possession of the mind even of a writer like Bishop Lightfoot, so eminently careful and cautious in the handling of historical evidence, that in his criticism of the chronology of the early Roman succession, he writes ' The date of Clement's epistle is fixed with a fair degree of certainty at 95 or 96 A.D., *as it was written during or immediately after the persecution under Domitian.* This year therefore must fall within the episcopate of Clement.' [1] But surely this is something like arguing in a circle, for I venture to say that there does not exist any definite evidence, internal or external, that the epistle was written during or immediately after the persecution of Domitian. It will be my object to show that such evidence as we possess points to a very different conclusion, viz. that when Clement gave literary expression to the message from the Church in Rome to the Church in Corinth he was not yet the official head of the Roman Church, and further that the probable date of the epistle is the early months of 70 A.D.

It will be necessary to deal with the arguments for and against *seriatim.*

The cause of the writing of the epistle was the outbreak of schism and dissension in the Corinthian Church described by the writer as ' that abominable and unholy sedition, foreign and strange to the elect of God, which a few head-strong and self-willed persons have kindled to such a pitch

---

[1] Lightfoot, *Apost. Fathers*, part i. vol. i. p. 342. The italics are mine. Among the older writers Hefele in his *Prolegomena* to the Epistle (1855) writes as to the date ' tota haec quaestio facillime posset dissolvi si tempus Clementis episcopatus plane constaret.' Workman (*Persecution n the Early Church*, p. 206) writes : ' As I incline to a later date for the epistle of St. Clement, I see no reason to reject the succession of bishops as Linus, Cletus, Clement. . . . The question of succession is bound up with the date of the Epistle.'

of madness, so that your name, once respected and widely
spoken of and worthily beloved of all men, hath been greatly
defamed.'¹ The cause of this sad change is ascribed to
jealousy and envy, and the examples of Cain and Abel, of
Jacob and Esau, of Joseph, of Moses, and of David and Saul
are brought forward as warnings of the evil consequences
which indulgence in jealousy and envy produces. The
writer then proceeds: ' But let us cease to speak of examples of ancient days, and let us come to those who very
recently were athletes [of the faith] ; let us take the illustrious examples of our own time. Through envy and
jealousy the greatest and most righteous pillars were persecuted and contended even unto death. Let us take
before our eyes the good apostles.'² Then follow references
to the martyrdoms of St. Peter and of St. Paul. This
epithet ' good ' has exercised the minds of critics, but there
seems to be no doubt that it is the true reading. Lightfoot
remarks ' Such an epithet may be most naturally explained
on the supposition that Clement is speaking in affectionate
remembrance of those whom he had known personally,
otherwise the epithet would be out of place.' Does not
the same comment apply, it may be asked, to the readers
of the Epistle? Peter and Paul were regarded as the
founders of the Corinthian as well as of the Roman Church,
and the epithet points to their memory being still quite
fresh. Then in the following chapter Clement gives a
description of the climax of the Neronian persecution;

¹ Clement, I Cor. i. 1.
² Ibid. v. 1 : ἀλλ' ἵνα τῶν ἀρχαίων ὑποδειγμάτων παυσώμεθα, ἔλθωμεν ἐπὶ τοὺς
ἔγγιστα γενομένους ἀθλητάς· λάβωμεν τῆς γενεᾶς ἡμῶν τὰ γενναῖα ὑποδείγματα.
Lightfoot translates τοὺς ἔγγιστα γενομένους ἀθλητάς ' those champions who
lived very near to our time ' ; Gregg (Early Church Classics) : ' those great
ones, who are nearest to our time '; Hippolyte Hemmer, Clément de
Rome (1909) : ' venons en aux athlètes tout récents.' τῆς γενεᾶς ἡμῶν
can only mean ' our own time,' i.e. the time in which all of us are living,
not a period thirty years ago. When John the Baptist cried ' O generation
of vipers,' or our Lord ' Whereto shall I liken this generation ? ' or ' An
adulterous generation seeketh after a sign,' or St. Peter ' Save yourselves from this untoward generation,' they were speaking to and of the
living men and women they saw around them, and so does Clement in this
passage.

briefly but with graphic strokes he tells us how ' to these men of holy living was gathered together a great multitude of the elect, who having suffered through jealousy many indignities and tortures became very splendid examples amongst ourselves. Persecuted through jealousy, women after having suffered in the guise of Danaids and Dirces terrible and monstrous outrages attained the goal which made sure to them the race of faith and those who were weak in body received a noble reward.' ⌐If any one were to read those paragraphs for the first time without any presuppositions or *arrière-pensées*, would they doubt that they told of scenes of horror which not only the author but all those in whose name he wrote had literally before their eyes, and which still haunted the minds of the witnesses ?⌐

⌐Further, if Clement had just passed through the persecution of Domitian in which so many Christians of illustrious rank suffered, with whom as bishop he must have had intimate relations, is it conceivable that none of their examples should have been brought forward, but only those of an already distant persecution, whose memory more recent events must have tended to throw into the background ?⌐ But it is said that Clement is speaking of what happened under Domitian in the sentence which follows the opening salutation—' by reason of the sudden and successive troubles and calamities which have befallen us, we consider that we have been somewhat slow in giving attention to the questions in dispute among you.' [1] But it may be asked, is it possible to read into these words so large a reference ? The Domitianic persecution, when it came, must have touched Clement himself and his fellow-Christians at Rome far too severely and closely for the subject to have been dismissed thus casually and once for all in the ten opening words of a sentence containing fifty-nine words ? When one considers that according to the opinion of the critics this Epistle was written almost

---

[1] διὰ τὰς αἰφνιδίους καὶ ἐπαλλήλους γενομένας ἡμῖν συμφορὰς καὶ περιπτώσεις, ἀδελφοί, βράδιον νομίζομεν ἐπιστοφὴν πεποιῆσθαι περὶ τῶν ἐπιζητουμένων παρ' ὑμῖν πραγμάτων.

immediately after the death of Domitian the Persecutor, it seems mere trifling to suppose that the deep sorrow and keen sense of bereavement that must have been filling the Roman Church at the sad fate of so many of its foremost members could not have found here or elsewhere in this lengthy letter more fitting expression.⌐ But if the date of the document be, as I hold that it is, the early·months of 70 A.D., then the reference to ' the sudden and successive troubles and calamities, which have befallen us ' receives a natural explanation, one written large in the historical records of the time,[1] and a mere allusion to which would be sufficient to account to the Corinthians for the delay of the Roman Church in dealing with the questions on which its advice had been sought.[2]⌐ In the whole course of its long and chequered history the city of Rome has never experienced so many ' sudden and successive troubles and calamities ' as befell it in the course of the year 69 A.D., and the brief reference to them by the writer of this Epistle is seen to be as aptly as it is tersely phrased.

The internal evidence of the Epistle is in many important respects strongly in favour of the early date.⌐ In the organisation of the Church only ' bishops and deacons ' are mentioned, exactly as they are in St. Paul's Epistle to the Philippians, while the title ' bishop ' is to the same extent interchangeable with that of ' presbyter ' as it is in the Acts and the Pauline epistles, and the word ' rulers ' has the same sense as in the Epistle to the Hebrews.[3] ⌐ The Apostles

---

[1] See Lecture VI, pp. 168-170. Also Tac. Hist. i. 2 . Philostratus, Apollonius of Tyana (ed. Phillimore, ii. p. 58) : ' Galba was killed at Rome itself after grasping at the Empire ; Vitellius was killed after dreaming of empire ; Otho, killed in lower Gaul, was not even buried with honour, but lies like a common man. And destiny flew through all this history in one year.'

[2] Unless the advice of the Church at Rome had been sought, there could have been no reason to excuse delay in attending to the matter. Zahn, Intr. to N.T. vol. i. p. 269, holds that Fortunatus, who is mentioned in Clement's Epistle lxv. brought the news of the Corinthian dissensions to Rome. See also Stahl, Patristische Untersuchungen, 1901.

[3] Clement, I Cor. xlii. 4, 5 ; xliv. 1. 4, 5 ; liv. 2 ; lvii. 1, for rulers. ἡγούμενοι i. 3, προηγούμενοι xxi. 6.

derive their authority directly from Jesus Christ, the
presbyter-bishops and deacons from the Apostles, who
are described as having gone through town and country
preaching the good tidings that the kingdom of God was
about to come.[1]   All this is thoroughly primitive.   It is too
the mark of a very early date that while Clement three
times speaks of the Lord Jesus as ' child or servant of God '—
παῖς Θεοῦ—only once is the word son—υἱός—used, and
that in a quotation from the second Psalm taken direct from
the Epistle to the Hebrews.[2]   Again as to Clement's references
to the canonical writings of the New Testament, Dr. Lightfoot, though on other grounds he supports the late date for
this Epistle, writes thus—' one important test of date in
early Christian writings lies in the *Biblical quotations*—both
the form and the substance. ⌠Now the quotations from the
Gospels in this letter exhibit a very early type.   They are
not verbal ; they are fused ; and they are not prefaced by
" It is written " (γέγραπται) or " The Scripture saith "
(ἡ γραφὴ λέγει) or the like, but a more archaic form of
citation is used, " The Lord spake " (ὁ Κύριος εἶπεν) or
some similar expression.' [3] ⌡ A very considerable admission.
On the other hand the abundant use that is made of the
Pauline epistles, especially Romans and 1 Corinthians,
of 1 Peter, and more than any other of the Epistle to the
Hebrews, is very natural in one who was the disciple and
companion of St. Peter and St. Paul, and whose conversion
tradition assigns to St. Barnabas.[4]

It is difficult to see how the evidential value of c. xli.
can be explained away.   It is so important as a witness
for the early date that it must be given in full.   ' Let each

[1] *Ibid.* xlii. 2, 3 : ὁ Χριστὸς οὖν ἀπὸ τοῦ Θεοῦ καὶ οἱ ἀπόστολοι ἀπὸ τοῦ Χριστοῦ
. . . . ἐξῆλθον (οἱ ἀπόστολοι) εὐαγγελιζόμενοι τὴν βασιλείαν τοῦ Θεοῦ μέλλειν
ἔρχεσθαι.

[2] *Ibid.* lx. 2. 3, 4, xxxvi. 4 ; Heb. i. 5.

[3] Lightfoot, *Apost. Fathers*, part i. vol. i. p. 353.

[4] Of the four epistles named, 1 Corinthians dealt with a situation in
some respects similar to that described by Clement and in the same town.
Romans and Hebrews were addressed to Rome, and 1 Peter written in
Rome.   The use made by Clement of Hebrews strengthens the argument
for its Barnabas authorship.

o

of you, brethren, in his own order give thanks[1] [at the Eucharist], keeping a good conscience without passing beyond the appointed rule of his service[2] with reverence. Not in every place, brethren, are the perpetual daily[3] sacrifices offered, or the free-will offerings or the sin offerings and the trespass offerings, but in Jerusalem alone, and there not in every place is it offered, but before the sanctuary in the altar-court ; after the victim which is being offered has been inspected for blemishes by the high priest and the aforesaid ministry. They then who do anything contrary to the seemly order of His [God's] will have death as their punishment. Ye see, brethren, how in proportion as we have been deemed worthy of fuller knowledge, so much the greater is the danger to which we are exposed.' Those who cling to the Domitianic date for this Epistle are driven to strange shifts to find any plausible argument for denying to this passage its obvious sense, that at the time when it was written the Temple at Jerusalem was still standing, and the daily sacrifice had not ceased. Lightfoot and others bring forward Josephus' account of the Mosaic sacrifices ('Ant.' iii. cc. 9, 10) written in 93 A.D., in which the historic present is freely used. But as Hefele[4] pointed out some years ago, there is a wide distinction between the two cases. Josephus, in describing a ritual system that had passed away, employs a well-known artifice of the historian in

[1] εὐχαριστείτω, perform his act of Eucharistia.

[2] λειτουργία, a word transferred to Christian ministerial services, especially that of the Eucharist, from the LXX. where it signifies the ' service ' of the priests in their Temple duties.

[3] ἐνδελεχισμόν. This word is used in the LXX. to distinguish the sacrifices that were obligatory every day from those of free will. See Ex. xxix. 42, xxx. 8 ; Numbers, xxviii. 6.

[4] Hefele, *Patrum Apost. opera* (1855), xxxiv. : ' Sed res utraque, Iosephi et Clementis, longe dissimilis est. Iosephus, sacros populi sui ritus describens, per figuram, historicis non inusitatam, praesenti, quod dicimus, historico utitur. Clemens, autem, ut Corinthos ad ordinem servandum adducat, lectoribus ordinem Iudaici cultus ante oculos ponit. Quodsi autem templum iam fuisset destructum, tota S. Patris argumentatio fuisset infirma, ipsaque adversarios invitasset, ut dicerent : En, eversione templi Hierosolymitani Deus ipse testatus est, talem ordinem sibi non esse exoptatum.'

order to lend vividness to his narrative. Clement on the other hand brings before the eyes of his readers the fixed order of the Jewish worship with the purpose of showing to them that the maintenance of such order was a Divine institution. But if the Temple had been destroyed and that order of worship had been violently brought to an end, would not his whole argument fall to the ground and his opponents be able to retort that the complete disappearance of the Jewish sanctuary, its official hierarchy and ordered ritual was a proof that such a system no longer could claim the divine sanction ?

Once more as to the dissensions at Corinth, little is told as to their cause and character, except that the action of certain ' headstrong and reckless persons ' had led to some of the duly constituted presbyters being expelled from their office, and that the ringleaders were few in number.[1] Perhaps the example held up before the authors of the discussion of the hierarchical order of the Mosaic cult at Jerusalem may point to these ' headstrong persons ' being Judaeo-Christians, who had strong opinions about the absolute equality of all members of the Christian community, or possibly without going so far as to object to the existence of the office of presbyter they may have protested against the appointment of uncircumcised Gentiles to this office. Moreover, while we have no information to throw light upon the state of Corinth at the end of Domitian's reign, that town had been the scene of stirring events and activities some thirty years earlier. In the autumn of 66 A.D. Nero went to Greece. In November 67 A.D. he witnessed at Corinth the Isthmian games, and in that city conferred freedom upon Achaia, a privilege which was not revoked until six years later by Vespasian, because of the disorders that broke out. What is even more important, Nero at this time seriously set about the formidable engineering task of cutting a navigable canal through the Isthmus.[2] For

[1] Clement, I Cor. i. 47.
[2] Henderson, *Life and Principate of Nero*, pp. 392 ff., 495 ff. ; Philostratus, *Apollonius of Tyana* (Bewick), p. 216.

this purpose no fewer than 6000 Jewish prisoners, captured by Vespasian in a battle at Tiberias on the Sea of Galilee, were sent by that general to Corinth to carry out the excavations,[1] and at the time of Nero's death a considerable part of the work had been completed. It was, however, then abandoned, with the result that a very large body of fanatical Jewish Zealots must have remained at Corinth as slaves or freedmen, their fierce patriotism still glowing unquenched by defeat and bondage.   Here then in 69 A.D. were present all the elements for fomenting such an outbreak of strife and discord as actually took place.

Or take the well-known reference to the story of the Phoenix,[2] and the analogy that it offers to the Resurrection. In recounting this legend Clement was no more credulous than his contemporaries, one of whom, Pliny the Elder, tells us in his ' Natural History ' ' that a phoenix was brought to Rome in the censorship of the Emperor Claudius (47 A.D.) and that it was exposed to public view in the Comitia,' adding ' this fact is attested by the public annals.'[3]   Now Clement, as a boy, may have actually seen this publicly exhibited wonder, and the vivid impression made on the youthful imagination here finds expression some twenty-two years later.   It is just one of those little touches that give added life to the narrative and connect the personality of the writer with the events of his time.   It is to be noted that Clement does not hint at there being anything of a miraculous character in the resurrection of the Phoenix, he speaks of it as a fact of natural history.

Let us now turn our attention to the passages on which the advocates of a late date have chiefly relied.   The beginning of chapter xliv. runs thus : ' Our Apostles also knew through our Lord Jesus Christ, that there would be strife about the dignity of the bishop's

---

[1] Josephus, *Bell. Iud.* iv. 10 : ' Out of the young men he chose 6000 of the strongest and sent them to Nero to dig through the isthmus of Corinth.'

[2] Clement, 1 *Cor.* xxv.

[3] Pliny, *Nat. Hist.* x. 3 (Bostock's tr., p. 481) ; compare Tac. *Ann.* vi. 28.   Pliny was himself a sceptic—' there is no one but doubts it was a fictitious phoenix only.'

office.[1] For this reason then having received perfect fore-knowledge they appointed the aforesaid [bishops and deacons] and then they further laid down regulations [2] that if they [any of these bishops and deacons] should fall asleep, other tried men should succeed to their ministry. Those then who were appointed by them or afterwards by other men of repute with the approval of the whole Church, and have ministered unblameably to the flock of Christ in all humility, peaceably and without arrogance [3] and who have for many years received high testimony from all [4]—we do not consider it just that these men should be ejected from their ministration.' Here the words ' our Apostles ' clearly signify St. Peter and St. Paul, held to be the joint founders of both the Churches of Rome and Corinth. The careful advice and warnings addressed by both these Apostles to the presbyter-bishops in their extant writings are a proof of the truth of Clement's assertion as to their having pre-vision about the difficulties which might arise in the future concerning the authority and position of these ' rulers ' of the Church. But it does not follow, because the Apostles laid down regulations for the filling up of these offices, whenever they became vacant by death, or because, at the time when Clement was writing, some of the holders of these offices had been appointed by the Apostles, others by the choice of the presbytery with the consent of the Church, or because among these were men who for many years had been honoured and respected by all, that there-fore the Epistle was written some decades after the Apostle's martyrdom. Those who use this argument overlook the possibility that the first presbyters of the Roman Church were appointed by St. Peter about 44 or 45 A.D., and those of Corinth by St. Paul about 51 or 52 A.D. Most of these would be literally ' elders '—men well advanced in

---

[1] 1 Pet. v. 1-6 ; 1 Tim. iii. 1-13 ; Tit. i. 5-11 ; compare 1 Cor. xi. 18, 19 ; Rom. xii. 6-8 ; Eph. iv. 11-12 ; Heb. xiii. 17.

[2] The reading here ἐπινομην is probably corrupt. The translation of L. *legem dederunt* has been adopted.

[3] ἀβαναύσως, the opposite disposition to those having βάναυσος, arrogance, pride ; compare 1 Pet. v. 3. [4] μεμαρτυρημένους πολλοῖς χρόνοις ὑπὸ πάντων

198   CHURCH OF CORINTH REBUKED

years when first they took office—and in the interval between
these dates and 70 A.D. there must have been many vacancies
by death and fresh appointments, some directly by the
Apostles, others in their absence by the Churches in the
manner ordained by Apostolical authority.

Again in chapter xlvii., after condemning in the
strongest terms the strifes, parties, and divisions which
were tearing to pieces the Corinthian Church, Clement
continues : ' Take up the epistle of the blessed Paul the
Apostle. What was it that he first wrote to you in the
beginning (ἐν ἀρχῇ) of the Gospel ? In truth under the
inspiration of the Spirit he sent you a letter concerning
himself and Cephas and Apollos, because that even then
you had given way to party spirit.' Clement then proceeds
to compare the apostles of renown, the great leaders of those
days (just mentioned), with the present instigators of schism
and dissension, and he denounces their conduct in the words
'It is shameful, beloved, very shameful and unworthy of
Christian conduct that it should be reported that the very
steadfast and primitive (ἀρχαίαν) Church of Corinth should by
one or two persons have been induced to rebel against its
presbyters.'   Now far too much stress has been laid by the upholders of the Domitianic hypothesis upon this word ἀρχαίαν
as signifying ' ancient,' and it is said that such a description
could not have been given of a Church only twenty years
old.   But is it not evident that the word ἀρχαία was
suggested by the previous word ἀρχή, and that it means no
more than that the foundation of the Church at Corinth
took place in the earliest days of the preaching of the Gospel
in Europe ? [1]

[1] St. Paul (Phil. iv. 15) in his Epistle to the Philippians writes : 'and
ye yourselves also know, ye Philippians, that in the beginning of the
Gospel (ἐν ἀρχῇ τοῦ εὐαγγελίου), when I departed from Macedonia, no church
had fellowship with me in the matter of giving and receiving, but ye
only.' And in his Second Epistle to the Corinthians (xi. 9) : 'when
I was present with you and in want, I was not a burden on any man ;
for the brethren when they came from Macedonia supplied the measure
of my want.' We thus see that St. Paul himself applies the expression
ἐν ἀρχῇ τοῦ εὐαγγελίου to his first visit to Corinth. Compare St. Luke,
i. 2 οἱ ἀπ' ἀρχῆς αὐτόπται.

The following particulars concerning the envoys who were the bearers of this epistle to Corinth have been held to necessitate a late date. 'We have sent faithful and discreet men who have passed their lives blamelessly in our midst from youth to old age.' And again ' Send back to us quickly in peace and with joy our envoys Claudius Ephebus and Valerius Bito together with Fortunatus also.' 1 Now the conjecture of Lightfoot that the names of Claudius Ephebus and Valerius Bito point to their being freedmen of the Imperial household at the time when Messalina was Empress is probably correct.2 But if they received their manumission about 45 A.D., they may well have been from thirty-five to forty years of age at that date, and so more than sixty in 70 A.D. As there is reason to believe that Christianity was first brought to Rome shortly after the death of St. Stephen, and as St. Peter's first visit took place at the very time when Messalina was at the height of her power, there is no difficulty in giving these two men a place among the very first converts to the faith. Fortunatus is separately mentioned, and we may infer that he was not a Roman envoy but a Corinthian, and if a Corinthian, then although the name is not uncommon, his identification with the Fortunatus mentioned by St. Paul in his First Epistle to the Corinthians is more than a possibility.3 It is, how- ever, extremely unlikely that the Fortunatus whose coming to Ephesus refreshed St. Paul in 54 A.D., was still active and travelling to and fro as an emissary between his native town and Rome in 96 A.D., more than forty years later.

The assumption so commonly made that the Epistle, the actual authorship of which by universal consent is

1 Clement, 1 Cor. lxiii. and lxv.
2 Lightfoot, Apost. Fathers, part i. vol. i. p. 27 ff.
3 τοὺς δὲ ἀπεσταλμένους ἀφ' ἡμῶν Κλαύδιον Ἔφηβον καὶ Οὐαλέριον Βίτωνα σὺν καὶ Φορτουνάτῳ. The words σὺν καὶ place Fortunatus in a different category from Ephebus and Bito. Th. Zahn (Intr. to N.T. vol. i. p. 269) holds that Fortunatus was a delegate from Corinth and that it had been he who had brought the news of the dissensions to Rome. Lightfoot also (part i. vol. i. p. 29 and vol. ii. p. 187) is of opinion that Fortunatus was a Corinthian and that there is no improbability in identifying him with the Fortunatus of 1 Cor. xvi. 17.

attributed to Clement, the third in order of succession of the
Roman bishops, must have been written during the period
of his episcopate, 92 to 101 A.D., has in fact really no justification. There are very strong arguments (besides those
already brought forward) to be urged against it, both
negative and positive. The Epistle is written in the name
of the Church of Rome, and is throughout anonymous.
From the first line to the last there is not a single phrase
which hints at the individuality of the writer or gives any
indication that he was a man of mark and authority, the
personal pronouns used are always ' we ' and ' us.' Now
such self-effacement would be perhaps natural in the young
Clement of 70 A.D. It is quite in accordance with what
Epiphanius tells us (quoting apparently the lost memoirs of
Hegesippus) about his voluntary refusal to accept the post
of presiding-bishop after the death of the Apostles,[1] 'lest
he should cause strife and division,' and of his withdrawal
in favour of his seniors, first of Linus, then of Anencletus.
But tradition asserts with no uncertain voice that Clement
held a place apart in the Roman Church as the first century
began to draw to its close.   It was not his 'Epistle to the
Corinthians ' which gave him fame, and which caused a
plentiful crop of legends to grow up around his name, but
his distinction first as being a personal disciple of St. Peter,
by whom he was ordained to the presbyterate, and also a
fellow-worker with St. Paul, and secondly from the high
social position and family connexion   which   tradition

---

[1] See the most interesting chapter on the *Hypomnemata* of Hegesippus
in *Eusebiana*, by H. J. Lawlor (Clarendon Press. 1912).   Mr. Lawlor
produces very strong arguments and evidence (pp. 73–94) to show that
Epiphanius in writing his *Panarion* had before him a copy of Hegesippus'
Memoirs, and further that those Memoirs contained a great deal of information about the early history of the Churches of Jerusalem, Corinth, and
Rome : ' We find that, just as in the case of Jerusalem and Corinth, so
in that of Rome, what he [Hegesippus] wrote was mainly a *résumé* of the
history of the Christian community, special attention being paid to the
circumstances under which each bishop succeeded to his charge ' (p. 85).
Among other passages of Epiphanius that which explains how it was that
Clement though appointed bishop by the Apostles Peter and Paul was not
first but third in succession, *i.e.* the story of his resignation in favour of
Linus and Anencletus, was probably taken from Hegesippus (p. 9).

assigns to him, a tradition which I believe to be in substance correct.[1] |The Clement, then, who became bishop in 92 A.D. was an Apostolical man of exceptional authority, whose personality would not lend itself to concealment. If he wrote the Epistle in 96 A.D., his name would give added weight to the advice of the Church over which he presided. Moreover are there not strong grounds for holding that during the quarter of a century of Flavian rule, at Rome and elsewhere, the office of bishop had been growing in importance and respect and dignity, and was gradually becoming monarchical in character? ⌠Can any unprejudiced person read the language of Ignatius without perceiving that the primitive organisation of the Roman and Corinthian Churches, as depicted in Clement's Epistle, could not have still subsisted unchanged until 96 A.D. ?⌡ Ignatius, remember, was a contemporary of Clement, his letters were written not more than seven or eight years after Clement's death, and in these letters the authoritative and autocratic position of the bishop is set forth again and again in terms that admit of no qualification. ' Let no man do aught pertaining to the Church apart from the bishop '—' it is not lawful apart from the bishop either to baptise or hold an *Agape* '—' whenever you are subject to the bishop, you appear to me not to be living the ordinary life of men, but after the manner of the life of Jesus Christ.' It is quite clear that in such statements as these Ignatius is not speaking of any new thing. With him the office of bishop is of the very *esse* and not merely of the *bene esse* of the Church. Without the three orders of bishop, presbyters, and deacons ' there is ' he declares ' no Church deserving of the name.' In another passage he speaks of ' the bishops established in the furthest quarters as being in the mind of Jesus Christ as Jesus Christ is the Mind of the Father ' and of the ' presbytery that is worthy of God being fitted to the bishop as the strings to a harp.' [2] These words preclude

---

[1] See ' Clementine ' *Homilies* and *Recognitions*, the *Epistles to Virgins*, the *Apostolical Constitutions*.

[2] *Smyrn.* 8 ; *Trall.* 2. 3, 4 ; *Eph.* 3, 4 ; *Magn.* 3, 6, 7 ; *Philad.* 4, etc.

any mere local reference, and when one considers how close was the intercourse between Antioch and Rome, it will be seen how extremely difficult it would be to conceive of the Great Roman Community, for which Ignatius himself expresses the utmost veneration,[1] as not possessing that qualification without which ' it would not be deserving the name of a Church.' ⌈In other words in the year 96 A.D. the organisation of the Roman Church was not that which we find in Clement's Epistle, nor was the position which Clement with his antecedents must at that date have held consistent with the entire absence of the personal note in the letter which he wrote to Corinth.⌋

The case in fact against this Epistle having been written by Clement during his episcopate is very strong. It only remains to draw attention to two pieces of documentary evidence, both of which indirectly confirm the conclusion at which we have arrived. In a passage from the letter of Dionysius, bishop of Corinth, to Soter, bishop of Rome, which has been preserved to us by Eusebius, the words occur ' to-day we have spent the Lord's Holy Day, in which we have read your epistle ; reading which we shall at all times receive admonishment, as also [is the case] with the former epistle written to us by Clement.'[2]   Dr. Bigg in the introduction to his Commentary on the First Epistle of St. Peter compares the Greek words here used ἡμῖν διὰ Κλήμεντος γραφεῖσαν with those of St. Peter : ' I have written to you by Silvanus ' —διὰ Σιλουανοῦ ὑμῖν ἔγραψα, and he holds that the two passages must be understood in the same way, and he says that Dionysius's words ' mean clearly that Clement was the mouthpiece or interpreter of the Church of Rome.'[3] This implies that Clement, though no doubt a leading official, was in putting into literary form and with a free hand the general instructions he had received, only the servant, not the head of the Church acting on his own initiative.

---

[1] *Romans* (salutation) : ἥτις καὶ προκάθηται ἐν τόπῳ χωρίου 'Ρωμαίων, ἀξιόθεος, ἀξιοπρεπής, ἀξιομακάριστος, ἀξιέπαινος, ἀξιεπίτευκτος, ἀξίαγνος καὶ προκαταθημένη τῆς ἀγάπης, Χριστώνομος, Πατρώνομος.

[2] Eus. *Hist. Eccl.* iv. 23.   [3] Bigg, 1 *Peter*, Intr. p. 5.

The evidence of Hermas has a double interest from
the light that it throws both on the date of 'The Shepherd'
and upon the position of Clement. With the date of 'The
Shepherd' I shall deal in the next lecture. I will merely state
here that my contention will be that that part of Hermas'
work known as 'The Visions' and possibly the whole of it was
written in the course of the first decade of Domitian's reign.
The reference to Clement occurs at the close of the Second
Vision. In the Vision an old woman, representing the
Church, had given to Hermas a small book containing a
revelation, which at her command he had copied out letter
by letter. This done the aged woman again came to him
and asked him if he had already given the book to the
presbyters. On his replying that he had not, the aged woman
said—I quote the exact words—'Thou hast done well, for I
have words to add. When then I shall have finished all
the words, by thee it shall be made known to all the elect.
Thou shalt therefore write two little books and shalt send
them to Clement and to Grapte. Clement will then send
to the cities that are without, for to him this [charge] has
been entrusted; and Grapte will admonish the widows
and the orphans. But thou shalt read [the words] unto this
city before the presbyters, who preside over the Church.' [1]
This passage has been variously interpreted, but it is
allowed by the great majority of critics that it contains a
definite historical allusion to Clement, the author of the
Epistle from the Roman Church to the Corinthians, and the
comment of Lightfoot is perfectly just—'the allusion in
Hermas seems to be an obvious recognition of the existence
of this letter. . . . Clement is represented as the writer's
contemporary, who held a high office, which constituted
him, as we might say, foreign secretary of the Roman
Church.' [2] Precisely. But such a description surely implies
that at the time Clement was occupying what can only be

---

[1] Hermas, *Vision* iii. 4 : γράψεις οὖν δύο βιβλαρίδια καὶ πέμψεις ἐν Κλήμεντι
καὶ ἐν Γραπτῇ. πέμψει οὖν Κλήμης εἰς τὰς ἔξω πόλεις, ἐκείνῳ γὰρ ἐπιτέτραπται·
Γραπτὴ δὲ νουθετήσει τὰς χήρας καὶ τοὺς ὀρφανούς· σὺ δὲ ἀναγνώσῃ εἰς ταύτην τὴν
πόλιν μετὰ τῶν πρεσβυτέρων τῶν προϊσταμένων τῆς ἐκκλησίας.

[2] Lightfoot, *Apost. Fathers*, part i. vol. i. p. 348.

described as a subordinate position, since he was charged with secretarial duties entrusted to him by others. The particular charge was one that might very well be assigned to a younger member of the presbyterate distinguished among his colleagues for wider culture and greater familiarity with literary Greek. ⌈The mere fact that his name is here coupled with that of Grapte, apparently a deaconess, is of itself a proof that the Clement of Hermas' second Vision had not yet become at the close of a long and honoured career the venerated bishop of 96 A.D.⌋

Nothing is known of Grapte outside of this reference, and some critics have supposed that the name was not that of a real woman, but is used here allegorically. But if so, then is it not reasonable to suppose that the whole passage is allegorical, not historical?   If Grapte be a mere creature of Hermas' imagination, why not Clement ?   But those who seek in this way to evade the difficulties attending this passage, which is so important for fixing the dates both of Clement's Epistle and of 'The Shepherd,' have really no justification for taking refuge in allegory. The names Graptus and Grapte though rare are both of them to be found in contemporary inscriptions. One of these inscriptions is particularly interesting,[1] as it brings into collocation the names of Clemens and Graptus. It tells how a certain Julius Graptus adorned a mausoleum with plantations in

---

[1] *C.I.L.* xii. 3637 :

m. ARRECINO CLEMENTE II
L. BAEBIO HONORATO
cos
IVLIVS.GRAPTVS.MAG.
MAESOLEVM.EXCOLVIT.ET.VT.ESSET.FRVns
ornaviT.POSITIS.ARBORIBVS.VITIBVS.ROSAriis idem
OBLATA.SIBI.A.COLLIBERTIS.IMMVNITATE ET TITVLO.
qVO.BENIVOLENTIA.EIVS.CONTINERETVR
ne.QVA.PARTE.VTILITATIBVS.EORVM.
qvAVIS.VIDERETVR.IMMVNITATEM
reMISIT.ET.TITVLO.QVEM.DE.SVO.
posVIT.   CONTENTVS.FVIT.

                              Emended by Mommsen.

the year when M. Arrecinus Clemens was consul for the second time, in other words in the year 93 A.D. Another inscription,[1] a fragment, contains the words *Grapte uxor.* This Julius Graptus and Grapte the deaconess may well have been the children of Nero's freedman Graptus, described by Tacitus as active in his master's service in the year 59. Arrecinus Clemens was a near relation of the imperial Flavians; if he were at the same time an elder brother of Clement the bishop, then at once the mystery of the high family connexion which the Clementine romances have woven around the name of the bishop disappears and becomes explicable. That such a relationship existed is no mere random suggestion. It is one which, as I shall endeavour to show elsewhere, is well deserving of careful examination.[2]

[1] *C.I.L.* xii. 4822 :   GRAPTE
                             VXOR
[2] See Lecture VIII. pp. 227–35, and Note D of the Appendix.

LECTURE VIII

Daniel, xi. 3, 6 : 'And the king shall do according to his will; and he shall exalt himself, and magnify himself above every god till the indignation be accomplished.'

DURING the period which followed the accession of the Flavian dynasty to the Imperial throne the Church in Rome seems to have lived in comparative repose. For more than a quarter of a century after the martyrdom of St. Paul there is no record of any violent persecution of the Christians. But there is no reason to believe that the ban under which those professing the Christian faith lay since the Neronian persecution of 65 A.D. was in any way lightened or removed. The Christians were then condemned for crimes which were summed up by Tacitus as constituting ' hatred of the human race,' in other words they were condemned as enemies of the Roman state and people. The mere confession of the Christian name henceforth in itself entailed punishment. The principle of action, which Tertullian calls *the Neronian Institution*, continued to be the settled policy of the Roman government. This did not mean that the Christian so long as he lived quietly and did nothing to bring himself under the notice of the police was sought out and dragged before the magistrate. But it did mean that he was an outlaw, liable as such at any moment to be dealt with summarily by the authorities, as a mere matter of police administration. No regular judicial trial was needed, the inquiry (*cognitio*) was confined to the establishment of the charge of being a Christian, and once established by the confession of the accused the death penalty followed.

The policy of the Flavian emperors, Vespasian, Titus,

and—during the first part of his reign—Domitian, was on the whole both towards Jews and Christians one of singular moderation. After the merciless suppression of the terrible revolt in Judaea and the destruction of Jerusalem and its Temple, the position of the Jews in the empire was however no longer the same. ⌈ As a political entity, a nation in any sense of the word, they had ceased to exist, they were but a number of separate communities scattered throughout the Roman world. ⌋ But Vespasian granted to them a continuation of the religious privileges they had hitherto enjoyed ⌈ on condition that all Jews were registered and paid to Roman officials as a tax for the maintenance of the temple of Jupiter Capitolinus the *didrachma* that they had previously contributed for the support of the Temple at Jerusalem.[1] But the very fact of this registration for fiscal purposes served to accentuate the distinction between Jew and Christian the more clearly.   The Christian Church could no longer find shelter under the shadow of the privileges of the synagogues.

That Titus was himself well aware of the difference, and that he was personally hostile to Christianity, is shown by an interesting passage in the fourth-century historian, Sulpicius Severus, which in the opinion of scholars is generally regarded as an extract from one of the lost books of Tacitus. It tells of a council held by Titus at the time of the final storming of Jerusalem to decide whether the Temple should be destroyed or not.   Titus himself, it is reported, with some of his officers held that it was necessary, ' so as to abolish more completely the religion both of Jews and Christians, since these religions, although opposed to

---

[1] Josephus, *Bell. Iud.* vii. 6. 6 ; Dion Cassius, lxvi. 7.   This conciliatory attitude of Vespasian and Titus to the Jewish *Diaspora* was due in part to the fact that the non-Palestinian Jews had taken no share in the revolt and that they were financially useful, in part to the influence of Agrippa II and his sister, who lived at Rome on terms of close intimacy with the Imperial family.   Vespasian had also special cause to be grateful to the Jew, Tiberius Alexander, who was the first to proclaim him emperor at Alexandria and who secured the allegiance to him of the legions in Egypt, 1 July 69. See Tac. *Hist.* ii. 79.

each other, both sprang from the same origin ; the Christians
had issued from the Jews ; if the root were taken away, the
stem would quickly perish.'[1] With the destruction of the
Temple and the crushing out of the revolt, however, the
situation was changed, moderate and statesmanlike views
prevailed, the Jews secured religious toleration and lenient
treatment, and no systematic persecution was directed
against the Christians so long as Titus lived or for some years
after his untimely death.

There is no contemporary Christian writing which throws
any light upon the state of the Church during this time,
unless it be 'The Shepherd' of Hermas. ⌠This remarkable
work bears every mark from internal evidence of being a
product of the Flavian age.⌡ We have already seen in the
last lecture that the author speaks of a certain Clement, who,
if not the well-known writer of the 'Epistle to the Corinthians,'
which is the general opinion, must be a fictitious personage.
Were it not for certain statements in the documents known
as the 'Muratorian Fragment on the Canon' and the 'Liberian
Catalogue' probably few would have given to 'The Shepherd'
a later date than the beginning of the second century.
The reference to Hermas and his book by the Muratorian
writer runs thus :[2] '. . . very lately in our times Hermas
wrote "The Shepherd" in the city of Rome while his brother
Pius, the bishop, was sitting in the chair of the Church of
the city of Rome, and therefore it ought to be read ; but it

[1] Sulp. Severus, *Chron.* ii. 30. 6 : ' Fertur Titus adhibito consilio prius
deliberasse . . . at contra alii et Titus ipse evertendum templum in primis
censebant quo plenius Iudaeorum et Christianorum religio tolleretur ;
quippe has religiones, licet contrarias sibi, iisdem auctoribus profectas :
Christianos ex Iudaeis extitisse : radice sublata, stirpem facile perituram.'
[2] . . . ' pastorem uero
nuperrim e temporibus nostris in urbe
roma herma conscripsit sedente cathe
tra urbis romae aeclesiae pio eƥs fratre
eius et ideo legi eum quidē oportet se pu
plicare vero in eclesia populo neque jnter
apostolos in finē temporum potest.'
Zahn, *Gesch. N.T. Kanons*, ii. p. 8 ; both Zahn and Lightfoot render
nuperrime by νεωστί.

cannot, to the end of time, be placed either among the prophets who are complete in number, nor among the Apostles for public lection to the people in church.' Zahn in his 'Geschichte des Neutestamentlichen Kanons' makes this comment :ʃ 'Careful and impartial reading of "The Shepherd" would have shown the Fragmentist that the same must have been written a considerable time before the episcopate of Pius. He who holds the book, despite the name of Clement (*Vis.* ii. 4) and many other signs, as a work dating from about 145, must hold it to be a pseudepigraphic fiction, which the Fragmentist throughout does not.' [1] ʃThe statement in the Muratorian extract quoted above is in fact, from whatever point of view it be regarded, a blunder of the writer who is called by Zahn 'the Fragmentist.' The dilemma is one from which there seems to be no possibility of escape.

ʃ Dr. Lightfoot has very convincingly shown that this Muratorian document contains a literal translation into Latin (somewhat corrupted in transmission) of a Greek metrical original, and also that there are strong reasons for assigning the authorship to Hippolytus.ʃ The literary activity of this famous Roman writer during the closing years of the second and the first quarter of the third century was very great. ʃThe 'Muratorian Canon' may probably be dated from 185 to 200 A.D.[2]ʃ The 'Liberian Catalogue,' it is generally agreed, was largely dependent on a later work of Hippolytus, the 'Chronology.' Now in the 'Liberian Catalogue' to the notice of Pope Pius I the following statement is appended : 'under his pontificate his brother Hermes wrote a book in which is contained the *Mandate* which an angel gave to him, when he came to him in the garb

---

[1] 'Denn aufmerksame und unparteiische Lesung des Hirten würde dem Frg. gezeigt haben dass derselbe geraume Zeit vor dem Episkopat des Pius geschrieben sein will. Wer das Buch trotz des Namens Clemens (*Vis.* ii. 4) und vieler anderer Anzeichen für ein Werk aus der Zeit vom 145 hielt, musste es für eine pseudepigraphische Fiction halten, was der Frg. durchaus nicht thut.'—Zahn, *Gesch. N.T. Kanons*, ii. 113.

[2] Lightfoot, *Apost. Fathers*, part i. vol. ii. pp. 405-13.

P

of a shepherd.' [1] ⌐The two passages, Muratorian and Liberian, are derived in fact from a common source, most probably Hippolytean.⌐But an examination of the character of this source may well make one distrustful of its strict accuracy as regards names and dates.⌐The ' Liberian Catalogue ' contains a number of strange errors. The deaths of St. Peter and St. Paul are stated to have taken place in 55 A.D. Clement succeeds Linus in 67 A.D., and Anencletus, the real successor of Linus, is duplicated and follows Clement, first at Cletus, then as Anacletus. ⌐Clement's death is recorded as having occurred sixteen years before he became bishop according to the generally received date.[2] ⌐ Nor were the errors confined to the first-century episcopates. The Hippolytean source is not even accurate about Pope Pius himself, who in the words of the 'Muratorian Fragment' lived ' very recently in our own times.' Hegesippus and Irenaeus, both of whom stayed some time in Rome soon after the death of Pius, both give the order of succession as Pius, Anicetus, Soter, Eleutherus.[3] The ' Liberian Catalogue ' makes Pius the successor of Anicetus instead of the predecessor. The conclusion then that we are compelled to draw is that this particular piece of external evidence for the date of ' The Shepherd ' cannot be accepted as authoritative in face of the internal evidence of the book itself. Probability points to its having arisen through a confusion between the name of the author and the title of his work. Bishop Pius according to a very ancient tradition had a

---

[1] ' Sub huius episcopatu frater eius Ermes librum scripsit, in quo mandatum continetur, quod ei praecepit angelus, cum venit ad illum in habitu pastoris.' Lightfoot, *Apost. Fathers*, part i. vol. i. p. 254. Lelong, *Le Pasteur d'Hermas*, p. xxvi. Duchesne, *Lib. Pont.* vol. i. p. 4. Harnack, *Chronologie*, pp. 175 and 258-9.

[2] In 76 A.D. instead of 92 A.D.

[3] Hegesippus visited Rome when Anicetus was bishop and was acquainted with Soter and Eleutherus. Eus. *Hist. Eccl.* iv. 22. Irenaeus also spent some time in Rome, probably in the episcopate of Soter 169-175. In his work on *Heresies* he gives the order of succession of the Roman bishops : ' . . . then Pius, then Anicetus, then Soter ; lastly the twelfth in order from the Apostles, Eleutherus, who now holds the office of bishop.' Eus. *Hist. Eccl.* v. 6 ; Iren, *Haer.* iii. 3.

brother named Pastor, who was a presbyter.[1] Now in the Latin version known as 'Vulgate,' which probably dates from the end of the second century, the title of Hermas' book is 'Liber Pastoris.'[2] This version was thus contemporary with the 'Muratorian Fragment.' It required but a single step therefore to identify the presbyter Pastor with the author of the allegory. The 'Liber Pontificalis,' while embodying the biographical notice of Pius I which is found in the 'Liberian Catalogue,' prefaces it by another paragraph in which this Pope is spoken of as 'the brother of Pastor.' There is no attempt to fuse this statement with that concerning Hermas—they are separated from one another by intervening matter. Indeed in the two earliest forms of the 'Liber Pontificalis' that we possess, the so-called 'Felician' and 'Cononian' abridgements, the compiler of the 'Cononian,' evidently perceiving the incongruity of the double reference to a brother, deliberately refuses to apply the term to Hermas, the words 'frater ipsius' being omitted.[3]

---

[1] [The Acts of Pastor and Timothy, though apocryphal, are of great antiquity.] The ecclesia Pudentiana, the foundation of which in the Baths of Novatus by Pope Pius I is recorded in these Acts, still exists as the Church of St. Pudentiana—see note in Lib. Pontificalis under biographical notice of Pius. 'Hic ex rogatu beatae Praxedis dedicavit ecclesiam thermas Novati, in vico Patricii, in honore sororis suae sanctae Potentianae, ubi et multa dona obtulit ; ubi saepius sacrificium domino offerens ministrabat. Immo et fontem baptismi construi fecit.' According to tradition Pius erected this Church into a titulus, and appointed as its presbyter his brother Pastor. The provision of a baptismal font probably means that this church became at this time the Metropolitan Church of Rome. Inscriptions have been found in which this church is styled 'titulus Pudentis.' In the excavations now being carried out for the building of the new Ministry of the Interior it is hoped that discoveries may be made throwing further light on these traditions. Galland, Bibl. Patrum, i. 672 ; De Rossi, Bullettino, 1867, pp. 49–58 ; Marucchi, Elém. d'Arch. Chrét. ii. pp. 381–3, iii. pp. 364–373 ; Hefele (Patrum Apost. Op. xcv) quotes from Galland 'Presbyter Pastor titulum condidit et digne in Domino obiit.' See Appendix, Note C, The Legend of Pudens.

[2] Lelong, Le Pasteur d'Hermas (1912), Intr. cv : 'La Version Vulgate (L¹) remontant peut-être à la fin du 11e siècle, en tout cas très ancienne . . . nous est parvenue dans de nombreux manuscrits.'

Duchesne, Lib. Pont. p. 58. The passage stands thus in the Felician Abridgement : 'Pius, natione Italus ex patre Rufino, frater Pastoris, de

The earliest patristic references to ' The Shepherd ' point to its having been written considerably before the pontificate of Pius I (140–155 A.D.) Irenaeus, whose sojourn in Rome took place less than twenty years after the death of Pius, quotes the opening sentence of the ' First Mandate ' as Scripture —' Well then spake the Scripture, which saith.'[1] Before a document could be thus—plainly, simply, and without periphrasis—accepted as Scripture, it must needs have been of some considerable antiquity, and indeed it may be regarded as evidence that Irenaeus looked upon Hermas as an ' Apostolical man,' the Hermas in fact mentioned by St. Paul in his Epistle to the Romans.

Clement of Alexandria in Egypt and Tertullian in Western Africa, in writings which date about twenty years later than that of Irenaeus just quoted, and almost contemporary with the first publication of the ' Muratorian Canon,' both speak of ' The Shepherd ' as ' Scripture.' Of Clement Dr. Salmon says [2] : ' The mutilated commencement of the " Stromateis" opens in the middle of a quotation from " The Shepherd " and about ten times elsewhere he cites the book, always with a complete acceptance of the reality and divine character of the revelations made to Hermas.'

civitate Aquileia, sedit ann. xviii, mens. iiii, dies iii. Fuit temporibus Antonii Pii a consulatu Clari et Severi. Sub huius episcopatu frater ipsius Hermis librum scripsit in quo mandatum continetur quod praecepit angelus Domini cum venit ad eum in habitu pastoris et praecepit ei ut sanctum Paschae die dominica celebraretur.' The *Cononian Abridgement* omits *frater ipsius*. Pius is the first of the Roman bishops after Clement to bear a Latin name. If he were, as stated above, an Italian by birth, it is in the last degree unlikely that he was the brother of a slave who had the Greek name Hermas, and who seems to hint that he was of foreign origin. There is no reference to the Easter controversy in *The Shepherd*.

[1] Irenaeus, *Haer*. iv. 20. 2 : καλῶς οὖν εἶπεν ἡ γραφὴ ἡ λέγουσα· Πρῶτον πάντων πίστευσον . . . from Hermas, *Mand*. i. 1.

[2] Article on ' Hermas ' in Smith and Wace's *Dictionary of Christian Biography*. Hilgenfeld in the *prolegomena* to his edition of *Hermae Pastor* 1881, p. v), after giving a list of the passages in which Clement of A. quotes *The Shepherd*, concludes : '. . . Clemens Alex. igitur integro Pastore usus de divinis eius revelationibus ne dubitavit quidem neque Hermam apostolorum temporibus posteriorem existimasse potest.'

Tertullian [1] before he became a Montanist in his treatise ' De Oratione ' rebukes the custom of sitting down for prayer, the origin of which he attributes to the opening words of the fifth Vision of ' The Shepherd.' This assigns to ' The Shepherd ' an authority which could only belong to a book long received as the work of an inspired man. Origen [2] somewhat later in the third century gives as his opinion (based no doubt on tradition) that the Hermas mentioned in the Epistle to the Romans was the writer of ' The Shepherd ' and adds ' this scripture seems to me very useful and as I think divinely inspired.' Such testimonies —and there are none of like date (save the ' Muratorian Fragment ') of an adverse character—if not conclusive, point unmistakeably to the work of Hermas having already about it the hallowing consecration of age and the reverence due to a sub-apostolic writing.

The contents of this strange book are divided into two parts. The first part contains a series of five Visions. In the last of these Visions a noble-looking man in the garb of a Shepherd, and who is named the Angel of Repentance, appears to Hermas, and bids him write down a series of Precepts or *Mandates*, and of Parables or *Similitudes*,

---

[1] Tertullian, *De Oratione*, xii. : ' Quod assignata oratione assidendi mos est quibusdam, non perspicio rationem, nisi quod pueri volunt. Quid enim, si *Hermas* ille cuius scriptura fere *Pastor* inscribitur, transacta oratione non super lectum'assedisset, verum aliud quid fecisset, id quoque ad observationem vindicaremus ? ' The actual words of the Latin version of the *Pastor* referred to occur at the beginning of the Fifth Vision : ' quum orassem domi, et consedissem supra lectum, intravit et quidam reverenda facie etc.' See Hefele, *Patr. Apost. Op.* p. 345. Hilgenfeld's comment is ' non vero " scripturae " auctoritatem ipsam sed solum argumentum inde haustum [Tertullianus] impugnavit.' *Proleg.* iii. That Tertullian used the Latin version of Hermas—*i.e.* the Vulgate version, and that this *Liber Pastoris* was read publicly in the Churches of Provincial Africa at the opening of the third century, is the opinion of Harnack. Introd. to edition of Hermas' *Pastor* by Gebhardt and Harnack, p. xlviii.

[2] Origen, *Comm. on Rom.* xvi. 14 : ' quae scriptura valde mihi utilis videtur et ut puto divinitus inspirata.' Hefele, *Proleg.* xciii. Again in his *Comm. on Hosea* Origen refers to the building of the tower in Hermas, *Vis.* iii. ii. 16, 17 in a passage beginning with καὶ ἐν τῷ Ποιμένι and ending with σημαίνει ἡ γραφή. See Hilgenfeld, p. 15. This expresses his attitude to *The Shepherd* throughout his works.

which he had come to deliver to him. The second part of the work contains the twelve *Mandates* and the ten *Similitudes*, which he received from the mouth of the Shepherd. It is not my intention to discuss the question whether the autobiographical details in this book belong to the real life-story of a genuine Hermas, nor again the question whether the two parts of the work are from the hand of the same author. ⌐There are few in the present day who have doubts on either of these questions, and I shall assume the unity of authorship of a man, who while conveying instruction and warning, moral and doctrinal, under alle-, gorical forms is dealing all the time seriously with the religious experiences and spiritual failings and trials of his own personal life and of the contemporary life of the Christian Church in Rome.[1] ⌐But these assumptions being granted, it will at once be seen that the use that can be made of ' The Shepherd ' as an illuminating historical document depends almost entirely upon its date.

It has already been suggested that the Muratorian Fragmentist blundered in his assertion that the work of Hermas was written during the episcopate of his brother Pope Pius I, because he confused the author of ' The Pastor ' with a well-known brother of the bishop, who actually bore that name. Now the very first line of Hermas' book compresses into the briefest compass the life-story of the writer's youth. ' He who brought-me-up sold me into Rome to a certain Rhoda.' [2] This implies that Hermas had either been born a slave in the house of the vendor, who did not live at Rome, or what is from the form of the expression— ὁ θρέψας—quite probable, that he had been a castaway

---

[1] The question of the unity of the work has been set at rest by Link, *Die Einheit des Pastor Hermas*, 1888, and Baumgaertner, *Die Einheit des Hermas Buchs*, 1889.

[2] ὁ θρέψας με πέπρακέν με 'Ρόδῃ τινὶ εἰς 'Ρώμην. *Vis.* i. 1. θρεττός = Lat. *verna*, a slave born and brought up in a house. Hilgenfeld quotes Pliny, *ep. ad Traian.* 66 : ' quos vocavit θρεπτούς qui liberi nati expositi, deinde sublati a quibusdam et in servitute educati sunt.' The preposition εἰς here seems to be used as meaning that Hermas was brought to Rome from elsewhere to be sold.

child whom the above-mentioned master had taken care of and brought up as a slave. In the last case his parentage would be unknown and he would have no brother. If, however, he were born a slave, three things must be postulated before the Muratorian statement can be accepted : (1) that in this slave household relationships were recognised ; (2) that both Hermas and his brother must have been sold in Rome and afterwards became freedmen ; (3) that the brother laid aside his original Greek slave name for that of Pius. Negative evidence is never conclusive, but it is certainly very strange that, if Hermas wrote his book during his brother's episcopate, there should not be a single reference to that brother's existence in a work in which the author several times speaks of his family and, as has been said, repeatedly deals with the condition, organisation, and affairs of the Church.

The allusion to Clement as a living man, entrusted with the task of communicating with foreign cities, seems to fix the date at which the Visions were written, as being previous to the accession of the said Clement to the episcopate, i.e. before 92 A.D. How hopeless is the attempt to combine a belief in the historicity of this personal reference to Clement, as a contemporary occupying an important position in the Roman Church, with an acceptance even in a modified form of the statement of the Muratorian Fragmentist is exemplified by Harnack in his ' Chronologie der Altchristlichen Literatur.' [1] Harnack will not admit for a moment that the paragraph about Clement and Grapte is ' fiction,' [2] so he meets the difficulty first by extending the life of Clement to 110 A.D., then by imagining the ' Shepherd ' to have been written in instalments during a period of some thirty-five years, the original ' little book ' consisting of a portion of Vision II only. But while admitting that the work of Hermas shows evident traces of

---

[1] Harnack, *Chronologie*, pp. 262–7.

[2] Harnack, *Chronologie*, p. 265 : ' Dass diese Worte [the passage about Clement and Grapte] eine " Fiction " seien, ist eine Annahme, die sich nicht begründen und die sich nicht halten lässt, wenn man sie durchdenkt.'

gradual growth to completion, it seems to me quite clear
that no great interval of time can have separated the first
portion written from the last. From beginning to end the
same conditions obtain throughout both as regards Hermas
personally and as regards the internal condition and the
trials of the Church. In that very Vision II which
Harnack regards as the oldest part of the book, ' a great
tribulation ' is announced as coming, and in Vision IV
the announcement is repeated ; but although past persecutions are described in the earliest ' Visions ' and latest
' Similitudes,' [1] they differ in no way in character, and there
is nowhere any allusion to the ' great tribulation ' as having
come. Again in the ' Visions ' [2] Hermas is represented as
having lost his wealth and been ruined because of the
wrong-doings of his family. This punishment has fallen
upon him for his neglect in not admonishing his children,
who are invited to penitence and are promised forgiveness,
if from their heart they repent. In ' Similitude VII ' we
learn that the children have repented from their heart, and
Hermas complains to the Shepherd Angel that nevertheless
his afflictions have not ceased. The reply is ' Dost thou think
that the sins of those who repent are straightway remitted ? '
The very essence of this rejoinder lies in the fact that the
time of Hermas' affliction—i.e. the period covered by the
book—had been short.

The past persecutions described by Hermas agree with all
we know of the Neronian persecution and its consequences.
In Vision III mention is made of those who have suffered
' scourges, imprisonments, great afflictions, crosses, wild
beasts for the Name's sake.' [3] In Sim. IV. we read of
' sufferers for the sake of the name of the Son of God, who
suffered willingly with their whole heart and gave up their
lives. These when brought before the authority and

---

[1] Compare *Vis.* ii. 2. 7 and iii. 2. 1, with *Sim.* viii. 3. 6, 7, and ix. 28.

[2] *Vis.* i. 3, ii. 2. 2–5, 3.1 ; iii. 6. 7, with *Sim.* vii. τῶν οὖν μετανοούντων
εὐθὺς [εὐθέως] δοκεῖς τὰς ἁμαρτίας ἀφίεσθαι; ' Numquid ergo,' ait, ' protinus
putas aboleri delicta eorum, qui agunt poenitentiam ? '

[3] *Vis.* iii. 2. 1 : μάστιγας, φυλακάς, θλίψεις μεγάλας, σταυρούς, θηρία.   See
also *Vis.* ii. 2.

questioned did not deny, but suffered readily '; of others as ' fearful and hesitating, who reasoned in their hearts whether they should deny or confess before they suffered ' ; of others again—' the double-minded '—who at the first rumours of persecution ' through cowardice sacrifice to idols and are ashamed of the name of their Lord.' We find in these references a remarkable agreement with the references to the Neronian persecution in 1 Peter, Hebrews, the Apocalypse, 1 Clement and the ' Annals ' of Tacitus, both as to the punishments inflicted, and the various categories into which the accused were divided, the willing and courageous martyrs, the more timid and doubtful sufferers, and the renegades and apostates, who denied their faith.[1] It may be gathered also from various passages of ' The Shepherd ' that persecution was not confined to the one violent outburst, but that at the time when Hermas was writing those who professed the Christian faith were living if not in peril yet in continual insecurity, liable at any moment to be called upon to confess or deny their faith. Such was the state of things which

---

[1] *Sim.* ix. 28, *passim* : ὅσοι ἐπ' ἐξουσίαν ἀχθέντες ἐξητάσθησαν καὶ οὐκ ἠρνήσαντο ἀλλ' ἔπαθον προθύμως . . . ὅσοι δὲ δειλοὶ καὶ ἐν δισταγμῷ ἐγένοντο καὶ ἐλογίσαντο ἐν ταῖς καρδίαις αὐτῶν, πότερον ἀρνήσονται ἢ ὁμολογήσουσι καὶ ἔπαθον . . . ὑμεῖς δὲ οἱ πάσχοντες ἕνεκεν τοῦ ὀνόματος δοξάζειν ὀφείλετε τὸν θεὸν . . . δοκεῖτε ἔργον μέγα πεποιηκέναι ἐάν τις ὑμῶν διὰ τὸν θεὸν πάθῃ. *Sim.* ix. 19. 1 : ἐκ τοῦ πρώτου ὄρους τοῦ μέλανος οἱ πιστεύσαντες τοιοῦτοί εἰσιν· ἀποστάται καὶ βλάσφημοι εἰς τὸν Κύριον, καὶ πρόδοται τῶν δούλων τοῦ θεοῦ. τούτοις δὲ μετάνοια οὐκ ἔστι, θάνατος δὲ ἔστι. *Sim.* viii. : τινὲς δὲ αὐτῶν εἰς τέλος ἀπέστησαν· οὗτοι οὖν μετάνοιαν οὐκ ἔχουσιν· διὰ γὰρ τὰς πραγματείας αὐτῶν ἐβλασφήμησαν τὸν Κύριον καὶ ἀπηρνήσαντο. Compare 1 Pet. iii. 13–17 : ἀλλ' εἰ πάσχοιτε διὰ δικαιοσύνην, μακάριοι. τὸν δὲ φόβον αὐτῶν μὴ φοβηθῆτε, μηδὲ ταραχθῆτε . . . ἕτοιμοι δὲ ἀεὶ πρὸς ἀπολογίαν παντὶ τῷ αἰτοῦντι ὑμᾶς, and iv. 12–19 : εἰ ὀνειδίζεσθε ἐν ὀνόματι Χριστοῦ, μακάριοι. . . . εἰ δὲ ὡς Χριστιανός, μὴ αἰσχυνέσθω, δοξαζέτω δὲ τὸν Θεὸν ἐν τῷ μέρει τούτῳ. Heb. vi. 4–8 : Ἀδύνατον γὰρ τοὺς ἅπαξ φωτισθέντας . . . καὶ παραπεσόντας, πάλιν ἀνακαινίζειν εἰς μετάνοιαν . . . τὸ τέλος εἰς καῦσιν. x. 32 : πολλὴν ἄθλησιν ὑπεμείνατε παθημάτων . . . ὀνειδισμοῖς τε καὶ θλίψεσι θεατριζόμενοι· . . . τὴν ἁρπαγὴν τῶν ὑπαρχόντων ὑμῶν μετὰ χαρᾶς προσεδέξασθε. Hermas himself appears to have been among those who had lost their possessions for their faith. *Vis.* ii. 2 (1, 2) ; iii. 6 (6, 7). Rev. xii. 11 : οὐκ ἠγάπησαν τὴν ψυχὴν αὐτῶν ἀχρὶ θανάτου. Also xiv. 9–13, xx. 4, and 1 Clement v. and vi. Tacitus, *Ann.* xv. 44 : ' Nero subdidit reos et quaesitissimis poenis adfecit, quos per flagitia invisos vulgus Christianos appellabat . . . igitur primum correpti qui fatebantur, deinde indicio eorum multitudo ingens. . . . .'

there is good reason to believe subsisted throughout the first two decades of Flavian rule. The constitution of the Church is a subject that has no direct interest for Hermas. The almost chance references to it in the pages of ' The Shepherd ' are however of considerable significance and value. The condition of things, we find, has altered little since Pauline days. ⌠ The charismatic ministry of apostles, prophets, and teachers are working side by side with the hierarchical officials—bishops, presbyters, and deacons. ⌡ In Vision III. 5, the white stones used for the building of the tower, which is the Church, are described as being ' the apostles, bishops, teachers, and deacons, who have walked in godly gravity, and who have discharged their duties as bishops, teachers, and deacons for the good of God's elect. Some of these have fallen asleep, some still are with us.' [1] Now this passage, which recalls the language of 1 Cor. xii. 28 and Eph. iv. 11, clearly implies that of the original apostles, bishops, teachers, and deacons there were some still living when Hermas wrote. It will be noticed that Hermas omits from this list ' the prophets,' and elsewhere throughout this work, but in Similitude XI he treats at length of the difference between true and false prophets. He was himself a prophet and he is at pains to claim for himself inspiration and a position of authority. He does not classify ' the prophets ' with the apostles and teachers, because he regards the prophets apparently as possessing gifts which place them in a category apart. From a number of passages it may be seen that Hermas, as a prophet, both claimed and exercised the right of delivering charges and admonitions to the rulers of the Church, and of speaking publicly in the assemblies.[2]

Apostles and teachers are mentioned several times in Similitude IX. In one curious passage Hermas tells how those of these apostles and teachers ' who had fallen asleep

---

[1] Vis. iii. 5: οὗτοί εἰσιν οἱ ἀπόστολοι καὶ ἐπίσκοποι καὶ διδάσκαλοι καὶ διάκονοι οἱ πορευθέντες κατὰ τὴν σεμνότητα τοῦ θεοῦ καὶ ἐπισκοπήσαντες καὶ διδάξαντες καὶ διακονήσαντες ἁγνῶς καὶ σεμνῶς τοῖς ἐκλεκτοῖς τοῦ θεοῦ, οἱ μὲν κεκοιμημένοι, οἱ δὲ ἔτι ὄντες.

[2] Vis. ii. 2. 6 ; 4. 2–3 ; iii. 8. 11 ; 9. 7–10 ; Sim. ix. 31. 6.

in the power and faith of the Son of God preached to those
who had fallen asleep before them and themselves gave
them the seal of their preaching,' i.e. baptised them.[1] From
this it has been inferred that all the Twelve Apostles were
dead when these words were written. But surely this is
not so. The ' apostles ' of Hermas were the whole body of
those chosen and sent out as missionaries by the Churches.
Only those who had ' fallen asleep ' could follow in their
Master's steps and preach to the dead. The position of the
charismatic ministry in the days of Hermas seems in fact
to have changed little since St. Paul wrote his First Epistle
to the Corinthians.

Very important historically, however, are certain hints
which may be found in ' The Shepherd ' about changes at
work in the constitution of the official hierarchy. Twice
Hermas refers to the hierarchy under the general title of
' chiefs of the Church,' [2] using the same Greek term as is
employed in the Epistle to the Hebrews and in 1 Clement.
Only once does the word *presbyters* occur as the designation
of this official class, when the aged woman, the Church,
bids Hermas read the book she has given him—' to this city
with the presbyters that preside over the Church.' And here
the word for ' those who preside ' [3] is a technical word found
several times in the same sense in St. Paul's epistles. The
references of Hermas therefore to the constitution of the
Church are thus thoroughly primitive, and the picture
drawn by him of the local organisation essentially the same
as that which we find in the Pauline epistles. It is clear for

---

[1] *Sim.* ix. 16. 5 : οὗτοι οἱ ἀπόστολοι καὶ οἱ διδάσκαλοι οἱ κηρύξαντες τὸ
ὄνομα τοῦ υἱοῦ τοῦ θεοῦ, κοιμηθέντες ἐν δυνάμει καὶ πίστει τοῦ υἱοῦ τοῦ θεοῦ ἐκήρυξαν
καὶ τοῖς προκεκοιμημένοις καὶ αὐτοὶ ἔδωκαν αὐτοῖς τὴν σφραγῖδα τοῦ κηρύγματος.
In this passage the numbers of these ' apostles and teachers ' is given as
forty, and in the previous paragraph (4) the words ἡ σφραγὶς τὸ ὕδωρ ἐστίν
explain the meaning of ' the Seal.' The ' apostles ' throughout *The
Shepherd* is used in the wider sense of ' missionaries ' except in *Sim.*
ix. 17. 1.
[2] οἱ προηγούμενοι. *Vis.* ii. 2. 6 ; iii. 9, 7. Compare 1 Clem. xxi. 6.
οἱ ἡγούμενοι is found 1 Clem. i. 3 and Heb. xiii. 7, 17, 24.
[3] *Vis.* ii. 4. 2 : οἱ προιστάμενοι ; see 1 Thess. v. 12 ; Rom. xii. 8 ;
1 Tim. v. 17.

instance that the title *episcopus* was not yet confined to a single individual, but was still the common designation of all presbyters who were charged with the cure of souls. Nevertheless there are signs that an evolutionary movement was already in progress, which was preparing the way for that transformation in the signification of the word ' bishop,' which we find already accomplished at the time when Ignatius wrote his epistles towards the end of the first decade of the second century. This seems to be the fair and legitimate interpretation of certain passages of ' The Shepherd,' to which we will now turn our attention.

Sternly does the Prophet in Vision III rebuke the dissensions among those who sit in the foremost seats.[1] Again in Similitude VIII the Shepherd-Angel speaks of certain men ' who, though always faithful and good, were jealous one of another about the first places and a certain dignity '[2] (δόξης τινός). ' But these,' he continues, ' are all foolish to contend thus for the first places. Nevertheless, when they heard my commands, being good men they cleansed themselves and repented quickly.' Now knowing, as we do, on grounds approaching to historical certainty that from the time of the deaths of the apostles Peter and Paul a succession of presbyters occupied a post of pre-eminence and dignity among their fellows—that of presiding bishop and official head of the local Church—is it not permissible to read between the lines that, around this office, heart-

---

[1] *Vis.* iii. 7, 9 : νῦν οὖν ὑμῖν λέγω τοῖς προηγουμένοις τῆς ἐκκλησίας καὶ τοῖς πρωτοκαθεδρίταις· μὴ γίνεσθε ὅμοιοι τοῖς φαρμακοῖς . . . βλέπετε οὖν, τέκνα, μήποτε αὗται αἱ διχοστασίαι ὑμῶν ἀποστερήσουσιν τὴν ζωὴν ὑμῶν . . .

[2] *Sim.* viii. 7: 4 : ἔχοντες ζῆλόν τινα ἐν ἀλλήλοις περὶ πρωτείων καὶ περὶ δόξης τινός. Harnack (*Gesch. d. Altchrist. Lit.* 1,' Chronologie,' p. 175) after quoting these passages writes : ' die zuletzt angeführten Stellen mögen darauf hinweisen, dass der monarchische Episkopat damals in Anzug war ; aber von diesem selbst ist in dem Buche keine Spur zu finden.' It is curious that a critic of the calibre of Harnack should not see that the statement in the last clause does not and cannot weaken in the very least the force of the admission previously made. Hermas felt it was his duty to rebuke the rivalries and dissensions to which the growing power of the bishop gave rise, but why should he, writing for Roman Christians of his own day, and not for the enlightenment of far distant posterity, inform his contemporaries of a fact which was a matter of common knowledge ?

burnings and jealousies not unaccompanied by cabals and intrigues had arisen ? During the two long episcopates of Linus and Anencletus, each of twelve years according to tradition, the office that they held had, we can scarcely doubt, been gradually drawing to itself more and more of initiative and authority, and becoming more monarchical in character. If then Hermas wrote, as I am now contending he did, during the closing years of Anencletus, the long immunity from violent persecution which the Church in Rome had then enjoyed was precisely a period when in such a large and mixed community, containing unstable and doubtful elements, strifes and dissensions about precedence might arise, and ambitious presbyters be found ready to assert with acrimony and self-assertion their equality of privilege with one who was nominally only one of themselves, *primus inter pares* it might be, but still a *presbyter* like the rest.

The immunity from persecution, to which I have referred, was, however, not long to endure, and the severe trial through which the Church had to pass before the end of Domitian's reign would doubtless be more effective in purifying and cleansing it from those jealous, self-seeking, and factious elements of which Hermas speaks, than his rebukes and upbraidings. The coming tribulation, which he predicted as being at hand, was no doubt that tribulation [1] which first-century Christianity expected would precede, in accordance with the Lord's words, the Second Advent and the final consummation of all things. The prophecy proved true, however, though in a different sense from that which the prophet intended.

Christian writers have been accustomed to couple together the names of Nero and Domitian, as the first two persecutors of the Church. It has already been shown that although the attack of Nero on the Christians was but the violent outburst of a tyrant, anxious to divert public odium from himself against a body of sectaries who were generally hated and despised, it had permanent results and

[1] St. Matt. xxiv. 21, 29 ; St. Mark, xiii. 24 ; compare 2 Thess. i. 4–10.

marked the real beginning of what was to be the continuous policy of the Roman State. The persecution of the adherents of the Christian faith by Domitian was far less direct, and did not, as may be gathered from the letter of Pliny to Trajan about sixteen years later, establish any fresh precedents; for had such fresh precedents been established they would not have escaped the notice of this writer, who was a contemporary and, as his correspondence proves, a close observer of current events.

The origin of the persecution of Domitian was not so much religious as fiscal. The Imperial treasury had been emptied by a series of extravagances. In his search for fresh sources of income, Domitian bethought him of the tax which Vespasian had in 70 A.D. imposed upon the Jews, commanding them, as a condition for their religious privileges being respected, to pay henceforth, as already stated, the *didrachma* they had become accustomed to contribute for the support of the Temple and its worship at Jerusalem to the Roman authority for the maintenance of the Temple of Jupiter Capitolinus. Hitherto the collection of this tax had been leniently carried out and had been only demanded from those circumcised Jews who were professed members of the synagogues. Domitian determined that all who lived *more Iudaico*, including the large class of 'God-fearers' and indeed all who to a greater or less extent followed Jewish customs, should be liable, and a strict inquisition was in consequence made.[1] The exact date is not accurately known, but what followed was the bringing to the notice of the Government the existence of a body of people living after the Jewish fashion but repudiating any connexion with the synagogues and therefore having no right to shelter themselves behind the Jewish privileges. Against them the charge of 'atheism and Jewish manners' was accordingly preferred, and out of the fiscal demand there came a series of arrests and trials in which many Christians suffered.

[1] Suet. *Domitian*, 12: 'Praeter caeteros Iudaicus fiscus acerbissime actus est; ad quem deferebantur qui vel improfessi Iudaicam viverent vitam, vel, dissimulata origine, imposita genti tributa non pependissent.' See Martial, vii. 55. 7.

It must, however, be borne in mind that there does not seem to have been any organised attack upon the Christian faith as such, but rather that a number of individuals, both of high rank and of low, became for various causes, during the reign of terror which marked the closing years of Domitian's rule, suspect to the government, and paid by their lives or their exile, and in both cases by the confiscation of their property, the penalty for exciting the fears, the jealousy, or the rapacity of the tyrant.[1] Moreover to a man whose proclamations began with the words ' our God and Lord Domitian,' and who ostentatiously made the restoration of the national religion one of the aims of his policy, it was easy under the charges of ' atheism and Jewish manners ' or ' of being movers of innovations '[2] to strike at those who held aloof from taking part in Caesar-worship or in the religious festivals and spectacles.

Very little, practically nothing, is known of the extent to which the general body of Christians suffered under Domitian. In as far as persecution fell upon the humbler classes, it arose, as I have pointed out, not as part of a systematic attack on the Christian religion as such, but as a result of the stricter exaction of the *didrachma* tax. And it was by no means confined to Rome. Wherever colonies of Jews were settled the fiscal inquisition would be made, and thus the presence of Christian communities brought to the official notice of the magistrates. In their case the procedure would be summary. The mere confession of the Name was sufficient to place the Christian outside the law. He would be asked either to deny the faith or to suffer martyrdom, and among the large number of those who were but half and half Christians, doubtless very many conformed to the request and saved their lives. Eusebius in his ' Chronicle ' quotes the historian Bruttius as stating that many Christians suffered under Domitian, but the expression

---

[1] Suet. *Domitian*, 3: ' Virtutes quoque in vitia deflexit; quantum coniectare licet, super ingenii naturam inopia rapax, metu saevus.' Orosius, vii. 10: ' Nobilissimos e senatu, invidiae simul et praedae causa . . . interfecit.'   [2] *Ibid.* 10: ' molitores novarum rerum.'

is a very vague one,[1] and obviously the chief interest of the passage to Eusebius, as it is to us, is its reference to the important fact that among the many high and influential persons whom the tyrant visited with death or banishment were certain of his own near relatives who were Christians. It is around the names of a very small group of individuals that the chief interest of the Domitianic persecution centres, an interest which has been greatly increased by recent archaeological discoveries.

The passage from the 'Chronicle' of Eusebius merely tells us the name of one of these relatives of Domitian who, according to his authority Bruttius, suffered banishment because she was a Christian. Her name was Flavia Domitilla, and she is described in Jerome's Latin version as ' being a niece of Flavius Clemens the consul by his sister.' Her place of banishment was the island of Pontia. The Armenian version of the 'Chronicle' suggests that there may be in this passage some corruption of the text,[2] nevertheless its general correctness is confirmed strongly by the parallel passage from the ' History' of Eusebius, where that writer basing his statement on the evidence of heathen historians, prominent amongst whom would be the Bruttius named in the 'Chronicle,' states that ' in the fifteenth year of Domitian amongst many others who suffered persecution was Flavia Domitilla, a daughter of the sister of Flavius Clemens, one of the consuls at Rome at that time, who for her witness to Christ was banished as a punishment to the island of Pontia.' [3]

---

[1] According to the Latin Hieronymian version (ed. Schöne, ii. p. 163) : 'Scribit Bruttius plurimos Christianorum sub Domiciano fecisse martyrium, inter quos et Flaviam Domitillam Flavii Clementis consulis ex sorore neptem in insulam Pontianam relegatam quia se Christianam esse testata sit.' See Lightfoot, *Apost. Fathers*, part i. vol. i. p. 108.

[2] In the Latin translation of the Armenian version of the *Chronicle* (ed. Schöne, ii. p. 160) we find : ' refert autem Brettius, multos Christianorum sub Dometiano subiisse martyrium ; Flavia vero Dometila et Flavus Clementis consulis sororis filius in insulam Pontiam fugit quia se Christianum esse professus est.' Lightfoot, *ibid.* p. 105. In the Syrian Epit. (ed. Schöne, p. 214) : ' Flaviam Domitillam, filiam sororis Clementis consulis.' [3] Eus. *Hist. Eccl.* iii. 18.

Now this evidence of Eusebius, when compared with certain passages in the pages of Dion Cassius and Suetonius, requires very careful attention. Dion writes (I quote the abridgement of Xiphilinus)—'in this year (95 A.D.) Domitian put to death Flavius Clemens, being then consul, his cousin, and Flavia Domitilla, his relation and the wife of the same [Clemens]. Both were condemned for the crime of "atheism." On this charge were condemned many others who had adopted Jewish customs ; some were put to death, others punished by confiscation. Domitilla was only transported to the island of Pandateria.'[1] Now the relationship of this Domitilla to Domitian is revealed to us plainly by Quintilian,[2] who was tutor to the sons of Flavius Clemens and who states that they were the grandchildren of the Emperor's sister, who also bore the name of Flavia Domitilla. This daughter of Vespasian died before her father, but the name of the grand-daughter appears on several extant inscriptions, from which we learn that the Christian catacomb in which many members of the Flavian family were buried, and which dates from the first century, was excavated on her property.[3] There can be no doubt that she was a Christian and that the faith of Christ had been adopted by others closely related to Domitian. Whether Flavius Clemens himself was actually a baptised Christian and suffered martyrdom, it is very difficult to say. The complete silence of Eusebius and of Christian legend and tradition would rather lead to the conclusion that, though the consul may have been well-disposed towards Christianity and even lived after the Christian manner, and so have incurred the charge of ' atheism,' yet this was not the real cause which

---

[1] Dion Cassius, lxvii. 14 : κὰν τῷ αὐτῷ ἔτει ἄλλους τε πολλοὺς καὶ τὸν Φλαούϊον Κλήμεντα ὑπατεύοντα, καίπερ ἀνεψιὸν ὄντα καὶ γυναῖκα καὶ αὐτὴν συγγενῆ ἑαυτοῦ Φλαουΐαν Δομιτίλλαν ἔχοντα, κατέσφαξεν ὁ Δομετιανός· ἐπηνέχθη δὲ ἀμφοῖν ἔγκλημα ἀθεότητος, ὑφ' ἧς καὶ ἄλλοι ἐς τὰ τῶν Ἰουδαίων ἔθη ἐξοκέλλοντες πολλοὶ κατεδικάσθησαν, καὶ οἱ μὲν ἀπέθανον, οἱ δὲ τῶν γοῦν οὐσιῶν ἐστερήθησαν· ἡ δὲ Δομιτίλλα ὑπερωρίσθη μόνον ἐς Πανδατερίαν.

[2] Quint. Inst. Orat. iv. prooem.: ' Cum mihi Domitianus Augustus sororis suae nepotum delegavit curam.'

[3] See Appendix, Note F, The Cemeteries of Priscilla and Domitilla. C.I.L. vi. 948, 949, 8942, 16246.

led to his being executed. Like his brother Flavius Sabinus
before him he stood too near the throne for the suspicious
and childless tyrant to endure the presence in Rome of
those whose blood-relationship made them possible rivals
and successors. This is borne out by the statement of
Suetonius, who after describing the morbid state of fear and
suspicion, amounting almost to semi-madness, in which
Domitian spent his last years, living in constant dread of
conspiracy and assassination, proceeds—' finally he suddenly
put to death on the faintest suspicion, when he had only
just ceased to be consul, Flavius Clemens, his cousin-german,
a man of the most contemptible inactivity, whose sons, then
of very tender age, he had openly destined for his successors,
and, discarding their former names, had ordered one to be
called Vespasian, the other Domitian.   By this violent act
he very much hastened his own destruction.' [1]   It was in
fact by the hand of Stephanus, a freedman and steward of
Domitilla, Flavius Clemens' wife, that the tyrant was stabbed
a few months later.

Now Suetonius had previously given an account of the
murder of Flavius Sabinus, the elder brother of Flavius
Clemens, by his cousin Domitian for no other reason than a
mistake of a herald, who on Sabinus being chosen at the
consular election, inadvertently proclaimed him to the people
not as *consul* but as *imperator*,[2] and in the passage quoted
above the historian clearly implies that it was on some
similar very slender ground of political suspicion that Flavius
Clemens fell a victim to Domitian's jealousy.   Possibly his
Christian principles, however laxly held, may have compelled
him during his tenure of office to hold aloof from certain
religious ceremonies and spectacles, thus bringing down
upon him the imperial anger.   The words of Suetonius that
he was ' a man of most contemptible inertia '[3] represent a

---

[1] Suetonius, *Domitian*, 15-17 : ' repente ex tenuissima suspicione
tantum non in ipso eius consulatu interemit.'

[2] Suetonius, *Domitian*, 10.

[3] ' Contemptissimae inertiae.'   Compare Tacitus' words in reference
to his father, *Hist.* iii. 65 : ' mitem virum abhorrere a sanguine et
caedibus '; 73 : ' Flavium Sabinum inermem neque fugam coeptantem

charge which was frequently brought against the Christians, because their religious scruples prevented them from taking an active part in the political life and still more in the cruel and vicious amusements of their time. The same charge is brought by Tacitus against Flavius Sabinus, the City Prefect during the latter years of Nero. He was the elder brother of Vespasian and the father of the Sabinus and Clemens put to death by Domitian. He perished in defending the Capitol against the German mercenaries of Vitellius in 69 A.D. Tacitus describes him as at the close of his life ' mild in character, averse to bloodshed, and sluggish.' He must in his official capacity have taken part in the persecution of 65 A.D., and the effect of what he witnessed may well have been the conversion wholly or in part of the unwilling persecutor.

The theory of the identity of Flavius Clemens the consul put to death in 95 A.D. with Clement who was bishop of Rome at that period was at one time seriously put forward by a number of eminent German scholars,[1] but it has now been generally abandoned. It was pointed out with a certain amount of plausibility that the later Clementine legend ascribing to the bishop a close connexion with the imperial family was due to the fact that he was a mere duplication of the consul, and that it was unlikely that there should be at once in Rome two persons bearing the same name, one of whom occupied one of the highest official positions in the state, and the other was the official head of the Christian community. Dr. Lightfoot was able to show conclusively that this theory of duplication had no foundation and was untenable, but his own solution of the mystery surrounding Clement the bishop's personality, ' that he was a man of Jewish descent, a freedman or the son of a freedman

circumsistunt'; 75 : after stating that Flavius Sabinus had served the state in thirty-five campaigns and with distinction at home and abroad, Tacitus proceeds : ' in fine vitae alii segnem, multi moderatum et civium sanguinis parcum credidere.' It was a change of disposition that was observed at the close of the life of this tried servant of the State. See Allard, *Hist. d. Persécutions*, i. pp. 81–115 (ed. 1892).

[1] Lipsius, Volkmar, Hilgenfeld, Erbes, at one time Harnack.

belonging to the household of Flavius Clemens,' [1] is equally if not more impossible. Dr. Lightfoot seems to have forgotten that Flavius Clemens was quite a young man, probably not more than thirty, when he died.[2] ⌐Clement the bishop, unless all that tradition relates of him be false, must have been at least fifty in 95 A.D. He could not in any case have been the son of a freedman of the younger man⌐ Again if a freedman he would not have adopted his master's *cognomen*, but would have retained his own slave name as *cognomen*, preceded by the *nomen* Flavius.

It is somewhat strange, however, that while so many attempts have been made either to identify the two Clements mentioned above or at least to connect them in some way with each other, the presence of a third contemporary Clement, who undoubtedly played a much larger part in Roman public life than either of the other two, has been overlooked. Yet I am now going to ask you to fix your attention upon this man and his family relationships, for I believe that by doing so we shall find the clue to the solution of many difficulties and shall be able to clear up a number of doubtful points in the history of Roman Christianity at the end of the first century. Here in the lecture itself I can only indicate briefly and in outline the hypothesis which I am putting forward, and am perforce reserving for a special note in the Appendix the fuller discussion of details and of the authorities on which the various statements and suggestions are based.[3]

M. Arrecinus Clemens was the son of M. Arrecinus Tertullus Clemens, Praetorian Prefect under Caligula. From Josephus we learn that this Tertullus Clemens was privy to the conspiracy which resulted in the murder of that Emperor, and connived at it. From the same authority comes the information that after the assassination Herod

---

[1] Lightfoot, *Apost. Fathers*, part i. vol. i. pp. 59–61.

[2] Tac. *Hist.* iii. 69 : 'eoque, concubia nocte, suos liberos Sabinus, et Domitianum, fratris filium in capitolium accivit.' The children of Sabinus were quite young in 70 A.D., and Clemens was younger than Sabinus. His own sons were children under a tutor in 95 A.D. The fact that he did not become consul till that date is of itself a proof of his youth. The Flavian emperors as a rule reserved the consulships for members of their own family. [3] Appendix, Note D, The Family of Clement the Bishop.

Agrippa was allowed to act as an intermediary between the Praetorian troops and the soldiery who obeyed the Senate. The result was that Claudius who had been acclaimed Emperor in the camp became quietly possessed of the reins of power without bloodshed. He owed thus his peaceful accession to the throne in no small measure to the authority exercised by the Praetorian Prefect. How great that authority and influence was may be gathered from the fact that his son thirty years later was welcomed by the guards as their Prefect because the memory of his father was still fresh among them.

It should be noted that it is from the Jewish historian, Josephus, only that the information comes as to the parts played by Arrecinus Tertullus Clemens and Herod Agrippa before and after Caligula's death, and it seems to me a perfectly legitimate inference that the Prefect was a friend of Agrippa and may indeed like many other well-to-do Romans have felt the attraction of the synagogue and to a greater or less extent been a ' God-fearer.' Be this as it may, it is certain that Titus Flavius Vespasianus was a relative of Tertullus Clemens. Vespasian, Suetonius tells us, was brought up from early childhood by his grandmother Tertulla, a name which suggests not merely the bond of kinship between the Prefect and the future Emperor but the likelihood that in their youth they were closely associated. Evidence of the friendliness of the relations which continued to subsist between the two men in later life is not wanting. Titus, the son of Vespasian, was born in 39 A.D. in very poor circumstances, but shortly after the accession of Claudius both Vespasian himself and his elder brother T. Flavius Sabinus obtained commands in the expedition to Britain under Aulus Plautius. In his father's absence we find Titus at Court, as the companion of Britannicus, the son of Claudius. Can we not see here signs that Clemens to whom Claudius owed so much had used his influence with the Emperor on behalf of his kinsmen ? As a further mark of the closeness of the relations between them we find that Titus, while still little more than a boy, was married to Arrecina Tertulla, daughter of Clemens. Domitian, the younger son of Vespasian, was not born until 51 A.D., after his father's return from Britain, and he seems to have found a home with his uncle, T. Flavius Sabinus, during the years 57–69 A.D., when Vespasian was abroad and Sabinus filled the post of Prefect of the City. This elder brother of Vespasian did not marry till late in life, probably not until after he settled in Rome in 57 A.D. at the close of his governorship of Moesia, for, as we have already seen, his children were still young when he was murdered in December 69 A.D. Domitian, then aged eighteen, was with his uncle in the Capitol, when it was stormed by the Vitellian troops, and narrowly escaped with his life, to be immediately afterwards saluted as Caesar and invested with consular authority. One of his first acts was the appointment of his relative, M. Arrecinus Clemens, who is described by Tacitus as being in very great favour with Domitian, to the post of Praetorian Prefect, formerly held by his father. This younger Arrecinus Clemens was afterwards twice consul (suffect) in 73 A.D. and 94 A.D., and from 82 A.D. onwards a member of the Imperial Council. Shortly after his second consulship he was suddenly condemned and put to death by Domitian, who, as Suetonius tells us, treated him with every mark of regard up to the last. The death of this active and prominent man can therefore have occurred only about a year before that of Flavius Clemens.

It is not surprising that there should be confusion and mistake on the part of later Christian writers, who knew nothing of Clemens the consul of 94 A.D., the man of twenty-five years' official experience, but attributed all references in heathen writers to a consul of that name to Flavius Clemens, thereby creating entanglements and difficulties. For instance it has been seen that Eusebius, referring to Bruttius [1] as his authority, both in his ' History ' and in his

---

[1] At Torre Marancia, on the Via Ardeatina, on a plot of land adjoining the entrance to the cemetery of Domitilla, a burial place of the Bruttian *gens* has been discovered. The historian was probably Bruttius Praesens, the friend of Pliny the Younger. De Rossi, *Bull. Arch. crist.* 1865, p. 24 ; 1875, p. 74. Marucchi, *Roma Sotterranea Cristiana*, N.S. tom. i. 22–23, 29–30. See also App. Note F, Cemeteries of Priscilla and Domitilla.

'Chronicle,' states that Flavia Domitilla, the niece [the sister's child] of Flavius Clemens, one of the consuls at that time, had been exiled because of her profession of the Christian faith to the island of Pontia. There is no mention in either passage of the death of Flavius Clemens. Further, Jerome, in one of his epistles giving a description of the visit of a certain Paula in 385 A.D. to the island of Pontia, declares that she saw there the cells in which Flavia Domitilla had spent a long exile.

On the other hand Suetonius and Philostratus record the death of Flavius Clemens without any hint of any punishment falling upon any Flavia Domitilla. Dion Cassius, however, declares that both Flavius Clemens and his wife Flavia Domitilla were accused of the crime of 'atheism' and that he was executed, while his wife was banished to the island not of Pontia but of Pandateria.

This is all very puzzling, but there is yet another source of information available to us—the legendary 'Acts of Nereus and Achilles.' These 'Acts,' though late in date and as regards many details pure fiction, rest nevertheless on a solid basis of real fact, for a memorial of Nereus and Achilles (according to the story the martyred chamberlains of a Flavia Domitilla, whose mother Plautilla was the sister of Clemens the Consul) has been found in the cemetery of Domitilla, where the 'Acts' tell us the bodies were laid. Flavia Domitilla herself, so runs this narrative, had been banished to the island of Pontia because as a Christian she wished to live in virginity, and had refused to marry in accordance with the Emperor's commands. To say that such an incident is one common to early Christian hagiography is no argument against its authenticity in this or any particular instance. It is a simple matter of fact that the precepts of St. Paul on the subject of virginity had a far-reaching influence, and that during the age of persecution many Christian women did regard the state of life commended by the Apostle as the highest ideal of discipleship. Plautilla's name, I can see no reason to doubt, was found in the original source which furnished the materials for the sixth-century 'Acts of Nereus and Achilles.' I am inclined, however, to connect the disobedience and banishment of Domitilla the virgin with the sudden disgrace and execution of Arrecinus Clemens, she being his niece and Plautilla his sister. Eusebius states that the Domitilla banished to the island of Pontia was the niece of Flavius Clemens, and he quotes the contemporary historian Bruttius as his authority. Apart from other reasons for believing that Eusebius must have made a mistake, to which I shall refer directly, I think it more than likely that he never saw the original narrative of Bruttius at all, but only some Greek extract from it at second hand, in which the mother of Domitilla was described, just as she is in ' The Acts of Nereus and Achilles,' simply as the sister of Clemens the consul. He naturally would interpret this as a reference to Flavius Clemens. The same error was committed by the author of the 'Chronicon Paschale,' who records that Flavius Clemens was consul both in 93 A.D. and 95 A.D., whereas it is certain that he was consul for the first time in 95 A.D., the consul in 94 A.D. being Arrecinus Clemens.

There is every mark (except the duplication of names) that the account given by Dion Cassius of the execution of Flavius Clemens and the condemnation of his wife, Domitian's niece, to exile in the island of Pandateria is quite distinct from that recorded by Eusebius on the authority of Bruttius, and with fuller detail in ' The Acts of Nereus and Achilles.' Eusebius in mentioning the name of Flavius Clemens could surely not have refrained from speaking of his fate had the passage from Bruttius that was before his eyes made any allusion to this last and crowning act of Domitian's cruelty. No, the incidents connected with the sentences on the two Flavia Domitillas seem to have been separated by an interval of some twelve months or more from each other.

Circumstantial evidence is in favour of the conclusion I have adopted. In 95 A.D. Flavius Clemens was, as I have said, still quite a young man. It is therefore extremely improbable that he should have had a niece of sufficient age and standing to have aroused the resentment of Domitian, or that she should have been accompanied into exile by two soldier-chamberlains, the historical reality of whose martyrdom and subsequent burial in the cemetery of Domitilla extant memorials testify. Dr. Lightfoot [1] sees a discrepancy in the representation of these two men both as soldiers of the guard and as chamberlains of Domitilla. It is rather an undesigned piece of confirmatory evidence, if, as I am assuming, this Domitilla were the niece and the granddaughter of two Pretorian Prefects, one of whom had just served the office of consul.

But further light may, I think, be thrown upon her personality, which will reveal still more clearly the causes for the confusion of names to which I have referred. It never seems to have struck any of the numerous critics and commentators who have dealt with these questions, that 'Clemens' was not a *cognomen* in use among the Flavian family. If the second son of T. Flavius Sabinus received the *cognomen* Clemens, the inference is that he derived it from his mother.

The name of the wife of Flavius Sabinus, the brother of Vespasian, is not recorded, but he married late in life, and if that wife were Plautilla, daughter of the Praetorian Prefect, Tertullus Clemens, and sister of Arrecinus Clemens the consul of 93 A.D., it seems to me that not merely the difficulties attaching to the scanty historical references to the Domitianic persecutions, but also those connected with the more or less legendary traditions relating to the same period, will be largely removed. Let us examine some of the consequences of the hypothesis that I have put forward as to Plautilla having been the wife of Titus Flavius Sabinus, the Prefect of the City from 57 to 69 A.D. According to 'The Acts of Nereus and Achilles' she was a Christian convert and died the same year that St. Peter was martyred. Sabinus was murdered in 69 A.D. and as I have already pointed out there are hints in the narrative of Tacitus that he,

[1] Lightfoot, *Apost. Fathers*, part i. vol. i. p. 51.

too, may in his last years have imbibed Christian principles. The natural guardian of his orphan children would be their uncle M. Arrecinus Clemens, the Praetorian Prefect of 70 A.D. The two sons as they grew up would no doubt pass under the direct care of Vespasian himself, but the daughter, Flavia Domitilla, would remain with her uncle, and would thus be rightly described not as the sister of Flavius Clemens but as the niece of Arrecinus.

Again, the name Plautilla suggested to De Rossi that her mother's name was likely to be ' Plautia.' This suggestion I shall adopt by the further assumption that the wife of Tertullus Clemens was a sister of Aulus Plautius the conqueror of Britain, and therefore a relative of Plautia Urgulanilla the second wife of Claudius and sister-in-law to Pomponia Graecina, whose conversion through Judaism to Christianity may be dated as having taken place early in Claudius' reign. That Tertullus Clemens either personally or through his wife had some special Jewish connexion has already been suggested as an explanation of the particular knowledge shown by Josephus about the part played by this Praetorian Prefect at the time of the assassination of Caligula ; and if his wife were the sister of Aulus Plautius not only is there a possibility that she may have shared the religious views of Pomponia Graecina, but a further reason is adduced for the appointment of both Vespasian and his brother Sabinus to posts in the army of Britain under that general.

Thus a scheme of relationship between the Flavian and Arrecinian families has been drawn up, which has at least the not inconsiderable merit of co-ordinating a number of isolated facts and bringing them into harmony with one another. It will be found that it is able to answer to a further and still more trying test of its general accuracy. I have suggested at the close of the last lecture that Clement the Bishop was a younger brother of M. Arrecinus Clemens the consul. It will be found, as I then said, that such a suggestion was in no way a random conjecture. The high position which the famous bishop held, according to all the traditions that have come down to us, in the estimation of later generations was due not to his being the author of the Epistle sent by the Roman Church to the Church at Corinth, but to his being a personal disciple of St. Peter and at the same time a man of distinguished birth and family connexion. In the ' Acts of Nereus and Achilles ' the bishop is described as being ' the son of a brother of Clemens the consul.' The relations between him and St. Peter, the evidence for which is strong and convincing, render it more probable that he was the younger brother of Arrecinus. This would be in accordance with what we find in the Clementine ' Homilies ' and ' Recognitions.' In their accounts of the early life of the bishop, which are derived from a common earlier source, Clement is represented as the youngest of his family. In these romances, the biographical chronology is hopeless. The names of the parents and brothers of the bishop belong to the period of Hadrian and the Antonines, while his conversion takes place in the reign of Tiberius. The statement, however, that the father of Clement was a near relative and foster-brother of an emperor and that his mother was likewise a kinswoman of Caesar can scarcely be the pure invention of a writer of fiction. There could be no object in a romancer going out of his way to make such an assertion unless it had behind it a genuine historical tradition. If Clement, however, were the son of Arrecinus Tertullus Clemens and of Plautia the sister of Aulus Plautius, his father was a relative and possibly the foster-brother of Vespasian, his mother a kinswoman of Claudius. It is an interesting thought that with such parentage he may have gained his early knowledge of the Jewish scriptures and of the principles of Christianity at the feet of Pomponia Graecina.

Among the victims of Domitian in 95 A.D. was a member of one of the most illustrious families in Rome—M' Acilius Glabrio.[1] While he was consul in 91 A.D. as the colleague of M. Ulpius Trajanus, the future emperor, he appears to

---

[1] Gsell, *Le Règne de l'Empereur Domitien*, pp. 294-6; Allard, *Hist. des Persécutions*, pp. 111-115.

have excited the suspicion and dislike of Domitian, who in order to humiliate and degrade him compelled Glabrio to fight with wild beasts in the amphitheatre adjoining the imperial villa at Albanum. He was victorious but was afterwards exiled. This punishment did not, however, satisfy the vindictive spirit of the Emperor. Dion Cassius, after telling of the execution of Flavius Clemens and the banishment of his wife upon the charge of 'atheism and Jewish manners,' says that he also caused Acilius Glabrio to be put to death for the same crimes. Suetonius likewise states that Acilius Glabrio in his place of exile and several others of senatorial and consular rank were executed as 'instigators of novelties '—*molitores rerum novarum*.[1] The character of these charges had for some time given rise to something more than a suspicion that this M' Acilius Glabrio may have been a Christian. This suspicion has been converted almost into certainty by the discovery in 1888 by De Rossi in the first-century cemetery of Priscilla of a gamma-shaped crypt formerly richly adorned with frescoes, now in a state of ruin, but containing many fragments of inscriptions showing that this was a burial place of the Acilii Glabriones and other members of the Acilian Gens.[2] It has been a great misfortune that in this catacomb, as in that of Domitilla, so much wanton destruction should have been wrought by the searchers for relics (especially at the beginning of the seventeenth century)/in ignorant disregard of the inestimable historical value of these precious archaeological records of primitive Roman Christianity.] The name Priscilla was not uncommon in the Acilian family, and it is thought that the particular Priscilla from whom the catacomb derives its name may have been the mother of M' Acilius Glabrio, the consul of 91 A.D. These two cemeteries of Priscilla and Domitilla even in their present devastated

---

[1] Dion Cassius, lxvii. 12, 14 ; Suet. *Domitian*, 10, 19 ; Juvenal, iv. 93–103 ; Fronto, *Ep. ad M. Caesarem*, v. 23.

[2] De Rossi, *Bull. di Arch. Crist.* 1888–89, pp. 15–66, 103–133 ; *Roma Sotterranea*, p. 319 ; Lanciani, *Pagan and Christian Rome*, pp. 4–8 ; Wahl, *Römische Quartalschrift*, 1890, iv. pp. 305 ff ; Marucchi, *Arch. Chrétienne*, ii. pp. 422–7. See App. Note F, Cemeteries of Priscilla and Domitilla.

condition bear witness, which cannot be gainsaid, to the hold which Christianity had obtained among the upper classes in the reign of Domitian.

This account of the Church in Rome in the first century has had to be compressed into eight lectures. Now compression implies that certain matters have been passed over lightly, others selected for special and detailed treatment. This is a true description of the method that I have followed, and it has consisted in choosing for more exhaustive and careful examination precisely those questions and subjects round which controversies have arisen and on which there have been and are strong differences of opinion. It is, for instance, of vital importance to a right understanding of the growth of Christianity in the centre of the empire, that the contemporary documents which throw light upon it should be correctly dated, and to this question of dates much attention, perhaps some may think a disproportionate amount of attention, has been given. That, however, depends entirely upon the results achieved by arguments whose force and validity rest upon the patient unravelling and disentanglement of a quantity of involved, obscure, and sometimes apparently contradictory evidence. This I will venture to say, that while only too deeply conscious of the limitations of my knowledge, it has been my endeavour in these lectures freely, and without prejudice, to give expression to the conclusions which close personal study of the documentary and epigraphic evidence has led me to form, in the hope if not of convincing or converting those who have adopted different views, at least of stimulating inquiry and arousing fresh interest in some questions that have been regarded as *choses jugées,* and to remind those who may do me the honour of reading these pages, that experience has taught that there are very few indeed even of the so-called ' accepted results of criticism ' which can be received without the mental reservation of a note of interrogation.

APPENDICES

NOTE A.

CHRONOLOGICAL TABLE OF EVENTS MENTIONED IN THE LECTURES.

The Crucifixion	Passover, 29 A.D.
Martyrdom of St. Stephen . .	33 A.D.
Accession of Claudius . . .	January 24, 41 A.D.
Imprisonment of St. Peter . .	Passover, 42 A.D.
St. Peter's 1st visit to Rome . .	Summer, 42 A.D.
Death of Herod Agrippa . . .	Spring, 44 A.D.
Prophecy of Agabus	44 A.D.
Famine in Judaea	45–46 A.D.
Queen Helena in Jerusalem . .	45 A.D.
St. Mark's Gospel written at Rome .	44–45 A.D.
St. Peter with St. Mark leaves Rome .	45 A.D.
St. Peter at Jerusalem . . .	Spring, 46 A.D.
Barnabas and Saul bring alms from Antioch to Jerusalem (visit of Gal. ii. 1–10)	Pentecost, 46 A.D.
Barnabas and Saul with Mark sail from Antioch to Cyprus	Spring, 47 A.D.
St. Peter makes Antioch the centre of his missionary work . . .	47–54 A.D.
Barnabas and Saul return from their missionary journey . . .	Autumn, 49 A.D.
Encounter of St. Peter and St. Paul at Antioch (Gal. ii. 11–14). . .	49 A.D.
Council at Jerusalem . . .	late 49 A.D.
Jews expelled from Rome by Claudius	49 A.D.
St. Paul starts from Antioch on his 2nd Missionary Journey with Silas .	after Passover, 50 A.D.
St. Barnabas and St. Mark go to Cyprus	,, ,, 50 A.D.

St. Paul at Corinth	Summer, 51 A.D.–Spring, 53 A.D.
Gallio arrives in Achaia . . .	April or May, 52 A.D.
St. Paul at Jerusalem . . .	Passover, 53 A.D.
Accession of Nero	October 13, 54 A.D.
St. Peter and St. Barnabas at Corinth	late 54 A.D.
St. Peter and St. Barnabas in Rome and Italy	early 55 A.D.–56 A.D.
St. Paul at Ephesus . . .	Autumn 53 A.D.–Spring 56 A.D.
1st Epistle to the Corinthians from Ephesus	Autumn 55 A.D.
St. Paul in Greece	early summer, 56 A.D.–Passover, 57 A.D.
Epistle to the Romans from Corinth .	early in 57 A.D.
St. Paul at Jerusalem . . .	Pentecost, 57 A.D.
St. Paul's imprisonment at Caesarea .	57 A.D.–59 A.D.
St. Luke's Gospel	58 A.D.–59 A.D.
St. Paul arrives in Rome . . .	February, 60 A.D.
St. Paul's captivity in Rome . .	60 A.D.–62 A.D.
The Acts of the Apostles . . .	before 62 A.D.
Death of Festus	Summer of 62 A.D.
St. Peter in Rome (3rd visit) . .	63 A.D.–65 A.D.
The Great Fire of Rome . . .	July, 64 A.D.
Persecution of the Christians by Nero	Spring, 65 A.D.
The Vatican fête	May, 65 A.D.
1st Epistle of St. Peter . . .	June, 65 A.D.
Martyrdom of St. Peter . . .	Summer, 65 A.D.
Apollonius of Tyana in Rome . .	66 A.D.
Epistle to the Hebrews . . .	late in 66 A.D.
Martyrdom of St. Paul . . .	67 A.D.
Death of Nero	June 9, 68 A.D.
Burning of the Capitol and storming of Rome	Dec. 19–21, 69 A.D.
Domitian in power at Rome . .	January–June, 70 A.D.
Clement's Epistle to the Corinthians .	February, 70 A.D.
St. John exiled by Domitian to Patmos, where he writes the Apocalypse. .	Spring, 70 A.D.
Destruction of the Temple by Titus .	September 7, 70 A.D.
Nerva consul	January to April, 71 A.D.
St. John released from Patmos . .	Spring, 71 A.D.

Anencletus succeeds Linus as 2nd bishop
of Rome   .   .   .   .   . 80 A.D.
Domitian becomes emperor   .   . September 13, 81 A.D.
"The Shepherd" of Hermas   .   . about 90 A.D.
Clement becomes 3rd bishop of Rome. 92 A.D.–101 A.D.
M' Acilius Glabrio consul .   .   . 91 A.D.
M. Arrecinus Clemens consul suffect. . 94 A.D.
T. Flavius Clemens consul   .   . 95 A.D.
Domitianic persecution   .   .   . 94 A.D.–96 A.D.
Assassination of Domitian .   .   . September 18, 96 A.D.

NOTE B

AQUILA AND PRISCA OR PRISCILLA

IN 1888 G. B. de Rossi discovered in the *Coemeterium Priscillae*
a crypt belonging to the *Acilian* gens dating from the first
century, but in a very ruinous condition. Among the broken
inscriptions of many members of this noble family one finds
the names of Acilius Glabrio and of Priscilla. Both Priscus
and Priscilla or Prisca are *cognomina* used by this family, as may
be seen by a reference to Pauly's ' Real-Encyclopädie ' under
Acilius. The existence of this elaborately decorated burial-
place containing a large number of *sarcophagi* seems to point to
M' Acilius Glabrio, the Consul of 91 A.D. who was accused of
' atheism and Jewish manners ' and put to death by Domitian,
having been a Christian. It has been conjectured therefore
that the Priscilla after whom the cemetery is named, and who
must have been the owner of the property beneath which the
excavations were made (property which was part of the extensive
possessions of the Acilii Glabriones) was a near relative—aunt
or sister—of the victim of Domitian. In this cemetery,
according to the witness of the ' Liberian Calendar,' of the
' Itineraries ' and of the ' Liber Pontificalis,' reposed the bodies
of Aquila and Prisca (Marucchi, ' Eléments d'Archéol. Chrét.' ii.
p. 385) with many other saints and martyrs. The biographical
notice of Leo IV (847-55 A.D.) in the ' Liber Pontificalis ' states
that that Pope removed many bodies within the walls to save
them from possible desecration by the Saracens (Duchesne, ii.
p. 115), among these the bodies of Aquila and Prisca.
The supposition that these two companions of St. Paul were
freedmen of the family of the Acilii Glabriones or connected
with them by ties of clientship is highly probable. Prisca or
Priscilla appears to have been a Roman and by the precedence
of her name over that of her husband, as already stated, it has
been assumed that she was of higher position and that the
house at Rome was her property. This suggests that she may
have been a daughter of a freedman of the *Acilian* Priscilla who
was the founder of the cemetery. The Priscilla of the Acts
was so named after her. Aquila was a Jew and a native of

Pontus. Of his Jewish name we are ignorant. He may have been taken to Rome as a slave and been a freedman of one of the Acilii. Quite possibly, however, he may have settled in Rome, like so many others, as a craftsman and trader, and his connexion with the powerful family, perhaps through the influence of Priscilla, have been one of clientship. As to the name Aquila, the following quotation from a poem of Ausonius with the title 'Acilio Glabrioni, grammatico Jun. Burdigalensi' [214. 3. 4] may explain its origin :

> Stemmate nobilium deductum nomen avorum
> Glabrio Aquilini Dardana progenies.

The contention of De Rossi, Marucchi and others that the ancient church of St. Prisca on the Aventine covers the site of the church in the house of Prisca and Aquila will not bear serious investigation. Of the St. Prisca, virgin and martyr, who gave her name to the church nothing is really known, but she was a different person from the Prisca of the Acts and the Pauline epistles. From the fourth to the eighth century the church is always described as *titulus Priscae* (Duchesne, ' Lib. Pont.' i. 501, 517). It was not until the Pontificate of Leo III (795-816 A.D.) that the name *titulus Aquilae et Priscae* first appears (Duchesne, ii. p. 20) : ' fecit in titulo beatis Aquile et Priscae coronam ex argento pens. lib. VI.,' but in this same notice of Leo III occur the words ' basilica beate Priscae ' and Duchesne remarks that Prisca was still ordinary at this time (p. 42).

In a MS. preserved in the Bibliothèque Nationale at Paris (Cod. lat. 9697 p. 78) an account is given of the discovery in 1776 of the ruins of a Roman house and Christian oratory close to St. Prisca with frescoes of the fourth century, but this ruin was unfortunately destroyed and no trace of it remains. In Bianchini's edition of the ' Liber Pontificalis ' (*P.L.* cxxvii. col. 1315) mention is made in the notice of Pope Zephyrinus (198-217) of a Christian ' glass '[1] found ' intra antiquae ecclesiae rudera prope S. Priscam ' (de Rossi in ' Bull. di Arch. Crist.' 1867, p. 48). These things prove the existence on this spot of a very ancient Christian place of worship, but nothing more.

---

[1] The words of the *Lib. Pont.* itself ' Et fecit constitutum in ecclesia et patenas vitreas ante sacerdotes in ecclesia, et ministros supportantes, donec episcopus missas celebraret, ante se sacerdotes adstantes, sic missae celebrarentur,' are an interesting reference to the rites attending the celebration of the Mass at Rome in early times. Duchesne, *L: P.* i: p: 140, makes the comment ' la mention de patènes de verre est à remarquer ; elles n'étaient certainement plus en usage à la fin du Vᵉ siècle.'

NOTE C

THE PUDENS LEGEND

THE name of a certain Pudens occurs in St. Paul's Second Epistle to Timothy (iv. 21) : ' Eubulus greeteth thee, and Pudens and Linus and Claudia.' He is not mentioned elsewhere in the New Testament, but a large number of traditions have grown up about him, which connect him with St. Peter rather than with St. Paul ; and in these traditions there is in all probability a basis of historical fact. In modern times the theory met with strong support, especially among English writers, that Pudens was the husband of Claudia. They were identified with the Pudens and Claudia of Martial's ' Epigrams ' (iv. 13, xi. 53), and Claudia was held to be a British maiden and a daughter of a British chief named Cogidubnus (Martial, xi. 53, ' CIL.' vii. 11). But it is needless to discuss this hypothesis, for it has been conclusively shown that the ' Epigrams ' were not written until many years after the death of St. Paul. The name Claudia moreover was then not uncommon, and the fact that the names Pudens and Claudia in the salutation are not coupled together, but separated by the name Linus, is a strong objection *prima facie* to their being husband and wife.[1]

The ground document for the Pudens Legend is the very ancient ' Acts of SS. Pudentiana and Praxedis,' or as it is sometimes called ' the Acts of Pastor and Timothy.'[2] These ' Acts ' consist of a letter from a presbyter named Pastor (this Pastor appears in the ' Liber Pontificalis ' as brother of Pope Pius I) to another presbyter named Timothy and the reply of the latter. The letters are followed by a short appended narrative. The date of these ' Acts ' is uncertain, and the letters in their present form are undoubtedly fictitious, but they embody, as can be proved by existing memorials, a genuine tradition treated as to its details with the usual inventive freedom and chronological inexactitude.

[1] See Lightfoot, *Apost. Fathers*, part i. vol. i. pp. 76–79.
[2] Bollandist *Acta SS. Maii*, iv. 297–301.

The story as told in these ' Acts ' is as follows : a certain Pudens, whose mother was named Priscilla, a Christian of property, who had shown great zeal in entertaining Apostles and strangers, after the death of his wife consecrated his house as a church of Christ. This church in the house of Pudens in the Vicus Patricius was erected into a Roman parish under the name of *titulus Pastoris* (the Pastor who wrote the letter being the presbyter placed in charge of this parish). Here with his two daughters Praxedis and Pudentiana, who as chaste virgins spent their lives in prayer, fasting, and charitable deeds, Pudens passed his remaining days. The daughters after his death not only obtained the consent of Pope Pius to the building of a baptistery adjoining the church, but the bishop drew the plan with his own hand, and frequently visited the church and offered there the sacrifices to God. On the decease of Potentiana the letter of Pastor informs us that he and the surviving sister Praxedis placed the body by the side of that of her father in the Cemetery of Priscilla[1] on the Via Salaria.

Here begins what in some MSS. is called the ' Acts of Praxedis.' Many noble Christians including Pope Pius came to console Praxedis on her loss, among them a certain Novatus, described as the brother of Timothy, but nowhere in these ' Acts ' as the brother of Praxedis and Pudentiana. This is an important point to remember, for most modern writers following later Martyrologies describe Novatus and Timothy as sons of Pudens.[2] Novatus having fallen ill, Praxedis and Pastor visited him in his sickness, and the issue was that he left to them the whole of his property. The letter containing all this information was sent to Timothy to know what he would wish that they should do in the matter of his brother's estate. Timothy replies that he is rejoiced at what his brother has done, and leaves the entire disposition in the hands of Praxedis and Pastor. The contents of these letters in fact make it absolutely clear that there was no relationship between the sisters Praxedis and Potentiana and the brothers Novatus and Timothy.

After the letters comes a narrative by the hand of Pastor of what followed. Praxedis asked Bishop Pius that the Baths of

[1] It is evidently intended that the Priscilla who gave her name to the cemetery was the mother of Pudens.
[2] A note in the Bollandist *Acta SS. Maii*, iv. p. 301, states for instance : *Colitur S. Novatus* 20 *Iunii etiam Martyrologio Romano adscriptus et dicitur* ' filius S. Pudentis Senatoris et frater Sancti Timothei Presbyteri et Sanctarum Virginum Praxedis et Potentianae, qui ab Apostolis eruditi sunt in fide,' *quorum nihil probamus.*

Novatus, which at that time were not in use, should be consecrated as a church. Pius consented and dedicated in the name of Praxedis the Baths, as a church, within the city in the *Vicus Lateranus* and he erected it into a Roman parish, *titulus*, and consecrated a baptistery to it. That this is the true meaning of the original and that the words in brackets are a later gloss interpolated by the writer to explain the existence in his days of a church of St. Pudentiana in the *Vicus Patricius* as well as a church of St. Praxedis in the *Vicus Lateranus* is almost self-evident. It runs thus : ' Quod et placuit Sancto Pio Episcopo ; thermasque Novati dedicavit ecclesiam sub nomine beatae Virginis [Potentianae in vico Patricio. Dedicavit autem et aliam sub nomine sanctae Virginis] Praxedis infra urbem Romam, in vico qui appellatur Lateranus.' The ' Acts ' had already given an account of the dedication of the church in the *Vicus Patricius* at a much earlier period before the death of Novatus. The ' Acts ' conclude with an account of the burial of Praxedis by Pastor in the cemetery of Priscilla by the side of her father and sister.

The mistake, which led to the interpolation above mentioned caused the following note to be appended to the biography of Pope Pius in two MSS. (and their derivatives) of the ' Liber Pontificalis ' : ' Hic [Pius] ex rogatu beate Praxedis dedicavit aecclesiam thermas Novati in vico Patricii, in honore Sororis suae sanctae Potentianae, ubi et multa dona obtulit ; ubi saepius sacrificium Domino offerens ministrabat '; Duchesne commenting on this writes : ' L'auteur de la note paraît avoir mal compris le texte des *Acta*, car il ne parle que de l'une des deux églises, rapportant à celle du Vicus Patricius ce qui est dit de l'intervention de Praxède et des thermes de Novatus ' (Duchesne, ' Lib. Pont.' i. 133). This note has also misled most modern writers on the subject.[1] The two Churches of St. Pudentiana and St. Praxedis are at this day two of the most interesting churches in Rome, and undoubtedly stand on the sites of those mentioned in the 'Acts,' and there is a record of St. Pudentiana having been restored by Pope Siricius (384–398 A.D.). It is quite certain, however, that this church was not named after a daughter of Pudens but after Pudens himself. An inscription ' Hic requiescit in pace Hilarus Lector tituli Pudentis ' bears the date 528 A.D. and shows that this was

---

[1] See De Rossi, *Bullettino di Arch. Crist.* 1867, pp. 49–65 ; Marucchi, *Eléments d'Arch. Chrét.* ii. 364 ff. ; *Mem. degli Apost. Pietro e Paolo*, pp. 110–116 ; Lanciani, *Pagan and Christian Rome*, pp. 110–115 ; Barnes, *St. Peter in Rome*, pp. 72–78 ; Spence-Jones, *Early Christians in Rome*, pp. 263–7, &c.

the correct style. Another inscription of 384 A.D. is ' Leopardus Lector de Pudentiana ' and in the mosaic of the apse (the oldest mosaic in a Roman church) the Saviour holds an open volume with the words ' Dominus conservator ecclesiae Pudentianae.' As Lanciani remarks ('Pagan and Christian Rome,' p. 112) : ' In course of time the ignorant people changed the word Pudentiana, a possessive adjective, into the name of a Saint ; and the name Sancta Pudentiana usurped the place of the genuine one. It appears for the first time in a document of the year 745.' An inscription of 491 A.D. speaks of certain presbyters ' Tituli Praxedis.'

The existence, however, of both sisters receives substantiation from the fact that their tombs and that of Pudens are mentioned in the ' Liberian Calendar ' and in the ' Pilgrim Itineraries ' as existing in the fourth and fifth centuries in the Cemetery of Priscilla, where according to the ' Acta ' they were buried. Paschal I in his great translation of the remains of saints from the catacombs into the city in 817 A.D. brought the *sarcophagi* of SS. Pudentiana and Praxedis from the catacomb to the Church of St. Praxedis, and the names of both are recorded on a catalogue inscribed on a marble slab to the right of the altar and their portraits appear in the mosaics of this date, which adorn the Church (Marucchi, ' Elém. d'Arch. Chrét.' iii. 325–332).

It is thought that Justin Martyr, when on his trial in 160 A.D. he declared, being interrogated by the Judge as to his dwelling place, that he lived close to the baths called ' the Timotine,' may have been referring to the baths of Novatus as the place where he was accustomed to worship. As Timothy was the brother of Novatus it is a possible supposition.

The question now arises, was this Pudens of the ' Acta ' identical with the Pudens of the 2nd Epistle to Timothy. The Bollandists say No. De Rossi, Marucchi, and many others say Yes, and they get over the chronological difficulty by urging that Pudentiana and Praxedis may have lived to a very advanced age. But the probabilities against such a view are almost insuperable. It is much more likely that the Pudens of the Epistle and the Pudens of the ' Acta ' were father and son. At one time it was the opinion of De Rossi and his school that the first-century cemetery of Priscilla was the property of the family of Pudens. He and his daughters were buried in the cemetery and his mother's name is given in the ' Acta ' as Priscilla. But the discovery of the crypt of the Acilian gens in this catacomb seemed to render it almost certain that the cemetery must have belonged to the family of Acilius Glabrio, the Consul of 91 A.D., in which the names of Priscus, Priscilla and Prisca are found. De Rossi therefore suggested that Pudens may have himself been an Acilius. I have however already made another suggestion, i.e. that Priscilla the mother of Pudens according to the ' Acta ' was an Acilia, and perhaps the aunt or sister of M'Acilius Glabrio.

The traditions which connect the name of Pudens with the early history of the Church in Rome are persistent and numerous quite apart from what is recorded in the ' Acta ' that we have been considering. It is said that the house of Pudens (the elder Pudens mentioned by St. Paul) was during his stay in Rome the home of St. Peter. The *sella gestatoria*, or St. Peter's chair, the oak framework of which is of great antiquity, is said to have been originally the senatorial chair of Pudens. The wooden altar at the St. John Lateran again has been in continuous use there since the fourth century, when it was removed from St. Pudentiana, and that despite the fact that Pope Sylvester in 312 A.D. ordered that all altars should henceforth be of stone. Many indeed had been so before, for the word *titulus* which signifies a consecrated parish church implies its possession of a stone altar. In the Church of St. Pudentiana at the present time there is preserved within the altar a single wood plank reputed to have been left at that church as a memorial when the altar itself was removed. When Cardinal Wiseman was titular cardinal of St. Pudentiana he had the plank examined and found that the wood was identical with that of the altar at the Lateran Church. The reason of its preservation was the tradition that this altar had been used by St. Peter when he celebrated the Eucharist in the oratory in Pudens' house. When St. John Lateran replaced St. Pudentiana as the Cathedral Church of Rome the bishop and the altar moved there together.[1]   These

---

[1] Concerning the term *titulus*, Barnes (*St. Peter in Rome*, p. 75) writes : ' A great deal has been written on the origin and use of this word, but it is probable that it is really derived from its occurrence in the Old Latin version, in the account of the setting up by Jacob of the altar at Bethel after his wonderful dream : an account which to this day is read in the service for the consecration of an altar in a church. " And Jacob said : How terrible is this place ; this is no other but the house of God and the gate of heaven. And Jacob arising in the morning took the stone which he had laid under his head and set it up for a title (*erexit in titulum*), pouring oil upon the top of it." A " title " therefore, in early Christian usage, came to be nothing else but a stone altar duly consecrated, and, in a wider sense, the church that contained that altar and drew its own sanctity from it.'

In the *Liber Pontificalis* (Duchesne, tom. i. p. 126) of Evaristus, the successor of Clement as bishop in 101 A.D., it is recorded ' hic titulos in urbe Romae divisit presbyteris.'

traditions have historically small value in themselves, but it
may safely be said that they could never have arisen and obtained
the vogue which we find them to have had in comparatively
early times, had not the Pudens of Apostolic times and his
family after him been active and leading members of the
primitive Christian community in Rome.[1]

[1] Bianchini in his *Anastasius Bibliothecarius* (edn. of *Liber Pontificalis*
in 1718) made the suggestion that Pudens was a member of the *Gens
Cornelia*. In 1778 in the primitive Christian oratory discovered in immediate proximity to the Church of St. Prisca (*supra*, p. 243) a bronze
tablet was found to one Caius Marius Pudens Cornelianus offered to this
man by a town in Spain expressing gratitude for services rendered during
the time when he filled the office of legate, and stating that he (Pudens)
had been chosen as 'patron' by the citizens. The date of this *tabula
patronatus* is 222 A.D., and its presence gives strong grounds for assuming
that the house containing the Christian place of worship was his property.

The following inscription is of great interest as it belongs to the reign
of Vespasian and contains the names of an Amaranthus, a T. Flavius,
a Q. Cornelius Pudens, and a Chrestus. Marucchi (*Rom. Sott.* N.S.
i. p. 30) states that immediately adjoining the Cemetery of Domitilla
excavated beneath Flavian property lies a property known as *Tor
Marancia* from a certain Amaranthus; on this are a number of pagan
sepulchres belonging to the Bruttian family; while Eusebius tells us that
he derived his information about the Flavian Christians from an historian
named Bruttius [see Note D, p. 256, and Note F, p. 279].

HILARITATI PVPLIC · · ·
IMP · CAES · VESPASIANI · · ·
SACRVM
TRIBVL · SVCC · CORP · IVN *

T : COMINIVS AMARANTH : : : ·
T : FLAVIVS · T : F : LVSCV : · : ·
Q : CORNELIVS · Q : F : PVDENT : · ·
CVRATORES : LIBEROR : TRIB : SVC : COR : IVNIOR : : · ·

On the other face occur the words:

PONEN · CVR ·
C · NYMPHIDIVS · CHRESTVS ·

DEDIC · XVII K · DEC ·
L · ANNIO · BASSO ·
C · CAECINA · PAETO ·   COS ·   (i.e. 70 A.D.)

* Tribules succussani. Corpus juniorum.—Muratori, tom. i. p. cccviii.

THE FAMILY CONNEXION OF CLEMENT THE BISHOP.

A TABULAR STATEMENT OF THE SCHEME OF RELATIONSHIP (SET FORTH IN LECTURE VIII) BETWEEN THE ARRECINIAN AND IMPERIAL FLAVIAN FAMILIES.

THE ARRECINIAN FAMILY.

(1) M. Arrecinus Tertullus Clemens = (2) *Plautia*(?)

3) M. Arrecinus Clemens

(4) Plautilla = (11) T. Flavius Sabinus

(5) Arrecina Tertulla = (19) Titus Flavius Vespasianus [The Emperor Titus]

(6) Clement the Bishop

THE FLAVIAN FAMILY.

(7) T. Flavius Petro = (8) Tertulla

(9) Titus Flavius Sabinus = (10) Vespasia Polla

(11) T. Flavius Sabinus = (4) Plautilla (?)

(12) T. Flavius Vespasianus [The Emperor Vespasian] = (13) Flavia Domitilla

(14) T. Flavius Sabinus (15) Flavia Domitilla the virgin = (21) Julia Augusta

(16) T. Flavius Clemens = (24) Flavia Domitilla

(17) Vespasianus (18) Domitianus

(19) T. Flavius Vespasianus [the Emperor Titus] = (5) Arrecina Tertulla
= (20) Marcia Furnilla
(21) Julia Augusta = (14) T. Flavius Sabinus

(22) Flavia Domitilla = (23) unknown

(24) Flavia Domitilla = (16) T. Flavius Clemens

(25) T. Flavius Domitianus = Domitia Longina [The Emperor Domitian]

NOTE D

(1) M. Arrecinus Tertullus Clemens, Prefect of the Praetorian Guard in 41 A.D. (Josephus, ' Ant.' xix. 1. 6, 7, and Tac. ' Hist.' iv. 68.) It is from Josephus that we learn that Clemens was privy to the conspiracy of Chaerea and others against Caligula and connived at his assassination. It appears from Josephus that Herod Agrippa came to the Praetorian camp, where the troops had acknowledged Claudius as emperor, and successfully acted as mediator between them and that portion of the army that obeyed the Senate (Josephus, ' Ant.' xix. 3. 1, 3 ; 4. 1, 2, ff.). This information exclusively reported by Josephus may be taken to imply that Clemens had some connexion, possibly as a ' God-fearer,' with the Jewish community at Rome, and that he was a friend of Herod Agrippa.

From Tac. ' Hist.' iv. 68 it appears that this Prefect was so much beloved by his troops that his son's appointment as Prefect in 70 A.D. was hailed with joy in the camp, because the father's memory after so long an interval of time was still held in regard. Suetonius (' Titus ' 4) tells us that his name was Tertullus, that he belonged to the Equestrian order, and that his daughter Arrecina Tertulla was the first wife of the Emperor Titus. An inscription ' CIL.' vi. 12355 gives his *praenomen* as Marcus.

(2) Plautia. The name of the wife of (1) is actually unknown. The reasons for assigning to him, as his wife, a sister of Aulus Plautius, the conqueror of Britain, are stated in Lecture VIII. Plautia would be the sister-in-law of Julia Pomponia Graecina, and a relative of Plautia Urgulanilla, the second wife of Claudius.

(3) M. Arrecinus Clemens, son of (1), described by Tacitus ' Hist.' iv. 68 as ' domui Vespasiani per adfinitatem innexum et gratissimum Domitiano, Praetorianis [Domitianus] praeposuit, patrem eius, sub Caio Caesare, egregie functum ea cura, dictitans, laetum militibus idem nomen.' The relationship

with the Imperial Flavian House may be traced back to (8) Tertulla, the grandmother of Vespasian, by whom from childhood he was brought up. Tertullus Clemens (1) the Prefect was probably Vespasian's cousin and the companion of his boyhood. Arrecina Tertulla (5), daughter of (1) and sister of (3), married Titus (19). She died while Titus was quite young. M. Arrecinus Clemens (3) was Consul Suffectus in 73 A.D. (' CIL.' vi. 2016 and xiv. 2242) and a second time with L. Baebius Honoratus (' CIL.' xii. 3637). This second consulship appears to have been most probably in 94 A.D. The *Fasti Consulares* are admittedly imperfect with regard to the names of the consuls suffect. But the names of both the ordinary Consuls Collega and Priscus and of the three suffects for 93 A.D. have been preserved. In 94 A.D. Asprenas and Lateranus were ordinary consuls.[1] In some lists Arrecinus Clemens appears, however, as the colleague of Asprenas (see Dion Cassius, ed. Lipsiae, 1829, iv. p. 84). The ' Chronicon Paschale ' (extract given in Lightfoot, ' Clement of Rome,' i. p. 110) has the following entries : 93 A.D. Domitian Augustus XIII and Flavius Clemens, 94 A.D. Asprenatus [Asprenas] and Lateranus, 95 A.D. Domitian Augustus XIV and Flavius Clemens II. This is an instance of that confusion of Arrecinus Clemens with Flavius Clemens which has been the fruitful source of difficulties. Flavius Clemens was consul only once and in 95 A.D., Arrecinus Clemens for the second time in 94 A.D. He was a member of the Imperial Council from 82 A.D. and also *Curator Aquarum.* His name appears ' CIL.' vi. 199 xi. 428 and xv. 7278. He was put to death by Domitian 94 A.D. or 95 A.D. (Suet. ' Domitian,' 11.)

(4) Plautilla. The ' Acts of Nereus and Achilles ' represent these martyrs as at first servants of Plautilla, the sister of Clement the Consul, and afterwards of her daughter Domitilla the virgin. The ' Acts of Petronilla,' which are incorporated

---

[1] The most complete *Fasti Consulares* for the Flavian Period are found in a contribution by Asbach in *Jahrbücher des Vereins von Altertumsfreunden im Rheinlande* [Bonn] vol. 79, p. 60 ff. Asbach has only discovered the name of one *Suffectus* in 94 A.D., but he quotes Prosper as making Clement the colleague of Asprenas. It is almost certain that in a year when the Emperor did not assume the consulship there would be several *Suffecti*. In Muratori, *Nov. Thes. Vet. Inscr.* tom. i. p. cccxlv, the full list for 93 A.D. is preserved. Consules 93. *Pompeius Collega, Cornelius Priscus, quibus suffecti fuerunt. M. Lollius Paullinus, Valerius Asiaticus Saturninus. Horum uni suffectus erat, C. Antistius Iulius Quadratus.* So in 94 A.D. M. Arrecinus Clemens and L. Baebius Honoratus were *suffecti* to Asprenas and Lateranus. The *suffect* mentioned by Asbach—Silius Italicus—may have taken the place of Clemens in the last months of 94 A.D.

with those of Nereus and Achilles, state that these three saints were all buried in the crypt of Domitilla. That they were real historical persons has been proved in recent years by the discovery by De Rossi [1] of their memorials in the cemetery of Domitilla. It is at least possible, therefore, that Plautilla is likewise an historical person, and the presumption is increased by the fact that she is definitely in these Acts represented as the sister of Clement the Consul. De Rossi himself believed in her real existence, and many others have followed him in the assumption, which I have adopted, as also his suggestion that her mother's name was Plautia. I differ, however, in my interpretation of the words ' sister of Clement the Consul ' in making her the sister not of Flavius but of Arrecinus Clemens. If the historicity of the statement of the ' Acts of Nereus and Achilles ' about Plautilla be accepted, it should be accepted as a whole. Now stress is laid on the fact that the Plautilla of these Acts died in the same year as St. Peter suffered martyrdom. The words are explicit : 'eodem anno dominus Petrus apostolus ad coronam martyrii properavit ad Christum et Plautilla corpus terrenum deseruit.' Plautilla therefore could not well be the sister of Flavius Clemens, the younger of the two sons of Flavius Sabinus, as these sons are described as children at the time of their father's murder in December 69 A.D. The hypothesis that she was the daughter of M. Arrecinus Tertullus Clemens the Praetorian Prefect of 41 A.D., and therefore sister of M. Arrecinus Clemens the Consul of 73 A.D. and 94 A.D., and that she was the wife and not the daughter of her cousin Flavius Sabinus, the brother of Vespasian, and that, through her, T. Flavius Clemens, her son, Consul in 95 A.D., obtained his *cognomen*, has about it impress of verisimilitude.

(5) Arrecina Tertulla.—The first wife of the Emperor Titus. She died quite young. See ' CIL.' vi. 12355, 12357.

(6) Clement the Bishop.—In the ' Clementine Homilies ' and ' Clementine Recognitions,' which are in reality Petrine romances derived from a common original and dating from the beginning of the third century, Clement is represented as a Roman by birth and of the kindred of Caesar. His father is a relative and foster-brother of an emperor, and his mother likewise connected with Caesar's family. The name of the father is Faustus (' Homilies '), Faustinianus (' Recognitions '), Faustinus (' Liber

---

[1] De Rossi, *Bull. di Arch. Crist.* 1874, pp. 5 ff., 68 ff., 122 ff. &c. *Roma Sotterranea*, tom. i. pp. 130 ff. See also Lipsius, *Apokryphen Apost. Geschicht.* II. i. p. 205.

Pontificalis '), of two elder brothers Faustinus and Faustinianus ('Homilies '), Faustinus and Faustus ('Recognitions '), of the mother Mattidia. Now these names belong to the period of Hadrian and the Antonines. Faustina (died 141 A.D.) was the wife of the Emperor Antoninus Pius, and her daughter of the same name (died 175 A.D.) was the wife of his adopted son and successor, Marcus Aurelius. Mattidia was the niece of Trajan, and her daughter Sabina the wife of the Emperor Hadrian. As the romances throughout make Clement to have been the disciple and companion of St. Peter and he is spoken of as being already grown up at the time of the Crucifixion, it will be at once perceived that the compilers of this Clementine literature were, in the use that they made of tradition, absolutely indifferent to chronological considerations. That they gave voice to a genuine tradition both as regards Clement's discipleship to St. Peter and his relationship to the family of the reigning Caesars is rendered in the highest degree probable from the fact that the Clementine story is merely a framework for the Ebionite or Helchasaite version of Peter's travels, preaching and controversies with Simon Magus, which forms the real subject-matter of this literature. [Hort, 'Clementine Recognitions.'] M. Arrecinus Tertullus Clemens was the kinsman of Vespasian, and as that emperor was brought up not in his paternal home but by his grandmother Tertulla, it is quite possible that they were actually foster-brothers. Tertullus was one of the Flavian *cognomina.* Q. Flavius Tertullus was consul *suffect.* in 133 A.D. ('CIL.' vi. 858). Plautia was a relative of Plautia Urgulanilla, the second wife of Claudius, her daughter Arrecina Tertulla the wife of Titus.

In the 'Acts of Nereus and Achilles' Clement the Bishop is addressed as the nephew of Clement the Consul: 'patris tui fuisse germanum.' In the Clementines he is represented as considerably the youngest of his family. It is for various reasons more probable that he was the younger brother than the nephew of M. Arrecinus Clemens, and such I have assumed him to be.

(7) T. Flavius Petro.—The name of the famous saint, Petronilla, who was buried in the Flavian cemetery of Domitilla, was probably derived from this Flavian *cognomen.* A crop of legends grew up around her name, as being a daughter of St. Peter. It is possible that she may have been a spiritual daughter of the Apostle, as having been converted and baptized by him.

(8), (9), (10). Titus Flavius Sabinus and his wife, according to Suetonius, left Italy to live among the Helvetii ; their son Vespasian was educated by his grandmother Tertulla upon a family estate at Cosa in the Volscian territory. (Suet. ' Vespasian,' 2, 3.)

(11) T. Flavius Sabinus, the elder son of (9) and (10). After serving the State in thirty-five campaigns with distinction (Tac. ' Hist.' iii. 75) and having been Governor of Moesia for seven years, Sabinus was appointed in 57 A.D. Prefect of the City. He held this important office for twelve years continuously save for a brief interval in the short reign of Galba. As Prefect of the City he must have taken part (perhaps passively) in the persecution of the Christians in 65 A.D. and been the witness of the courage with which so many martyrs faced torture and a horrible death. Some have supposed that in his latter years he may to a greater or less extent have fallen under the influence of the Christian Faith. His whole career proclaims him· to have been during the greater part of his life a man of action. Tacitus speaks of his being ' invalidus senecta ' and describes him at this stage as ' mitem virum abhorrere a sanguine et caedibus ' (' Hist.' iii. 65). When the Vitellians stormed the Capitol, ' Flavium Sabinum inermem neque fugam coeptantem circumsistunt ' (' Hist.' iii. 73). And again after his murder, ' in fine vitae alii segnem, multi moderatum et civium sanguinis parcum credidere ' (' Hist.' iii. 75). All these traits do not prove much in themselves, but the fact that several of his descendants and relatives were undoubtedly Christians lends a certain probability to the supposition that this mildness, sluggishness, and unwillingness to resist arms in hand may have been due to the acceptance of Christian principles. Sabinus apparently did not marry till late in life, possibly not till after he settled at Rome in 57 A.D., as his children were quite young at the time of his murder in December 69 A.D. If Plautilla were his wife, she died four years before her husband, leaving two sons and a daughter, the younger son receiving his grandfather's *cognomen* Clemens.

(12) The Emperor Vespasian appears to have been in considerable poverty at two periods of his life. His eldest son, Titus (19), was born December 30, 39 A.D. : ' prope Septizonium sordidis aedibus cubiculo vero perparvo et obscuro.' (Suet. ' Tit.' 1.) Yet a few years later we find him being educated in the palace with Britannicus. It is suggested that this change may have been partly brought about by the influence

on behalf of his kinsman of the Praetorian Prefect Arrecinus Tertullus Clemens. At a later period, before he went as Proconsul to Africa in 61 or 62 A.D., he was in such bad circumstances that he had to mortgage his entire property to his brother in order to raise money. (Tac. ' Hist.' iii. 73.) His wife (13) and his daughter (22), both named Flavia Domitilla, predeceased him. His younger son Domitian (25) seems when Vespasian was abroad in Africa and Judaea to have lived with his uncle Sabinus and to have been under his care. Titus (19) was, while still a youth, married to his relative Arrecina Tertulla (5). Domitian (25), born October 25, 51 A.D., was twelve years younger than his brother. From the end of December 69 A.D. to the following June as Praetor with full consular power he with Mucianus exercised in the absence of Vespasian in Egypt and Titus in Judaea the imperial authority at Rome.

(15) Flavia Domitilla, spoken of by Eusebius, ' Chronicon ' (Jerome's Lat. vers. ed. Schöne ii. p. 163), thus :—' Scribit Bruttius . . . Flaviam Domitillam Flavii Clementis consulis ex sorore neptem in insulam Pontianam relegatam, quia se Christianam esse testata est.' A similar reference derived no doubt from the same source is found in ' Hist. Eccl.' iii. 18, where the meaning of the word *neptem* is made clear : Φλαυΐαν Δομετίλλαν . . . ἐξ ἀδελφῆς γεγονυῖαν Φλαυίου Κλήμεντος, ἑνὸς τῶν τηνικάδε ἐπὶ 'Ρώμης ὑπάτων. Eusebius states that this took place in the fifteenth year of Domitian, but, as I have pointed out in Lecture VIII, it is almost certain that Eusebius has here misread his authority and that the Consul to whom Flavia Domitilla was niece was Arrecinus Clemens the Consul of 94 A.D., and not Flavius Clemens the Consul of 95 A.D. The family of Flavius Sabinus (11) were children in 70 A.D. ; it is scarcely possible therefore that this Flavia Domitilla should have been old enough to occupy such a position of importance as is here assigned to her, and still more so in the ' Acts of Nereus and Achilles.' In those ' Acts ' she appears as the daughter of Plautilla, sister of Clement the Consul, and is clearly a woman of property with chamberlains of her own. In the ' Chronicon Paschale ' the same passage of Bruttius, about the persecution of the Christians by Domitian, as Eusebius quotes is referred to, but the notice of it appears under the fourteenth year of Domitian, which began in September 94 A.D. The banishment of this Domitilla to the island of Pontia I believe to have taken place at the end of 94 A.D., after Arrecinus Clemens was Consul and before Flavius Clemens entered on his consulship.

The fact that Eusebius neither in the ' Chronicle ' nor ' Ecclesiastical History' makes any mention of the execution of Flavius Clemens or the banishment of his wife seems to me inferential evidence that his authority Bruttius did not here record an event which Eusebius could scarcely have overlooked in one or other of his two historical works. In my Table of the Flavian Family I have made Flavia Domitilla [the virgin] the daughter of Flavius Sabinus (15) and of Plautilla (4), the sister of Arrecinus Clemens (3). I have further suggested in Lecture VIII that after the murder of Sabinus, Plautilla being already dead, the maternal uncle (3) undertook the charge of the orphan children. The two sons as they grew up would in due course be cared for by the Emperor Vespasian, as being the nearest male representatives of his family, his own two sons having no male heirs, the daughter remaining still in the wardship of the maternal uncle who had brought her up. It would be only natural therefore in such circumstances for Bruttius to speak of her as the niece of Arrecinus, rather than as the sister of Flavius.

The sudden condemnation to death of Arrecinus Clemens by Domitian, as recorded by Suetonius (' Domit.' 11), may well have been connected with the same causes which led to his niece Domitilla's banishment, i.e. her profession of the Christian faith and her contumacy in refusing to marry at the Emperor's bidding.

(22), (23), (24) Dion Cassius (lxvii. 14) relates that Domitian put to death his cousin Flavius Clemens while consul [Suet., ' Domit.' 15, says almost before his consulship had ended] and that he sent his wife Flavia Domitilla, also a relative, into exile on the island of Pandateria. Suetonius does not mention the wife's banishment, but remarks that ' this violent act— i.e. the execution—very much hastened his own destruction ' and then tells us of the tyrant's assassination by Stephanus the steward of Domitilla. Philostratus (' Apollonius,' viii. 25) in his account says that Stephanus was the freedman of Flavius Clemens' wife. Quintilian, who was the tutor of Flavius Clemens' young sons (of very tender age, Suet. ' Domit.' 15), makes it clear that their mother was the daughter of Domitian's sister : ' cum vero mihi Domitianus Augustus sororis suae nepotum delegaverit curam ' (' Inst. Orat.' Prooem. 2). This sister of Domitian died before her father Vespasian became Emperor in 70 A.D. For epigraphic evidence of the existence of this Flavia Domitilla, wife of Flavius Clemens, see ' CIL.' vi.

948, 8942 and 16246. The first of these as restored by Mommsen stands :

> Flavia Domitilla FILIA.FLAVIAE.DOMITILLAE.
> Imp. Caes. VespasiANI.NEPTIS.FECIT.GLYCERAE.L.ET.

The name of the NEPTIS is given in ' CIL.' vi. 8942 :

> FLAVIAE.DOMITIL
> VESPASIANI.NEPTIS

There were thus four Flavia Domitillas: the wife of Vespasian (13), her daughter (22), her granddaughter (24), and her niece (15).

NOTE E

THE TOMBS OF THE APOSTLES ST. PETER AND ST. PAUL

' IF thou wilt go to the Vatican or to the Ostian road thou wilt find the trophies of the Apostles who founded this Church.' These words of the Roman presbyter Gaius (identified by Dr. Lightfoot[1] with the well-known Hippolytus bishop of Portus) in his treatise against the heretic Proclus are a positive testimony to the existence at the end of the Second Century of trophies or *memoriae*—*i.e.* small oratories—over the graves of the Apostles Peter and Paul. It further indicates in what localities these visible monuments were to be found. Eusebius, to whom we are indebted for the preservation of this piece of valuable evidence, makes the further statement that the names of the Apostles were to be seen in the cemeteries of Rome in his day.[2]

The ' Liber Pontificalis ' contains what appears to be an authentic record of the construction of one of these *memoriae*. Of bishop Anacletus (Anencletus) it is said ' Hic memoriam Beati Petri construxit et composuit.' The erection of these monuments may therefore be placed in the early years of Domitian's reign.

The evidence from traditional sources as to the exact position of the spots where the two Apostles were martyred and afterwards buried is very detailed and complete, and, as is usual in topographical references, is accurate, even though the narratives, in which these references occur, are in the main apocryphal fictions of a late date.

The principal authorities in the case of St. Peter are as follows :

' Liber Pontificalis ': [Petrus] ' sepultus est via Aurelia in templum Apollinis, iuxta locum ubi crucifixus est, iuxta palatium Neronianum, in Vaticanum, iuxta territorium Triumphale.'

Jerome, ' De Viris Illustribus ': ' Sepultus est in Vaticano iuxta viam triumphalem totius orbis veneratione celebratur.'

---

[1] *Apost. Fathers*, part i. vol. ii. pp. 318, 377–83.
[2] *Hist. Eccl.* ii. 25.

' Martyrium Beati Petri Apostoli ': ' ad locum qui vocatur Naumachiae iuxta obeliscum Neronis in montem.'

' Acta Petri ': ' apud palatium neronianum iuxta obeliscum inter duas metas.'

' Liber Pontificalis ': [Cornelius] ' posuit iuxta locum ubi crucifixus est, inter corpora sanctorum episcoporum, in templum Apollinis, in monte aureo, in vaticanum palatii neroniani.'

' De locis S.S. Martyrum ': ' Petrus in parte occidentali civitatis iuxta viam Corneliam ad milliarium primum in corpore quiescit.'

From these notices it will be seen that three roads are mentioned—the Via Aurelia (Nova), the Via Triumphalis, and the Via Cornelia. These three roads met at a point close to the Pons Neronianus or Triumphalis. Between the Via Aurelia Nova and the Via Cornelia stood the Circus of Nero, between the Via Cornelia and the Via Triumphalis the Vatican hill. The Circus of Nero was the scene of the Games at which a multitude of Christians perished by horrible tortures in the spring of 65 A.D., and here according to the ' Acta Petri ' suffered St. Peter ' iuxta obeliscum inter duas metas '—that is on the *spina* at a point equidistant from the two goals, where the obelisk stood, the same obelisk removed in 1586 to the front of the Basilica. The *palatium Neronianum* and the *Naumachia* were appellations given in later days to the remains of the Circus, which was destroyed when Constantine built the first Basilica above St. Peter's tomb. The Mons Aureus (a corruption of Aurelius) was so called from its proximity to the Via Aurelia Nova, later the name was extended to the Janiculum also, the southern part of which is still called Montorio.[1]

Templum Apollinis. Duchesne writes (' Lib. Pont.' i. 120) : ' Quant au temple d'Apollon, il y a, dans cette désignation, un souvenir du célèbre sanctuaire de Cybèle, qui s'élévait tout près du cirque et de la basilique, et qui fut, jusqu'aux dernières années du ive siècle, le théâtre des cérémonies sanglantes du *taurobolium* et du *criobolium*. . . . Le Collège des xv. *viri sacris faciundis*, qui était chargé du culte de cette déesse, étaient aussi directeurs du culte d'Apollon.' In any case there was a building on this spot popularly known as the *templum Apollinis*, witness the notice in the ' Liber Pontificalis ' of Pope Silvester (314–335 A.D.) : ' eodem tempore Augustus Constantinus fecit basilicam

[1] For the tradition connected with S. Pietro in Montorio and its origin see Lanciani, *Pagan and Christian Rome*, p. 128 ; Barnes, *S. Peter in Rome*, p. 98.

beato Petro apostolo in templum Apollinis.' (Duchesne, ' Lib. Pont.' i. 176.)

The body of St. Peter then was buried in a small cemetery on the Vatican hill close to the place where he was crucified. Over this tomb Anencletus erected his *memoria*, and in the immediate vicinity the first twelve bishops of Rome, with the exception of Clement and Alexander, were according to the ' Liber Pontificalis ' laid to rest—in each case the phrase recurs ' sepultus est iuxta corpus beati Petri in Vaticanum.' In time the entire space available was filled up. Zephyrinus was the first to be buried in 217 A.D. on the Appian Way, and his successor Calixtus created the crypt in the great subterranean cemetery called after his name, where he himself and a number of his successors were interred. The crypt of the Popes was discovered in 1854 by De Rossi, and the inscriptions on the broken coverings of the Sarcophagi of several of the bishops may still be seen. Excavations made near the Great Altar of St. Peter's in the early seventeenth century by Paul V and Urban VIII revealed many interesting facts. A large coffin was found made of great slabs of marble containing a mass of half-charred bones and ashes, pointing to the probability that Peter was interred close by the remains of the martyrs who had perished as living torches at the Neronian Vatican fête. All round the ' Confessio ' in which the Apostle's relics were supposed to rest were placed coffins side by side against the ancient walls, containing bodies swathed in Jewish fashion. On the slabs that covered them were no inscriptions, save in one case where the name Linus could be deciphered.[1] Whether these were the bodies of the earliest bishops of Rome it is impossible to say, but the discovery, taken in conjunction with the statements of the ' Liber Pontificalis ' which topographically are so often correct, makes the supposition credible. The evidence is far from complete, but it is weighty. The historical character of the notices relating to the Vatican interments in the ' Liber Pontificalis ' is borne out by the remarkable omission of Clement and also of Alexander. The legend of Clement's martyrdom in the Chersonese is fictitious. It may be taken as certain that he did not die in Rome. In the ' Liber Pontificalis ' we read concerning Alexander— ' sepultus est via Numentana, ubi decollatus est, ab urbe Roma

---

[1] The evidence of Torrigio (but see below Drei's plan) is not clear, whether the name Linus was a separate word, or the termination of such a name as Marcellinus. The tomb of Linus appears however to have been known in the ninth century according to the poet Rhabanus Maurus. *Acta Sanct.* 6 Sept. p. 543.

non longe, miliario VII.' In the Itinerary or Pilgrim Guide of William of Malmesbury : ' In septimo miliario eiusdem viae [Nomentanae] s. papa Alexander cum Eventio et Theodulo pausant' (De Rossi, ' Rom. Sott.' i. 179).[1] Again the later notices as to the burials of Zephyrinus, of Callistus and their successors not on the Vatican but upon the Appian Way have been verified by De Rossi and other modern archaeologists. The statements as to the discoveries made in the excavations of 1615 and 1626 rest on contemporary authorities. Francesco Maria Torrigio, who was with Cardinal Evangelista Pallotta an eye-witness of the exhumations of 1615, has given an account of them in his work ' Le sacre Grotte vaticane,' 1639; and Giovanni Severano also relates what he had heard in his ' Memorie sacre delle sette chiese di Roma,' 1629. The master mason Benedetto Drei, who was likewise an eye-witness of the discoveries made in 1615, has left an engraved plan originally intended for Torrigio's book ; one copy of this, in the British Museum, is of exceptional interest, for it is covered with auto-graph MS. notes in the handwriting of Drei himself.[2] In this one can see how the tombs are so arranged round the central shrine that the bodies seem to surround that of St. Peter ' like bishops assisting at a council.' An account quite as circumstantial and authentic is given by a certain R. Ubaldi, canon of the basilica, of the excavations made in 1626. The MS. containing this narrative lay forgotten in the Vatican Archives until it was discovered by Professor Gregorio Palmieri in recent years and was transcribed and published by Cavaliere Mariano Armellini in his work ' Le Chiese di Roma,' 1891. An English version may be found in A. S. Barnes, ' St. Peter in Rome,' pp. 315–338, a work full of interesting material and valuable research.

Let us now turn to the tomb of St. Paul on the Ostian Way. The Apocryphal Acts all declare that St. Paul as became his *status* as a Roman citizen suffered martyrdom by decapitation—*honestiores capite puniantur*, and that he was led out to a place known as *Aquae Salviae*, near the third mile-stone on the Ostian Way. This tradition has not been seriously disputed. In the Greek Acts the addition is made that the Apostle suffered under a pine-tree—εἰς μάσσαν καλουμένην Ἀκκούαι Σαλβίας πλησὶ τοῦ δένδρου τοῦ στροβίλου. An extant inscription of Gregory the

---

[1] There is some doubt about Alexander. Marucchi, *Élém. d'Arch. Chrét.* i. p. 28.

[2] An excellent reproduction of this will be found in Barnes's *St. Peter in Rome*, facing p. 304. Drei's MS. notes confirm the reading Linus.

Great, 604 A.D., records the gift by him of a piece of land at the *Aquae Salviae* to the basilica of St. Paul—' Valde incongruum ac esse durissimum videretur ut illa ei specialiter possessio non serviret in qua palmam sumens martyrii capite est truncatus ut viveret, utile iudicavimus eandem massam quae Aquas Salvias nuncupatur . . . cum Christi Gratia luminaribus deputare.'[1] A memorial chapel was built here in the fifth century, whose remains were discovered in 1867 under the present Church of S. Paolo alle Tre Fontane, and in 1875 in the course of some excavations for a water tank behind this church a number of coins of Nero were found together with several pine-cones fossilised by age.

The body of St. Paul according to tradition was buried by a Christian matron of the name of Lucina in a plot of ground, which was her property, about a mile nearer to Rome. It was not a subterranean cemetery but one on the surface, and the piece of land was confined, being hemmed in between the Ostian Road and another road, which has since disappeared, known as the Via Valentiniana.[2] This spot in the time of the presbyter Gaius, about 200 A.D., was marked like that of St. Peter on the Vatican by a memorial oratory (trophy) probably erected by Anencletus at the same time as the Petrine *memoria* already referred to.

That the bodies of the Apostles did not continuously remain undisturbed in their first resting places is one of those traditions which can be supported by a body of evidence, leaving indeed some points doubtful and obscure, but as regards the main fact almost conclusive. In that Kalendar of the Church known as the ' Feriale Philocalianum ' (about 354 A.D.) under the heading ' Depositio Martyrum ' occurs the following entry :

' III. Kal. Iul. Petri in Catacumbas et Pauli Ostense—Tusco et Basso cons.'

The names of the Consuls fix the date as 258 A.D. and show that this entry is taken from some official source. It is clearly unintelligible as it stands. De Rossi however discovered at Berne a Codex of the ' Martirologium Hieronymianum ' which exhibits the same entry in a fuller form :

' III. Kal. Iul. Romae natale apostolorum sanctorum Petri et Pauli—Petri in Vaticano via Aurelia Pauli vero in Via Ostensi,

[1] Marucchi, *Elém. d'Arch. Chrét.* ii. p. 74; De Rossi, *Roma Sotterranea,* i. p. 182; *Bullet. di Arch. Crist.* 1869, pp. 81 ff.; Lanciani, *Pagan and Christian Rome,* pp. 156-7.
[2] Stevenson, ' L'area di Lucina sulla Via Ostiense ' in *Nuovo Bullett. di Arch. Crist.* 1898, pp. 68 ff.

utrumque in Catacumbis, passi sub Nerone, Basso et Tusco consulibus.'[1]

This can only mean that on June 29 the Feast of the Apostles was kept in three places or stations—at the Vatican, on the Ostian Road, and in a place known as the Catacombs in memory of some event which took place in the consulate of Tuscus and Bassus, 258 A.D. The words *passi sub Nerone* must be regarded as a parenthesis. The existence of these three stations is proved by a hymn of pseudo-Ambrose for June 29, as these lines show :

> Tantae per urbis ambitum
> Stipata tendunt agmina ;
> Trinis celebratur viis
> Festum sacrorum Martyrum.

Now it can be proved that these consular dates in the Kalendar signify in other cases a translation of remains, and the conclusion is that a translation of the bodies of St. Peter and St. Paul to the Catacombs took place in 258 A.D.

There are many testimonies to the fact that the bodies of the two Apostles did actually rest in the cemetery *ad Catacumbas*, but the authorities differ as to the period at which the translation took place and also as to the duration of time during which the relics remained in their temporary tomb. The story contained in the Apocryphal ' Acta Petri et Pauli ' speaks of certain unknown people from the East who after the Apostles' martyrdom attempted to carry off the bodies to their own country, but being overtaken by an earthquake the people of Rome took the bodies from them at the third milestone on the Appian Way at the place called *ad Catacumbas*. Here the remains were deposited for one year and seven months until tombs were built for them on the Vatican and the Ostian Way. Now this story, of which there are several slightly differing versions, is almost certainly based upon a real historical event, the translation which took place in 258. The late writers of the ' Acta ' were utterly indifferent to chronology, and the deposition in the cemetery on the Appian Way when Tuscus and Bassus were consuls was associated with the martyrdoms and relegated with the accompaniment of many confused and legendary details to the time of Nero. All probability is against the story of the ' Acta.' Even if the Apostles were put to death at the same time, and I have shown that there is a very strong presumption that St. Peter's death preceded that of St. Paul by two years, nothing could be more

---

[1] Duchesne, *Lib. Pont.* i. p. cv.

unlikely than the bringing back of their bodies to be interred in
the vicinity of their places of execution when once they had been
laid safely to rest in the cemetery on the Appian Way. There
were as yet no sacred associations connected with the Vatican
Hill and the Ostian Way to move the Roman Christians to act
in the manner described in these apocryphal narratives.[1]
The cause of the translation of 258 A.D. is not difficult to
divine, for this was the year of the outbreak of the persecution
of Valerian. An Edict had been issued against the Christians,
forbidding their meetings in the cemeteries. It might well
be that fears were aroused lest the sacred tombs of the Apostles
should be desecrated, and so the bodies were removed to a place
of greater safety. The researches of archaeologists have
shown that the cemetery *ad Catacumbas* must in those days
have been admirably adapted for the purpose. It was ancient
already, it lay apart from other cemeteries, and it resembled
rather a pagan than a Christian place of burial (Duchesne,
' Lib. Pont.' cvii). It has been in recent years most carefully
examined and studied and in the chamber known as the Platonia
or Platoma a double tomb may still be seen, said to be that in
which the bodies were placed.[2] Here Damasus (366–387 A.D.)
built a basilica, which until the eighth century was known as
the Basilica of the Apostles, and on the walls of the Chamber
he placed an inscription in verse. In the ' Liber Pontificalis '
we read—' Hic fecit basilicas duas : una beato Laurentio iuxta
theatrum . . . et in Catacumbas ubi iacuerunt corpora sanctorum
apostolorum Petri et Pauli, in quo loco platomam ipsam, ubi
iacuerunt corpora sancta, versibus exornavit.' This poem of
Damasus has fortunately been preserved. The text runs thus :

Hic habitare prius sanctos cognoscere debes
Nomina quisque Petri pariter Paulique requiris
Discipulos oriens misit quod sponte fatemur
Sanguinis ob meritum Christum qui per astra secuti
Aetherios petiere sinus regnaque piorum
Roma suos potius meruit defendere cives
Haec Damasus vestras referat nova sidera laudes.[3]

Those words *discipulos oriens misit* may possibly have given
rise to the later apocryphal fictions about the unknown men
from the East, who tried to carry off the bodies of the Apostles.

[1] A letter of Gregory the Great to the Empress Constantina about
600 A.D. shows that the legend of the early translation was current in
his time and accepted by him. *Opp. St. Greg.* ii. cp. 30.
[2] Dr. A. De Waal, *Die Apostelgruft ad Catacumbas an der Via Appia*;
Marucchi, *Le Memorie degli Apostoli Pietro e Paolo in Roma*, 1903,
pp. 75–92.   [3] De Rossi, *Inscr. Crist.* ii. p. 52.

Damasus however here clearly means by these words the Apostles themselves, the word *discipulos* being used instead of *Apostolos* through the exigencies of the metre. He says in effect that though the East had sent the Apostles, Rome, which had been the scene of their labours and their deaths, had the best claim to retain them.

But even if it be granted that the notices in the 'Feriale Philocalianum' and the 'Hieronymian Martyrology' contain an official authentic statement that a translation of the relics to the cemetery *ad Catacumbas* took place in 258 A.D., as such authorities as the Abbé Duchesne, Monsignor de Waal, Professor Marucchi, and Father A. S. Barnes admit, there are other difficulties to be overcome, and they differ from one another in their interpretation of documentary evidence, and in their views as to whether there were two translations or one only, and as to the duration of the sojourn of the relics in the *Platonia*. The Apocryphal 'Acta' say that the bodies were taken to the Catacombs immediately after the martyrdom of the Apostles and were removed to the tombs that had been prepared on the Vatican and on the Ostian Way one year and seven months afterwards. The Itineraries or Pilgrim Guides of the fifth and sixth centuries make the sojourn to be forty years : 'Et iuxta eandem viam (Appiam) ecclesia est S. Sebastiani martyris, ubi ipse dormit, et ibi sunt sepulchra Apostolorum Petri et Pauli; in quibus xl annos requiescebant ('De locis S.S. Martyrum'); 'Postea pervenies via Appia ad S. Sebastianum martyrem, cuius corpus iacet in inferiori loco, et ibi sunt sepulchra Apostolorum Petri et Pauli in quibus xl annos requiescebant' ('Salzburg Notitia'). As Duchesne and Barnes say, the term forty years is here undoubtedly intended as a round number, though the former is inclined, it seems to me, to extend it too widely.[1] The exact number of forty years would bring us to an impossible date, the height of the fiercest persecution which the Christian Church had to endure—that of Diocletian. The period of one year and seven months mentioned in the Apocryphal 'Acta' has, I have little doubt, some historical basis, which now it is impossible to discover,[2] but that the relics of the Apostles remained in the Platonia at least until the year 284 the 'Acta' of St. Sebastian testify. According to these 'Acta' the Saint was buried in the Catacomb which still bears

---

[1] Duchesne (*Lib. Pont.* cv and cvii) suggests a date after 313 A.D., Barnes (*St. Peter in Rome*) 308 or 309 A.D.

[2] See suggestion *infra*, p. 269.

his name close to the *Platonia* because he had in a vision expressed the wish that his body might lie near the *vestigia* of the holy Apostles.[1] There is another difficulty to be surmounted. In the biography of Pope Cornelius, 251–253 A.D., in the ' Liber Pontificalis ' the statement is made that at the request of a certain matron Lucina by name the bodies of the blessed Apostles Peter and Paul were taken up by night ; and that Lucina first buried the blessed Paul in her own ground (*in praedio suo*) on the Ostian Road and then that Cornelius placed the body of Peter close to the spot where he was crucified among the bodies of the holy bishops—' in templum Apollinis, in Monte Aureo in Vaticanum palatii Neroniani iii Kal. Iul.' Now it is clear that if the bodies of the Apostles were only brought to the cemetery *ad Catacumbas* in 258 A.D., they cannot have been restored to their former tombs some years earlier. Duchesne, Marucchi, and Barnes are all of opinion that this paragraph in the notice of Cornelius has been somehow misplaced.[2] Further it is stated that after the martyrdom of this Pope this same Lucina gathered together his remains (*cuius corpus noctu collegit*) and buried it in her own ground (*praedio suo*) in a crypt close to the Cemetery of Callistus. Apparently therefore Lucina had property, which she converted into a cemetery, both on the Ostian and the Appian Way.

Now Barnes has proposed a solution of this difficulty which is both ingenious and well worthy of consideration.[3] He suggests that in some worn MS. the name Marcellus has been read as Cornelius and that the passage relating to the restoration of the bodies of the Apostles to their original tombs belongs to the biography of Marcellus. The Pontificate of Marcellus is separated from that of his predecessor Marcellinus by an interregnum due to the persecution of Diocletian, and its date was probably 306–309 A.D. In the biography of this Pope there is again mention of a certain matron, Lucina, the widow of a man named Marcus. On the martyrdom of Marcellus she gathered together his remains (*cuius corpus collegit*) and buried it in the Cemetery of Priscilla. Lucina, it is said, gave all her property to the Church, and a comparison of the various documents seems to point to that portion of the cemetery of Priscilla on the *Via Salaria Nova*, where Marcellus and his successors were

[1] *Acta Sanctorum*, Jan. 2, p. 622.
[2] Duchesne, *Liber Pont.* i. p. 151; Marucchi, *Le Memorie degli Apostoli Pietro e Paolo*, p. 56; Barnes, *St. Peter in Rome*, pp. 116 ff.
[3] *St. Peter in Rome*, pp. 119–127.

buried, having been the property of this Lucina. By the time of the accession of Marcellus the bodies of the Apostles had been in the Platonia nearly 50 years. The abdication of Diocletian in 305 A.D. led to peace [1] being restored to the Christian Church in Rome by the advent of Maxentius to power. This then would be a very fitting time for a new pope to prepare the removal of the Apostolic relics from the catacomb to their original tombs. There is extant an inscription of Damasus [2] which tells us that the severity of Marcellus to those who had lapsed in the persecution stirred up violent strife and discord leading to sedition and the shedding of blood.

> Veridicus rector, lapsos quia crimina flere
> Praedixit, miseris fuit omnibus hostis amarus ;
> Hinc furor, hinc odium sequitur, discordia, lites,
> Seditio, caedes ; solvuntur foedera pacis.
> Crimen ob alterius, Christum qui in pace negavit,
> Finibus expulsus patriae est feritate tyranni.
> Haec breviter Damasus voluit comperta referre
> Marcelli ut populus meritum cognoscere posset.

This inscription contains no reference to Marcellus having brought back the bodies of St. Peter and St. Paul to the Vatican and the Ostian Way, but the brevity of the poetical encomium of Damasus, as he himself states, made him confine himself to praising those actions of the bishop which were the cause of the suffering and exile that befell him.[3] I would suggest, however, that in these discords and tumults, to which the inscription refers, may be found perhaps an explanation of the delay of one year and seven months in the entombment of the Apostles of which the Apocryphal ' Acta ' (*Passio Petri et Pauli*) speak. The strange passage, which tells of how ' while the bodies of the Apostles were being carried off by the Greeks to be taken to the East, there was a great earthquake and the Roman people ran out and seized them in the place which is called Catacumba

---

[1] Gibbon, *Decline and Fall*, vol. ii. p. 161 : 'The revolt of Maxentius immediately restored peace to the Churches of Italy and Africa, and the same tyrant who oppressed every other class of his subjects showed himself just, humane, and even partial towards the afflicted Christians.'

[2] De Rossi, *Inscr. Crist.* ii. pp. 62, 103, 138.

[3] That there is confusion in the traditions relating to Cornelius and Marcellus is evident from the fact that in the *Liber Pontificalis* Cornelius is beheaded in Rome, in the *Liberian Catalogue* in exile at Centumcellis, *cum gloria dormitionem accepit.* Damasus makes Marcellus apparently die in exile. In the *Liber Pontificalis* he is condemned to tend horses in stables at Rome and dies of ill-usage. The inscription of Damasus is however authentic, as is the extant slab containing the words Cornelius Martyr, in the crypt where this Pope was buried.

at the third milestone on the Via Appia, and the bodies were
kept there for one year and seven months, until the places were
built in which their bodies were placed, and then they were
brought back with glory of hymns and were deposited that of
St. Peter in the Vatican and that of St. Paul on the Ostian Way
at the second milestone,' may well be a distorted and misdated
version of events that really took place in the days of Marcellus.
Let us suppose that on the first anniversary day of the Apostles,
June 29, after the accession of Maxentius an attempt was made
to remove the relics from the Catacombs, but that it was frus-
trated by the sudden attack of a hostile crowd, from whose hands
the bodies were with difficulty rescued and taken back to the
Platonia. Then about a year and a half later after all prepara-
tions had been carefully made the translation was successfully
carried out. Now in the ' Liberian Catalogue ' under the heading
depositio martyrum the entry occurs ' viii. kl. Martias Natale
Petri de Cathedra,' and this commemoration Professor Marucchi
states was according to ancient documents observed from the
Fourth century with such feasting that it gained the popular
name of ' dies sancti Petri epularum.' [1] Further in the *Later-
culum* of Silvias, 448 A.D., it is said that in earlier times this
commemoration, held on February 22, was a joint festival of
SS. Peter and Paul.[2] Was it not then on this date that after a
year and seven months the actual translation took place ?

What may be called the Marcellus hypothesis remains
however little more than a plausible conjecture, for no positive
evidence can be brought forward to establish its truth.

Nevertheless an examination of the Apocryphal ' Acta '
reveals the fact that a certain Marcellus was supposed to be the
writer of the ' Passio Petri et Pauli ' from which the extract
quoted above about the attempt to carry off the Apostles' bodies,
and about their lying for a year and seven months in the Catacombs, is taken. Marcellus it is who after the martyrdom
takes the lead in burying St. Peter ' near the Naumachia in the
place called the Vatican.' Lipsius in his work on the Apostolic
legends devotes a whole section to what he styles ' der so-
genannte Marcellustext.' [3] Nor is this all. On late authority

---

[1] Marucchi, *Elém. d'Arch. Chrét.* ii. pp. 453-6; De Rossi, *Bullett. d.
Arch. Crist.* 1890, p. 72 ff.
[2] Blunt, *Annot. Book of Common Prayer* (' The Conversion of St. Paul')
[3] Lipsius, *Die Apokryphen Apostelgeschichten und Apostellegenden,*
2er Band 1e Hälfte, pp. 284-386. One MS. *Cod. Urbin.* is headed—' III.
Kl. Iulii Passio beatorum Petri et Pauli a Marcello discipulo Petri edita
quique idem interfuit passioni.'

St. Paul was said to have been buried by a certain matron Lucina in her own property (*in praedio suo*) on the Ostian Way.[1] In the 'Liber Pontificalis' the Lucina of the Cornelius biography buries St. Paul on the return from the Catacombs on the Ostian Way 'in praedio suo.' The Lucina of the Marcellus biography is the widow of Marcus, in the 'Passio Petri et Pauli' Marcus is the father of Marcellus. In all probability the three Lucinas are one and the same person, whose activity was connected with the life of Pope Marcellus. If this should be so, it will at once appear that a strong case is made for placing the return of the relics from the Platonia in the pontificate of Marcellus, about 307 A.D.

That the bodies of the Apostles were believed to lie in the tombs on the Vatican and on the Ostian Way when Constantine determined to erect basilicas over their remains is certain. The exact year in which these were built is unknown, except that it was in the Pontificate of Pope Silvester, 314–335. The words of the 'Liber Pontificalis' (Duchesne, i. 176 and 178) tell us that the object of the Emperor was to do honour to the sacred tombs of the Apostles. The sarcophagus which contained the body of St. Peter he enclosed in bronze from Cyprus and fixed it at the central point of a cubical chamber of masonry—' cuius loculum undique aere Cypro conclusit, quod est immobile ; ad caput, pedes V ; ad pedes, pedes V ; ad latus dextrum, pedes V; ad latus sinistrum, pedes V ; subter, pedes V ; supra, pedes V ; sic inclusit corpus beati Petri et recondit.' He then placed on the coffin a cross of gold (with an inscription)—' super corpus Petri, supra aera quod conclusit, fecit crucem ex auro purissimo, pens. lib. cl. in mensuram loci, ubi scriptum est hoc CONSTAN-TINVS AVGVSTVS ET HELENA AVGVSTA HANC DOMVM REGALEM SIMILI FVLGORE CORVSCANS AVLA CIR-CVMDAT, scriptum ex litteris nigellis in cruce ipsa.'

Constantine likewise built a basilica on the Ostian Way to the memory of St. Paul, whose sarcophagus was, like St. Peter's, enclosed in bronze and a cross of gold placed over it ' cuius corpus ita recondit in aere et conclusit sicut beati Petri . . . et crucem auream super locum beati Pauli apostoli posuit pens. lib. cl.' The scrupulous care that was taken not to disturb the tombs in any way was conspicuously shown in the instance of the Constantinian basilica of St. Paul. It was the custom in the early basilicas that the altar upon the tomb of the saint or

---

[1] De Rossi, *Roma Sotterranea*, ii. p. 262 ; Stevenson, 'L'area di Lucina sulla Via Ostiense,' *Nuovo Bullett.* 1898, p. 60 ff.

martyr to whom the church was dedicated should be placed at
the west end at the central point of the chord of an apse round
which the clergy sat on either side of the bishop or other dignitary.
The Celebrant stood with his back to this apse facing eastward
with the congregation before him in the nave. Now the tomb
of St. Paul lay so near to the Ostian Way, one of the main roads
from Rome, that this first basilica was of diminutive proportions.
Before however many years were past it was felt that so small
a church was unworthy of St. Paul, and another basilica on the
same scale as that of St. Peter was erected in 386 A.D. To effect
this without touching the tomb and altar led to a completely
new departure in the internal arrangements of the basilica,
a new departure that was to have permanent results by being
generally adopted.[1] The church was reversed, the apse was now
placed at the east end, but the celebrant still stood on the west
side of the altar facing eastwards, with result that he looked
towards the clergy in the apse and had his back to the congregation in the nave : a custom which has since become universal.
Another innovation arose from the desire to cover all the
consecrated ground, where the first basilica had stood, and a
transverse nave at right angles to the main nave was built, and
thus came into existence in 386 A.D. the earliest known example
of a cruciform church. No stronger evidence could be brought
forward to show the scrupulous and reverential care with which
the early Christians cherished and guarded the burial places of
their dead. In this they were aided by the laws of the State,
which declared every tomb to be ' locus sacer, locus religiosus,'
and there is seen to be no impossibility in the assumption that
the *sarcophagi* which Constantine enclosed in bronze really
contained the bodies of the Apostles. Whatever care was be-
stowed on other tombs, those of St. Peter and of St. Paul would
from the first be regarded with exceptional veneration, and be
watched over and tended with peculiar devotion, so that it would
be most unlikely that those who translated the relics to the
catacombs in 258 A.D. should have made any mistake.
  The question whether these sarcophagi encased in bronze
by Constantine are still in existence, or whether they were
destroyed by the Saracens in 846 A.D. or by the soldiery of
Bourbon in 1527, can only be answered positively by excavations
which it may safely be said will never be undertaken. Probability on the whole seems to be that, though the shrines were

---

[1] Barnes, *St. Peter in Rome*, p. 215 ff. ; Belloni, *Della grandezza et la
disposizione della primitiva Basilica Ostiense.*

plundered and destroyed, the tombs themselves were untouched. If the story told by Bonanni,[1] who professes to be giving from the MS. of a contemporary of the event (Torrigio) the evidence of eyewitnesses, be true, then in some alterations that were being made in 1594 by the orders of Pope Clement VIII to the altar of the Confession an aperture was opened through which the sarcophagus of St. Peter with the gold cross gleaming upon it was seen by the Pope himself, and Cardinals Bellarmine, Antoniano and Sfondrato. By Clement's command the aperture was filled up with cement and has not been opened since. Further in the excavations by Paul V in 1615 and by Urban VIII in 1626, in the immediate vicinity of the shrine conclusive evidence was obtained that the early Christian sepulchres which clustered round the sacred resting place of the Apostle had never been disturbed.

In the case of St. Paul's shrine a very interesting discovery made in 1835, when the basilica was being rebuilt after the great fire of 1823, points to the conclusion that the tomb had not been interfered with since the fourth century. A slab of marble measuring seven feet by four feet was uncovered with the simple inscription

PAVLO
APOSTOLO MART.

The opinion of archaeologists who have examined the slab is unanimous that the character of the inscription and the form of the letters fix the date as belonging to the age of Constantine. Under the name[2] is a round aperture, the ancient *billicum confessionis*, sometimes called the *fenestrella* or *little window*, through which handkerchiefs or other objects were lowered so as to be hallowed by contact with the sarcophagus.

[1] Bonanni, *Temp. Vatic. Historia*, published in 1696, p. 149.
[2] There are also two square apertures of later date, purpose unknown.

NOTE F.

THE ROMAN CATACOMBS.
THE CEMETERIES OF PRISCILLA AND DOMITILLA.

DURING the first century of our era the Romans almost universally practised cremation for the disposal of their dead. The law of the XII Tables supposes inhumation as well as cremation to be in use ; but cremation gradually became the vogue and it was not until the age of the Antonines that, largely through the influence of Christianity and other Oriental cults, a reversion to the practice of inhumation began to take place. The early Christians from the first adopted the Jewish custom of burial, and their tombs were, whenever circumstances permitted, fashioned after the likeness of those in Palestine, sepulchres like that of the Lord Jesus Christ. No burials were permitted within the city of Rome ; but the beds of soft volcanic tufa which lay beneath the soil of the suburban area afforded easy facilities for the excavation of subterranean galleries, vaults, and crypts in which to lay the dead. Hence gradually in the course of the first four centuries came into existence that vast underground city of the dead, often incorrectly spoken of as the Roman Catacombs. The word Catacombs strictly applies to one small cemetery only, the *locus ad catacumbas*[1] where the bodies of St. Peter and St. Paul in 258 A.D. found a temporary resting-place. The first Christian cemeteries differed in no way from those of the Jewish community, three of which have been discovered and explored.[2] There has been much written on the subject of the Roman Catacombs which does not need consideration here. The cemeteries of the first century, whatever may have been the case later, were the property of private persons of rank and wealth, and were intended in the first place for the use of the family to which the owners belonged, also for that of their clients, freedmen and slaves, and by permission

---

[1] The meaning of the term is uncertain. De Rossi gives it a hybrid derivation from κατά and *cubitorium*, but this is very doubtful.

[2] Raffaele Garrucci, *Cimeteri degli antichi Ebrei*; Orazio Marucchi, *Elém. d'Arch. Chrét.* ii. 208-226, 259-276.

T

for other poor persons belonging to the Christian brotherhood. As yet there was no question of the formation of *Collegia funera-tica* or Burial Guilds, though it is regarded as highly probable that such organisations with their collective ownership and special privileges did exist in the third century; indeed it is known that the several cemeteries were each attached to a *titulus*—or parish church. But this was not the case in the period with which we are dealing, when the places of assembly for congregational worship were still private houses—*ecclesiae domesticae.* The most ancient parts of the cemeteries of Priscilla and Domitilla and the crypt of Lucina, which date from Apostolic times, were family vaults constructed beneath the property of the person after whose name they are called, and granted by that person, as a ' locus sacer ' placed under the protection of the Roman Law (*lex monumenti*). Henceforward the tomb was held inviolable, whatever might be the religion of those interred in it. The plot of ground (*area*) was often enclosed by walls, or its dimensions were engraved on boundary stones. Sometimes the inscription is found ' Sibi suisque, libertis libertabusque posterisque eorum,' sometimes the letters H.M.H.N.S.—' hoc monumentum haeredem non sequitur.' The administration of the *leges monumentorum* lay within the jurisdiction of the *pontifices*, who were thus the legal guardians of the inviolability of the burial-places thus granted, and their leave was required for the deposition of the bodies in the tombs or their translation, or indeed for the holding of anniversary festivals or rites or for any changes in the construction or character of the monuments. These powers do not seem to have been arbitrarily or vexatiously used, but it must always be remembered that they did exist and that the catacombs were in no sense secret and unknown hiding-places of the early Christians, but, with the exception perhaps of a few small subterranean crypts carefully concealed, like the *Platonia* chamber in which the bodies of the Apostles for awhile were laid, were registered and thus known to the magistrates.

The Roman Catacombs are one of the wonders of the world. It has been calculated that the length of the galleries in the cemeteries excavated within three miles of the Gates of Servius amounts to 540 miles, the quantity of material removed by excavation 96,000,000 cubic feet, and the number of bodies interred at the very least 1,700,000.[1] Of this vast network

[1] Lanciani, *Pagan and Christian Rome*, pp. 320-1. The estimate is that of Michele Stefano de Rossi made in 1860.

of subterranean galleries only a comparatively small portion has been explored, though progress is being made year by year, and unfortunately all the cemeteries as they have been opened out have been found to be in a miserable state of ruin and devastation. Nevertheless, the Catacombs even in their present condition contain in the inscriptions and frescoes that still cover the walls, and in the remains of the shrines of saints and martyrs, a most precious record not merely of the names of the Christians who in the ages of persecution found their last resting-place in the *loculi* arranged along the walls of these crypts and galleries, but of their beliefs, prayers, rites, worship, and modes of thought. Historically we are here in the presence of a crowd of witnesses who though dead yet speak to us, of a mass of evidence that is incontrovertibly authentic.

By far the larger part of the tombs in the Catacombs belong to the century and a half which preceded the peace of the Church under Constantine, 313 A.D. But after the middle of the fourth century, although by the care of Pope Damasus (366–384 A.D.) and others basilicas were erected over the most venerated remains of famous martyrs, and the chapel-crypts in which the bodies actually lay were adorned with rich shrines and mural decorations, subterranean interment gradually ceased [1] and in the fifth century the Catacombs had become simply sanctuaries, whither pilgrims resorted to pray before the tombs of the martyrs. For three centuries a continual stream of pilgrims made their way to Rome for this purpose, and some of the Itineraries or guide-books that they used still exist. Meanwhile the cemeteries were already in the seventh century beginning to be robbed of their precious contents, as in 645 A.D. and in 652 A.D. a number of the bodies of martyrs were removed from the Catacombs into Rome in order to save them from pillage and desecration at the hands of barbarian invaders. Finally in the time of Paschal I (817–824 A.D.) this translation to churches within the city walls was carried out on an extraordinary scale. It is said that the remains of no fewer than 2300 martyrs were deposited in one single church, that of St. Praxedis. Henceforward the pilgrimages came to an end, the Catacombs were deserted, and in time their very existence was forgotten. The accidental re-opening of a Christian cemetery by some workmen in the Vigna Sanchez on the Via Salaria in 1578 led to a revival of interest. It was part of what is now known as the Catacomb of the Jordani, but a landslip, owing to the rough carelessness of those who first examined these crypts,

---

[1] No inscription has been found of a later date than 410 A.D.

completely destroyed them and no trace of them now remains. It was fortunate that at the beginning of the seventeenth century a really intelligent and scientific exploration of the Catacombs was undertaken by Antonio Bosio, died 1629 A.D., who devoted thirty years to the study of the subject and was the real founder of Christian archaeology. He had great difficulties in his way owing to lack of resources for the purposes of excavation, but his ' Roma Sotterranea,' published after his death in 1632, is of very great value owing to the wanton destruction during the next two centuries of monuments and works of art, which had survived as memorials of early Christianity in Rome. The one object of the exploration of the Catacombs, even on the part of those who did seriously study Christian archaeology and whose writings are a proof of the interest they felt in their subject—Aringhi, Boldetti, Bottari [1] and others—was the discovery of the relics of saints. To effect this purpose the cemeteries were pillaged and ravaged, the *loculi* broken open, their contents carried away, the inscriptions broken to pieces or removed wholesale, the precious works of art found in the tombs—gold and silver vessels, lamps, medallions, engraved seals, precious stones, and personal ornaments—stolen and scattered far and wide. Some of these are to be seen to-day in museums and private collections, but the greater part have disappeared. Not until the middle of the nineteenth century was a successor found who approached the study of the Catacombs in the scientific spirit of Bosio, and with far greater genius. Giovanni Battista de Rossi (1822–94), whose early interest in the subject of Christian archaeology had been aroused by the labours of P. Marchi,[2] whose pupil indeed he was, gave his whole life with a thoroughness and industry which could not be surpassed to the investigation of all known sources which threw light upon the topography and history of subterranean Rome. He possessed in a peculiar manner a special combination of gifts—patience, imagination and insight, and the results of his labours have been not merely fruitful in discovery and in additions to our knowledge of early Christianity, but they have proved that the so-called legends of the ' Acta Sanctorum,' though late in date, are never to be regarded as simply fictitious romances, the efforts of imaginative invention. On the contrary, however great the accretion of legendary details, largely thaumaturgic, these stories deal with

---

[1] Aringhi, *Roma Sotterranea*, 1651; Boldetti, *Osservazioni sopra i cimeteri di santi martiri ed antichi cristiani di Roma*, 1720; Bottari, *Sculture e pitture sacre extratte dai cimeteri di Roma*, 1757.
[2] *I monumenti delle arti cristiane primitive nella metropoli di Cristianesimo*, 1844.

real historical persons and have been built up on a basis of genuine fact. Of De Rossi's method of working and the materials that he used in his researches—*i.e.* the Pilgrim Itineraries of the seventh century, five of which are still preserved in monastic libraries, the ancient topographies, the 'Sillogae Epigraphicae' drawn up in the eighth and ninth centuries, the famous Monza papyrus containing a list of the sacred oils from the various shrines sent by Gregory the Great to the Lombard Queen Theodelinda, the notices in the 'Liber Pontificalis,' the Hieronymian Martyrology, the lists in the Liberian Catalogue entitled 'Depositio Episcoporum' and 'Depositio Martirum,' and the 'Acta Sanctorum' themselves—a full account is given by himself in his published works,[1] which should be consulted. References have already been made to the most important of the discoveries which have in recent years rewarded the explorers of the first century cemeteries of Priscilla and Domitilla under De Rossi's inspiring guidance, and it is unnecessary to restate at length what has been written. The bearing however of these and other discoveries in the same localities on the history of the Christian Church in Rome during the second half of the twelfth century is of such an interesting character that a brief recapitulation of results may be of service.

The vast cemetery of Priscilla lies on the Via Salaria Nova on the north side of the city. It consists of two stories, in each of which is found a network of galleries and crypts. The present entrance is modern (1865), the ancient door stands on the opposite side of the road, above which can be still read the inscription in the red letters which denote great antiquity, COEM. PRIS-CILLAE. It was in 1888 that De Rossi in the course of excavations discovered the crypt and chapel of the Acilian *gens*. The explorers first came across a broken marble slab containing the words ACILIO GLABRIONI FILIO, and afterwards the ruined crypt was unearthed and other fragments of inscriptions to members of various branches of the Acilian family. Formerly the walls had been encrusted with marble or coated with fine plaster and covered with frescos and mosaics, but everything had been smashed to pieces by the hands of relic and treasure hunters in the middle of the seventeenth century. Nevertheless

---

[1] *Roma Sotterranea Cristiana*, 1864-77. *Inscriptiones Christianae urbis Romae VII° saeculo antiquiores*, 1861-88. *Il museo epigrafico cristiano pro-laterense*, 1878. *Musaici delle chiese di Roma anteriori al seculo XV*, 1872. Especially *Bullettino di Archeologia cristiana*, 1863-94. The *Bullettino* has been continued with the title *Nuovo Bullettino* under the editorship of Professor O. Marucchi, the pupil and fellow-worker of De Rossi.

the historical value of this signal find is great. It may be held to establish the fact that M' Acilius Glabrio, the consul of 91 A.D., who was put to death by Domitian accused of following 'Jewish manners and strange superstitions' and of being 'an inciter of innovations,' was a Christian, and not merely so but that in the second century many members of this distinguished family belonging to the high aristocracy of Rome had embraced the Christian faith. It seems to follow that this cemetery was excavated under property belonging to the *Acilian House*. The names of Priscilla and Prisca are found on inscriptions as in use among members of this family, and the Priscilla who was the donor of the ground and founder of the cemetery was doubtless a near relative of the Consul. In the preceding Note on the 'Legend of Pudens' it has been pointed out that there is no necessary inconsistency in the two statements that Priscilla was mother of Pudens and sister or aunt of M' Acilius Glabrio. Indeed there are signs that the Acilian crypt and the primitive cemetery of Priscilla, though closely adjoining, were originally separated, the crypt being approached by a distinct staircase. If so, it is quite possible, as the 'Acta' seem to indicate, that the cemetery may have been through his mother the property of Pudens, the crypt at its side constructed beneath land belonging to Glabrio. Above the cemetery of Priscilla, after the peace of the Church, was built a basilica, afterwards known as St. Sylvester,[1] into which the bodies of many martyrs and saints were translated from the crypts below in the fourth century. The bodies however of Pudens and his daughters and of Aquila and Prisca were left undisturbed until the time of Leo IV in the middle of the ninth century. Leo IV appears to have made a careful exploration of the cemetery, but after his days it fell into disuse and complete abandonment. Beneath the story where these bodies lay is a second story, consisting of a long gallery out of which open some twenty transversal galleries as yet very imperfectly explored. Of this second story deep down below the surface and approached by two or more staircases from the upper galleries Marucchi writes: 'On peut dire sans exaggération que c'est la region cimetériale la plus vaste et la plus régulière de toute la Rome souterraine. Ses inscriptions gravées sur marbre, ou peintes en rouges sur des tuiles comme au premier étage, attestent qu'au moins en partie elle remonte

---

[1] The basilica of St. Sylvester suffered complete destruction during the period of the Barbarian invasions. Its very existence had for long centuries been forgotten, until De Rossi unearthed its ruins in 1889.

à la plus haute antiquité. A mon avis, il y eut là un noyau cimetérial dès le IIe siècle.'[1] One of the most remarkable features of the cemetery of Priscilla is the existence of two large tanks, one on each floor, besides several smaller ones. ҀThese two large tanks were almost certainly ancient baptisteries.ǀ Marucchi has written learnedly, and with a considerable measure of success, to identify the cemetery of Priscilla with the ' *Cymiterium Ostrianum, ubi Petrus apostolus baptizavit*' of the apocryphal ' Acta Liberii.' This cemetery also was called *ad Nymphas* or *ad Fontes S. Petri*, names which might well be derived from the tanks just mentioned. One of the principal pieces of evidence adduced by Marucchi is found in the Catalogue of Monza containing a list of the phials of sacred oil taken from the different shrines and sent to Queen Theodelinda by the direction of Gregory the Great. Under the heading ' Salaria Nova ' follows : ' Sedes ubi sedit Sčs Petrus ex oleo Sči Vitalis Sčs Alexander Sčs Martialis Sčs Marcellus Sči Silvestri Sči Felicis Sči Filippi et aliorum multorum Sčorum. . . .' All these saints mentioned were buried either in the Cemetery of Priscilla or its immediate vicinity.[2] In any case we are in the presence here of the most ancient of Roman baptisteries.

The Cemetery of Domitilla lies to the west of the Via Ardeatina (a road which ran parallel to the Via Appia) close to the point where it is crossed by the modern Via delle Sette Chiese. The cemetery extends under a property known as the *Tor Marancia*, a name doubtless derived from a certain Amaranthus.[3] In excavations made on this property a number of pagan tombs were found, which gave the clue to De Rossi that he was seeking in order to locate the cemetery of Domitilla mentioned in the ' Acts of Nereus and Achilles.' One of these discovered in 1772 contains the words

FLAVIAE · DOMITILLAE
VESPASIANI · NEPTIS
EIVS · BENEFICIO · HOC · SEPVLCRVm
MEIS · LIBERTIS · LIBERTABVS · POsuit.

Another found in 1817 records how a certain Calvisius Philotas

[1] Marucchi, *Elém. d'Arch. Chrét.* ii. 459.
[2] Marucchi, *Di un antico battistero recentemente scoperto nel cimetero apostolico di Priscilla e della sua importanza storica*, 1901. *Le Memorie degli Apostoli Pietro e Paolo in Roma*, 1903, pp. 93–108. In *Roma Sotterranea Cristiana*, nuova serie, tom. i. p. 10, Marucchi writes ' Spero di pubblicare un nuovo lavoro su questo stesso argumento.'
[3] *Supra*, p. 249.

made this tomb for his brother Sergius Cornelius Julianus, for
his wife Calvisia, and for himself

EX INDVLGENTIA FLAVIAE DOMITILL.

In close vicinity to these were discovered four inscriptions to
members of the Bruttian gens. One of these makes mention
of a Bruttius Praesens.

D M.
BRVTIO · VENVSINO
C · BRVTTIVS · PRAESENS
PATRONVS · LIBERTO
BENE · MERENTI · FECIT.

Now Eusebius in his ' Chronicle ' tells us that he derived his
information about the Domitianic persecution and the banishment of Flavia Domitilla to the island of Pontia from an historian
named Bruttius, who may possibly be identified with C. Bruttius
Praesens, who was consul for the second time in 139 A.D. This
group of indications led De Rossi to suspect that the cemetery
which lay beneath the Tor Marancia was none other than the
Cemetery of Domitilla, in which, according to the ' Acts of
Nereus and Achilles,' those martyrs were buried.

Acting on this hypothesis the Commission of Sacred Archaeology under the direction of De Rossi began a systematic exploration of the cemetery in 1852. At first progress was but slow,
owing to the difficulties placed in the way of research by the
then proprietor of the property. Tor Marancia was however
in 1873 purchased by Monsgr. Francesco de Merode, with the
aim of forwarding the work by every means in his power.
Already in 1865 De Rossi had re-discovered the original entrance
to the Catacomb hewn out of the side of a low cliff. It must
always have been a conspicuous object to the passer-by, and
is a proof of the great security which was felt in the protection
and immunity from disturbance afforded by the law to all places
of burial. This entrance opened into a vestibule adorned with
biblical frescoes, which were plainly visible from outside through
the door. To this vestibule De Rossi gave the name of *Il
vestibulo dei Flavi;* its construction is assigned to the first
century. The inscription above the entrance was missing, but
in 1874 in the ruins of the basilica of St. Petronilla only a very
short distance from the entrance was a fragment of marble

containing a portion of a title, which De Rossi has restored thus :

SepulcRVM
FlaviORVM

Below this is the Christian symbol, an anchor. In 1873 De Rossi was rewarded by the discovery of the basilica of Nereus and Achilles, which had been one of the special objects of his search. There could be no doubt on the matter, for a portion of an inscription of Pope Damasus was found, the contents of which are known, for a copy exists in the Pilgrim Itinerary of Einsiedeln, and a small column was unearthed on which is represented a scene of martyrdom and above it the word ACILLEVS. According to the ' Itineraries ' the tomb of the famous martyr Petronilla lay behind the altar which covered the remains of Nereus and Achilles. The explorers were able to verify this indication. In a cubiculum behind the apse of the basilica, and approached by a short passage, a fresco was discovered on the wall filling the front of the *arcisolium* where the sarcophagus had lain ; the painting showed two female figures standing, an elder and a younger woman with their names inscribed

VENERANDA · DEP · VII · IDVS · IANVARIAS ·
PETRONELLA MARTYR.

In or close by this *cubiculum* was therefore, it may be safely inferred, the burial place of PETRONILLA. Her sarcophagus was actually removed to the Vatican at the request of the King of France at a time when many such translations were made by Pope Paul I (755-756).

The inscription on the sarcophagus.

AVRELIÁE · PETRONILLAE · FIL · DVLCISSIMAE ·

may be taken as indicating that she belonged to the Aurelian *gens*, several of whose members are buried in this cemetery, and that she was related to the Flavian imperial family, one of whose *cognomina* was Petro.

The legend that she was the daughter of St. Peter has no foundation other than the name.

One of the most ancient portions of the cemetery situated in the immediate vicinity, and to the south of the remains of the basilica of Nereus and Achilles (or as it is sometimes called of Petronilla), is that styled the Region of the Flavii Aurelii.

It contains the inscription ΦΛ. SABEINOS· KAI TITIANH ADELΦH· not improbably the grandchildren of Flavius Clemens and of Flavia Domitilla the founder of the crypt.

Another of the earliest and most interesting crypts in this Catacomb was discovered in 1881. The decorations of this sepulchral chamber are elaborate and rich, resembling those of a room in a Pompeian house, and belonging to the same period. Above the *arcisolium* inscribed on marble is the single word AMPLIATI. 'Les lettres de cette courte épitaphe,' remarks Marucchi, 'sont très soignées et d'une forme paléographique certainement antérieure à la seconde moitié du IIᵉ siècle ; on peut la juger sans témérité de la fin du premier.'[1] It is remarkable too that such prominence should be given to a single name bespeaking probably a man of servile origin. A further mark of the regard in which this tomb was held is the existence of a staircase of later date, cut through the rock to provide a direct way of approach from the Via Ardeatina to the pilgrims. That the man thus honoured was the Ampliatus mentioned by St. Paul in the salutation in chapter xvi. of the Epistle to the Romans is therefore not an unreasonable supposition. A later inscription in the same crypt records that a certain Aurelius Ampliatus with Gordianus his son have erected a memorial to Aurelia Bonifatia, his incomparable wife. This Aurelius Ampliatus may have been a descendant of the Ampliatus who was a contemporary of the Apostles, and very probably a freedman of the Aurelian family, many members of which family, as this Catacomb bears witness, had been among the early converts to Christianity.

The precious medallion in bronze, containing the earliest representation in existence of the heads of the two Apostles Peter and Paul, now in the Sacred Museum of the Vatican Library, was found by Boldetti in the Cemetery of Domitilla.[2]

[1] *Elém. d'Arch. Chrét.* ii. 118.
[2] *Osservazioni sui cimeteri*, 1720, p. 192.

INDEX

ACHAIA, 195

Achilles, 231, 233, 252-3, 280, 281

Acilii Glabriones, crypt of the, 52 *n.*[1], 236, 242, 247-8, 277

Acilius Glabrio, 52 *n.*[1], 235-6, 242, 248, 278

Acta Liberii, cited, 117 *n.*[3]

Acts of Nereus and Achilles, cited, 231-5, 252 *et seq.*

Acts of Pastor and Timothy, cited, 211 *n.*[1], 244

Acts of Petronilla, 252

Acts of SS. Pudentiana and Praxedis, 244-5 *passim*.

Acts of the Apostles, the narrative of, 30 *et seq.*, 87 *et seq.*, 101-2; character and object of, 30; for whom written, 30, 33; silences of, suggestive, 30, 33; authorship of, 31-2; date of, 32-3, 67 *n.*[4]; St. Peter in, 30-1, 34, 43; omission of reference to the Church in Rome, explanation of, 33; account of Simon Magus in, 38, 61; sequence of events in, frequently misunderstood, 73; otherwise mentioned, 7 *n.*[1], 28, 138, 186, 192

Acts, Passions and *Travels* of the Saints and Martyrs, traditions in, 46 *and n.*[1]; 54-5 *and notes*; 80-1 *and notes*; 147

Actus Petri Vercellenses, 107 *and n.*[1]

African races, traditional records among, *cited*, 44

Agabus, prophecy of, 74

Agrippa. *See* Herod Agrippa.

Agrippina, 99 *n.*[1]

Alexander (pope), 261

Alexandria:
 tradition as to Mark's work in, 106, 107
 Pauline authorship of *Hebrews* accepted in, 156 *and n.*[2]
 government in, 185-6

Alexandrians, 36 *and n.*[3]

Allard, Paul, *cited*, 6 *n.*[4], 53 *and n.*[1], 227 *n.*, 235 *n.*[1]

Ampliatus, 282

Ananias, high priest, 90

Andronicus, 16, 25-6, 26 *n.*[1], 35, 57

Anencletus (pope), 49, 72, 84, 180, 200, 210, 221, 259, 261, 263

Anicetus, 210 *and n.*[3]

Annaean gens, the, 113 *n.*[2]

Annianus, 106

Antichrist, 164, 172-3

Antioch, 41 *n.*[3]; evangelisation of, 39 *et seq.*, 56-7, 73; work of Barnabas, and Paul in, 41 *and n.*[3], 73; famine relief fund at, 74; Peter's episcopate in, 50, 77

Antioch in Pisidia, 101

Antonius Primus, 169

Apocalypse of St. John, the: date of, 140, 164, 167 *et seq.*, 178; length of, 157 *n.*[1]; authorship of, 164-7; evidence for the late date, 167; the name of Antichrist in, 164, 172-3; the number of the Beast in, 165, 173, 175; references to Neronian persecution, 140, 168; and events of contemporary history, 164, 168 *et seq.*; external evidence for the early date, 169 *et seq.*; examination of crucial passages, 172; central theme of, 172; influence of Daniel and Ezekiel in, 173; influence of first century Apocalypses, 174; historical background of, 174; a Neronian document, 174, 175; the 'Nero legend' in, 174-6; the 'ten horns and ten diadems' in, 176; Armageddon in, 176; a record of political and physical catastrophes, 177-9; other references, 47, 120, 144, 181

Apollonius of Tyana, 21, 36 *n.*², 65 ;
action of Tigellinus against,
134-5, 135 *n.*¹ ; on Nero, 135,
173 *n.*² ; banished, 160 *n.*⁴, 162
Apollos, 11, 12, 65
Apostle, explanation of the term,
25
Apostles, the twelve, 35-7 ; dispersion of, 36, 43, 57-8 ; widespread activities of, 79 ; false
estimate of activities of, explained, 105
Apostolic rule of action not to
build on another man's foundation, 82
Apostolic times, great facilities for
intercourse in, 21
Appii Forum, 96 *and n.*¹
Aquila, 10, 11 *n.*² ; status of, 11,
85, 242, 243 ; exiled under
Claudius' edict, 10, 11, 24 ; and
Priscilla at Ephesus, 12 ; the
church in their house, 12, 22-4,
181, 243 ; relations with Paul,
13, 21, 22 ; return to Rome, 13,
22, 83 ; tomb of, 22 *n.*¹, 52 *n.*¹,
242, 278
Otherwise mentioned, 21, 22,
82, 83, 163, 181, 243 ; *see
also* Priscilla
Aristarchus, 65, 96, 98 *and n.*¹, 104
Aristobulus, 26, 113
Arrecina Tertulla, 229, 250-4
passim
Arrecinus Clemens, 205, 228, 230-4,
250 *et seq. passim*
Arrecinus Tertullus Clemens, 228-9,
233, 234, 250 *et seq. passim*
Asbach, *quoted,* 252 *n.*¹
Ascension of Isaiah, the, *quoted,*
48 *and nn* ¹ *and* ³, 149 *and n.* ¹,
174 *n.* ², 175 *n.*¹
Asia Minor, St. Paul's work in,
28, 105
Asiarchs, 13
Athenagoras, 117 *n.*³, 135, 136 *n.*¹
Augustine, St., *cited,* 143, 150 *n.*¹
Augustus, 3 *and n.*³, 5, 26, 97, 176
Aulus Plautius, 85, 229, 234, 250
Ausonius, *quoted,* 243

Babylon, a common synonym for
Rome, 47 *and n.*⁵, 120, 168
Barnabas, 40 *and n.*², 159 ; selected
to go to Antioch, 40 *and nn.* ¹
and ², ·57, 73 ; with Paul as
bearers of relief fund to Jerusalem, 75 ; missionary journey with

Paul 76, 77 ; work in preparing
the way for Paul, 40 ; relations
with Paul, 40, 65, 74-6, 104,
106-7 ; work with Paul in
Antioch, 41, 73 ; at Corinth, 79,
80 ; traditions associating him
with Rome and Italy, 16 *and
n.,* 80 *and n.*² ; 81, 82 *n.*¹,
107-8, 159, 160 ; with Peter at
Rome, 81, 107 ; *Datiana Historia*
cited on, 81 *n.* ; relations with
Mark, 106-8 ; and the authorship
of *Hebrews,* 108, 157-60 *passim,*
193 *and n.*⁴ ; as mediator between
the Hebrew and Gentile Christians, 40, 159. *See also under
heading* Hebrews
Barnabas, the aunt of, 43, 66
Barnes' *St. Peter in Rome,* cited,
149 *n.*², 248 *n.*¹, 262, 266-7
Bartlett, Prof. Vernon, *quoted,*
161 *n.*³
Baur, Christian, 60 *and n.*⁴, 118,
121, 161 *n.*³
Bedriacum, battle, 117
Bianchini *cited,* 249 *n.*¹
Biblical quotations, as test of date
in early Christian writings, 193
Bigg, Prof., *cited,* 105 *and n.*¹, 119
*n.*², 187 *nn.*¹ *and* ², 202
Bishop, 185, 192, 196-7, 220 ; grow-
ing importance of the office of,
201, 220-1 ; the title not applied
to St. James, 43
Bithynia, 119 *and n.*²
Bosio, Antonio, 276
Britannicus, 229, 255
Bruttius, 223, 224 *nn:* ¹ *and* ², 230
*and n.*¹, 232, 280
Burial customs in the first century,
271, 273-4
Burrhus, 13, 99 *and n*¹., 113 *and n.*²

Caesar's Household, 20 *n.*², 26 *and
n.*¹, 112-3
Caesar worship, 5, 6, 223
Caligula, 5, 6 *n.*¹, 10, 41-2, 91 *n.*¹,
228-9, 250
Callistus (pope), 261, 262
Catacombs, origin of, 273 ; laws
relating to, 274 ; the Roman
catacombs, 274 *et seq.* ; the
Platonia chamber, 265, 274 ;
testimony of, to truth of Christian
tradition, 118, 236-7, 275 ; wanton destruction of, 236 ; St.
Jerome's record of visit to, 69
*and n.*³

Cemetery ad Nymphas, 55, 117 n.³, 279

Chapman, Dom John, *cited*, 66 n.¹, 164 n.¹, 184 n.¹

Charles, Dr., *cited*, 174 n.², 175 n.¹

Chrestus, Chrestianos, 9–10 *and notes*, 24

Christian :
Archaeology, confirmatory of Christian tradition, 47, 118
Church, established throughout Judaea, Galilee and Samaria, 38 ; and written records in the first century, 45 ; early records destroyed by fire and accidents ; 45 *and* n.², 46 n.¹, 54 n.¹ ; organisation of the Early, 181 *et seq.*, 192, 218 *et seq.*; formed on Jewish model, 180, 181, 185 ; gradual acquisition of Gentile characteristics, 181–2 ; the *ecclesia*, 181, 182 ; the presbyters, 181 *et seq.*, 219 ; the *episcopus*, 182–4, 220 ; government of, after martyrdom of the Apostles, 185, 220 ; the president bishop, 185 ; analogy of government with that of cities like Alexandria, 185 ; the prophet in, 186, 218 ; criticism of evidence of the 'Didache,' 186–7
Communities, in Rome, 181 ; organisation of the early, 181 ; the first organised community was at Jerusalem, 35
Name of, punishment for confession of, 136–9, 206, 223

Christiani, the nickname, 41, 73, 138

Christians :
Burial places, care of early Christians for, 271
Charges against :
Atheism, 136
—— and Jewish manners, 222, 223
contemptible inertia, 226–7
hatred of the human race, 128, 136, 137
incendiarism, 127, 128, 133, 137
magic, the crime of, 136
de maiestate, 137
movers of innovations, 223

Christians—Charges against :
name, crimes adhering to the, 117, 127, 135–40 *passim*, 162, 206, 223
Oedipodean intercourse, 136
Thyestean feasts, 117, 136
Jews and, dissociation of, 86, 101 ; difference between, accentuated under Flavian emperors, 207
Persecutions of. *See under headings* Diocletian, Domitian, Herodian, Neronian, Valerian
Status of early, 85

Christianity, expansion of, not confined to sphere of Paul's activity, 30 ; explanation of false estimate of, 105 ; beginnings of, in Rome, 8–9 *and* n.¹, 57, 199 ; official Roman attitude to : regarded as a Jewish sect, 9, 11, 13 ; dissociation of Judaism and, 86, 101, 207 ; policy of the Roman State towards, 222 ; and the upper classes in the reign of Domitian, 236–7, 278

Chronicon Paschale, cited, 232, 252, 256

Chronological table of events, 239–41

Church. *See* Christian Church
—— in Rome. *See under* Rome.

Cicero, *cited*, 3 n.³, 4 n.², 96 ¹

Claudia, 163, 244

Claudius Caesar, 6, 13, 23, 26, 42, 63, 65, 78 n. ¹, 80, 114 n., 126 n. ¹, 176, 229, 234, 250

Claudius Ephebus, 199

Clement, of Alexandria, *cited*, 36 n.², 55 n.¹, 67 *and* n.², 166, 167

Clement (of Phil. iv. 3), 111, 112

Clement of Rome, the Episcopate of, 49, 72 *and* n.; 84 *and* n.¹, 180, 210 ; withdrawal of, in favour of Linus and Anencletus, 200 *and* n.¹; tradition as to social and ecclesiastical position of, 85, 200–1, 234–5 ; identity of, 227–8 ; family connexion of, 234–5, 251, 253–4 ; disciple and companion of Peter, 235, 254 ; reference to, in Hermas, 122 n.¹, 203, 215 ; in Muratorian fragment, 210, 215 ; tradition as to the conversion of, 81 *and* n.² ; *Epistle to the Hebrews* attributed to, 155 ; death of, 261

Clement of Rome:
Otherwise mentioned, 112, 113, 155 n^3, 156, 162 and n^3.
Epistle to Corinthians of, 180, 188 ; date of, 188 *et seq.*, 202 *et seq.* ; authorship of, 122 *n.*[1], 188, 199–200 ; cause of writing of, 189–90 ; references to the martyrdom of SS. Peter and Paul in, 47, 141 and *n.*[1], 145, 147–8, 148 *n.*[1], 190 ; description of climax of Neronian persecution in, 141 and *n.*[1], 190 ; internal evidence for date, 192 ; references to our Lord in, 193 ; Biblical quotations in, 193 ; use of the Epistles in, 193 ; reference to the Temple worship, 194–5 ; the dissensions at Corinth, 195–8 ; the story of the Phoenix, 196 ; the evidence for the late date, 196 *et seq.* ; significance of the word ἀρχαίαν, 198 ; the bearers of the epistle, 199
Other references, 119 *n.*[1], 160 and n^4.
Clementine *Homilies* and *Recognitions*, 81 and *n.*[1], 107, 201 *n.*[1], 235, 253–4
Cletus. *See* Anencletus
Cohors Italica, 57 and *n.*[1]
Colossians, Epistle to, 102, 121
Constantine, Emperor, builds basilicas to the Apostles, 270
Consuls, lists of, *cited*, 252 and *n.*
Corinth, Church in, 15, 79, 145, 194, 195, 200 *n.*[1]; a primitive (ἀρχαίαν) church, 198 ; divisions and party spirit in, reproved by St. Paul, 78, 198 ; custom of reading Clement's epistle, 146 ; schism in, 189–90, 198 ; first presbyters of the, 197 ; organisation of, 201
Corinthians, Epistles to, cited, (first) 12, 22, 78, 80, 193 *n.*[4], 199 ; (second) 25, 83
Cornelius, the centurion, 38–9, 57
Cornelius (pope), 267, 268 *n.*[3]
Cyprian, St., 150 *n.*[2], 157
Cyrenians, 37

DAMASUS, pope, 68–9, 265 *et seq. passim*, 275
Demas, 104, 163
Demetrius, 13
De Rossi,G.B., work of, in Christian Archaeology, 276–7, 279 *et seq.*, *cited*, 86, 118 *n.*[2], 147, 236, 242, 243, 247, 248, 253 ; *quoted*, 54 *n.*[2]
Didache, the, 186, 187 ; date of, 187 and *n.*[2]; unreliable, 186, 187 ; the prophet in, 186
Didrachma tax, the, 222, 223
Diocletian persecution, 46 and *n.*[1], 54 *n.*[1], 266, 268
Dion Cassius, 10 and *n.*[3], 23 and *n.*[2], 162 *n.*[4], 170, 225 and *n.*[1], 231, 232, 236 and *n.*[1]
Dionysius of Corinth, 48 and *n.*[3], 79, 122 *n.*[1], 145–6, 148–9, 149 *n.*[1], 202
Domitian, 170, 171, 172 *n.*[1], 221–3, 226, 230, 236, 256, 257
Persecution under, 164 *et seq.*, 191–2 ; origin of, 222 ; not an organised attack on the Christian faith, 168, 222, 223 ; procedure in, 223 ; certain of the Emperor's own relatives affected, 168, 224 and *nn.*[1] and [2], 225–6, 233 ; other distinguished victims, 236
Otherwise mentioned, 169, 188, 189, 207 *et passim*
Domitilla catacomb, 52, 231, 236, 253, 274, 279
Drusilla, 91–2, 93 and *n.*[1]
Duchesne, Abbé, 49 *n.*[2], 68 and *n.*[2], 70 and *n.*[1], 71 and *nn.*[1] and [3], 77 *n.*[1], 149 *n.*[2], 150 *n.*[2], 211 *n.*[3], 242, 243 and *n.*[1], 246. *See also* heading Liber Pontificalis

EBIONITE *Preaching of Peter*, the, 55 and *n.*[1]
Ecclesia, the, 181, 182
Eleutherus, 49, 210 and *n.*[3]
Elymas, 93 *n.*[1]
Epaphras, 65, 104
Epaphroditus, 108, 110 and *n.*[1]
Ephesians, Epistle to, 102, 121
Ephesus, 83
Epiphanius, 200 and *n.*[1]
Episcopal succession in Rome, order of, 49, 72 and n^1, 180; 210 and n^3
Episcopus, significance of the word as applied to St. Peter, 70 ; signifi-

cance in the LXX, 182 ; used by St. Paul, 182, 184 *n.*[2] ; function of the, 183-5 ; distinguished from the ordinary presbyter, 183 ; the two aspects of the office of, 183, 185 ; an inner Presbyterate, 84-5, 185 *and n.* ; Peter's exhortation to, 184; received a stipend, 185; the Bishop *primus inter pares,* 85, 185, 220-1

Epistles. *See distinguishing headings*

Eubulus, 163 and *n.*[3], 244

Euodia, 111, 112

Eusebiana, 200 *n.*[1]

Eusebius : lists of the Roman bishops in, 49 *and nn.*, 71 ; the *Chronicle* of, 49 *n.*[2]; basis of the evidence of, 59 *and n.* ; on Simon Magus, 60 *nn.*[1] *and* [2]; on St. Mark, 67 *and nn.* [1], [2], [3], 106 *and nn.*[1] *and* [2] ; the Petrine tradition in, 70-2 *and* 70 *n.*[2]; .on Peter and Paul, letter of Dionysius to Soter, *quoted,* 79 *and n.*[3]
  Quoted, 48 *n.*[3], 146 *and n.*[1], 165 *and n.*[1], 202 *and n.*[1], 224 *and n.*[3], 230, 232
  Cited, 66 *n.*[1], 74 *nn.*, 112, 117 *nn.*[1] *and* [3], 122 *n.*[1], 148 *n.*[2], 149 *n.*[1], 156 *and n.*[2], 210 *n.*[3], 223, 224, 259

Ewald, *cited,* 161 *n.*[2]

FELIX, 88 *et seq. passim,* 93 *n.*[1], 98

Festus, 88, 90, 93-4, 98, 115

Flavia Domitilla (virgin), 224, 225, 231-4, 252, 256, 257, *passim*
——————— (wife of Clemens), 225, 231, 232, 257

Flavian and Arrecinian families, scheme of relationship between, 234 *and Appendix* Note D

Flavian emperors, policy of, to Jews and Christians, 129, 206-7

Flavius Clemens, theory of identity with Clement of Rome, 227 ; Dr. Lightfoot's theory, 227-8 ; other references, 224-6, 230-6, 253, 257 *passim*

Flavius Sabinus (T.), (i) 255
——————— (ii) 226 *n.*[3], 227, 229, 230, 233, 234; 253, 255; 256, 257
——————— (iii) 226, *n*[3].

Fortunatus, 192 *n.*[2], 199

Fronto, 236 *n.*[1]

Furius Dionysius Filocalus, 69

GAIUS, presbyter, 146, 259

Galatians, Epistle to, 75, 77 *and n.*[2]

Galba, 176, 192 *n.*[1]

Galilee, 35 *and n.*[1]

Gallio, 78 *and n.*[1], 87, 113 *n.*[2]

Gentiles in the Church, Apostolic council in Jerusalem, on, 76

Ghetto, Transtiberine, the, 5 *n.*[1], 8 *n.*[1], 127, 155

' Godfearers,' 7, 8, 18, 115, 222, 229

Gog and Magog, 176-7

Grapte, 203, 204-5, 215

Graptus, 203, 204-5

Greek language in Rome, 4 *and n.*[1]

Greeks, evangelisation of, 39 *n.*[2]

Gregory the Great, 277, 279

Grenfell, *Amhurst Papiri* cited, 48*n.*[1]

HARNACK, Adolf, on Luke and Acts, 31 *and n.*[2], 32 *and n.*[1], 33 ; on Mark's Gospel, 67 *and nn.*[2] *and* [4]; on Barnabas, 80 *n.*[2], 82 *n.*[1]; on Hermas, 215-6 *and nn.* Other references, *cited,* 65 *and n.*[2], 77 *n.*[2], 186 *and n.*[3] ; *quoted,* 19 *n.*[3], 36 *n.*[2]

Harris, Prof. Rendel, 93 *n.*[1]

Haruspices, 65

Hatch, Dr., *cited,* 182 *n.*[4], 186

Hausrath, *cited,* 161 *n.*[2]

Hebrews, Epistle to the, 108 ; date of, 119 *n.*[1], 140 ; addressed to Roman Christians, 153-5, 193 *n.*[4] ; widespread knowledge of, among Roman Christians, 155-6 ; ascribed to Paul by Alexandrian and Eastern Churches, 156-7 ; but not by Roman and Western Churches, 156-7 ; ascribed to Barnabas, 157 *and n.*, 193 *n.*[4] ; influence of Stephen observable in, 158 ; an *Eirenicon,* 159 ; personal references in, support Barnabean authorship, 159, 160 ; characteristics of, 159 ; references to Neronian persecution and concurrent persecution in the provinces, in, 134, 140, 144. Otherwise mentioned, 185, 193 *and n.*[4]

Hefele, *Patrum Apost. Opera,* 189 *n.*[1], 194 *n.*[4], 211

Hegesippus, 59 *n.*[1], 200 *and n.*[1], 210 *and n.*[3]

Helena, Queen, 74

Helius, 162 *and n.*[6]

Henderson's *Life and Principate of the Emperor Nero,* quoted, 88 *and n.*[3], 89 *n.*[1], 142, 166

Heracleon, *cited*, 55
Hermas, 212, 218
The Shepherd of, 188 ; date of,
203, 204, 208, 215, 221 ; confusion of its author with
Pastor the brother of Pius I,
209-11 ; earliest patristic
references to, 212 ; referred
to as Scripture, 212 ; contents of, 213 ; the auto-
biographical details in,
214-6 ; Harnack's views
as to, 215-6 ; the reference
to Clement in, 203 *and n.*[1],
215 ; references to the
Neronian persecution, 216 *et
seq.* ; on the constitution of
the church, 218-9
Otherwise mentioned, 122
n.[1], 134
Herod Agrippa I, 41 *n.*[4], 42 *and n.*[2],
43, 91 *n.*[1], 229, 250
Herod Agrippa II, 89, 93, 95, 115,
116, 138, 207 *n.*[1]
Herodian family in Rome, 6 *and n.*[3],
207 *n.*[1]
Herodian persecution, 42-3 ; effect
of, 37, 39 *n.*, 56, 58, 73
Herodion, 26
Hieronymian Martyrology, quoted,
149 *n.*[2]
Hilgenfeld, *quoted*, 212 *n.*[2], 214 *n.*[2],
227 *n.*[1]
Hilkiah, 115
Hippolytus, Bishop of Portus,
cited, 49 *n.*[2], 50, 63 *and nn.*[2], [3], [4],
83, 156, 161 *n.*[1], 259
Hort, Dr., *quoted*, 61 ; *cited*, 81 *n.*[1],
119 *n.*[2] *et passim*

Ignatius, 201 ; on the constitution
of the Church, 201 ; Epistles of,
quoted, 48 *and n.*[2] ; *cited*, 188,
220
Irenaeus, 49, 146 ; on the Apocalypse, 164-5, 165 *n.*[1], 173 *and
n.*[2] ; on Hermas, 212 *and n.*[1] ;
on order of the Roman bishops,
49, 180, 210 *and n.*[3] ; on SS. Peter
and Paul, as founders of the
Roman Church, 48-9 *and n.*[1],
64, 146 *and n.*[2] ; on Simon
Magus, 60, 63, 64
Otherwise mentioned, 50, 66
and n.[1], 156
Ishmael, son of Fabi, 89, 90, 115,
116

James, St. (son of Zebedee), 42,
43, 165
James, St. (the Lord's brother),
position of, in the Early Church,
43, 76, 180, 181 ; martyrdom of,
117 ; *Epistle of*, cited, 120 *n.*[3]
Jerome, St., 69 ; evidence of, as to
the Petrine tradition, 50-1, 58,
68 *et seq.* ; on martyrdom of the
Apostles, 150 *and n.*[2] ; on the
Apocalypse, 166, 167 ; *cited*,
36 *n.*[2], 59 *and n.*, 106 *n.*[1], 171 *n.*[1],
231
Jerusalem, famine in, 74-5 ; condition of, in time of Felix, 88-9 ;
quarrel between priestly party
and Agrippa in, 115-6 ; outburst
of fanaticism against Christians
in, 117 ; siege and destruction of,
172, 207 ; destruction of the
Temple, 172, 207-8
Apostolic centre, as, 35, 36,
43, 57
Church in, 35, 200 *n.* ; constitution of, 43, 180, 181
Jesus Justus, 104
Jewish Christians, the, two groups
of, 17 ; the Judaising group
opposing St. Paul, 17, 18 *and n.*[1],
25, 110, 154-5 ; persecution of,
154-5 ; attitude to Gentiles in the
Church, 19, 195 ; views of, as to
equality in the Church, 195
Otherwise mentioned, 159
Jewish *Diaspora*, 34, 181, 207 ;
synagogues of, in Jerusalem, 36
Jewish Zealots, 88, 196
Jews in Alexandria, *cited*, 8 *n.*[1],
36 *n.*[3]
Jews in Rome and the Empire,
numbers of, 6-7, 36 *n.*[3], 37 *n.*[1] ;
the colony in Rome, 4-6, 8 *n.*[1] ;
the Transtiberine Ghetto, 5 *n.*[1],
8 *n.*[1], 127, 155 ; attitude of
the Romans to, 6-7 ; synagogues in Rome, 8 *n.*[1] ; attitude of, to Christians, 9-10,
17, 116-7, 117 *n.*[2], 127 ; edict
of expulsion of, under Claudius,
9-10, 13 ; Jewish converts to
Christianity, how regarded by
the orthodox Jews, 116 ; attitude
of the Flavian emperors to, 206-
7 ; the *didrachma* tax, 222. See
also Jerusalem, Judaea, Judaism
John, St. (the Presbyter), 35 *n.*[4], 56,
65, 66, 76, 164 *and n.*[1], 165 *et seq.*,
171 *and n.*[1], 181, 184 *and n.*[1] See
also under Apocalypse

John, St., Gospel, 48; evidence of historical character of, 120 *n.*[3]
Jones, Rev. A. S. Duncan, *cited*, 187 *n.*[2]
Josephus, *cited and quoted*, 5 *nn.*[3] *and* [4], 26 *n.*[2], 37 *n.*[1], 42 *and nn.*[1] *and* [2], 74 *and n.*[2], 88–95 *passim*, 115, 116 *nn.*, 117 *n.*[1], 194, 196 *n.*[1], 228, 229, 234, 250 *et passim*
Jost, *Geschichte des Judenthums*, cited, 42 *n.*[2]
Joyce, *South American Archaeology*, quoted, 44
Judaea, condition of, in time of Felix, 88 *et seq. passim*; revolt in, suppressed by Titus, 207–8; *and see under* Jerusalem
Judaeo-Christians. *See* Jewish Christians
Judaism, attractiveness of, as a religious cult, 6, 7, 65; efforts of Jews to dissociate Christianity from, 101, 127
Judas of Galilee, 88
Julia Pomponia Graecina, 85–6. *See* Pomponia.
Julius Caesar, 3, 5 *and n.*[3]
Julius, centurion, 90, 97, 98
Julius, dictator, 7
Junias, 16, 25 *and n.*[3], 26 *and n.*[1], 35, 57
Justin Martyr, *cited and quoted*, 60 *and n.*[2], 61–3, 117 *n.*[3], 247
Juvenal, 4 *n.*[1], 9 *n.*[2], 236 *n.*[1]

LACTANTIUS, 10
Lake, Kirsopp, *quoted*, 20, 28 *n.*[1], 64, 75 *n.*[2] *et passim*.
Lanciani, *quoted*, 26, 27 *n.*[1], 47, 51, 52 *n.*[1], 147, 155 *and n.*[2], 247
Last Supper, tradition as to place of the, 40 *n.*[1]
Lateran Church, altar at, 248
Laureolus, the, 9 *and n.*[2]
Lawlor, H. J., *quoted*, 200 *n.*[1]
Le Blant, Edmond, *cited*, 54 *n.*[1]; *quoted*, 80 *and n.*[1]
Lehmann, H., *Claudius und seine Zeit*, 42 *n.*[1], 65 *n*[1].
Lelong, *Le Pasteur d'Hermas*, cited, 211 *n.*[2]
Leo IV, 242
Liberian, or Filocalian, Catalogue, the, 70; sources of, 71, 83, 149 *n.*[1], 210; the Petrine tradition in, 70–2, 84; errors in account of the Roman episcopate in, 72, 84, 210; date of martyr-

dom of Peter and Paul in, 149; on Hermas, 188, 208, 209, 211; *cited*, 150 *n.*[2], 242
Liber Pastoris, 211
Liber Pontificalis (*see also under* Duchesne); tradition as to compilers of, 69; basis of, 70, 149 *and n.*[2], 150, 211; the Petrine tradition in, 68 *and n.*[2], 70–1, 77 *n.*[1], 84 *and n.*[3]; martyrdom of the Apostles, date of, 149, 150 *and n.*[2]; on Hermas, 211 *and n.*[1]; the Cononian and Felician abridgements of, 211 *and n.*[3]; *cited* 52 *n.*[1], 243 *and n.*[1]
Libertines, the, 34 *and n.*[1], 36, 57
Lightfoot, Dr., *Apostolic Fathers* on the order of succession of the Roman Bishops, 72 *n.*[1]; on Clement of Rome, *cited*, 180 *n.*[1], 188, 194; *quoted*, 189 *and n.*[1], 190, 193 *and n.*[2], 203 *and n.*[2], 227, 228 *and n.*[1]; mentioned, 49 *n.*[2], 113 *n.*[2] *et passim*.
Linus, 49, 50, 71, 84, 122 *n.*[1], 163 *and n.*[3], 180, 200, 210, 221, 244, 261
Lipsius, Richard A., 60 *and n.*[5], 107 *n.*[1], 118, 152 *n.*[1], 227 *n.*[1]
Livia, 26
Lucina, 263, 267, 270; crypt of, 86, 263, 267, 274
Luke, St., and the authorship of the third Gospel and the Acts, 31; literary plans of, 33, 102, *and n.*[1]; date of *Gospel* and *Acts*, 67 *n.*[4]; use of the Marcan lections, by, 67 *n.*[4]; chronological expressions in writings of, 73; accuracy and historical value of writings of, 32, 87, 89 *and n.*, 97; characteristics of writings, 10, 11 *n.*[2]; accompanies St. Paul to Rome, 96, 98 *and n.*[1], 104. Otherwise mentioned, 65, 105, 108, 163
Lysias, 89, 90

MACCHI, Carlo, *quoted*, 55 *n.*[2], *cited*, 66 *n.*[1];
Marcellus (pope), 267 *et seq.*
Mark, 66, 121; cousin of Barnabas, 104 *et seq.*; disciple and interpreter of St. Peter, 64, 66, 67, 75–6, 122; a living bond between St. Peter and St. Paul, 64, 122; his gospel, 66–7, 67 *n.*[4], 68; journey with Barnabas and Paul,

U

76; tradition as to work of, in Alexandria, 106, 107; with Barnabas and Paul in Rome, 104 ff.

Martial, *Epigrams* of, *cited*, 244

Martin, P., *cited*, 51 *n.*¹, 147 *n.*²

Marucchi, O., 46 *n.*¹, 52 *n.*¹, 53 *and nn.*² *and* ³, 117 *n.*³, 118 *n.*², 227 *n.*¹ *et seq.*; *et passim*

Mary, mother of John Mark, house of, in Jerusalem, 42-3, 66

Maxentius, 268 *and n.*³

Messalina, 85, 199

Mommsen, *cited*, 49 *n.*², 70 *n.*¹, 97, 128-9 *and nn.*

Mount Athos, discovery of manuscript of Hippolytus at, 63

Mucianus, 169, 170, 171, 256

Muratorian fragment, date of, 161 *and n.*¹, 209, 212; on Hermas, 188, 208-9, 214; mentioned, 113

NARCISSUS, 26, 113

Nereus, 231, 233, 252-3, 280, 281

Nero, accession of, 13 *and n.*¹; and the burning of Rome, 123 *et seq.*; persecution of Christians a personal act of, 129-31, 142, 221 (*and see* Neronian persecution, *infra*); participates in Vatican Gardens fête, 128, 141; visit to Greece, 162, 195-6; death of, 174; popular belief as to, at time of death, 174-5; a matricide, 48 *n.*³, 173 *n.*²; identified with Antichrist of the Apocalypse, 134, 166, 172, 173

Otherwise mentioned, 48, 50, 99 *n.*¹, 113, 115, 120 *and n.*², 141, 148

Neronian persecution, the description of, in Tacitus, 124 *et seq.*; date of, 125, 141, 143, 144; description of, climax of, 128, 140-2, 143, 191, 216-8; spread of, to Asia Minor, 140 *and n.*²; and the provinces, 143, 144, 151; the Great Fire and the accusations against the Christians, 124, 125, 127; period between the fire and the holocaust, 125; the charge of incendiarism a pretext, 127, 131-2; not a normal repressive measure, 129; a personal act of Nero, 129-31, 142, 221; character of the charges against the Christians in, 132 *et seq.*; explanation of confession

of incendiarism, 133, 137; the Neronian ordinance, 137-8, 206; permanent results of, in Roman policy, 222

Mommsen's views on, *cited*, 129

Nerva, 166, 171, 172 *n.*¹

Novatian, 157

Novatus, 245; the Baths of, 245-6, 247

Nymphidius Sabinus, 162

OCTAVIA, 115

Onesimus, 103

Oriental cults, vogue of, in Rome, 65

Origen, *cited*, 55 *n.*¹, 112, 148 *n.*², 156 *and n.*², 165, 213

Orosius, 132 *and n.*², 143 *and n.*, 144, 223

Otho, 176, 192 *n.*¹

Our Lord's Ministry, testimony to the Johannine account of, 35 *nn.* ¹ *and* ⁴

PAMPHYLIA, 76 *and n.*¹

Pantaenus, *cited*, 156

Papias, 66 *and n.*¹, 67

Paschal I, 247

Passio Petri, quoted, 152 *n.*¹

Pastor (Presbyter), 210-11, 244 *et seq.*

Pastor and *episcopus*, 85, 184

Pastoral Epistles, 161, 183

Paul, St., at Corinth, 10; relations with Aquila and Priscilla, 10, 11, 12, 21 *et seq.*, 83; at Ephesus, 12-13 *and n.*⁴, 75, 83; journey *via* Macedonia to Corinth, 13, 14, 82, 83; his desire to visit Rome, 10, 13, 14, 27, 55; delay due to the restriction not to build on another man's foundation, 27-8, 56, 82-3; intention in visiting Rome, 28; fears regarding his reception in Rome, 15, 18, 21; enmity of the Judaeo-Christians for, 17, 18, 25, 110, 117 *and n.*³, 154-5; attack on his doctrine of Justification by Faith, 18; attitude of, to Judaism and Christianity, 18-19, 117 *n.*²; the *Epistle to the Romans*, 14 (*and see heading* Romans); journey to Jerusalem, 13, 86; the tumult in the Temple Courts, 89; captivity of, in Caesarea, 87, 89;

treatment of, by the authorities, 87, 90-2, 97-9; status and financial resources of, 90 et seq., 103, 110 n.[1]; the charge against political, not religious, 93, 94-5; appeals to Caesar, 94-5; his knowledge of the Latin language, 94 n.[2]; journey to Rome, 87, 95-6; delivered in charge to the *Stratopedarch*, 97; captivity of, in Rome, 97 et seq.; interview with Jewish leaders, 98, 99-101; breach with official Judaism, 101; the epistles written during captivity, 102 et seq.; trial of, 109 et seq.; acquittal, 113, 114; date of release, 115-6; journeyings of, 113-4, 160-1; second imprisonment in Rome, 160-2; sense of desertion, attitude of Roman Christians to, 163; martyrdom of, 47, 141 et seq., 163, 171 n., 190; date and manner of, 147-8, 148 n.[2], 150; tradition of anniversary with Peter, 50, 84, 147-50, 264; tomb of, 146, 149, 259, 262 et seq.; translation of relics of, 263 et seq.; basilica of, 270-1, 272; his name coupled with that of St. Peter as joint founders of Roman Church, 48-9, 79, 146, 190; and of the church at Corinth, 48, 79, 80, 190

Characteristics of, revealed in the epistles, 100
Christianity preached by, essential note of the, 101
Likenesses of, in Rome, 51-2 and n.[1], 282
Tübingen theories, the, 60-1, 64
Otherwise mentioned, 30, 37, 105, 120, 159, 186-7, 193, 199, 206, 212, 231

Paula, 231
Peru, pre-Hispanic civilisation of, *cited*, 44
Peter, St., the narrative in the Acts, 34-43; meeting of, with Simon Magus in Samaria, 38, 61; advance of, in casting loose from Jewish prejudice, 38; visit to Cornelius, 38, 57; defence to the brethren, 39; imprisonment by Herod and escape, 42-3, 51, 58; after-life of, 44

Relation of Peter to the Roman Church, 28-9, 44, 48-51, 59; his name coupled with

that of Paul as joint founders, 48-9, 79, 146, 190; evidence for considerable residence of Peter in Rome, 47, 51-5, 118, 120, 248; likenesses of, in Rome, 51-2 and n.[1], 282; appearance of name Peter on early Christian tombs, 52; representations on sarcophagi, 53; evidence in legends and apocryphal literature, 54-5; date of arrival of Peter in Rome, 58, 70; encounters Simon Magus, 62-5, 68; first Roman visit, 50, 51, 66, 75 and n.[1], 199; relations with Paul, 61, 64, 77-8, 121; relations with John Mark, 66-8; Evidence of St. Jerome as to tradition current in the pontificate of Damasus, 68-70, 72; the standard Roman tradition, 68; Liberian Catalogue and Eusebian Chronicle versions, 70-72; Hieronymian-Eusebian version irreconcilable with narrative in Acts, 72; hypothesis of a previous sojourn at Rome, 56, 59, 72-3, 75; date and length of 'episcopate,' 49 and n.[2], 50, 70-1, 77, 84; founds Antiochean Church, 70; 'episcopacy' of Antioch, 50, 68, 72, 77 and n.[1]; Peter, with Paul, regarded as founders of Corinthian Church, 48, 79, 190; with Barnabas in Corinth, 80, 82; gives to Roman Church its organisation, 84, 197; ordination of presbyters by, 84; date of last visit to Rome, 118; evidence for death of, in Rome, 47-8, 50, 118, 190; date and manner of martyrdom, 47, 48, 50, 70, 118, 141, 143, 145 et seq., 171 n.; survived the Vatican fête, 151; the *Quo Vadis?* story, 55, 151 et seq.; tradition of anniversary with St. Paul, 50, 84, 147-150, 264; tomb of, 146, 149, 259 et seq.; translation of relics of, 265 et seq.; basilica of, 270

Peter St. (cont.) :
 Chair of, in basilica, 55, 248
 Mental characteristics of, as exemplified in 1 Peter, 121; effect
  of St. Paul's epistles on, 121
  and n.[1]
 Missionary labours of, 72, 76-9
  passim, 119
 Tübingen theory as to, 60-1, 64,
  119, 121
  Otherwise mentioned, 107,
   159, 181, 183, 184, 193,
   248, 254 et passim
Peter, First Epistle of : written from
 Rome, 47, 193 n.[4]; historical
 value of, 119; salutation of,
 119; indebtedness to other New
 Testament writings, 120 and n.[3];
 reminiscences of our Lord's words
 in, 120 n.[3], 183 n.[3]; references
 to St. Paul's epistles in, 64, 121-
 122; circumstances in which it
 was written, 120, 151; references
 to persecutions in, 139-40; exhortations in, 140; the amanuensis
 of, 64, 122; mentioned, 144,
 183 n.[3]; Second Epistle cited, 48
Petronilla, 254, 280, 281
Pfleiderer, 161 n.[2]
Philemon, 102, 103-4
Philip the Evangelist, 37-8, 56, 61,
 68 n.[1]
Philippi, Church of, 108, 111
Philippians, Epistle to, 102, 107-
 112 passim, 154, 160, 183, 192
Phillimore, Prof. J. S., cited, 135 n.[1]
Philo, cited, 5 n.[1], 6 n.[1], 36 n.[3]
Philostratus, cited, 21, 65, 134,
 135 n.[1], 160 n.[4], 177 n.[4], 195
 n.[2], 231; quoted, 173 n.[2], 192 n.[1]
Pisonian conspiracy, 126, 127, 137,
 141, 142
Pius I, 208-12 passim, 244, 245, 246
Plautia, 234, 250, 254
Plautia Urgulanilla, 234, 250, 254
Plautilla, 231-4, 252 et seq. passim.
Pliny (the Elder), quoted, 3 n.[3], 196;
 cited, 123 n.[1], 133 and n.[2], 138 n.
——— (the Younger), cited, 98 n.[1],
 124 n.[1], 135, 138, 222
Polycarp, 146, 164
Polynesians, cited, 44
Pomponia Graecina, 85-6, 138 n.,
 234, 250
Pontia, island, 231
Pontus, 119 and n.[2]
Popes, crypt of the, 261-2
Poppaea Sabina, 115, 116 and nn.[1]
 and [2]

Praxedis, 245 ff., 278
——— St., Church of, 246 ff., 275
Presbyter, the, 181 et seq.; distinction between Christian and
 Jewish, 181, 185; p. without
 specific local charge, 184; functions of, 185, 186; the word used
 by Hermas, 219; see also under
 Episcopus
Praetorian Prefects, the, 99 n.[1]
Prisca, Priscilla, 10, 11 n.[2]; exiled
 under Claudius' edict, 10, 11, 24;
 status of, 11-12, 24, 85, 242;
 precedence of her name over that
 of Aquila, 11 and n.[2], 24, 242;
 the church in the house of, 12, 22,
 23-4, 181, 243; relations with
 Paul, 13, 21 et seq., 83; return to
 Rome, 13, 22, 83; tomb of,
 22 n.[1], 52 n., 242, 278
 Otherwise mentioned, 21, 22,
  82, 83, 163
Prisca, St. (virgin and martyr),
 243
——— Church of, 23 n.[1], 24, 55, 243,
 249 n.[1]
Priscilla (Acilia), founder of the
 cemetery, 242, 278; mother of
 Pudens, 245, 247, 248, 278
Priscilla, cemetery of, description
 of, 277 et seq.; mentioned, 22 n.[1],
 23 n.[1], 52, 117 n.[3], 236, 242, 245
 and n.[1], 247, 267, 274
Profumo, A., quoted, 138 n., cited,
 172 n.[1]
Prophet, the, in the early church,
 186, 218
Proselytes of the Gate, the, 7 n.[1]
Prudentius, cited, 150 and n.[1]
Pudens, identity of, 247-8, 249 n.[1];
 the Pudens legend, 244-9; traditions connecting the name with
 early history of the Church in
 Rome, 248-9; mentioned, 24,
 163 and n.[3], 278
Pudenziana, St., Church of, 24, 55,
 211 n.[1], 245 et seq., 278; wooden
 altar of, 248
Puteoli, 95-6; Christian community at, 96

Quintilian, quoted, 225 n.[2], 257

Ramsay, Sir Wm., cited, 3 n.[1], 31
 and n.[1], 93 n.[1], 98 n.[1], 102 n.[1],
 161 and n.[3]; quoted, 45 and n.[1],
 74 nn.[1] and [2], 97 and n.[2]

Renan, *quoted*, 119 *n.*[1], 161 *n.*[2], *cited*, 177

Rhoda, 42

Robinson, Armitage, *cited*, 187 *n.*[2]

Romans, Epistle to the, evidential value of, as to Christianity in Rome, 14–15, 24, 44, 55, 59 ; the note of *apologia* in, 15–16; the difficulties of interpretation, 16–18; groups of persons to whom the epistle is addressed, 17, 18, 19 ; the motive for writing, 18 ; the list of salutations in Chap. xvi., 17, 19 *et seq.*, 113 ; Tertius' interpolation in, 21–2 ; the autobiographic passage in Chap. xv., 17, 27, 82–3 ; absence of reference to St. Peter in, explained, 28 ; written in Corinth, 83 ; addressed to Rome, 82, 193 *n.*[4]; familiar to St. Peter, 121 *and n.*[1]

Rome, in the first century, 2 ; freedom of intercourse in, 2 ; essentially a Mediterranean power, 2 ; population of, at beginning of Christian era, 3 ; slaves in, 3 *and n.*[3]; paupers in, 3 ; manumission, custom of, in, 3 ; freedmen in, 3–4 ; foreign population of, 4 ; the Pretorian camp, 4 ; Greek the language of, 4 *and n.*[1] ; the Jews in, 4–6 ; burning of, 123 *et seq.* ; pestilence and calamities in, 143, 144, 169–170, 192. *See also under* Neronian, *and under Emperors' names.*

Rome, the Church in :

Beginnings of Christianity in Rome, 8–9 *and n.*[1], 57, 199; evidential value of *Epistle to the Romans* as to, 14–5, 24, 44, 55, 59 ; an established Christian community in, in 57 A.D., 14, 24, 44, 55 ; composition of the community, 14, 17, 20, 25 *and n.*[1]; places of assembly, 24 ; explanation of Paul's attitude of deference for, 27 ; relation of Peter to, 28–9, 44, 48–51, 59 ; founded by the Apostles Peter and Paul, 48–9, 79, 146, 190 ; eminence of, due to martyrdom and burial of Apostles there, 147 ; organisation given to, by Peter, 84–5, 197 ; the government passes to the inner committee of the presby-

terate, 85, 185; earliest official document of, 180 ; order of episcopal succession in, 49, 72 *and n.*[1], 180, 210 *and n.*[3]; the Bishop president, 185 ; primitive organisation of, illustrated in Clement's Epistle, 192–3 ; organisation in 96 A.D. according to Ignatius, 201–2 ; during the Flavian dynasty, 206, 208 ; constitution of, references in Hermas, 218–9 ; a period of immunity from persecution, 206, 221 ; persecution under Domitian, 221 *et seq.* ; persecutions of Nero and Domitian contrasted, 221–2

SALMON, Dr., *quoted*, 161 *n.*[2], 212

Samaria, evangelisation of, 56

Sanday and Headlam, *Commentary on Romans*, cited, 19 *n.*[1] *et passim*

Schürer, *cited*, 7 *n.*[1], 186 *n.*[1] *et passim*

Sebastian, St., 266

Seneca, 13, 91 *n.*[1], 113 *and n.*[2], 148 *n.*[2], 151 *n.*

Septuagint, *cited*, 182, 194 *nn.*

Sibylline Oracles, the, *cited*, 47 *and n.*[2], 120 *and n.*, 123, 174 *and n.*[2]

Sicarii, the, 88

Silas, 65, 104

Silvanus, 64, 119 *n.*[2], 122 *and n.*

Simon (Ετοιμος), 93 *n.*[1]

Simon Magus, 38, 50, 56, 57, 60–5, 66

Simonians, the, 62, 63

Siricius, pope, 246

Slaves in Rome, 3 *and n.*[3] ; Jews as, 4–5

Soter, Bishop, 79, 146, 202, 210 *and n.*[3]

South Galatian theory, *cited*, 28

Statilius Taurus, 27 *n.*[1]

Stephanus, 236, 257

Stephen, work and martyrdom of, 36–7 ; persecution and dispersion of his disciples, 37, 39 *n.*[2], 56, 73

Strabo, *quoted*, 178 *and n.*[4]

Stratopedarch, the, 97 *and n.*[1]

Subrius Flavus, 126, 127, 133

Suetonius, *quoted*, 5 *n.*[4], 24, 117 *n.*[3], 124 *n.*[1], 130, 136, 138, 143, 220 *et passim*

Sulpicius Severus, 132, 207
Sylvester, pope, 248
——— St., basilica of, 278 *and n.*
Synagogue, the original model of
    Christian organisation, 181 ;
    signification of the word, 182
——— of the Hebrews, 155 *and n.*[1]
Synagogues, in Rome, 8 *n.*[1]; of the
    Hellenists in Jerusalem, 36
Syntyche, 111, 112

Tacitus, *cited and quoted*, 5 *n.*[1],
    46 *n.*[1], 85–6, 88, 117 *n.*[3], 123–7,
    129–36, 140–3, 169, 207, 226–7
    and n., 228 *n.*[2] *et passim*
Tarsus, 89 *n.*[2]
Tertius, 22
Tertulla, 229, 254, 255
Tertullian, *quoted*, on the Neronian
    persecution, 130–1, 132 *and n.*[2],
    148 *and n.*[2]; the *Neronian
    Institution*, 206 ; on martyrdom
    of Peter and Paul, 148 *and n.*[2];
    on *Hebrews*, 156–8 ; on Hermas,
    213 *and n.*[1]; other references,
    cited, 9 *n.*[1], 117 *n.*[2], 130 *n.*[2], 136,
    171 *n.*[1]
Thera (island), 173 *n.*[1], 178–9
Thyestean feasts, 117, 136
Tiberius, 5 *and n.*[4], 91 *n.*[1], 176
Tiberius Alexander, 74 *and n.*[2],
    207 *n.*[1]
Tigellinus, 99 *n.*[1], 113, 131, 134,
    135, 137, 162
Timothy, Paul's amanuensis, 104,
    111 ; at Ephesus, 107–8 ; men-
    tioned, 64, 65, 107, 159 *n.*[1], 160,
    163, 183
Timothy, *Epistles to*, cited (first),
    112, 160 ; (second) 22, 108, 148,
    161 *and n.*[2]
Timothy (brother of Novatus), 245
Titulus, definition of, 248 *and n.*[1]
Titus (Paul's disciple), 65, 112, 183
Titus (Emperor), 229 ; and the
    distinction between Jew and
    Christian, 207 ; attitude to Jews

and to Christianity, 207–8,
    207 *n.*[1]; otherwise mentioned,
    170, 171, 172 *and n.*[1], 206, 250
    et seq. passim
Tradition, oral and written, 44, 77 ;
    early Christian records, 44–6 ;
    criteria in judging traditions,
    46–7, 51
Trajan, 99 *n.*[1], 129, 135, 138, 166,
    222, 235
Tres Tabernae, 96 *and n.*[1]
Tübingen School, theories of the,
    60–1, 118, 121
Turner, C. H., *quoted*, 146, 147 *and
    n.*[1], 150 *n.*[2]
Tychicus, 104

Valerian persecution, 149, 265
Valerius Bito, 199
Vespasian, 229 ; policy towards
    Jews and Christians, 206–7, 206
    n.[1], 222 ; otherwise mentioned,
    170–7 *passim*, 195, 196, 230, 234,
    254, 255–6, 257
Victorinus, *cited*, 166, 167
Vindex, 176
Vitellius, 169, 176, 177, 192 *n.*[1], 227,
    230

Wiseman, Cardinal, 248
Workman, *Persecution in the Early
    Church*, 6 *n.*[4], 189 *n.*[1]

Xiphilinus, abridgement of Dion
    Cassius, quoted, 225
Xystus I, pope, 71 *and n.*[1]

Zahn on Muratorian Fragmentist,
    quoted, 208 *n.*[2], 209 ; *cited*, 24 *n.*[1],
    120 *n.*[2], 192 *n.*[2], 199 *n.*[3] *et passim*
Zealots, the, 88, 196
Zephyrinus, pope, 146, 243, 261,
    262

INDEX OF SCRIPTURE REFERENCES

OLD TESTAMENT

EXODUS
	PAGE
xxix. 42 .	194
xxx. 8 .	194

NUMBERS
xxviii. 6 .	194

PSALMS
cviii. (cix.) 8 .	182

ISAIAH
vi. 9, 10 .	101
lx. 17 .	182

EZEKIEL
xxxiv. 11 .	182

DANIEL
vii. 25 .	172
xi. 3, 6 .	206
xii. 25 .	172

NEW TESTAMENT

ST. MATTHEW
xiii. 14 .	101
xvi. 18 .	53
xx. 22 .	165
,, 23 .	171
xxiv. 21, 29 .	221

ST. MARK
iv. 12 .	101
xiii. 24 .	221

ST. LUKE
i. 2 .	198
viii. 10 .	101
xii. 1-18 .	42
xxiv. 44-49 .	36
,, 50-53	33, 35, 102

ST. JOHN
xii. 40 .	101
xiii. 23-27 .	35
,, 36 .	148
,, 36, 37	152, 153
xiv. 16, 26 .	40
,, 26 .	36
xvi. 13 .	36
xviii. 15 .	35
xx. 3-10 .	35
xxi. 15-23 .	152
,, 18, 19 .	148
,, 20-24 .	35

ACTS
i. . .	102
,, 20 .	182

	PAGE
ii. . .	102
,, 32-36, 46 .	35
iii. 1, 14, 15 .	35
,, 20, 21, 26 .	35
iv. 10, 13, 33 .	35
,, 36, 37 .	159
,, 37 .	40
v. 12, 25 .	35
,, 30-32, 42 .	35
vi. 8 .	37
,, 9 .	.26, 35
vii. 54-60 .	37
viii. 1-3 .	37
,, 5-24 .	38
,, 14 .	35
ix. 25-27 .	41
,, 26-31, 32 .	38
xi. . .	75
,, 1-18, 19-27 .	39
,, 19-20 .	73
,, 26, 27 .	73
,, 26 .	41
xii. 1 .	73
,, 12 .	40
,, 25 .	73
xiii. 1, 15 .	40
xv. . .	75
,, 41 .	38
xvi. 6-7 .	28
xviii. 1 .	10
,, 11, 18, 19 .	12
,, 23 .	38
,, 24-27	.11, 12
xix. 10 .	12
,, 21 .	13
,, 22-24 .	87
,, 31, 33, 34 .	13
xx. 19-25 .	14
,, 28 .	182
xxi. 4, 11-14 .	87
,, 16 .	98
,, 37-40 .	89
xxii. 11-14 .	87
,, 22-30 .	89
xxiii. 5 .	90
,, 11 .	95
,, 12-22 .	90
xxiv. 22 .	91
,, 26 .	92
xxv. 12 .	94
,, 19 .	94
xxvii. 27 .	95
xxviii. 15 .	87, 96
,, 17-21 .	101
,, 23 .	98

	PAGE
xxviii. 29-31 .	33
,, 30	98, 102
,, 31 .	102

ROMANS
i. 1, 5 .	16
,, 8 .	1, 14
,, 10-12 .	82
,, 12 .	16
,, 15-16 .	100
ii. 17-29 .	18
iii. 1, 2, 8 .	18
iv. 1 .	18
ix. 1-3 .	100
,, 3 .	25
x. 1 .	100
,, 14 .	30
xi. 8 .	101
,, 13, 14 .	19
,, 17, 24 .	8
xii. 6-8 .	197
,, 8 .	219
xiii. 11-13 .	133
xv. 14 .	15
,, 14-29 .	27
,, 20 .	.27, 82
,, 23-24 .	82
,, 24 .	.15, 87
,, 30-31 .	87
xvi. 7 .	16
,, 19 .	15
,, 34 .	13

I CORINTHIANS
i. 10 .	180
ix. 6 .	79, 157
x. 4 .	53
xi. 18, 19 .	197
xii. 28 .	187, 218
,, 28-29 .	187
xiv. .	187
xv. 51-52 .	133
xvi. 17 .	199
,, 19 .	11, 12

2 CORINTHIANS
i. 8 .	13
ii. 4, 5, 13 .	14
iv. 8-11 .	14
viii. 23 .	25
x. 12-18 .	15
xi. 9 .	198
,, 27-28 .	14
xii. 10 .	14
,, 11-13 .	15

PAGE

xii. 11 . . 79
,, 14 . . 83
,, 20, 21 . 14
xiii. 1 . . 83

GALATIANS
i. 18 . .35, 38
,, 18–21 . . 41
,, 19 . . 181
ii. . . . 75
,, 1–10 . . 75
,, 9 . 35, 181
,, 12 . . 181

EPHESIANS
ii. 20 . . 187
iii. 5 . . 187
iv. 11 . 187, 218
,, 11–12 . . 197
vi. 19, 20 . . 103
,, 21, 22 . . 104

PHILIPPIANS
i. 12–15 . . 109
,, 13–14 . . 154
,, 14–18 . . 111
,, 15, 16 . . 18
,, 19–25 . . 109
ii. 11 . . 108
,, 17, 24 . . 109
,, 19–30 . . 109
iii. 1–6 . . 18
,, 2–3 . . 111
,, 2–5 . . 154
iv. 3 . . 112
,, 10–20 . . 110
,, 15 . . 198

COLOSSIANS
i. 1, 7 . . 104
ii. 1 . . 105
iv. 3 . . 103
,, 7, 8, 9 . 104
,, 10 . 104, 121
,, 12, 14 . . 104
,, 18 . . 103

1 THESSALONIANS
iv. 16–18 . . 133
v. 12 . . 219

2 THESSALONIANS
i. 4–10 . . 221
,, 7–10 . . 133

1 TIMOTHY
i. . . . 112
,, 3 . . . 160
,, 19, 20 . . 108
iii. 1–13 . . 197
,, 2 . . . 183
v. 17 . 183, 219
vi. 12 . . 160
,, 12–13 . . 134
,, 12–14 . . 108

2 TIMOTHY
PAGE
i. 15–18 . . 161
,, 15 . . 163
ii. 11 . . 108
iv. 9–11 . . 108
,, 9 . . 163
,, 10–13 . . 163
,, 11 . . 64
,, 17 . . 162
,, 19, 20, 21 . 163

TITUS
i. 5–11 . . 197
,, 7, 9 . . 183

PHILEMON
1 . . . 104
8–13 . . 103
10 . . . 104
19 . . . 103
22 . . 98, 103
23 . . . 104

HEBREWS
i. 5 . . . 193
iv. 14, 15 . . 140
v. 23–27 . . 140
vi. 2–6 . . 157
,, 4–6 . 134, 140
,, 4–8 . . 217
,, 6 152, 153, 154
ix. 37 . . 133
x. 23–27 . . 140
,, 26–29 . . 134
,, 32 . . 160
,, 32, 33 140, 154
,, 39 . 134, 154
xi. 9 . . 155
xii. . . 154
,, 1–13 . . 140
,, 15–25 . . 154
xiii. 3 . . 154
,, 7 . 154, 219
,, 12, 13 . 154
,, 17 . 197, 219
,, 23 108, 140, 160
,, 24 . . 219

1 PETER
i. 7 . . . 140
ii. 11–17 . . 140
,, 12, 14 . . 139
,, 12 . . 162
,, 19–21 . . 152
,, 25 . 183, 184
iii. 13–17 . . 217
,, 14–18 . . 152
,, 15–17 . . 139
,, 16 140, 162
iv. 7 . . . 133

iv. 12–19 . . 217
,, 12 . . 140
,, 13 . . 162
,, 14–16 . . 140
,, 15 . . . 139
,, 16 115, 152, 162
,, 19 . . 162
v. 1, 2 . . 184
,, 1–6 . . 197
,, 3 . . . 197
,, 12 . . 122
,, 13 . 120, 121

2 PETER
iii. 10–12 . . 133

REVELATION
ii. 3, 9, 10, 13 . 140
iii. 8–11 . . 140
vi. 9–11 . 140, 168
,, 12–17 . . 178
,, 14 . . 168
vii. 13–17 . 140
viii. 5–9 . . 178
,, 8, 9 . . 178
xi. 1, 2, 8 . 172
xii. 10, 11 . 140
,, 11 . 145, 217
xiii. . . 134
,, 1 . 173, 176
,, 7, 8 . . 140
,, 8, 9 . . 178
,, 15 . . 168
xiv. 8 . . 169
,, 9–13 . . 217
,, 17–20 . 169
xvi. 3 . . 178
,, 5–7 . . 168
,, 6 . . 140
,, 10 . . 134
,, 14–16 . 177
,, 18 . . 178
,, 19 . . 134
,, 20, 21 . 178
xvii. 3–7 . . 168
,, 5–9 . . 134
,, 6 . . 140
,, 9 . . 168
,, 12–13 . 176
,, 16 . . 169
,, 18 . . 59
xviii. . . 169
,, 1–21 . 133
,, 10 . . 170
,, 18 . . 176
,, 20 . . 169
,, 24 . 140, 168
xix. 20 . . 176
xx. 4 . 140, 217
,, 8 . . 177
xxii. 10–12, 20 . 133

15801864R00177

Made in the USA
San Bernardino, CA
06 October 2014